Butterfield Overland National Historic Trail
PASSENGER DIARIES & STORIES

Across Oklahoma, Arkansas, and Missouri
1858 - 1861
by Bob Crossman

First Printing • February 2024
Ingram Spark Press

John Butterfield, President, Butterfield Overland Mail Co.

Explore the Butterfield Overland National Historic Trail by also reading these books by Bob Crossman:

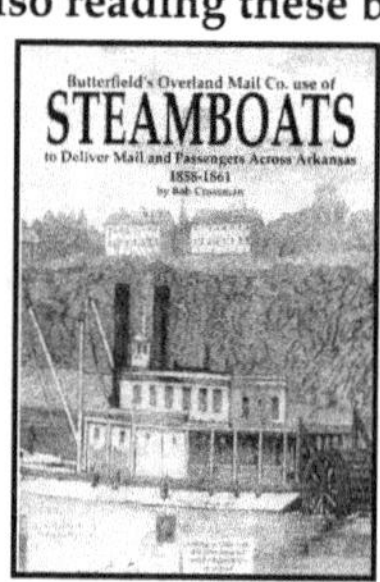

Cover Art: Journal image by Pexels on Pixabay.com
ISBN: 979-8-9885900-0-2 in hard cover
ISBN: 979-8-9885900-3-3 in soft cover

Forward

Butterfield's Overland Mail Company stagecoaches rolled across Oklahoma, Arkansas and Missouri one hundred and sixty five years ago as they connected with San Francisco.

Now that Congress has named the route "THE BUTTERFIELD OVERLAND NATIONAL HISTORIC TRAIL," it seems appropriate for the Butterfield passengers to tell us about their experience on the trail. The following pages contain reminiscences of first person observers in their own words.

In most chapters below I have attempted to only include portions of each original document that focus on passage through Missouri, Arkansas and the Indian Territory.

Some of these original documents are hundreds of pages long and include details of passage through Texas, New Mexico, Arizona, and California that are not included here.

Several of the articles were brief enough, *[such as Henry Everett, J. W. Farwell, Warren Baer, Thomas M. Johnston, and the speech by Waterman L. Ormsby]*, I included their remarks concerning the entire route from San Francisco to the Mississippi River.

Bob Crossman

"Butterfield Run Through the Ozarks" by Phillip W. Steele, 1966

T A B L E   O F   C O N T E N T S

Table of Contents

Page

Introduction & Passenger Count Article 6
The Butterfield Overland National Historic Trail Stations 17

Prologue

Randolph B. Marcy, 1849/1859 33
W. B. Parker, 1854/1856...35

1858

1. Observations of John Butterfield, Aug. 2, 1858 61
2. Passenger Letter to Mrs. Butterfield, Sept. 18, 1858 70
3. R. M. Brimmer, *Weekly Arkansas Gazette*, Sept. 25, 1858...........71
4. Speech by John Butterfield, Oct. 14, 1858................................72
5. Observations of A. H. Wilson, September, 1858 74
6. G. Bailey's trip for the Postmaster General, Sept., 1858...........78
7. Waterman Ormsby, *New York Herald*, Sept., 1858....................83
      Ormsby's Speech, *Daily Alta*, Oct. 12, 1858.......................118
8. Passenger / Employee Report, Oct. 10, 1858 123
9. John T. Chidester's Observations, Oct. 13 & 23, 1858 125
10. George S. Dana, *Daily Alta Californian*, Oct. 16, 1858 132
11. Wm. Hayes Hilton, Oct. 23, 1858 137
12. Letter to the Editor of the *Herald*, Oct., 1858....................144
13. J. M. Farwell, Nov. 6, 1858..146
14. Passenger observations, *Los Angeles Star*, Nov, 9, 1858.........161
15. J. B. Nichols' Report, Nov. 24, 1858 and June 10, 1859.........163
16. Milo June, Tipton Butterfield Agent, Nov. 6, 1858................165
17. Warren Baer, *Bulletin* Correspondent, Nov. 25, 1858............166
18. Butterfield Eastern Conductor, *Daily Alta*, Dec. 20, 1858.....184
19. In Pursuit of Her Husband, Dec. 23, 1858 185
20. D. Jones, *Weekly Arkansas Gazette*, Dec. 25, 1858 186

1859

21. Major Emory, *Missouri Republican*, Jan. 7, 1859....................187
22. Passenger, *Arkansas True Democrat*, Jan. 5, 1859 189
23. J. P. Myers, *Missouri Republican*, Jan. 7, 1859....................190
24. Passenger Letter, *Arkansas True Democrat*, Jan. 8, 1859.........192
25. John T. Chidester, *Memphis Daily Appeal*, Jan. 12, 1859 195
26. Passenger Observations, Jan., 1859....................................196
27. Correspondent, *Sacramento Daily Union*, Jan.-May, 1859.....199
28. Correspondent, *Memphis Avalanche*, Feb. 17, 1859................206
29. Major Ben McCulloch, Texas Ranger, Feb., 1859...................212
30. W. H. Walton, *Memphis Avalanche*, Feb. 25, 1859...................224
31. Rev. Thomas McConnell Johnston's Diary, Mar., 1859. 227

32. Jennie Whipple Passenger, *Arkansian*, March 23, 1859........232
33. Jennie Whipple Passenger, *True Democrat*, Mar. 26, 1859.....233
34. Passenger Report, March 30, 1859 234
35. A. G. Mayers, Fort Smith Postmaster, July 5, 1859 235
36. "Authentic Source," *Missouri Republican*, July 11, 1859. 238
37. John Russell Young, *The Press*, Aug. 4 & Oct. 9, 1859..........241
38. Henry Everett, Sept. 19, 1859 and Sept. 15, 1859 261
39. Albert D. Richardson, Sept. - Oct., 1859................272
40. Capt. Smith, *Glasgow Missouri Times*, Oct. 13, 1859 291
41. Goodrich, *The Hydraulic Press*, Oct. 15, 1859........................293

1860

42. Sarah Ann Harlan, *Chronicles of OK*, January 13, 1860(?).....294
43. Passenger, Overland mail stage, April 6 & 12, 1860..............299
44. Passenger in the 'Boot,' *Arkansian*, April 27, 1860 304
45. Rebecca Johnston Yoakum, Spring, 1860 305
46. Hiram Rumfield letters from June, 1860 to June, 1862........ 317
47. William Tallack, July 4, 1860 353
  William Tallack, *Savannah Morning News*, Dec. 25, 1903.370
48. S. P. Nott, Accident on Butterfield Stage, July, 1860 372
49. William Wallace, *St. Joseph Free Democrat*, Sept. 7, 1860.......375
50. Mountain Station Accident, *Messenger*, July 22, 1860...........377
51. S. H. Shock, *Missouri Republican*, Aug. 13, 1860 380
52. Letter to the Editor, *Press Argus*, Sept. 7, 1860.......................382
53. 1860 Presidential Campaign, Oct. 5, 1860...............................383
54. Ralph Pumpelly, Oct. 8, 1860 385
55. Henry Dwight Barrows, Dec., 1860 389

1861

56. Charles Babcock, *Santa Fe Gazette*, June 26, 1861 399
57. Butterfield Employee Recollections 400
58. Enslaved "Aunt Adeline" from Parks Station, Arkansas....417
59. Enslaved "Kiziah Love" from Colbert's Ferry 419
60. William Buckley, Supt. & Fred K. Cook, Treasurer, 1861.....421

Postscript

61. Wm Averell, April 17, 1861 *[30 days after last westbound stage]*.425
62. John Butterfield Jr. & Amos B. Stafford, April 24, 1903........431
63. Alexander Toponce, Employee, as told in 1919 440
64. Thomas Ranahan, Stage Driver, March 26, 1923...................442
65. Muriel H. Wright, The Butterfield Overland Mail 445
66. Tom Dillard, Overland Mails Memphis - Fort Smith..........447

About the Author/Editor 453

Introduction

The words on the following pages were written between 1857 and 1861 concerning Butterfield's Overland Mail Co. stagecoach route as it passed through Oklahoma, Arkansas and Missouri. Many of these are first person accounts; others are newspaper interviews.

The compiler of these journal, diaries, and newspaper accounts kept any editorial comments to an absolute minimum, thereby, allowing the reader of this book to experience the world of the Butterfield Overland National Historic Trail directly from passengers themselves. Photographs and engravings from the period have been added to help the reader imagine the setting.

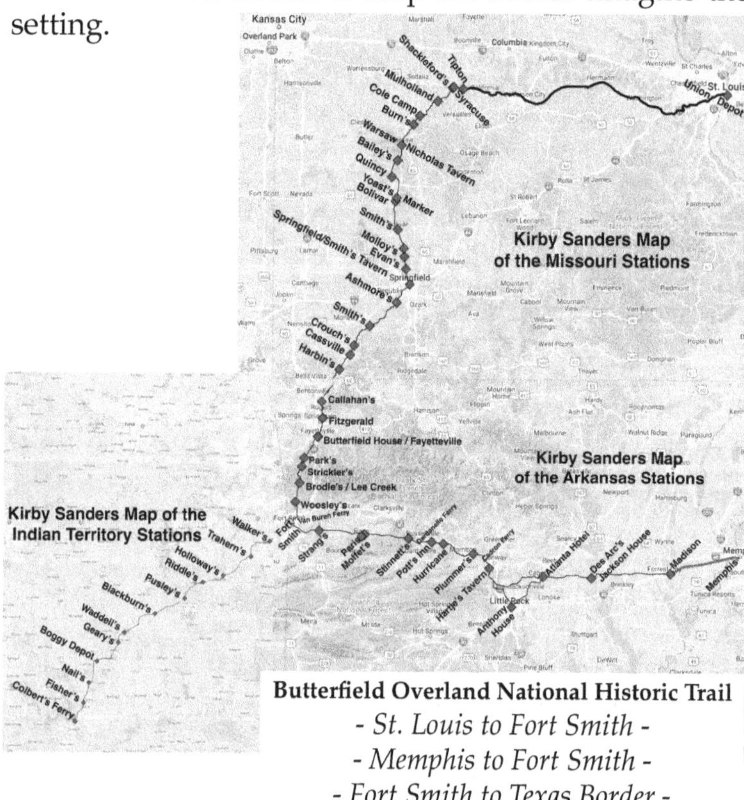

Butterfield Overland National Historic Trail
- St. Louis to Fort Smith -
- Memphis to Fort Smith -
- Fort Smith to Texas Border -
Image Source: Kirby Sanders

Upon picking up a book containing the diaries and stories of passengers on the Butterfield Overland National Historic Trail, it seems appropriate to ask:

How Many Passengers Rode the Butterfield?

As of today, no official records of the Overland Mail Company have surfaced that record the answer.

However, Rupert N. Richardson, in his 1925 article, *"Some Details of the Southern Overland Mail"* attempted to answer that question. The portion of his article dealing with passenger counts is reproduced below:

Rupert N. Richardson (April 28, 1891 - April 14, 1988)
Hardin-Simmons University, History Department
Dean, Vice-President, President

Some Details of the Southern Overland Mail
by Rupert N. Richardson, 1925

"...From the files of the Saint Louis and San Francisco papers, especially the Saint Louis *Missouri Republican* for 1858-1859, one may gather considerable information concerning the passengers that arrived at the two eastern termini, Saint Louis and Memphis, as well as those that reached San Francisco from the east. For the first year that the service was maintained, there are unusually complete accounts as to the passengers that arrived at Saint Louis. The number of passengers and generally their names were reported. When they reached Saint Louis, inquiring newspaper reporters generally met them and proceeded to gather from them all the information possible about their journey — the number of persons who left San Francisco, the number that joined the party or left it at the different way stations, the number that left the Saint Louis route at Fort Smith bound for Memphis, the destination of all parties, and their names and occupations. Thus it is for the first year of the Southern Overland Mail we have, in the files of the Saint Louis papers, definite accounts of the arrival of forty-seven of the possible one hundred four stage passenger parties that may have arrived.

In these forty-seven stage parties, there were eighty-five through passengers, who had come directly (or with short stop-overs at way stations to rest) from San Francisco or Los Angeles to Saint Louis or Memphis and about the same number of way passengers who had joined the stage party at some point on the line. The number of passengers starting from San Francisco who completed their journey before reaching Saint Louis or Memphis is not considered in this count but there were not many of this class.

From a similar perusal of the files of the *San Francisco Herald*, it seems that the number of west bound passengers at San Francisco did not greatly exceed, if, indeed, it equaled that of those going east. *[San Francisco Herald for January, June and August, 1859, and January and March, 1]* Frequently there were no through passengers from the east, and the number did not generally exceed two. There appeared to be more way passengers than through passengers arriving at that point. It would, therefore, be a safe conclusion that all through passengers did not amount to many more than one hundred fifty, each way, for the first year of the route, and that the way passengers arriving at Saint Louis and Memphis and those arriving at San Francisco did not greatly exceed this number.

As for passengers who patronized the line going from one way point to another, the number was, as we might expect, evidently decidedly greater. These people could not avail themselves of ocean or railroad transportation and the overland stage passing from their own to neighboring communities offered them a means of conveyance of incalculable benefit.

Stages arriving at San Francisco or Saint Louis carrying few or no through passengers often brought waybills showing that from twenty to thirty persons had used the stage on that trip.*[The waybill for the stage that arrived at San Francisco August 10 1859, showed 29 passengers; that for January 7, 1860, showed 27, and that for January 10, showed 23.]*

Compared with the thousands of persons who made the trip or from California every year by the Isthmus of Panama or the Tehuantepec routes or the thousands of others who followed the different overland routes by private conveyance, the few hundred persons who availed themselves of the stage for their trans-continental journey represent an almost negligible number.*[Nearly 1200 passengers for the Atlantic coast left San Francisco by steamers which departed on the 12th inst." Missouri Republican, March 31, 1859. "Nineteen hundred passengers arrived by the steamer John Stephens." San Francisco National, quoted by the Missouri Republican, May 25, 1859.]*

As the service continued, the number of through passengers seems to have diminished and the number of way passengers increased. Whether this decline was due to the disinclination of the public to attempt the journey after its hardships became known, or the inability of the company to transport more passengers is difficult to determine. Perhaps both causes must be taken into account.

It may be noted in this connection, however, that

in June, 1859, a weekly "accommodation stage" was put on the route between San Francisco and Los Angeles. The officials were reported as saying that this service might be extended to Saint Louis, thus giving a tri-weekly overland service for all the route; but it does not appear that this was ever done.

At first there was a sharp demand for seats at the San Francisco terminus, and one passenger reported that over one hundred persons were on the waiting list there when he left in November, 1858. *[Refers to the account given by Mr. Hough, a passenger. He also tells of one passenger who was forced to remain at a way station because he had gotten off there to rest and had been unable to secure a seat on the following stages although he offered a liberal bonus. He had been thus marooned a month. Missouri Republican, Dec. 12, 1858.]*

But it seems that this rush did not continue. *[This statement seems to be substantiated by the fact that way passengers increased after the route had been in operation for a while, and through passengers decreased somewhat proportionately. Since through passengers were given preference over way passengers, it was necessary for the number of the former to diminish before people along the route could use it at all.]*

Notwithstanding the comparatively small number of persons the company transported, the stage service was not without its value to the people of the nation. Army officers going to their posts or back to their homes took advantage of the service; politicians and lobbyists were frequently listed among the passengers; business men with pressing affairs frequently used it, because it offered a comparatively rapid means of transportation for various persons who needed to hurry. And, communities along the route, that would have been completely isolated without the stage found it a convenient means of conveyance for those of their citizens who needed to travel..."

Source: The Southwestern Historical Quarterly, July 1925, "Some Details of the Southern Overland Mail," Rupert N,. Richardson, pages 1-18.

TYPES OF STAGES USED ON THE BUTTERFIELD OVERLAND NATIONAL HISTORIC TRAIL

Butterfield used two types of stages: a mail stagecoach and a lighter weight Celerity wagon - both types ordered by John Butterfield from J. S. & E. A. Abbot Co. of Concord, New Hampshire.

Appearing in print for the first time in over a 120 years, shown below is the only existing image of a mail stagecoach used by Butterfield.

This image was re-discovered by Gerald T. Ahnert in December, 2023. Daguerreotype image Courtesy of The Post-Standard, April 24, 1904, page 12 In Sept. 1858, commemorating the first trip of the Overland Mail Co. between St. Louis and San Francisco, this daguerreotype image was taken in front of Charles E. Butterfield's residence in Fayetteville, Arkansas. John Butterfield Jr. is shown on the box, and A. B. Stafford holds the reins. Andrew Furlow stands at the head of the wheel horses. A second man, unnamed, standing near the rear wheel, may be passenger Waterman Ormsby. You can faintly see the lettering under the top railing: "Overland Mail Company."

Photo by Marilyn Heifner

This is Charles E. Butterfield's home as it appears today. This home, at 207 West Center Street, was re-discovered in Dec. 2023 by the research of Marilyn Heifner, president of THE BUTTERFIELD NATIONAL TRAILS Association. This "Walker-Stone" house is now the location of the Folk Art School of Fayetteville.

On rougher portions of the route, such as between Fayetteville and Fort Smith, and from Fort Smith to the California border, John Butterfield used a lighter weight stage called a "Celerity wagon" as shown below.

Below is the only photograph in existence of a Butterfield owned Overland Mail Company Celerity wagon.

The driver of the Celerity wagon shown above in the 'ten gallon hat' was David McLaughlin. This image was taken near the Cottonwood Stage Station, El Paso, Texas. This copy of a 1861 daguerreotype image is courtesy of the Nita Stewart Haley Memorial Library at Midland, Texas.

Deadwood Stagecoach in London during "Buffalo Bill's Wild West"
This is not a Butterfield owned stagecoach. However it is similar to the Concord stagecoaches Butterfield used on smooth portions of the route in Missouri, Central Arkansas and California. Buffalo Bill Cody (standing) and John Nelson (atop stage) Image source: taken during Wild West Show in London, ca. 1897

Letter from Buffalo Bill to Mr. Downing, stagecoach manufacturer of Concord, New Hampshire

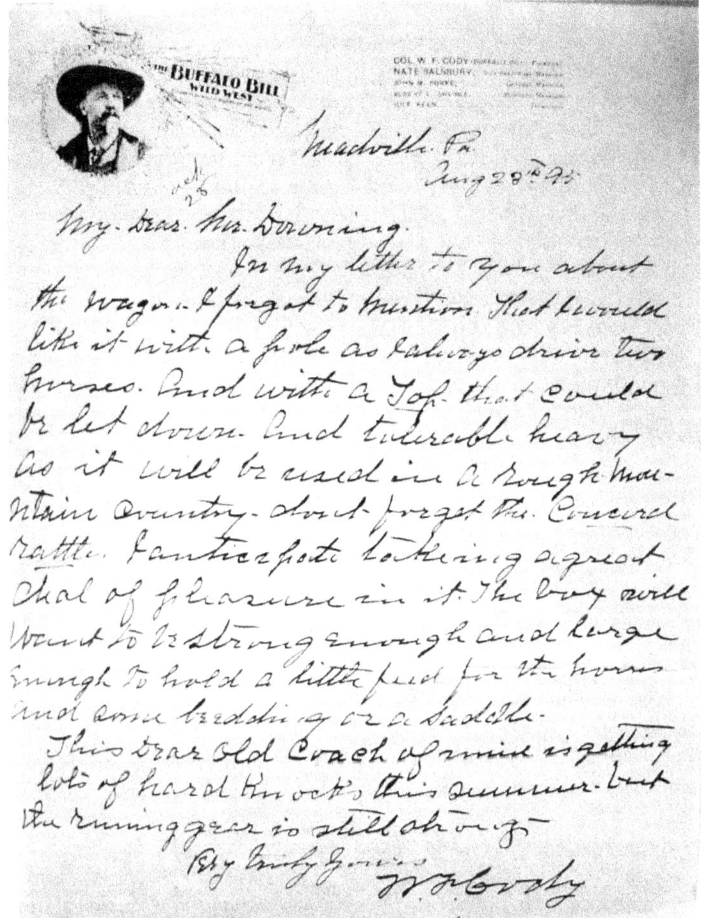

My Dear Mr. Downing,   Meadville, PA., Aug, 22, '95

In my letter to you about the wagon, I forgot to mention that I would like it with a pole as I always drive two horses. And with a top that could be let down. And tolerable heavy as it will be used in a rough mountain country — don't forget the Concord rattle. I anticipate taking a great deal of pleasure in it. The box will want to be strong enough and large enough to hold a little feed for the horses and some bedding or a saddle.

This dear old coach of mine is getting lots of hard knocks this summer but the running gear is still strong.   Very Truly Yours,
W. F. Cody

Image Source: Gerald T. Ahnert discovered in the files of the Abbot-Downing offices in Concord, New Hampshire

John Butterfield
November 18, 1801 – November 14, 1869

Bidding against eight others, John Butterfield was chosen September 16, 1857 by former Tennessee Governor, the Postmaster General Aaron Brown for a new Route #12578.

Concerning the selection of John Butterfield's bid over the competition, Gerald T. Ahnert, historian and authority on the Overland Mail Company, wrote: *"What was needed was someone with some of the most extensive experience in the United States."* [Source: "Butterfield Makes the Southern Overland Trail His Own, Gerald T. Ahnert, Overland Journal, Spring, 2020, pg. 13.]

Born in Berne, New York in 1801, Butterfield grew up on a farm located directly on a stagecoach route. By the age of 19, John was driving spring coaches for the Thorpe & Sprague Livery Stable in Albany. Moving to Utica he married Malinda Baker in 1822, eventually having eight children. To make ends meet he moonlighted at night driving a two-seat carriage. In 1825 John became manager of Parker and Co. Soon his enterprise grew into a boarding house, eastern stagecoach lines, packet boats and railroads.

"He had been a stagecoach driver when a young man, and had risen to be owner of nearly all the stage lines running in Western New York. In 1849 he was engaging in transporting freight across the Isthmus of Panama. He was also projector of the Morse Telegraph line between Buffalo and New York, and he not only built it, but also put it into successful operation. Enlisting others with him, he founded a line of Lake Ontario and St. Lawrence steamers, and in 1849 he formed the express company of Butterfield, Wasson and Co. We suppose he may claim to be founder of the American Express Company, for in 1850 he approached Henry Wells with the acceptable proposition that the three firms should be consolidated." [Source: Harper's New Monthly Magazine, Aug., 1875, p. 322]

In 1857, by the time John Butterfield was fifty-six he *"had accumulated a comfortable fortune, and it was widely known that no man in the country knew more about the ins and outs of horse-drawn transportation. He had an incredible memory and was a natural born leader, admired because of his basic generosity and genuine interest in public benefit. He was scrupulously fair... besides being deeply religious...*

A busy man in the field of stagecoach lines and transportation, Butterfield was able to attract and keep good workers. A successful businessman, he didn't seek glory and glamour but was much more interested in results. He had little formal education, but he made up for it with his natural organizational and managerial talents...

At a time when he should have retired to enjoy comfortable life with a comfortable fortune behind him, Butterfield instead chose to commit himself to the most outstanding achievement of his career: the Overland Mail Company..." [Source: "Butterfield Makes the Southern Overland Trail His Own, Gerald T. Ahnert, Overland Journal, Spring, 2020, pg. 13.]

Overland Mail Co.
1858-1864

The gold rush of 1848 began a mass migration of men to California, seeking fortune for themselves and their families back home. This migration put increasing pressure on Congress to improve mail delivery to the pacific coast.

Bidding against eight others, John Butterfield was chosen September 16, 1857 by former Tennessee Governor, the Postmaster General Aaron Brown for a new Route #12578. The six year contract, with a $600,000 annual payment, required Butterfield to carry mail and passengers, semi-weekly departing simultaneously from St. Louis & Memphis, merging in Fort Smith, then on to San Francisco in 25 days or less in comfortable four-horse stagecoaches.

In only 12 months, the Overland Mail Co. poured about three and a half million dollars into establishing the 3,000 mile route from the Mississippi River to the Pacific coast. Butterfield purchased 34 Mail Stagecoaches and 66 Celerity wagons from J. S. and E. A. Abbot of Concord New Hampshire, 1,800 horses and mules, and ordered delivery of 3,000 tons of grain and hay to the various stations along the route.

Butterfield established 139 stations in the beginning of service averaging about 15 miles apart, increasing to 175 stations within a year. The 34 Mail Stagecoaches, Celerity wagons, and 150 other vehicles were spread along the 3,134 mile route, *(including the 322 miles from Memphis to Fort Smith).*

John Butterfield employed almost 2,000 drivers, conductors, station-keepers, blacksmiths, mechanics, wheelwrights, helpers, hostlers, herders, veterinarians, armed guards, and harness makers along the route.

True to the contract, in mid September, 1858, almost simultaneously the Overland Mail departed San Francisco, St. Louis and Memphis — arriving at their destinations in less than 25 days.

On March 20, 1860 the Overland Mail Company Board decided to retain its structure, but remove John Butterfield as president. William B. Dinsmore was elected president in Butterfield's place.

After 130 weeks of operation on the southern route, at the dawn of the Civil War in March of 1861, the Southern Route was canceled. Butterfield's old six year contract was amended to the Central Route, entirely avoiding the southern states. This required John Butterfield to begin moving employees and equipment north to the Placerville — Salt Lake City — St. Joseph route.

The new Central Route contract required daily trips from St. Joseph, Missouri to Placerville, California. It also required Butterfield to oversea the once private Pony Express over that same route.

In mid 1864 when the six year contract was complete, John Butterfield ended his relationship to the Overland Mail Co. In August 1864, former board president Wm. Dinsmore organized a new Overland Mail Co. and continued seeking postal contracts. In December 1866 the Overland Mail Co. and several other stage lines were purchased by Ben Holladay. Within a few months, Holladay sold his entire stagecoach business to Wells Fargo & Company.

Butterfield Overland National Historic Trail

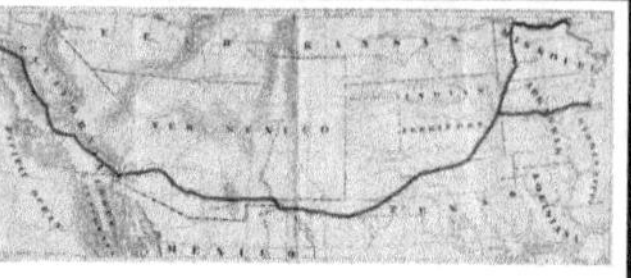

Approved by Congress, December 2022

On September 16, 1857 John Butterfield signed a contract with Postmaster General Aaron Brown for a new Postal Route #12578. That contract required the Overland Mail Co. to establish a route:

"from the Mississippi River to San Francisco, California, converging at Little Rock, Arkansas; thence, via Preston, Texas, or as near so as may be found advisable, to the best point of crossing the Rio Grande above El Paso, and not far from Fort Fillmore; thence, along the new road being opened and constructed under the direction of the Secretary of the Interior, to or near Fort Yuma, California; thence, through the best passes and along the best valleys for safe and expeditious staging, to San Francisco, California, and back, twice a week, in good four horse post coaches or spring wagons suitable for the conveyance of passengers as well as the safety and security of the mails..."

John Butterfield received permission for the St. Louis and Memphis stages to merge at Fort Smith instead of Little Rock, Arkansas.

From the Mississippi to Fort Smith, existing roads would be used. To determine the exact route west of Fort Smith, two expeditions were sent out by the Overland Mail Company on January 2, 1858.

Led by Marquis Kenyon, Frank DeRyther, S. L. Nellis, James Swart and John Butterfield, Jr. began their expedition out of San Francisco.

George Wood, Jesse Talcott and Charles P. Cole began their expedition out of St. Louis. The two expeditions were to meet at El Paso.

Completing their expedition, they returned to Fort Smith on April 24, 1858, "having made the trip from El Paso – a distance of 925 miles – in the unprecedented short time of twenty-five days, which we believe is the quickest trip ever made across the Plains."*(May 1, 1858 Arkansas Gazette)* On this return trip to St. Louis, Marquis L. Kenyon made significant changes to the route the westbound expedition had recommended.

In June of 1858, with the preliminary survey complete: 1) a team began in California and another in Fort Smith, renting existing buildings or building new buildings to serve as stations; 2) they began to distribute horses, equipment and spare replacement stages and stagecoaches along the route; and 3) Daniel Butterfield fixed the schedule, setting arrival and departures to the minute from each of the major stations.

Butterfield established 139 stations in the beginning of service averaging about 15 miles apart, increasing to 175 stations within a year. The 34 Mail Stagecoaches, Celerity wagons, and 150 other vehicles were spread along the route. John Butterfield employed almost 2,000 drivers, conductors, station-keepers, blacksmiths, mechanics, wheelwrights, helpers, hostlers, herders, veterinarians, armed guards, and harness makers along the route.

True to the contract, in mid September, 1858, almost simultaneously the Overland Mail departed San Francisco, St. Louis and Memphis — arriving at their destinations in less than 25 days.

As the months passed, there were several adjustments made to the route, but overall trail remained the same until it was relocated north to the St. Joseph, MO *via* Salt Lake to Placerville, CA Central "in the spring of 1861.

BRIEF DESCRIPTION OF
THE BUTTERFIELD OVERLAND NATIONAL HISTORIC TRAIL
STATIONS

The following stations [in plain text] are officially recognized by the National Parks System (www.nps.gov)

MISSOURI Stations
St. Louis, #56 Main Street
> *From St. Louis to Tipton, the mail was carried by the Pacific Railroad.*

Tipton / *Train Station*
   Syracuse/Train Station
   Smithton/Train Station
Schackleford's Station
Mulholland's Station
Burn's Station
Warsaw
Bailey's Station
Quincy
Yoast's Station
Bolivar
Smith's Station
Evan's Station
Springfield
Ashmore's Station
Smith's Station
Crouch's Station
Harbin's Station

ARKANSAS Northwestern Route
Callahan's Station
Fitzgerald's Station
Fayetteville
Park's Station
Brodie's Station (Lee Creek)
Woolsey's Station (Signal Hill)
Van Buren *Ferry*
Fort Smith

ARKANSAS Memphis Route
Memphis, TN Commercial Hotel
   Hopefield Train Station
Madison, Ark.
   Station south of Oakland
   Station south of Cotton Plant
Des Arc
   Hickory Plains Station

Atlanta *Hotel* (present-day Austin)
   Jacksonville Stage Station
   Anthony House Station
   Hartjie & Sevier Station
Cadron *Ferry*
Plummer's Station (Plumerville)
Lewisburg (Morrilton)
Hurricane (Atkins)
Pottsville Inn *Kirkbride Potts Inn*
Norristown (Russellville)
Dardanelle *Ferry*
Stinnett's Station
   Shoal Creek Station
   Creole Station
Paris *Moffett's Station*
Charleston *A. J. Singleton Station*
   Strang's Farm Station (Lavaca)
Fort Smith *City Hotel*
   St. Charles Hotel after the fire

OKLAHOMA Stations
Walker's Station (Skullyville)
Trahern's Station
Holloway's Station *(Brazil Station)*
Riddle's Station
Pusley's Station
Blackburn's Station
Waddell's Station
Geary's Station
Boggy Depot
Blue River Station *(Nail's Crossing)*
Fisher's Station
Colbert's Ferry

TEXAS Stations
Preston's Station
Sherman
Diamond's Station
Gainesville...

For balance of the list see:
www.nps.gov/articles/000/butterfield-overland-trail-stage-stations.htm

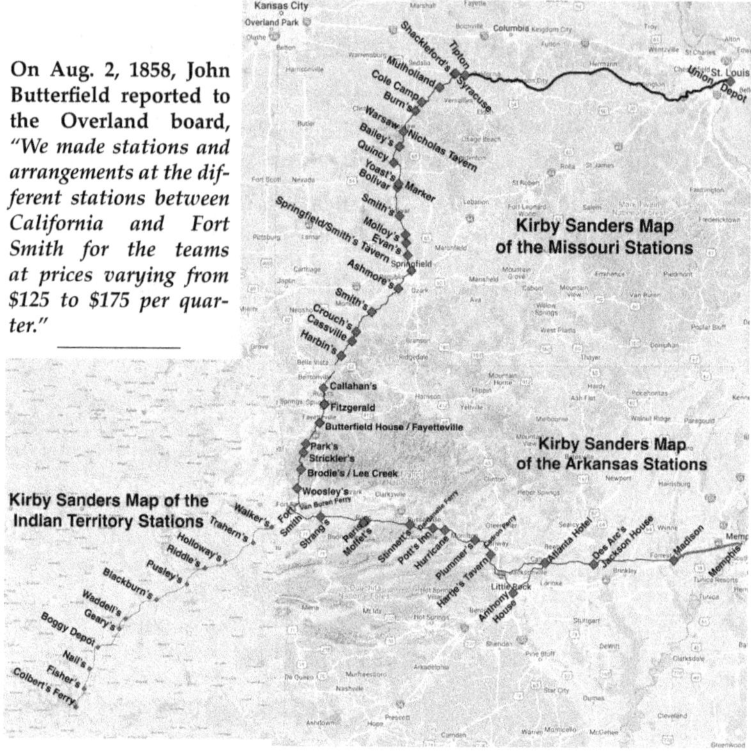

A Brief Description of the Stations from St Louis & Memphis to Fort Smith and the Red River

The St. Louis, Missouri offices of the Overland Mail Company were located at 56 North Main Street.

Passengers could purchased a $200 westbound ticket from S. M. Allen, agent for the Overland Mail Co. According to the schedule, at 8:00 a.m. every Monday and Thursday, passengers would ride a horse-drawn cab fourteen blocks to the train station on 14th Street.

At 9:00 a.m., the Pacific Railroad train would depart for Tipton, a 163 mile trip westward to the end of the tracks.

Jan. 1, 1859, Daily Missouri Republican
Appreciation is expressed to Gerald T. Ahnert
for finding this newspaper ad.

Jan. 10, 1859, Missouri Republican
giving departure days & times of
Pacific RR trains and stagecoaches

Route of Pacific Railroad
through St. Louis County

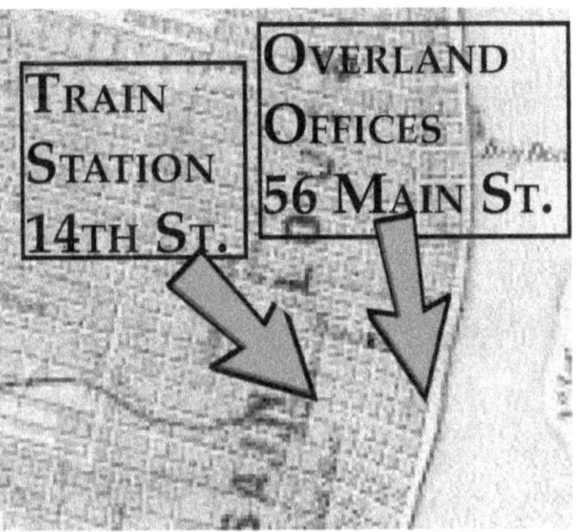

Train Station & Overland Office
in St. Louis, Missouri

1857 Map of Saint Louis County,
Courtesy of the Library of Congress

TIPTON STATION

When the train arrived at Tipton, American Express ticket agent Milo June would assist passengers transfer from the train to the Overland Mail Co. Concord stagecoach. The Overland stagecoaches departed Tipton every Monday and Thursday at 6 p.m. If the train arrived early, passengers could rest or eat at Tipton's Prairie House, where H. H. Newman was the proprietor.

Aug. 29, 1859, Weekly California News,
California, Missouri, page 4

1861 James T. Lloyd's Official Map of Missouri, Library of Congress

NOTE: At every station listed below, averaging 15 miles apart, the stage received fresh horses, and typically the axles greased as well. Every 50 to 60 miles, at a home station the stage received a fresh driver. Every 100 to 120 miles the stage received a fresh conductor. The old driver and old conductor would spend a few nights at that home station, taking charge of the next stage headed back in the opposite direction.

SYRACUSE STATION, June 1859

After nine months, the railroad tracks had been extended seven miles further west and the Butterfield terminus station and agent Milo June relocated to Syracuse in June of 1859. Gerald T. Ahnert recently discovered that the station agent at Syracuse was Isaac S. Coe.

Passengers arriving early at Syracuse could rest or eat at the Brayton House where Thomas R. Brayton was the proprietor.

According to the 2023 research of Gerald T. Ahnert, George Shackelford's served as the Syracuse station until August, 1859 when John Butterfield purchased 6 lots in Syracuse and built company owned stables.

Syracuse served as Butterfield's Overland Mail Co. transition station from June, 1859 to Feb. 5, 1861.

> **Stage for Springfield and Southwest Missouri, leaves Syracuse on Monday, Wednesday, Thursday and Friday evenings; and on every Monday and Thursday, P.M., the Overland Mail stages of Butterfield & Co. for Fort Smith, El Paso and San Francisco.'**

Feb. 4, 1861, Daily Republican, St. Louis, page 4

SMITHTON STATION, Feb. 6, 1861

On Feb. 6, 1861, with the tracks now extended farther west, the Overland Mail transition station relocated 13 miles west to Smithton, Missouri as indicated in the wording change within the newspaper ad below.

> **Stage for Springfield and Southwest Missouri, leaves <u>Smithton</u> on Monday, Wednesday, Thursday and Friday evenings; and on every Monday and Thursday, P.M., the Overland Mail stages of Butterfield & Co. for Fort Smith, El Paso and San Francisco.'**

Feb. 6, 1861, Daily Republican, St. Louis, page 4

This identical ad was running as late at June 28, 1861, indicating that the transition station did not relocate to Sedalia when it became the end of the tracks. As seen at the top of the ad below, Sedalia did have mail arrive by train, and stagecoaches carried that mail on to Lexington via Georgetown every evening - however this was a different stage line than Butterfield's.

> **Stages leave <u>Sedalia</u> daily, (on arrival of mail train from St. Louis.) for Independence, Kansas City, Leavenworth, Pleasant Hill, and Harrisonville.**
>
> **Stage for Lexington via Georgetown, leaves Sedalia every evening.**
>
> **Booneville stage leaves Tipton every evening, on arrival of trains.**
>
> **Stage for Springfield and Southwest Missouri, leaves <u>Smithton</u> on Monday, Wednesday, Thursday and Friday evenings; and on every Monday and Thursday, P.M., the Overland Mail stages of Butterfield & Co. for Fort Smith, El Paso and San Francisco.**

June 28, 1861, Daily Republican, St. Louis, page 4

Mulholland's continued to be the first stop for the southwest bound stagecoach from Smithton as it headed toward Springfield, and Fort Smith.

MULHOLLAND'S STATION

Departing the train station at Tipton, Syracuse or later Smithton, 13 miles south on the old Booneville Road, the stagecoach arrived at James P. Mulhollen's station.

BURN'S STATION

Departing Mulholland's station, 20 miles to the southwest the stagecoach arrived at Burn's station on

– 21 –

the outskirts of Cole Camp, Missouri.

WARSAW STATION

The stagecoach departed Burn's station for a 15 mile trip to Warsaw, typically arriving about 3:00 a.m. According to John Butterfield's letter of Aug. 2, 1858, he purchased a "stable and lot at Warsaw, MO... We keep our own teams buying the necessary hay and grass as required."

Leaving Warsaw, passenger Ormsby wrote, *"The road led through a ford of the Osage River and a dense forest, full of rocky hills, and the night was now dark as pitch. As we left Warsaw we had to be preceded by a man on horseback, with a light to show us the way through the ford... the water was not deeper than half the wheels."*

BAILEY'S STATION

Departing Warsaw on an 11 mile trip, crossing the covered bridge at Pomme de Terre River near Fairfield, the stagecoach arrived at E. K. Bailey's station.

QUINCY STATION

Ten miles south of Bailey's, the stage arrived at Quincy station which was a breakfast stop for passengers.

YOAST'S STATION

Departing Quincy for a 16 mile trip, the stagecoach traveled southwest through Wheatland and Elkton to arrive at Yoast's station.

BOLIVAR STATION

Traveling due south from Yoast's station for 16 miles, the stagecoach arrived at Bolivar station located near the Franklin Hotel where Ahab Bowen was the proprietor.

SMITH'S STATION

The stagecoach left Bolivar for a 12 mile trip to the James H. M. Smith station, two miles north of Brighton.

EVAN'S STATION

The next stop south of Smith's station was an 11

mile distance to Evan's station.

SPRINGFIELD STATION

Departing Evan's station, in 9 miles the stagecoach arrived on Booneville Road at Gen. Nicholas Smith's Tavern in Springfield, Missouri. According to John Butterfield's letter of Aug. 2, 1858, he purchased a "stable and lot at Springfield, MO... We keep our own teams buying the necessary hay and grass as required." At this point the Overland had traveled 143 miles from Tipton, in about 21 hours. According to the schedule, westbound stages departed Springfield on Wednesday and Saturday at 7:45 a.m.

ASHMORE'S STATION

Leaving Springfield, the route passed the home of John A, Ray which served as a post office from 1856 to 1866. Ray's was not a regular stop, however if mail or passengers were waiting, Ray's would place a flag out to signal the stagecoach to stop. Traveling 13 miles, the stagecoach arrived at John C. Ashmore's station.

SMITH'S STATION

The stagecoach left Ashmore's station, for a 20 mile trip to John I. Smith's station, which stood 7 miles west of Crane, Missouri.

CROUCH'S STATION

Leaving Smith's the stagecoach traveled southwest for 15 miles, to follow Flat Creek to John D. Crouch's station.

HARBIN'S STATION

Departing Crouch's station for a 16 mile trip, passing through Cassville, the stagecoach arrived at the last Missouri station - John G. Harbin's station which stood one mile south of Washburn, Missouri, and only 6 miles north of the Arkansas line.

[For more details on the Missouri portion of the Butterfield Overland Mail route, see *"The Butterfield Overland Mail, 1858-1861 and its Centennial Observance in Missouri,"* by Donald H. Welsh, *The Missouri Historical Review*, Vol. 52, No. 3, April 1858. Also refer to, *"Butterfield Run Through the Ozarks,"* by Phillip W. Steele. The information above, on the Missouri route, is based on these two sources.]

ARKANSAS
CALLAHAN'S STATION (Rogers, Arkansas)

After entering Arkansas, the stagecoach passed the 1833 Elk Horn Tavern built by William Ruddick. Although not an official station, Kirby Sanders refers to the tavern as a "flag station." Ten miles past the Elk Horn Tavern, the stagecoach crossed Little Sugar Creek and arrived at Dennis Callahan's Tavern.

FITZGERALD'S STATION

Leaving Callahan's, the stagecoach passed through Cross Hollows and Mudtown (modern day Lowell) and reached Fitzgerald's station. Butterfield contracted with Fitzgerald for permission to keep horses in the stone barn. That stone barn is still standing (as of 2023) along with an 1870's house.

FAYETTEVILLE'S STATION

Leaving Fitzgerald's, the stagecoach arrived in Fayetteville. In 1858, Butterfield bought 5 acres in Fayetteville and built a hotel at this station site and owned another stable on the west side of the square.

Butterfield's son Charles, who served as a Senior Superintendent, also built a home and lived in Fayetteville. According to schedule, westbound stages departed Fayetteville on Thursday and Sunday at 10:15 a.m.

PARK'S STATION

Leaving Fayetteville, the stagecoach passed Cato Springs and Hog Eye Tavern to arrive at John P. A. Park's station. At Park's station, mail and passengers were transferred from horse drawn Concord stagecoaches to the lighter weight mule drawn Celerity wagon due to the ruggedness of the route over Boston Mountain.

BRODIE'S STATION (Lee Creek)

Crossing Lee Creek on a 10 mile trip to Brodie's station, the Celerity wagon passed Strickler's flag station on the Bug Scuffle Road.

WOOSLEY'S STATION (Signal Hill)

Leaving Brodie's station, the stage continued south to George Woosley's station (sometimes mistakenly referred to at 'Oosley station.')

FORT SMITH'S HOME STATION

Continuing 10 miles south of Woolsey's, the Celerity wagon headed down the steep Signal Hill to reach the Van Buren ferry at about 2:30 a.m. Crossing the Arkansas River on the Van Buren Ferry, the Celerity wagon arrived at Fort Smith.

If the stage from Memphis had not yet arrived, passengers would rest and eat at John Roger's City Hotel, that housed the Butterfield offices.

After merging with the stagecoach from Memphis, a Celerity wagon would continue through Indian Territory toward San Francisco. According to the schedule, at 3:30 a.m. every Friday and Monday, a Celerity wagon departed for San Francisco.

[For more details on the Northwest Arkansas portion of the route, refer to *"Butterfield's Overland Mail Co. STAGECOACH Trail Across Arkansas, 1858-1861,"* by Bob Crossman.]

ARKANSAS'
MEMPHIS - FORT SMITH ROUTE

On average, the travel time from Memphis to Fort Smith took 91 hours, however poor roads and swampy conditions proved troublesome.

MEMPHIS' HOME STATION

The offices of the Overland Mail Company were at Memphis' Commercial Hotel, where D. F. Kandy was the Butterfield agent. According to the schedule, the Overland Mail left Memphis every Monday and

Thursday at 8 a.m. headed toward Fort Smith.

Arriving at the banks of the Mississippi River, passengers and mail crossed by ferry to arrive at the Hopefield train station. Boarding the train for a 24 mile trip, passengers and mail crossed the "Great Swamp" of the Arkansas delta to reach the end of the tracks. Transferring to a light vehicle twelve miles east of Madison, the Overland crossed the St. Francis River by ferry and traveled 50 miles to Des Arc.

The swing stations for a change of horses were typically 9 to 15 miles apart. So, most likely the 50 mile trip to Des Arc included a stop at the crossroads south of Oakland, and again south of Cotton Plant for fresh horses.

DES ARC STATION

Fifty miles west of Madison, the light vehicle crossed the White River ferry to arrive at Des Arc's Jackson House, where passengers and mail transferred to a Concord stagecoach. The twelve-room Jackson House was owned by M. M. Erin, where a 16' x 16' stage office was attached to the east side of the tavern.

When water levels were favorable, the Overland traveled by Butterfield's steamboat, the Jennie Whipple, from Memphis to Des Arc.

ATLANTA HOTEL (Austin, Arkansas)

Departing the Jackson House for a 26 mile trip to Oakland Grove's Atlanta House, most likely the stagecoach stopped halfway at Hickory Plain for a change of horses. J. J. Peebles' Atlanta Hotel, housed the offices of the Chidester, Reeside & Co. stageline.

During the first month of operation, the stagecoach went direct from the Atlanta Hotel to the Cadron ferry, bypassing the state capital of Little Rock. During September of 1858, mail and passengers were transported from Little Rock by Hanger's Stageline to meet the

Overland Mail stagecoach at the Atlanta Hotel.

During that first month, about halfway to the Cadron ferry, the stagecoach passed near Otto's Greathouse, where it may have stopped for fresh horses.

ANTHONY HOUSE STATION (Little Rock)

Starting in October, 1858, the stagecoach departed the Atlanta House and headed south, crossing the Arkansas River ferry to arrive at the Anthony House home station, William H. Dawson, proprietor.

It is about 30 miles from the Atlanta Hotel to the Anthony House, so most likely the stagecoach stopped half way at the Gray Township Stagecoach House (now called Jacksonville) for a change of horses.

When water levels were favorable on about 85 occasions, the Overland traveled by Butterfield's steamboat, the Jennie Whipple, from Memphis to Little Rock.

HARTJIE & SEVIER STATION

Leaving Anthony House, the stagecoach boarded the Arkansas River ferry, traveling northwest toward the next station. Crossing Palarm Creek's toll bridge, the stagecoach then stopped at August Hartje's 1854 tavern. About 1860, Mike Sevier built his tavern about 1½ miles to the south, and it apparently served as the Butterfield station beginning at that point.

CADRON STATION

Departing Hartje/Sevier Taverns, the stagecoach headed north 11 miles passing Round Mountain, Reedy Ridge, Gay Tavern, and Green Grove to reach the Cadron station and ferry. There may have been a Butterfield stage station atop Cadron Ridge.

PLUMMER'S STATION

Departing Cadron, rejoining the route initially used during the first month of operation, the Butterfield stagecoach continued west on the 1824 Old Military Road for 11 miles to reach Samuel's Plummer's station and leather shop. Plummer's leather shop is still standing (in 2023) but the station building collapsed in December of 2022.

LEWISBURG STATION (Morrilton, Arkansas)

Departing Plummer's station, the stagecoach continued west 7 miles to reach the Lewisburg station, a steamboat landing on the Arkansas River.

HURRICANE STATION (Atkins, Arkansas)

Leaving Lewisburg station, the stagecoach traveled 14 miles on the 1824 Old Military Road to reach the Hurricane station.

KIRKBRIDE POTTS' STATION

Continuing west 9 miles, the stagecoach reached Kirkbride Pott's 1858 home station. This structure is now restored, and serves as a museum. Pott's station is the only surviving unremodeled Butterfield station in Missouri, Arkansas or Texas.

NORRISTOWN (Russellville, Arkansas)

After a bite to eat at Potts Tavern, with a fresh driver and horses, the stagecoach continued west to Norristown. At Norristown, since 1824, the Old Military Road crosses the Arkansas River on the Dardanelle Ferry. One of the passenger accounts mentions that only passengers crossed on this ferry, and boarded a new stagecoach to continue toward Fort Smith, indicating that there may have been a stage station at Dardanelle.

STINNETT'S STATION

Departing the ferry at Dardanelle, passing Dardanelle Rock, the stagecoach continued west 10 miles to Moses' Stinnett's station for fresh horses.

SHOAL CREEK

Departing Stinnett's for a 17 mile trip, the stagecoach stopped at the Shoal Creek station for fresh horses.

CREOLE STATION

Departing Shoal Creek, the stagecoach stopped at the Creole station for a change of horses.

MOFFETT'S STATION (Paris, Arkansas)

With fresh horses, the stagecoach westward to Alfred Moffett's station, 27 miles west of Stinnett's station, 15 miles west of Shoal Creek station.

SINGLETON'S STATION (Charleston, Arkansas)

Departing Moffett's station, in 17 miles the stagecoach arrived at Andrew J. Singleton's station for another change of horses.

STRANG'S STATION (Lavaca, Arkansas)

Continuing west on the 1824 Old Military Road for 11 miles, the stagecoach arrived at James A. Strang's station. Kirby Sanders also mentions the presence of an alternate station owned by Bronson Andrews.

FORT SMITH STATION

Leaving Strang's station with fresh horses, the stagecoaches traveled 16 miles west to reach John Roger's **City Hotel** in Fort Smith where the Butterfield offices and stables were located, to merge with the Celerity wagon from St. Louis.

After the City Hotel was destroyed by fire on Sept. 15, 1860 the Butterfield offices were relocated a couple of blocks north to the **St. Charles Hotel**.

On about 4 occasions, when water levels were favorable, the Overland traveled by Butterfield's steamboat, the Jennie Whipple, from Memphis to Fort Smith.

[For more details on the Memphis to Fort Smith portion of the route, refer to *"Butterfield's Overland Mail Co. STAGECOACH Trail Across Arkansas, 1858-1861,"* by Bob Crossman.

For more details on Butterfield's use of his steamboat, the Jennie Whipple between Memphis and Fort Smith, refer to *"Butterfield's Overland Mail Co. use of STEAMBOATS Across Arkansas, 1858-1861,"* by Bob Crossman.]

INDIAN TERRITORY

Butterfield Overland National Historic Trail Through Oklahoma, by Susan Dragoo
Source: Map by JJ Ritchey. Originally published with Susan's wonderful
article in the Oklahoma Today magazine, July/August 2018.

The Indian Territory's twelve stage stations, across 192 miles of southeast Oklahoma, were established by contract with the Choctaw and Chickasaw Nations.

WALKER'S STATION (Skullyville, Oklahoma)
Departing Fort Smith with a fresh Celerity wagon, driver and horses, traveling west for 15 miles, the Celerity wagon arrived at Choctaw Governor Tandy Walker's station.

TRAHERN'S STATION (Latham, Oklahoma)
Departing Walker's station, the stagecoach crossed Brazil Creek, passing Brazil station, arriving at James N. Trahern's station. Trahern's was also the site of the Council House of the Moshulatubbe District of the Choctaw Nation.

HOLLOWAY'S STATION
Traveling southwest from Trahern's, passing the

trading post at Thomas Edwards' Store, the road reaches the Narrows and William Holloway's station.

RIDDLE'S STATION (Lutie, Oklahoma)

Departing Holloway's, the stagecoach passed present-day Red Oak, to reach Captain John Riddle's station for a change of horses.

PUSLEY'S STATION

Departing Riddle's, the stagecoach passed Mountain station, and crossed Gaines Creek to reach Silas Pusley's station.

BLACKBURN'S STATION

Traveling 17 miles southwest, the stagecoach left Pusley's station, through a valley along Buffalo Creek, to reach Casper B. Blackburn's station.

WADDELL'S STATION

Departing Blackburn's station for a 16 mile trip, along Brushy Creek to reach Waddell's station.

GEARY'S STATION (Chickasaw Creek)

Continuing southwest, the stagecoach left Waddell's station, passing Breadtown Creek (also known as Chickasaw Creek) to reach A. W. Geary's station.

BOGGY DEPOT

With another team of fresh horses, the stagecoach departed Geary's station to reach the capital of the Choctaw Nation and the Boggy Depot station at Guy's Hotel.

NAIL'S CROSSING STATION (Blue River)

Southwest of Boggy Depot, the stagecoach traveled to Jonathan H. Nail's station on the Blue River, also known as the Blue River Station.

FISHER'S STATION (Carriage Point)

Continuing southwest, the stagecoach left the Blue River station to reach Fisher's station.

COLBERT'S FERRY

Heading south from Fisher's station, the stagecoach

reached Benjamin F. Colbert's ferry to cross the Red River and continue across Texas, New Mexico, Arizona, and arriving at San Francisco, California.

[For more details on the Indian Territory portion of the route, refer to the wonderful article, *"Marking the Butterfield: Retracing the Indian Territory Segment of the 1858-61 Butterfield Overland Mail Stagecoach Road,"* by Susan Penn Dragoo, *The Chronicles of Oklahoma,* Spring 2019, Vol. 97, No. 1. The above information on the Indian Territory stations is based on Susan Dragoo's research.]

In December, 2023, Gerald T. Ahnert discovered this wonderful painting of Isaac S. Coe — the Syracuse, Missouri station keeper for Butterfield's Overland Mail Company.

Image courtesy of Gerald T. Ahnert Also at Syracuse, Mr. Milo June was the ticket agent with the American Express Co. and Ezra W. Houk was the Syracuse postmaster.

This is the blacksmith shop of Otto Mittag, grandfather of Bob Crossman. He was a wheelright, blacksmith, farrier, and tool and die maker.

He practiced his trade in Fort Smith, Arkansas and later in Houston, TX for Howard Hughes.

Years before his time, scattered along the trail, wheelwrights, blacksmiths, and farriers like him were engaged to keep the equipment in working order.

Randolph B. Marcy
(April 9, 1812 – November 22, 1887)

PROLOGUE

Below are two accounts of a journey through Indian Territory — from Fort Smith to the Red River ferry. The first is by Randolph B. Marcy, and the second is by his companion on the trip, W. B. Parker.

Their journey occurred in June, 1854, four years prior to Butterfield's Overland Mail Co. using basically the same route.

These two early accounts are included because they enhance the later Butterfield passengers diaries. In particular, this prologue includes W. B. Parker's rich and personal encounters with Choctaw residents on his journey through Indian Territory.

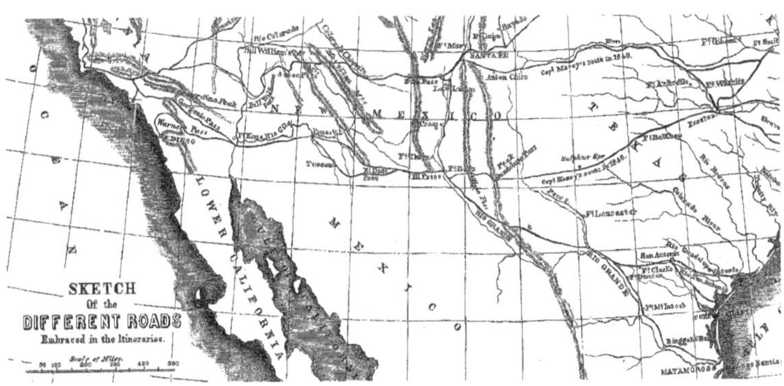

Marcy, R. B., The Prairie Traveler, 1859, New York: Harper and Brothers, p. 15

Note from Bob Crossman: I must express my appreciation to Susan Dragoo for introducing me to the Randolph B. Marcy travel journal.

Randolph B. Marcy, 1849/1859
*as reported in The Prairie Traveler, A Handbook for Overland Expeditions,
by Randolph Barnes Marcy, 1859.*

*[Marcy's recollections from an 1849 trip, is the earliest account included here,
of a passenger's report of travel basically over the route chosen by John Butterfield "for a great portion of the way to New Mexico."]*

Marcy writes:

EMIGRANTS or others desiring to make the overland journey to the Pacific should bear in mind that
there are several different routes which may be traveled with wagons, each having its advocates in persons directly or indirectly interested in attracting the
tide of emigration and travel over them. *[page 15]*

[page 17] The next route... is that over which the
semi-weekly mail *[Butterfield's Overland Mail Co.]* to California passes, and which, for a great portion of the way
to New Mexico, I traveled and recommended in 1849.
This road leaves the Arkansas River at Fort Smith, to
which point steamers run during the seasons of high
water in the winter and spring.

Supplies of all descriptions necessary for the overland journey may be procured at Fort Smith, or at Van
Buren on the opposite side of the Arkansas. Horses
and cattle are cheap here. The road, on leaving Fort
Smith, passes through the Choctaw and Chickasaw
country for 180 miles, then crosses Red River by ferry-boat at Preston, and runs through the border settlements of northern Texas for 150 miles, within which
distances supplies may be procured at moderate prices. This road is accessible to persons desiring to make
the entire journey with their own transportation from
Tennessee or Mississippi, by crossing the Mississippi
River at Memphis or Helena, passing Little Rock, and
thence through Washington County *[in 1860 Fort Smith was in
Sebastian County, and Van Buren was in Crawford County]*, intersecting
the road at Preston.

It may also be reached by taking steamers up Red River to Shreveport or Jefferson, from either of which places there are roads running through a populated country, and intersecting the Fort Smith road near Preston. This road also unites with the San Antonio road at El Paso, and from that point they pass together over the mountains to Fort Yuma and to San Francisco in California. *[page 18]*

The grass upon all the roads leaving Fort Smith is sufficiently advanced to afford sustenance to animals by the first of April, and from this time until winter sets in it is abundant. *[page 20]*

[For additional details, Marcy gives 'camping places' and distances on the road from Fort Smith to El Paso on pages 263-266 of his 1859 book, The Prairie Traveler, A Handbook for Overland Expeditions, by Randolph Barnes Marcy, 1859]

W. B. Parker, 1854 / 1856

as reported in "Notes Taken during the expedition *Commanded by Capt. R. B. Marcy* through Unexplored *Texas,* in the summer and fall of *1854"* *by W. B. Parker, 1856, pages 19 to 78.*

...arriving in **Fort Smith** on the 18th *[1854]*... by the 1st of June *[1854]* we were ready for our long journey.

The Fort Smith Commissary Building ca. 1838
This building was 20 years old when Butterfield offices were a few blocks away.
The building ca. 1945 and today preserved by the National Park Service.

The town of Fort Smith, (in the suburbs of which stands the garrison,) is a place of considerable commercial importance, doing a large Indian and up river trade. It stands upon the Arkansas river, near the mouth of the Poteau river, and contains about twenty-five hundred inhabitants.

The garrison is well and substantially built of brick, and was at the time, the head quarters of the seventh infantry, commanded by Colonel Wilson...

June 1st. — We left Fort Smith at noon, and crossing the Poteau river, immediately in rear of the garrison, entered upon the Choctaw Reserve, en route for Fort Washita, one hundred and eighty miles distant...

The road, which was narrow, with but a single track, ran through a rich alluvial bottom, overgrown with a dense, luxuriant growth of wild cane and immense cotton-wood trees, and owing to the prevalence of late rains, was one quagmire for ten miles...

June 2d. —... I met with a very agreeable surprise at an Indian house by the roadside, where I stopped to make some inquiries. My attention had been arrested in passing this house, during the storm and darkness of the previous night, by a merry ringing laugh, and cheerful conversation. On stopping this morning, I was met by a kind and courteous welcome from one of the inmates, (whose voice I recognized as the same,) who hearing my story, invited me to breakfast, and made me quite forget my cares, in the charm of her society. A prairie flower, brought up and educated upon the frontier, she had never been in a town of any size in her life, but though ignorant of the world, and forms of society, I found her a proud specimen of native grace, intelligence, and affability. A Cherokee, she owed her improvement in mind, to the excellent institution founded by Ross, at Tahlequah, her manners, however, were the result of no convention, but the gift of birth and blood. The daughter of a distinguished chief of her tribe, her soul was full of the ancient nobility of her race, whilst filled with indignation at their wrongs and present degradation, and her eye kindled, and her tongue became eloquent whilst dwelling upon their ancient grandeur, I was charmed beyond measure, surprised to a degree, for with a majority, I had hitherto considered Indian worth and character, a matter of tradition; it was like sunset upon a ruin, or like the last strains of distant melody, which linger upon the ear as if loathe to leave. Subsequent experience has proven to me, however, that she was but one in a thousand, — the death knell of Indian greatness has sounded, and ere long he will have vanished forever from the scene.

... The prairie, on which we were encamped, was about three miles wide, destitute of trees, but covered with rich grass, and beautiful flowers, among which the prairie pink, shone conspicuous, also a species of blue flag, very delicate, I made some selections of both. The soil was a dark loam. *[page 16]*

Chocktaw Agency, Skullyville, OK ca 1880's
Image courtesy of Oklahoma Historical Society Photograph Collection

June 3d. — A start at noon today, brought us to the **Choctaw Agency** at five P.M... We had previously seen two negroes chained together by the neck, and driven along the road, by several men; these proved to be the offenders, the one a freeman, the other a slave. It is optional with the owner, to allow the slave to be whipped or not, (the alternative being expulsion from the nation,) and in this instance he declined, but the free negro was undergoing the infliction of sixty lashes, laid on with an unmerciful hand, and to judge by his groans and cries, the punishment was full expiation for the offence...

The little town of Scullyville, where the agency is located, is a collection of log tenements, principally stores, where a large Indian trade is done. It stands about a mile from an extensive prairie, the road to which, like that from our late encampment, ran over a succession of hills of sand and clay covered with low post oaks.

Upon entering upon the prairie, we observed in the distance a crowd of natives in gay clothing, the brilliant colors blending with the verdure, and making at sunset a truly picturesque scene. Riding up, we witnessed a scene never to be forgotten. It was a ball-play. Described, as this sport has been, by the able pencil of Catlin, description falls far short of reality. About six hundred men, women and children, were assembled, all dressed in holiday costume, and all as intent upon the game as it is possible to be where both pleasure and interest combine. The interest, is one tribe against another, or one county of the same tribe, against a neighboring county; the pleasure, that which savages always take in every manly and athletic sport. In this instance the contestants were all Choctaws, practicing for their annual game with the Creeks, and I was struck with the interest taken by all the lookers on, in the proficiency of each of the players...

June 4th. — This (the first extensive prairie we had met) was about seven miles wide, surrounded by timber, and covered with flowers, among which the marigold and clematis were profuse; the soil was quite sandy. At dawn of day we were again en route. It was a beautiful sight in the dim light and bracing air of morning, to see the long line of white covered wagons rolling quietly over the slopes of the prairie; the lowing of the oxen, the snorting of the horses, the shouts and cracking of whips by the drivers, with all the bustle of breaking up camp made up an enlivening scene, which must be experienced to be enjoyed. One thing however marred its enjoyment to me, and that was the awful profanity of the drivers...

Being quite unwell — the result of the severe exposure of the last few days — I stopped in the course of the morning at an Indian hut to get some coffee, and had an opportunity to make some observations upon the indolence, carelessness, want of calculation and slovenly habits of this semi-barbarous people. The man had built his hut, which was new, about half as large as was necessary to accommodate his family, consisting of five adults and four children, and even this he was too indolent to finish. It had but one room, built of logs, roofed with a rude clap board, split from sapling oak. The floor was laid in puncheons-logs hewn on one side. He had hewed enough to cover all but a four feet square hole in the center, this was left open, and being convenient, was used as a receptacle for offal *[feeding dogs with by-products of butchered animals]* and a lounging place for dogs, of which I subsequently ascertained there are always a host about every Indian house. One can judge of the atmosphere of such a place. — Here they ate, drank and slept, and as philosophers say that man's comfort consists in his idea of what constitutes comfort, managed to live.

One of the squaws made coffee in an iron skillet, stirring it with an oaken paddle; when poured out it was of the consistency of corn gruel, but having called for it, I gulped it down for fear of giving offence, and paying my dime took my departure; my opinion, however, formed at the time, I have had no occasion to change from subsequent observations among them.

Our road, after leaving the prairie, ran over a succession of rough stony hills, covered with low oak trees. In descending one, the foremost wagon was disabled by the breaking of an axle-tree, and as the road was too narrow to pass, we were obliged to look out for camping ground, where there was water and grass to last until the damage could be repaired. These we found a quarter of a mile in advance, in a swamp, on the banks of the Brazil; so unhitching our oxen and unsaddling horses, we prepared to encamp. Shortly after a severe rain storm set in, so that with wet, gnats and mosquitoes, &c., the evening promised to be anything but pleasant, when just as we began to feel very melancholy...

June 5th. —...crossing the swollen Brazil, passed through several short prairies variegated with the wild sunflower, marigold and wild rose. A few hours brought us to the Narrows, where the road ran through a rugged mountain gorge, very difficult for wagons.

The locality is interesting from its geological formation. We found a vein of bituminous coal seventeen inches thick, and numerous fossils of limestone, the soil being argillaceous *[containing clay]*. Near the road, we passed an emigrant's grave, covered with a pent house of logs, and marked by the tailboard of a wagon, nailed upon a stake, upon which was rudely written with tar,*"George Bemshaus, born in Prussia, October 13th, 1812; died, March 2d, 1854."* Poor fellow! All his hopes of home and fortune in the land of freedom, lay here on a barren hillside in this wild Indian country, — such is life, a vision, a struggle, a grave.

...I have since constantly observed that these people have no idea of distance. When one gets information of this kind from them, it is best to multiply by two and add the original quantity, even then sometimes — as in our case — falling short of the fact. We rode twelve miles and then stopped for the night at an Indian hut. As we had eaten nothing since morning, we asked if we could have eggs and chickens for supper, having seen plenty of the feathered bipeds about, and were answered in the affirmative. With appetites sharpened by our exercise and long fast, we came to supper and found the eggs served up on the only piece of family plate, 'tis true, a glass dish, but fried in tallow, the chickens fried in the same, and a dish of sausages, made of the intestines of the hog, dried in the sun, a meal which a man might eat when in imminent danger of starvation, but which our day's fast had not quite toned our appetites to. We took a cup of coffee — the only thing swallowable, and went to the door to smoke and look at the moon, the odor of the viands being quite sufficient.

Edwards Store / Trading Post, Red Oak, Oklahoma (before restoration began) Although not mentioned in this travel journal, as the expedition neared Red Oak, they would have passed the site of this building that is still standing today. Built by Thomas Edwards 1850, establishing this trading post on the Fort Smith - Boggy Depot Road. This was a frequent stopping place for travelers.

Thomas Edwards and Nancy (Hardaway) Edwards
They were married in 1850 and established the Edwards Trading Post

Next, came our accommodations for the night. The hut had no windows in it, but to avoid stumbling over the living, snoring crew upon the floor, a pine knot blazed upon the hearth, and here, stowed in one corner, lay the Indian, his squaw, his daughter about nineteen years old, two young papooses, a negro slave with an infant at the breast, and two dogs, whilst on a kind of shelf, raised about two feet from the floor, were perched the writer and his friend, with our saddles for pillows, and our horse blankets for covering, for this privilege we paid two dollars.

June 6th. — When morning dawned, we wished to make our usual ablutions, but found that basin and towels, were not known in the domestic list; however the squaw offered us an old bake pan and a piece of cotton cloth, which she pulled off of a bundle in the hut, we declined the novelty, and preferred contenting ourselves until we joined the train. It was necessary to have some breakfast, however; so taking the experience of the supper for our guide, we superintended the boiling of some eggs in the shells, and with some corn dodgers and coffee made out very well.

Much to our surprise and satisfaction, our quondam host, who enjoyed the high-sounding name of George Washington, stirred himself this morning and procured from a neighbor what corn we wanted, so we waited here until the train came up. This neighbor called over to see us, and afforded us much amusement. He was a sub-chief of his tribe... *[page 27}*

Subsequent experience has proved to me that the invariable rules for safety, that should be followed by single individuals or small parties, when away from camp, and meeting parties of Indians, is to give them a wide berth, and for this reason — if sheer plunder is not the object of attack — according to their custom, young men cannot hold any position in their tribe, until they can show a scalp, and have stolen a number of horses. In consequence of this, two or three will start together, and sometimes be absent for a year, until they can return with these evidences of their manliness. The best plan is either to make the escape to camp, or else preserving a bold front, take care to have the first shot... *[page 30}*

Council House, at Nvnih Waiya, Indian Territory, abandoned about 1849
Image courtesy of Oklahoma Historical Society

A few miles travel brought us to the deserted **Coun-**

cil House of the nation, at the time occupied by an Indian family, the place of assembling in Council having been changed to Doaxville, farther south, It was a long, rambling building, built of logs, and not different, except in size, from their ordinary houses. Here I dug up a singular piece of pottery, of an antique form, and covered with various devices, but was unable to get any information about it from the family. They said they had never seen anything like it before, and did not know how it came there. Its shape and whole appearance proved it to be very ancient.

Our road from the stream was gradually ascending, and bounded on both sides by timber, when of a sudden we reached the top of the ridge and had a view of the largest prairie we had yet met. O, the glorious beauty of that scene. Fancy would in vain attempt to paint it! Below, stretching for twenty-five miles in length, and twelve in breadth, lay a sea of pale green, hemmed in by timber of a darker blue; flowers of every variety, shade and form, interspersed over the surface; a dark green belt of verdure here and there, marking the ravines and water-courses, and groves of trees, or clumps, or single trees, scattered in such perfect arrangement over the whole, as to seem as though some eminent artist had perfected the work. And truly so he did, for what artist can compare with the God who formed and arranged all these natural beauties now spread before us!... *[page31]*

Our whole command stopped involuntarily, in mute admiration; at last, one poor fellow, a rough, uncouth specimen of an ox driver burst, out, *"Oh, if I was only a lawyer, how I could talk about such a sight as this, but I havn't the larnin' to say what I want."* *[page32]*

...As every pleasure has its pain, every joy its sorrow, our feelings of admiration for the scenery, were soon merged into those of pity, for our horses, mules and oxen. The great drawback to pleasure, at this season, on the prairie, is the immense number of insects. Among these, is a large, **greenish brown horse fly**, the most inveterate blood sucker of the genus. So ravenous are they, that, after settling down to their bloody work, they will allow  themselves to be picked up in the fingers, making no effort to escape. At every stroke of their bills, the blood flows as if from a lancet, and they come in such myriads, that I have seen a horse bathed in his own blood.... *[page32]*

As we passed only along the edge of the prairie... we were stopped by the sudden announcement of five of our teamsters, that they would go no farther. These men, living a precarious but indolent life, upon the frontier of Arkansas, had joined the expedition with very romantic ideas, but the realities and discipline of camp life had cured them, and go any farther they would not; but leaving us upon the hillside, they turned their faces towards their accustomed lounging places, and were gone.... *[page33]*

The evening set in with a violent rain storm; so, to be as comfortable as possible during our detention, we took possession of an untenanted house on the premises, and building a fire in the hearth (for it was quite cold), we spread our blankets upon the floor and resigned ourselves to sleep, after a very good meal of milk, eggs, chickens, &c., which we procured from the farm house... *[page34]*

At an Indian house we passed to-day, I observed some little negroes, from two years old and under. They were naked, and were most singular and unsightly objects, from the distortion and protuberance of the stomach and abdomen. This is attributable to their being fed entirely on corn bread, causing enlargement of the spleen and other distresses. On speaking of this circumstance to the owner, he said,"*Well, may be so dey live, may be not;*" a matter of indifference to him, whose own stomach seemed well fed and healthy enough, but upon whom the natural consequences of cause and effect made no impression.

June 7th, 8th and 9th. — Our quondam *[former]* host was a full-blooded Choctaw. He served in the Creek war with General Jackson, and like all of his tribe, was very proud of the fact that they have always been allies of the United States. His wealth in cattle and horses, besides money (which was all hoarded, never, as is a general thing with Indians, put out at interest), was said to be over one hundred thousand dollars, and yet he was living not only in a filthy but most uncomfortable and disgusting manner, fond of nothing but gold and silver, which when we paid him the few dollars of expense incurred, he clutched with all the gloating of a miser, and shook with tremulous delight as he told them one by one into his greasy bag... *[page35]*

Some of the visitors got up a dance one evening. There were six dancers — three squaws and three men. The music was a droning discordance of sounds, drawn from an old cracked fiddle by the husband of one of the squaws, and the dance consisted in a monotonous bobbing up and down, like a bear on a hot plate, accompanied by yells, which grew louder as the night waxed older, and the whiskey began to take effect, so that long after we had retired to our blankets, we were roused when a louder yell than usual pealed out, or a heavier stamping announced that the orgy was becoming more fast and furious.

We met with, and in use, at this place, some vessels

of the same material and ancient shape, as the one I had previously dug up at the deserted Council House. Our host told us they were made of an admixture of clay and pounded muscle shells, but the art of making them was lost. They will stand the fire and would answer for crucibles as well as cooking pots... *[page36]*`

[page38] Most of the Choctaws hold slaves, but my observations both here and elsewhere, have convinced me that the general government would subserve the cause of humanity by prohibiting any Indians from holding them; they look upon them as mere beasts of burden, and treat them accordingly. At this place there were two slaves; one an old woman of seventy years of age, and lame with inflammatory rheumatism, the other a child of eight years old, who were compelled to do all the hard work about the farm. We saw the old woman sent out to catch and saddle a horse, and the boy, with no clothing on but a coarse, ragged, filthy tow shirt *[made of course fiber]*, chopping logs of wood, and then shouldering and carrying into the house, a log larger than himself... *[page39]*

Another of our party offered to buy the boy, but the avaricious *[greedy]* old wretch, immediately put up his price beyond his means, and upon being told that his price was unreasonable, merely replied,"*He good boy, may be so, somebody give it for him, may be not."*

Instances might be multiplied of great barbarities practiced; one, is that of an Indian in this nation, standing and enjoying the pastime of his half-grown boy, which consisted in practicing with bow and arrows, at a negro boy, as a target. Another, ordered a slave to shoot a man against whom he had a grievance, and upon refusal, whipped the slave to death. These are not isolated cases, but good specimens of their estimation of, and general treatment of slaves, and would seem to prove conclusively, that the Indian needs a master, as much, if not more, than the slave.

June 10th. — Having succeeded in filling the places of our shameless deserters *[who had left for home in Arkansas]*, we left the old man and his ill-enjoyed wealth, at an early hour this morning, and commenced the ascent of a steep, stony hill, on the opposite side of which slopes a prairie, extending down to Gaines' creek... *[page40]*

On reaching the creek *[west of Wilburton, OK]*, we found it too high to ford, and so encamped in a beautiful grove on the slope of the prairie, and a beautiful quiet evening we had, when the first clear moon for some nights, rose to hallow the peaceful scene below, the white tents, and the white covers of the wagons, peeping out from among the trees, the camp fires blazing, and the cattle feeding upon the green sward around us. We felt the soothing influence of the scene, after the rough times of the past week, and retired to our grassy couches with calmer thoughts for the morrow. *[page 41]*

June 11th — We found this morning, that the best horse we had, a noble sorrel, had been struck by a snake in the night, and could go no farther... The reptile is a small mottled snake, called Ground Rattlesnake. This is a misnomer, as it has no rattles, and strikes without warning. It is a species of the **Copperhead**, its bite very venomous, and generally attended with fatal results.

Southern Oklahoma Copperhead

At ten A. M., (the water having subsided to a fordable depth,) we crossed Gaines' Creek, and passing through several beautiful prairies, rich in pasture, and covered with those beautiful flowers which always delighted us so much... we came to a much more cultivated region. What first attracted our attention was a field of oats, a grain we had hitherto not met with, as the Indians raise nothing but corn.

"Aha," said I, the"*white man has had a hand in this,"* and so it proved to be the case. Several settlers from the States, who have married squaws, live here, the fact evidenced by the greater quantity of land cultivated, greater variety in the crops, the growth of vegetables, greater neatness about their buildings, and a general appearance of industry and thrift.

According to Choctaw law, no white man can marry until he has resided two years in the nation. He can then marry one of the tribe, and can fence in and cultivate as much as he pleases. There are many instances in the nation, and where ever met with, the difference from the native is very perceptible and striking.

Having learned, by the experience of the past, the phlebotomizing powers of the prairie-fly, we stopped at the first convenient place, and spent the rest of the day in making up muslin covers for our horses and mules, and during the day made some very interesting explorations and discoveries among the fossiliferous strata in the vicinity. *[page43]*

The soil is limestone, marked by the pellucid water and luxuriant vegetation. It yields, in ordinary seasons, forty bushels of grain to the acre; this season being unprecedentedly wet, the prospects were not so good.

Coal is found here in abundance, very bituminous, but used only by the few blacksmiths who live along the road. *[page 44]*

June 12th. — At daylight we were on the road, and commenced passing through a more broken, but still well cultivated and flourishing country, as there is quite a settlement — if distances of from ten to fifteen miles can be called a settlement — of white men with squaw wives...*[page44]*

Passing unobstructedly over so wide an extent, storms acquire terrific violence in this country, and leave indelible marks of their ravages. One of the settlers, an intelligent white man, had sixty acres of oats destroyed, and told us that hail was thick enough, in some places, to be shoveled up. He said he measured some of the stone, and one was eight inches long and five in circumference...

June 13th. — Our march today led us through an extensive prairie — covered as usual with a beautiful variety of flowers — where we found encamped a large party of emigrants, waiting for the subsidence of the waters of the Boggy, a stream more aptly named than pleasant to the traveler. They told us we could not cross, but we determined to make the attempt... *[page 45]*

A black, mucky deposit spread in width for two miles, and our hapless party went floundering and plunging on, sometimes brought to a dead stand, anon sinking to the saddle girths, then plunging into a slough and wondering what was to come next, until bedaubed and bespattered, breathless and half suffocated, we emerged upon the banks of the stream, and cast an involuntary glance backwards to see whether we had not left part of ourselves or our horses behind us.

With the loss of several horse and mule shoes, and the breaking of a swingletree *[a small wooden bar behind a harnessed horse]* in the ambulance, we got through, and arriving on the banks of the stream found it too high to cross with our wagons, and so set about to repair damages.

In course of the afternoon, we attempted to cross our horses over by swimming them, but on account of the bad landing on the opposite shore, were obliged to desist.

Having crossed myself, in a dug- out, in anticipation of my horse, I came near having an unpleasant adventure, *viz.*, a night alone in a Choctaw swamp.

Finding no likelihood of getting my horse, I started on foot for **Boggy Depot** — a collection of

Old Boggy Depot, 1837 by Vinson Lackey
Image courtesy of the Gilcrease Museum

dwellings and stores about a mile from the stream- as the most comfortable place to spend the night... *[page 46]*

June 14th. — The banks of the stream presented a wild and picturesque scene this morning. A high, steep bluff, on the opposite shore, was lined with over a thousand head of wild cattle, about to be driven across, on their way to Missouri and Illinois... *[page48]* It was an exciting sight, to see the herd plunge off the high bank-about fifteen feet perpendicular hight—and swim across, nothing appearing above water, but their taper heads and long thin horns.

The emigrants we had passed upon the prairie had also come down, determined to cross at all hazards. They had exhausted all their provisions, and were too impatient to wait until the stream was fordable. There were about four hundred of them, men, women, and children, and the scene of confusion, and damage to property, beggars all description. Their goods were saturated with water, the whole party wet to the skin; and in one instance a wagon sank entirely out of sight, and was only recovered by dint of diving and fastening ropes to it, when, with the assistance of several yokes of oxen, it was drawn ashore again... *[page49]* Their reason for emigrating was the cold and inhospitable climate of Missouri. One man told me that it was necessary to fodder cattle seven months in the year; a great difference to Texas, where cattle range in the pasture winter and summer, always fat and in good condition... *[page 50]*

The green flies — our quondam torturers — again made their appearance, and this time-it seemed to me-more famished than ever. Our lead horses, rendered half frantic, would dart first on one side of us, then on the other, sometimes come charging up to rub themselves against the ridden horse, who, rendered steadier by the rein, was of friendly assistance for this purpose then again, rolling upon the ground and jerking back, or pulling forward, until our arms were nearly dislocated, such is a faint picture of our situation, under circumstances.

Arrived on the banks of the Blue. (The streams all have appropriate names in this country, as for instance, the Boggy, whose peculiarities I have described; the Brushy, whose banks are tangled almost impassably, with briars and brambles, and the Blue, whose waters are a deep blue, from running over a bed of soft blue limestone and clay)... *[page 51]*

All would have gone well, had not my horse commenced floundering the moment his feet touched the soft clay at the bottom. In we went up to the neck, and whilst struggling to keep heads above water... I re-crossed and piloted the way to the *"terra firma"* of the most beautiful prairie we had yet crossed, the prairie, upon the outer edge of which stands **Fort Washita**, where we arrived at sundown, sore, sunburnt and fatigued, to experience all the comfort and pleasure, which unaffected and disinterested hospitality could offer and accomplish. *[page52]*

June 15th to 29th. — This post, established about twelve years since, was garrisoned by one company of the seventh infantry, commanded by Major Holmes, and one company of the fourth artillery, commanded by Major Hunt; Major Holmes commanding the post. Plain, but comfortable quarters, stand upon the brow of a hill, commanding a fine view of the plain. For ten miles, this rich, green velvet carpet is spread out, spangled with flowers of every hue, and interspersed with groves of timber. A little babbling brook meanders through the green sward at the foot of the hill, the whole forming a scene of picturesque beauty, compensating in some measure for the isolation from society and the daily peril concomitant to a frontier life. *[page53]*

Fort Washita, West Barracks, Durrant, Oklahoma
Established in 1842 to protect Choctaw and Chickasaw Nation
from the Plains Indians.

Poorly paid, and worse equipped, the soldiers of our republic never can receive too high a mete of praise for the choice that decided and the energy which marks their profession. Isolated from home and the world, they carry with them into these solitudes.... *[page54]*

Throughout our march we found in profusion flowers which, in the North and East, are cultivated with great care as ornaments for the drawing-room or conservatory. The Texas plume--a gorgeous flower of a brilliant scarlet, the red and white rose, the prairie pink, the verbena, the marigold of many varieties, the convolvulus, the ranunculus, · the sensitive and other liguminous plants, the flag, the sunflower and wild pea-all luxuriant in growth and brilliant in color--all bloom here together, and though" wasting their sweetness upon the desert air," still, as the occasional tourists wander among them, they stand the fragrant evidence of creative power, hallowing the scene and raising the thoughts from nature up to nature's God.

The timber found in the country passed through is the cottonwood, black jack, post oak, pecan, pride of China, and the" bois d'arc," or Osage orange, which occurs first at Boggy. The wood of this tree is the hardest and toughest known. It is used by the Indians for making their bows, (hence its name,) is very close grained, and of a deep-yellow color. It is also used for hedges. A very fine and lasting dye is also extracted from it. The foliage is very thick, leaf small and of a very deep-green, making it a handsome addition to the forest. It bears also a very large apple, which contains the seed, and which, when fully ripe, is a deep orange color.

The pecan, is very useful for mechanical purposes, as it can be split into very thin laths, and is very pliable. We also found some hickory and white oak, but very rare.

Although the soil is in general a black loam and the timber is short, except the cottonwood. *[page 56]*

The soil is well adapted for corn--the only thing the Indians raise... *[page 56]*

Sutler's Store, Fort Laramie, 1877
No image survives of the Sutler's Store at Fort Washita. It would have been similar to the Sutler's Store shown here at Fort Laramie.
The post sutler was a merchant or trader licensed by the Army to sell goods on military land. They were an important part of fort life, providing goods and services not available to soldiers through the regular army supply system.
Image courtesy of Historynet.com website

During our stay, many Indians came in to trade at the **Sutler's Store**. They were Caddo, Chickasaw and Witchita, a dirty, squalid and uninteresting set.

A party of Kickapoo also passed one morning, with pack mules. They were on their way down to Red River to barter for whiskey, the bane of the red man, but which he will have, despite of law and at the risk of starvation, a melancholy depravity, to our shame be it said, entailed upon him by the white man, against which no curse can be too loud or too bitter, no effort too strenuously exerted to eradicate... *[page 57]*

We had now passed one hundred and eighty miles through the Choctaw and Chickasaw Reserve, as fertile a country as ever the light of day rested upon... *[page 57]*

Their cattle and horses roam through the luxuriant pastures, which nature clothes in verdure and life, winter and summer, uncared for, except to be driven up and branded when necessary; their hogs subsist upon the mast, and with the corn, supply their eternal diet of hog and hominy. Thus their horses and cattle supply their hoard; their hogs and corn-the one fed from nature's bounty, the other, raised by the sweat of their slaves, in quantity sufficient to keep them from starvation- are their food; and the Indian can mount his pony and gallop whooping through the prairie, lounge dozing about his log hut, or taking his rifle, stroll listlessly about the country; in short, do any thing but work; that is a word not known in his vocabulary. *[page 59]*

The style of building among this people is peculiar; two square pens are put up with logs, and roofed or thatched. The space between the pens is covered in and serves for eating-place and depository of harness, saddles and bridles, &c. A door is cut in each pen, facing the passage. They have no windows, the door admitting all the light used. This style is called two pens

and a passage, and is, in fact, only a shelter for the family from bad weather, for of furniture
they have but little, and that of the rudest and most uncomfortable kind.

These buildings are stuck (almost invariably) upon the road; no neat door yard, with a substantial fence and neat gate, encloses them; no flower or vegetable garden is seen, but the ornamental figure of a half-starved hog, grunts lazily on one side, and a pack of miserable curs lounge pn the other, the whole presenting an untidy picture of squalid discomfort, which even its temporary appearance cannot deceive... *[page 60]*

{When there is illness or injury:] Near the hut where lies the patient, they erect a pole, from the top of which flaunts gay ribbons and pieces of gay cloth. At the foot of the pole stands a frame, to which is attached a bale of muslin or woolen cloth, ribbons, &c., and the door of the hut is festooned with ribbons and colored cloth. The mighty medicine man goes through with his mummeries, and leaves, taking the precaution to take with him, as perquisites, all the cloth, ribbons, & c., which have been used, and according to his wants, of muslin, woolen or ribbon, so will be the quantity required, and the quality of these infallible antidotes to the disease to be cured... *[page 61]*

Let us cherish the hope, that ere long the Indian representative may be found occupying his seat in our national legislature, to advocate his own cause and secure his rights from oppression... *[page 65]*

... a scheme of the white man to dispossess them of their lands. They say, *"We got land now, we keep him ; white man come, all is gone."* This idea is a necessary consequence of their inherent distrust of our race. At heart they hate us, and are only kept apparent friends by either fear or self- interest... *[page 65]*

June 29th. — At noon to-day we left our comfortable quarters at our friend S. H______'s, and bidding adieu to Washita, with its green plains, noble hearts and bright faces, we entered the timber, skirting the plain on the south-east, and commenced our long journey to unexplored Texas.

Fort Smith, Garrison Ave., 1864, 13th Regiment, Kansas Infantry
The 7th Infantry (at various times Company B, D, F and H) was stationed at
Fort Smith, May 8, 1854 to March 1, 1858
Image courtesy of the National Parks Service web site

Our military escort, which arrived on the twenty-eighth, consisted of forty non-commissioned officers and men, from the **7th Regiment** of infantry, commanded by Lieutenants P_____e and C____n of that regiment.

The command was a mixed one of Americans, Germans and Irish, a fine body of men, and as they had all volunteered for the expedition, we flattered ourselves that, should we get into a fight, we should have good material to depend upon.

The afternoon was oppressively hot, so we made but a short march, and on coming into camp found two- thirds of the command "hors de combat," from indulging too freely in whiskey, where obtained no one could tell, but the fact spoke for itself. *[page 67]*

During the evening a young Chickasaw — a very fine specimen of the Indian — came into our camp and asked for whiskey. He was quite drunk at the time, and we declined giving him any stimulant whatever. Very soon after he took a fancy to a calico shirt I wore, and offered a gaily trimmed hunting shirt in exchange. I gave him the shirt, and in a short time he jumped up suddenly to leave. Springing on his horse, we then observed that he had appropriated a knife belonging to Lieutenant P______e, and a buckskin coat belonging to our servant. We immediately charged him with the theft, when he flew into a terrible rage, swearing vengeance and heaping imprecations upon us. We advanced upon him in a quiet, but determined manner, when he threw down the coat, but galloped off with the knife, swearing bitterly all the while, and gesticulating violently as far as we could see him. We kept a good look out for him, but saw no more of him, though we learned in the morning, that he was one of the party who made the night hideous by their howls and yells around camp.

June 30th. — Our march today was very dull and uninteresting, our road at first, running over a succession of rough, steep hills, covered with low oaks; the weather oppressively hot, and the men suffering from their debauch.

Five miles brought us to a very wide prairie, which we crossed, admiring the beautiful flowers, as usual, and every moment starting quails or grouse from their hiding places in the rich grass.

This prairie was almost a level plain, extending to the horizon, and consequently not so attractive a view as those previously seen. *[page 69]*

After leaving it, we entered the timber, which lined the road all the way to Red River, and passing many Indian farms, all looking alike — to describe one is to describe all — we encamped upon the skirt of Red River bottom early in the afternoon, to allow the stragglers to come in, and to prepare for crossing the stream in the morning...

July 1st. — One would have supposed that the experience of the two last days would have been a sufficient lesson to our gallant sons of Mars, but the sequel of this day will prove the contrary.

We left camp at sunrise, and marching two miles through the low, sandy bottom, thickly wooded with cottonwood trees, with their limbs beautifully festooned with the trumpet creeper, in full bloom, we arrived on the shores of Red River, which we were obliged to cross by ferry boat, causing considerable delay from our numbers, and the weight of our wagons. *[page 70}*

We found ("en bivouac," upon the high bank), a party of Seminole Indians, men, women, and children, who had come a distance of one hundred and fifty miles, through the Reserve, to purchase whiskey on the opposite, or Texas shore of the river.

They were engaged in crossing it over in five gallon kegs. These they afterwards slung on their pack-horses in a netting made of raw hide. About fifty gallons were already piled upon the bank in kegs, and more arriving every hour or two. The women were quite the most industrious of the party, although assisting in procuring the cause of most of the brutal treatment they receive from their husbands.

Though not low enough to be fordable, the water was still low enough to cause much trouble in getting the large flat up to the bank, so, being impatient to cross, I stepped into a skiff, which held Indians and empty kegs, and was soon over... There is no means, at present, of preventing this traffic, the general government having no jurisdiction upon the Texas shore. All that can be done, is for the Light Horse to be vigilant and firm in the execution of the law.

The first person I met on landing, was the captain of the troop, a young Chickasaw, son of a chief. He was waiting patiently until the whole purchase should be crossed over into the Reserve, when he followed with his men, and promptly destroyed it all, amounting in value paid to one hundred and forty dollars. May he continue vigilant in this good cause, and perhaps, examples made, and the penalties suffered, may, in time, arrest this horrible evil.

The town of Preston, from which all this misery for the Red man emanates, is a collection of low groggeries *[tavern or bar]* and a few stores, lining the high bluff bank of the river.

It is notorious as the scene of some most cold-blooded and cruel murders, committed in open day, and with-up to that time-perfect impunity. This, together with the detestable traffic I have just alluded to, has brought such a stigma upon the place, that the very name is sufficient for all that is ruthless and vicious. *[page 72]*

[page 75] From Fort Washita to Red river, the soil is loam, with ridges of limestone. The timber, oak and pecan, with occasional Bois d'arc and cottonwood *[trees]*. The river takes its name from the color of its water, which is a dark maroon, full of sediment, and very unpalatable The Texas shore is very bold, presenting a stratification of red clay and white sand, giving a striking and very peculiar appearance in the distance, like chalk cliffs.

The stream *[Red River]* is but seldom in good boating order, rapid, and full of shifting shoals, making a very tedious ferriage *[tedious ferry ride]*...

[W. B. Parkers report of his trip from Fort Smith to the Texas border is found on pages 19 to 75 of his book, "Notes Taken DURING THE EXPEDITION Commanded by Capt. R. B. Marcy THROUGH UNEXPLORED Texas, IN THE SUMMER AND FALL OF 1854," by W. B. Parker, 1856.
On the above pages, that report has been shortened by about half. To read the full story, refer to W. B. Parker's original 1856 book. The reader might also be inter-

John Butterfield
(1801 - 1869, aged 67

CHAPTER ONE

Observations of John Butterfield, August 2, 1858

In September 1857, John Butterfield on behalf of his Overland Mail Company signed a contract with the Postmaster General to relay the mail twice a week between St. Louis & Memphis to San Francisco, and to have the infrastructure in place to start in exactly twelve months. After eleven months of preliminary set-up efforts, below is John Butterfield's personal on-site report to the Directors of the Overland Mail Company.

This letter was transcribed from the original letter, including the handwritten "Minute Book of the Overland Mail Company of New York" by the Historian of the Wells Fargo Museum in San Francisco, California in 2023.

To the Directors of the Overland Mail Company
New York, August 2, 1858

Gentlemen,

I herewith submit an informal report of a second trip to Fort Smith on the business of the Co. with such information as will convey a pretty correct idea of the present condition of our enterprise.

I left home on the 26th of May accompanied by Mr. Crocker. We met at St. Louis, Mr. Moore proprietor of the line from Jefferson City or more properly from the terminus of the Pacific Road to Springfield M.*[Missouri]* We purchased from him the entire property of the line with his mail contract to Warsaw MO., and goodwill.

The property consists of 100 horses with harness. Ten post coaches. Six wagons. Stable and lot at Warsaw MO. Stable and lot at Springfield MO. Price paid for contract etc $17,750.00 For the particulars of this purchase see the contract in the hands of the treasurer.

We made stations and arrangements at the different stations between California and Fort Smith for the teams at prices varying from $125 to $175 per quarter.

At Springfield MO. - Warsaw - Fayetteville - Fort Smith & California. We keep our own teams buying the necessary hay and grass as required. California, MO the present terminus of the Pacific RR will probably be discontinued as a station and Round Hill or Tipton be made the point of departure from the Pacific R. Road. The details for the arrangements for stations are all known to Mr. Crocker, the superintendent of that division, and it is not deemed necessary to particularize them here.

In addition to the Horses and property purchased of Mr Moore, we have purchased 182 horses at an average cost of $98.00 and 257 mules at an average cost of $102.54. Making in all 539 head. Every one of which we personally inspected and believe to be suited to our uses as serviceable animals. A detailed statement of these purchases is in the hands of the Treasurer.

Letters have been received from Mr Kinyon advising of the purchase by him of 220 horses. Further particulars of interest are contained in his letter to which is referred.

The aggregate of Kinyon's purchases and ours is 759 head. The balance of the stock necessary will be purchased and properly distributed previous to Sept. 15th the date of our commencement of service.

The details of the arrangement for working the line are as follows:

Under the Supervision of Hugh Crocker — the line from the RR terminus to Colbert's Ferry about 200 miles beyond Fort Smith being say 500 miles in all.

Under supervision of Henry Bates — the line from Colbert's Ferry to Fort Chadbourne 308 ¼ miles.

Under supervision of James Glover — the line from Fort Chadbourne to El Paso 413 ¾ miles.

Under supervision of Giles Hawley — the line from El Paso to Tucson 336 miles.

Under supervision of William Buckley — the line from Tucson to Fort Yuma 279 miles.

Under supervision of M. L. Kinyon and his apts — the line from Fort Yuma to San Francisco 664 miles.

About 2500 miles in all.

The estimate of stock etc required to run the entire route is attached hereto in Schedule A at the end of this report.

The wagons for the western end of the route are all dispatched and by this time are, accidents excepted, undoubtedly properly distributed. More horses will be sent on to that portion of the route for which the parties mentioned below have started from the stock purchased by me, heretofore mentioned as in the hands of the Treasurer in detail.

From Fort Smith we have started the various superintendents westward for their divisions as follows.

- James Glover with 21 horses and about 20 men
- Henry Bates with 21 horses and about 20 men
- William Buckley with 21 horses and about 20 men
- Giles Hawley with 21 horses and about 20 men

The line will be sufficiently well provided and stocked with teams and men to commence the service on the day named in the contract.

With regard to the line from Memphis to Fort Smith

I have deemed it prudent to wait and see what the condition of the river and the country would be when the late great floods shall have subsided their effects somewhat removed. Should the water prove to be too low in the Arkansas River a purchase of boats might prove injudicious. I am of the opinion still (expressed in my former report) that the boats should be purchased at $7,500 each and run upon the Arkansas River. I think this will be the best method of doing our business and will be one of the best if not the very best paying portion of our entire route.

Negotiations are in progress for the purchase of boats and for the men to run them. Discretionary powers have been left with Mr. Crocker. Should these negotiations and arrangements fail to produce the necessary facilities, on my return to Fort Smith I shall certainly see that portion of our contract fulfilled in proper shape.

The citizens and residents along the route have renewed their expressions of goodwill and interest in the success of our undertaking and have taken steps to make good their promises to put the roads in good order. In some instances, the money has already been raised and the making of the roads commenced.

In making this report I beg leave to state that the transaction of the Co. extending over so large a territory where there is no railroad or telegraph lines and mail connections by no means regular and at a slow pace where regular and the different superintendents moving on their separate divisions it cannot be expected to be as accurate and correct nor can estimates be made as correctly as to what will be needed for the service and what the expense will be as it can be after the men and teams shall have been stationed and an opportunity given to see where and what parts of the route will need double stock and men to run it with.

As the Superintendents are at work on their respective divisions placing their teams and arranging their stations and feed, it is confidently expected that all will be ready by the day stipulated in the contract. The wagons for the western division viz from El Paso to San Francisco that is as many as Mr Kinyon said he wanted have all been forwarded for his division.

In addition about one half of the wagons are ready for the Eastern Division and on the road to their destination and the balance will be forwarded without delay. As Mr. Abbott has assured Mr Holland that the balance shall all be ready and shipped by the 15th August that will give 30 days to get them on to the ground ready for service.

Since writing the above I have received several reports which are herewith attached.

Respectfully submitted

John Butterfield

Image Source: The Press Argus, September 19, 1958, Section A, page 1

Schedule A:
Estimate of men horses and wagons required for the overland mail company from California MO to San Francisco Cal.

		Miles	Drivers men	Horses	Wagons
California MO to H. Crocker Supt	Colbert's Ferry Texas	508	34	148	20
Colbert's Ferry Texas H Bates Supt	To Ft Chadbourne Tex	308 ¼	18	90	12
Fort Chadbourne Texas J. Glover Supt.	To El Paso or Franklin	413 ¾	21	115	13
El Paso or Franklin William Buckley and Giles Hawley Supt	To Fort Yuma	611	31	160	8
Fort Yuma M. L. Kinyon Supt	To San Francisco	664	84	260	11
Total		2505	188	773	64

Mr Corbin being present reported verbally that the subject of protection on the part of the government in substance that the Govt continued to profess to be willing to afford all the protection in their power but that no definite action had yet been ordered. The treasurer reported the condition of finances. The board then adjourned.

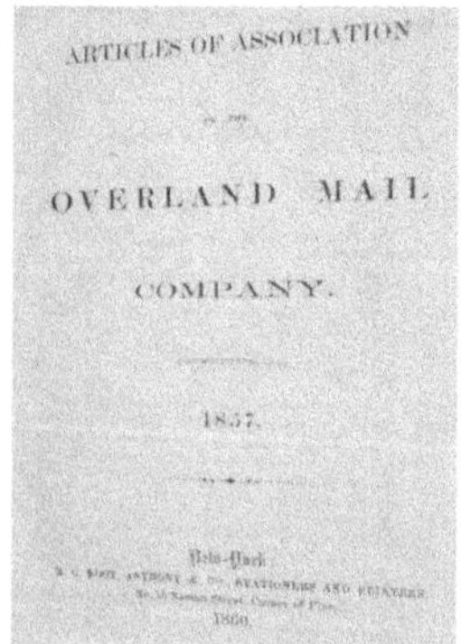

Livingston,
Secretary

Details about the legal structure of the Overland Mail Company are contained in a copy of "The Articles of Association of the Overland Mail Company, 1857" found in the collection of the Huntington Library of San Marino, California. The entire text of the Articles have been reprinted in "POSTAL HISTORY of John Butterfield's Overland Mail Co. on the Southern and Central Routes including Butterfield's Pony Express 1858-1864" by Bob Crossman, pages 270-278.

Defense of John Butterfield's Decisions
James Glover, Gayoso House, Memphis, Jan. 28, 1859
as as reprinted in The First Overland Mail: San Francisco to Memphis,
Walter B. Lang, 1945, pgs. 91-92.

You are no doubt aware that the company, believing that they could run light draught boats the year round on the Arkansas River, obtained the consent of the post master general to run boats between Little Rock and Fort Smith. This change was ordered too late for the company to have the class of boats which were necessary to run in low water with.

They sent to almost every boat-yard and city in the south and west, hoping to find some already built, but failed in finding any of light enough draught. They *[Overland Mail Co.]* continued this fruitless search until very near the time for the mails to commence running – too late for them to put stock and coaches on this arm of the route – and they were forced to make a contract with Messrs. Chidester, Rapley & Co., who were carrying tri-weekly mails from this place to Fort Smith, to carry their mails for them.

These gentlemen did all they could to put their mails through in schedule time, but their route was so circuitous, and they had to stop at so many offices, that they were unable to comply with this contract.

Failing in this, they *[Overland Mail Co.]* bought the contract from Dardanelle to Fort Smith, and put on their own stock, and made a contract with Chidester, Rapley & Co., to take their mails from Memphis to Dardanelle – the time allowed them being forty-five hours.

From Dardanelle the *[Overland Mail Co.]* company to carry them in their own stages to Fort Smith in fifteen hours; thus making the trip between Memphis and Fort Smith in sixty-hours – twenty-four hours less than that from St. Louis.　　　　**James Glover**

John Butterfield's Letter of Sept. 19, 1858
as reported in the Oct. 2, 1858 issue of the Weekly Jefferson Inquirer,
Jefferson, Missouri, page 2

FROM THE MISSOURI REPUBLICAN

SPEEDY LAND TRAVELS — PROGRESS OF THE OVERLAND MAIL

Mr. S. M. Allen, agent for the Overland Mail Company in this city, was yesterday advised by letter of the progress made by the train since its departure from St. Louis a short time since on the inaugural trip to the coast of the Pacific Ocean. —

His advices are contained in a **letter from Mr. Butterfield**, the President of the Company, written from Fort Smith under the date of the 19th inst. They are far more satisfactory when were anticipated at the setting out of the expedition. He states that the coaches arrive at that place *[Fort Smith]* at 2:55 Sunday morning, instead of 3:30 Monday morning which is the scheduled time — a gain of twenty-five hours.

The distance to Fort Smith from Tipton, the present terminus of the Pacific Railroad, is 475 miles, and from St. Louis over 600 miles. — This was accomplished in a little over three days — an exceedingly speedy land movement as is apparent from the above date.

If other divisions of the route are transversed as expeditiously as this one, and the saving time holds, San Francisco will be reached in about twenty-two days from St. Louis. This is less than the time consumed in the sea journey, and if kept up, must attract a large passenger travel to the overland route. The exactions and impositions so long practiced by the agents of the steamship lines and the Isthmus and the disadvantages of climate will be very potent to direct attention and custom to this new thoroughfare to the outer borders of our great west.

It is possible that Mr. Butterfield will not extend his journey beyond Fort Smith, but return hither from that place after some necessary business shall have been concluded. Six passengers, the letter says, were booked thorough to that post. *[Fort Smith]*

Two brief mentions of John Butterfield found in passenger interviews...

John Butterfield, Nov. 3, 1858
as reported in the New Orleans Commercial Bulletin, Nov. 3, 1858, page 2

Mr. Butterfield left Washington this afternoon for Memphis, and is to proceed to Little Rock, Fort Smith and other points to ascertain whether the mail route cannot be greatly improved.

Passenger Report, Oct. 16, 1858
as reported in the Oct. 16, 1858 issue of the Missouri State Times, page 2

...we left ...on Monday evening, per Pacific Railroad, via Tipton... On the *[train]* cars was the, at present somewhat celebrated MR. BUTTERFIELD, of the firm of Butterfield & Co., Overland mail contractors. MR. B was on his way to Fort Smith, to attend the celebration of the arrival of the Overland Mail at that point. Notwithstanding, his company has performed the almost incredible feat of transporting the mail between San Francisco and St. Louis in twenty-four days. He feels sanguine that he will soon reduce the time between these two points to *twenty days!* Our private opinion is, that if it can be done, MR. BUTTERFIELD will do it.

The train for California was under the charge of that clever and accommodating conductor, MR. WHIPPLE, who landed us "o' time" at Tipton. At this place we found our old friend of the "City," FRED HEPP, doing the honors of the Prairie House to a numerous body of guests. The table for supper was set; the gong gave notice that everything was ready; and with the fast crowd — fast as this young and thriving town — we rushed into the dining room...

MOTHER
MALINDA H. BAKER
WIFE OF
JOHN BUTTERFIELD
BORN OCT 23, 1799
DIED AUG 20, 1888

CHAPTER TWO

Passenger Letter to Mrs. Butterfield, Sept. 18, 1858
as reported in the Sept. 25, 1858 issue of the Albany Evening Journal
NOTE: Below is the first correspondence ever written by a passenger on a
Butterfield Overland Mail Company stage leaving Tipton,
Missouri. Probably written by Judge Wheeler's wife to Malinda Butterfield.

Appreciation is express to Gerald T. Ahnert for discovering this news article.

The Overland Mail—We are permitted to peruse a letter from St. Louis, dated Sept. 18th, concerning the opening of the Overland Mail, written to Mrs. Butterfield, by a person who went some distance on the first stage. We quote part of the letter: —

"The Great Overland Mail left St. Louis on the Pacific Rail Road at 8 A. M. on the 16th Inst. En route for San Francisco, under the personal charge of Mr. Butterfield. When the cars arrived at Tipton, 162 miles from St. Louis, and the end of the Rail Road, John Butterfield, Jr., drove along side of the platform a new Overland Stage drawn by six beautiful bay horses. Eleven persons, including Mr. Butterfield, Sen., took passage in and upon it, and John Butterfield, Jr., had the honor of driving the first six miles the first stage ever started from St. Louis for San Francisco. We reached Syracuse, 168 miles from St. Louis, at 7 P. M. and took supper. In fifteen minutes I shook hands with your husband and your son, and they started for Fort Smith under as bright a moon and on as beautiful a night as the Good Being ever granted to the sons of men. Mr. Butterfield told me, as he was getting into the stage:--'Write to my wife when we get to St. Louis and tell her how well I am, and that I believe we shall succeed.' Mr. Butterfield will proceed to Fort Smith, where he will meet the stage from San Francisco, and on the 10th of October he is expected on the return at St. Louis, with the first U. S. Overland Mail from San Francis-co."—[Utica Herald]

CHAPTER THREE
R. M. Brimmer, Sept. 25, 1858
as reported in the Des Arc Citizen; also
as reported in the article below from the Sept. 25, 1858 issue of the
Weekly Arkansas Gazette, Little Rock, Arkansas, page 2
The information in the article below was obtained in an interview with
passenger R. M Brimmer by the Des Arc Citizen newspaper.

THE GREAT OVERLAND MAIL. — The Overland California United States Mail left Memphis on Thursday morning last. It is brought by the Memphis and Little Rock Rail Road to within twelve miles of Madison, on St. Francis river, thence by light vehicles to Des Arc — thence by Messrs. Chidester, Reeside & Co.'s line of four horse U. S. Mail coaches to Fort Smith, where it meets the St. Louis mail. Messrs. Chidester, Reeside & Co., are sub-contractors under Butterfield & Co., from Memphis to Fort Smith; the whole then proceeds over the plains to El Paso and California.

R. M. Brimmer. Esq., of the firm of Chidester, Reeside. & Co., who came with the California Overland Mail early yesterday morning, has our thanks for Memphis papers of Thursday.

This, arrangement places Des Are within fourteen hours of Memphis. We are now "close neighbors" to the Bluff City. – *Des Arc Citizen.*

OVERLAND MAIL — Thursday last was the day on which the Overland Mail should have left St, Louis and Memphis, and San Francisco for this place*[Fort Smith]*. We expect the stage in this evening, from Memphis, and the one from St. Louis on Sunday morning. We look forward to the period as one of the greatest events in our history. Our citizens will make some public demonstration on their arrival from Memphis and St. Louis, but a general "turn out" is expected when they arrive from San Francisco, Cal., which will be about the 10th or 13th of October next. – *Fort Smith Times*

John Butterfield's Home in Utica, New York

CHAPTER FOUR
John Butterfield's Speech, Oct. 14, 1858

*John Butterfield Sr. was a passenger on the 1st westbound trip.
When the first eastbound stage arrived in St. Louis, Sunday, October 10, 1858
completing a twenty-four day journey, a celebration was held, and
John Butterfield was the keynote speaker. The Glasgow Weekly Times reported
on what Butterfield said in the following article.*

Glasgow Weekly Times
Glasgow, Missouri, Oct. 14, 1858, page 2
"First Trip of the Overland Mail"

The California overland Mail arrived at St. Louis Sunday, twenty-four days from San Francisco! The mail came through in four horse coaches, bringing four passengers.

The occasion was deemed worth of notice, and an impromptu celebration was arranged. A procession was formed in front of the Planter's House, and proceeded to the depot, where Mr. Butterfield, one of the contractors was welcomed in a neat speech by Hon. Jno. F. Darly.

He *[Butterfield]* replied briefly, as follows: —

Butterfield expressed the emotions which filled his heart at this demonstration of the good will and approbation of his fellow citizens, and said they were not the less pleasurable by being unexpected. He regarded it as the happiest moment of his life, in view of the fact that he had accomplished an object which had so long been desired by the citizens of St. Louis, and had received their hearty approval for his labor.

Great difficulties had lain in the way, but what obstacles, he continued, cannot be surmounted by American enterprise. (Applause.) He had entered upon the work with a determination to succeed, and by the help of his assistants (whom he complimented very highly) had succeeded. But the operations were as yet imperfect, this being the first trial. For the next six years, thirty thousand miles of mail traveling will be accomplished every day. Nations had taken hold of great works but had not reported. An Atlantic telegraph had been laid, it was true, but the Overland Mail was ahead of the submarine lightning at last, and had reported. (Applause.) He thanked the people and the committee for their cordial welcome, and concluded amid continued applause.

The first trip was highly successful. — Regular stations — over two hundred in number — have been established, and the line may be considered a fixed fact. The time through will be decreased several days, when everything gets in fair working order. No trouble was given by the Indians.

Upon the arrival of the mail, the President was notified by telegraph, to which he responded as follows:

WASHINGTON CITY, OCT. 7TH, 1858

John Butterfield, President Overland Mail Co.:

Sir: Your dispatch has been received. — I cordially congratulate you on the result. It is a glorious triumph for civilization and the Union. Settlements will follow the course of the road, and the East and the West will be bound together by a chain of living Americans which can never be broken.   JAMES BUCHANAN

Butterfield Overland Mail, 1858 to 1861
It took stagecoaches 21 ½ days to traverse the nearly 2,800-mile-long mail route from St. Louis and Memphis to San Francisco. The route was discontinued in early 1861 because of the impending Civil War.

Image source: United States Postal System

CHAPTER FIVE

Observations of A. H. Wilson, September, 1858

*The Ozarks Mountaineer, May 1955, page 3 within an article of F. P. Rose,
"Grand Welcome Given Butterfield," quoting from the original source:
"Personal Reminiscences and Fragments of the Early History of
Springfield and Greene County, Missouri"
Published 1914*

Personal Recollections of Early Settlers
Told at the Dinner of 1907
by A. H. Wilson

The enterprise that did most to push Springfield *[Missouri]* to the front in those days and give her a conspicuous place on the map of the nation was the Overland Mail Route, which was the forerunner of the Southern Pacific Railroad. This was accomplished by the arduous and unceasing efforts of the late Governor Jno. S. Phelps while in Congress. After the passage of the law, there was a very strong "pull" for the location of the point of departure for the Pacific Coast. Aaron V. Brown of Tennessee, President Buchanan's postmaster general, insisted that Memphis should be the starting point, while Governor Phelps and many prominent Missourians insisted on St. Louis. While

Gov. Phelps was in the west looking over the proposed route, the postmaster general was using every effort for Memphis. Gov. Phelps was hastily summoned to Washington, where, after a long and heated discussion, the latter was compromised with one line from Memphis—the other from St. Louis. The franchise or contract was awarded to Jno. Butterfield of New York, a life-long stage man of very limited education, but a man of wonderful energy and a prince of organizers. When he arrived in Springfield to look out a location for barn and shops, he created a great interest. Major D. D. Berry banqueted him and had many prominent Citizens to meet him.

John Butterfield, Sr.
was a short, thick man, and it being warm weather
he wore on the streets a linen duster down to his heels

He *[John Butterfield, Sr.]* was a short, thick man, and it being warm weather he wore on the streets a linen duster down to his heels. A good many young men about town got Butterfield Coats, among them Brannon Woodson, Billy Hornbeak, Jake Shultz, Jack Leathers and others. The fad was short lived. I think they were all discarded before frost.

Mr. Butterfield established his barn and shops on the lots now occupied by the Reps Dry Goods Co., and part of the lot covered by the Heer Dry Goods Co. Part of the property was owned by Jake Painter on which was his gunsmith shop. Mr. Butterfield was a man of few words, and approaching Mr. Painter said: *"I want to buy your lot."* Mr. Painter asked: *"What will you give?"* The answer was, *"One thousand dollars."* Mr. Painter replied, *"I will give you the deed tomorrow,"* and the transaction was closed, which I suppose is the shortest real estate deal ever made in Springfield.

The arrow points out Butterfield's Overland Mail Co. Station at Nicholas Smith's Union Hotel on Boonville Street (Old Wire Road) in Springfield, Missouri's downtown square. Image taken in early 1870. Courtesy of Greg Wadley.

Mr. Painter moved his shop to his home lot on the corner of Olive street and Patton alley, and it is said he was never again seen on the Public Square. I, myself, do not remember to have seen him away from his shop in the thirty years he lived in Springfield, after he moved from the Square.

**when the first Overland coach arrived
business houses were decorated,
and men, women and children
were out on the Public Square in force.**

It was a red letter day for Springfield, about the middle of August, 1858, when the first Overland coach arrived. The business houses were decorated, and men, women and children were out on the Public Square in force. If my memory serves me right, three coaches came in together — horses and coaches decorated with flags and ribbons, bugles sounding and horses came up

Boonville hill at a gallop. Young Jno. Butterfield was on the first coach, and it was said he made the entire trip through to California, but of course he was relieved for rest and sleep. The trip took about twenty-one days.

When Horace Greely of the Tribune and Sam Bowles of the Springfield, Mass., Republican came through Springfield in September, 1859, there was quite a turn-out to welcome them, but they were only here for a few minutes.

Warren H. Graves, who had taken much interest in establishing the line, on every trip received a bundle of daily papers that gave the later news than came in the regular mails, and there was always a rush to see the latest papers, and the interest never flagged as long as the mail was continued. Among the people who were most persistent to get the news were W. B. Logan, Jno. S. Kimbro and Col. M. Oliver.

There was always a crowd to welcome the coaches' arrival from either east or west; there was seldom a trip that did not bring one or more prominent men on the passenger list.

The saddest time came when in June, 1861, every day brought two or three coaches from the west, with a string of horses and men going north. And when the great war began in earnest, the glory of the Overland Mail had departed forever.

Within the *"Ozarks Mountaineer"* article, F. P. Rose added:
"Mr. Butterfield, described as a short, thick man, arrayed in a long linen duster reaching to his heels, a low flat-crowned wide brim hat, and boots was a most picturesque character. He was so greatly admired, it is said, that the store windows displayed coats, hats, shirts, cravats and boots, similar to the "Butterfield wardrobe," and that "no young man of any social standing whether attending church, a public function, or calling on his lady-love was considered correctly attired unless he appeared clad in Butterfield habiliments."

Image source: Pixabay.com

CHAPTER SIX

Observations of George Bailey, September, 1858
*as found in the Dec. 4, 1858 Report of the Postmaster General,
excerpts from pages 715, 718, 739, 740-44.
Also as reprinted in "The First Overland Mail: Butterfield Trail" by
Walter B. Lang, St. Louis to San Francisco, pages 105-110.*

REPORT OF THE POSTMASTER GENERAL.
Post Office Department, *December* 4, 1858.

To The President of the United States:

Sir: I have the honor to submit the following report of the operations and business of the Post Office Department since my communication to you of 1st December last...

OVERLAND MAIL ROUTE.

At the last session of Congress I reported fully the steps that had been taken to carry into execution the act of Congress, approved 3d March, 1857, authorizing the Postmaster General to contract for the conveyance of the entire letter mail between the Mississippi river and San Francisco.

The contract was executed on the 16th September, 1857, and service commenced within the twelve months, namely, on 15th September, 1858, agreeably to the provisions of said act.

The department is happy to announce its conclusive and triumphant success. Its departure and arrival were announced with unbounded demonstrations of joy and exultation. I submit a detailed report of Mr. Bailey, the agent of this department, who came over in the first line of stages which left San Francisco for St. Louis. It will be an important document, not less instructive at the present time than it may be interesting and curious to those who, in after times, may be desirous to know by what energy, skill, and perseverance the vast wilderness was first penetrated by the mail stages of the United States, and the two great oceans united by the longest and most important land route ever established in any country...

[From Geo. Bailey:]   W ASHINGTON, *October* 18, 1858.

S IR: I have the honor to submit herewith, in conformity to the instructions issued from your department on the 28th of June last, the result of my observations while passing over the mail routes between New York and San Francisco...

The establishment of a regular and permanent line of communication, overland, between the Atlantic States and California being a matter of general interest, some desire may naturally be felt to know how far the enterprise recently inaugurated under the auspices of your department has succeeded. I am induced, therefore, to reproduce, somewhat in detail, the notes I took while accompanying the first mail sent from the Pacific under the contract with the Overland Mail Company...

From Fort Belknap the road follows Captain Marcy's trail, portions of which the company have greatly improved at their own cost, and, passing through Gainesville and Sherman, crosses Red river at Colbert's Ferry. From Colbert's Ferry there is a direct route to Fort Smith, which would seem to be the natural terminus of the route on the east.

At this point the route branches, as you are aware, the mails being forwarded simultaneously to St. Louis and Memphis. It had been my intention to return by the Memphis branch, as being the shortest and most direct route, but I abandoned the idea on learning at Fort Smith that I should probably be subjected to some delay. It is to be regretted that the contractors on this route have exhibited so little energy in meeting the comparatively trifling difficulties they have had to encounter.

It is impossible that any road could be worse than that from Fort Smith to Springfield, Missouri, and a glance at the map will show that, so far as distance is concerned, theirs has greatly the advantage of the St. Louis route, yet they have been behind time on all their trips from Memphis to Fort Smith. So, at least, I was informed while at the latter place.

In conclusion, I have to report that, with the exception mentioned above, the company have faithfully complied with all the conditions of the contract. The road is stocked with substantially-built Concord spring wagons, capable of carrying conveniently four passengers with their baggage, and from five to six hundred pounds of mail matter. Permanent stations have been, or are being established at all the places mentioned in the memorandum before referred to; and where, in consequence of the scarcity of water, these are placed far apart, relays of horses and spare drivers are sent forward with the stage to insure its prompt arrival. The various difficulties of the route, the scant supply of water, the long sand deserts, the inconvenience of keeping up stations hundreds of miles from the points from which their supplies are furnished; all these, and the many minor obstacles, naturally presented to the successful management of so long a line of stage communication, have been met and overcome by the energy, the enterprise, and the determination of the contractors. Thus far the experiment has proved successful.

Whether this success is to be permanent; whether this great artery between the Atlantic and Pacific states is to pulsate regularly and uninterruptedly, does not, however, depend entirely upon the Overland Mail Company. They have conquered the natural difficulties of the route, but they have yet to encounter an enemy with whom they cannot successfully cope unaided. I refer, of course, to the tribes of hostile Indians through whose territory they necessarily pass. Their stations in Arizona are at the mercy of the Apache, and the Comanche may, at his pleasure, bar their passage through Texas.

The deep interest you have always manifested in this great enterprise renders it unnecessary for me to argue the importance of taking proper measures to guaranty its permanent success. What those measures should be it is not my province to suggest. My duty is ended with laying the facts before you, and adding my testimony to that already in your possession as to the necessity which exists for a prompt and effectual intervention on the part of government for the protection of the route.

With great respect, your obedient servant,
G. BAILEY, Special Agent, &c.

Memorandum of distances between the stations on the overland mail route from San Francisco to St. Louis, and of the time made on the first trip...

...SEVENTH DIVISION.

Colbert's Ferry to Fisher's, 13 miles; Nale's, 14; Boggy Depot, 17; Gary's, 16; Waddell's, 15; Blackburn's, 16; Pulsey's, 17; Riddell's, 16; Holloway's, 18; Trayon's, 19; Walker's, (Choctaw agency) 16; Fort Smith, 15.

Total, 192 miles. Time, thirty-eight hours.
EIGHTH DIVISION.

Fort Smith to Woosley's, 16 miles; Brodie's, 12; Park's, 20; Fayetteville, 14; Fitzgerald's, 12 ; Callaghan's, 22; Harburn's, 19; Couch's, 16; Smith's, 15; Ashmore's, 20; Springfield, Missouri, 13; Evans', 9; Smith's, 11; Bolivar, 11; Yost's, 16; Quincy 16; Bailey's, 10; Warsaw, 11; Burns', 15; Mulholland's, 20; Shackelford's, 13; Tipton, 7.

Total, 318½ miles.
Time, forty-eight hour and fifty-five minutes.
NINTH DIVISION.

Tipton to St. Louis, (by Pacific railroad,) 160 miles. Time, eleven hours and forty-five minutes.
RECAPITULATION.

	Miles.	Hours.
San Francisco to Los Angeles	462	80.0
Los Angeles to Fort Yuma	282	72.20
Fort Yuma to Tucson	280	71.45
Tucson to Franklin	360	82.0
Franklin to Fort Chadbourne	458	126.30
Fort Chadbourne to Colbert's Ferry	282½	65.25
Colbert's Ferry to Fort Smith	192	38.0
Fort Smith to Tipton	318½	48.55
Tipton to St. Louis	160	11.40
Total	2, 795	596.35

Deducting from this two hours and nine minutes for the difference of time between San Francisco and St. Louis, and reducing it to days, there results twenty-four days eighteen hours and twenty-six minutes as the time actually occupied in making the trip.

Waterman L. Ormsby

CHAPTER SEVEN

Observations of Waterman L. Ormsby, September, 1858
as found in "The First Overland Mail: Butterfield Trail" by
Walter B. Lang, St. Louis to San Francisco, pages 37 to 47.
Also as found in the "The Butterfield Overland Mail: Only Through Passenger
on First Westbound Stage," by Waterman L. Ormsby
Printed in the Oct. 2, 1858 edition of the New York Herald
Edited by Lyle H, Wright and Josephine B, Bynum
The Huntington Library, San Marino, California, excerpts from pages 1 to 38

NEW YORK HERALD, Sunday, September 26, 1858
OVERLAND TO SAN FRANCISCO
On the Way to San Francisco Overland
Sept. 16, 1858

...The operation in itself was simple enough; but, as the honest Irishman [railroad employee] passed the two diminutive bags to Mr. John Butterfield, the president of the Overland Mail Company... I could not allow the bags to pass me without copying the direction, just as a matter of history. Here it is, as it was branded on a stick tied to the bag: *San Francisco, California*
Per Overland Mail
St. Louis, Sept. 16, 1858
Return Label by Express

There were only two small bags, as the postmaster at St. Louis only put in such [envelopes] as were marked *"Per Overland Mail."* This was deemed advisable, so that in case of accident to the wagons the mail can be thrown across a mule, and proceed on its destination...

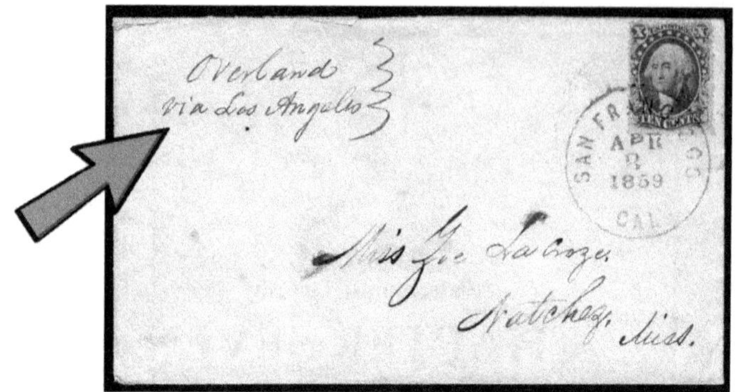

Example of an enveloped clearly marked "Overland via Los Angeles."
To be carried by Butterfield's Overland Mail Company from San Francisco to
Little Rock. Then by the regular postal system to Natchez, Mississippi.

Mr. Butterfield intended to have taken the bags from the post office at St. Louis himself, but the postmaster sent them to the railroad depot in the mail wagon, and Mr. Butterfield took charge of them there. He will accompany them as far as Springfield, MO.

The mail from Memphis, which is to meet this at Fort Smith and proceed with it to San Francisco, was to have started this morning. Should it, from any unforeseen cause, be detained, I understand the Postmaster General has given instructions to wait for it, if necessary, at least a day. But you may depend upon it that Mr. Crocker, who has that part of the line under his charge, will make every effort to be up to time, and nothing but accidents which would stop any route will prevent his appearance with the Memphis mail at Fort Smith when we get there...

We are now on the Pacific Railroad. But what's in a name? It is a single *[railroad]* track road, and only extends about a hundred and sixty miles west of St. Louis. It has nearly a due west course, following the course of the Missouri *[river]* to Jefferson City, the capital of the state... I had but a glance at Jefferson City as we stopped there but a few minutes, but the capitol can plainly be seen from the *[train]* cars...

At Tipton, Moniteau County, MO, the end of the Pacific Railroad *[tracks]*, the bags are first placed on the coaches *[stagecoaches]* of the Overland Mail Company.

In 1858 the Pacific Railroad from St. Louis arrived at Tipton, Missouri and John Butterfield personally carried the first mail bag, boarding an Overland Stagecoach headed through Fort Smith and on to San Francisco. Painted by Frank Nuderscher (1880 – 1959) for the Missouri Pacific Museum.

We left St. Louis this morning at eight o'clock, and are to leave Tipton at six P.M. Thus far we are up to time. I shall mail this *[letter]* at Tipton, and after that will write as the journey will permit. If I can write in the wagons *[stagecoaches]* with not less convenience than I have written this in the *[train]* cars, you will hear from me regularly.

New York Herald, Saturday, October 2, 1858
Overland to San Francisco
Special Correspondence of the New York Herald
In an Overland Mail Wagon,
Near Red River, Indian Territory, Sept. 20, 1858

My last letter was written on the Pacific Railroad, near the western terminus, and left us in anticipation of meeting the first overland mail stage at Tipton, about one hundred and sixty miles from St. Louis, which city, it will be recollected, the great overland mail left at 8 o'clock on the morning of the 16th inst. Since that time we have traveled day and night, across hills, mountains, and plains, as fast as four horses with constant relays could carry us. The teams have all been promptly ready to change, and I think that the facility of our progress has been even greater than the best hopes of the company anticipated. We are now nearly six hundred and seventy miles from St. Louis, or about one quarter of the distance of our journey.

Our general course has been west over the Pacific *[Railroad]* to a terminus, and southwest through Missouri, to Fort Smith on the Arkansas line, thence to the Red River, the border of Texas, crossing it a few miles below Preston. At Fort Smith we arrived just twenty-four hours in advance of the time allotted us in the time table which you have published, which made us due at 3:30 A.M. on Monday, while we had arrived and started before that time on Sunday. Much to our astonishment we found that the Memphis mail had beaten us fifteen minutes, though this was accounted for by the assertion that the Memphis postmaster had given up the mails before time. I was thus deprived of my anticipated privilege of writing you from Fort Smith, and, as since then the stages have gained nine hours more, you may readily believe I have had no opportunity to write.

To gain thirty-two hours, as we have, on the already close time table of the Overland Mail Company has not given us much time to go easy over the stones. I have given up several attempts to write, out of sheer despair, and perhaps your printers will wish I had given up this. Writing on Captain Rynder's back in the midst of a Tammany Hall row is not a circumstance to it. The only sleep I have had since last Thursday morning has been snatched in the *[Celerity wagons]* wagons, on roads which out — 'Connecticut' Connecticut. Yet the new scenes which constantly meet the view, the variegated aspect of the country, the curious characters to be met, and the novelty of roughing it overland, are, I think, quite a recompense for any slight inconvenience which may be experienced.

But, to the details of our journey.

The Pacific Railroad train, carrying the first overland mail, arrived at Tipton, the western terminus of the road, situated in Moniteau County, Mo., at precisely one minute after six o'clock P.M. of Thursday, the 16th inst., being several minutes behind time. We there found the first coach ready, the six horses all harnessed and hitched, and Mr. John Butterfield, Jr., impatient to be off.

Bob Crossman kneeling by the historical marker in Tipton, Missouri.

The town contains but a few hundred inhabitants, and all these seemed to have turned out for the occasion, though they made no demonstration on account of it. The place is, however, but a few months old, having been built since the completion of this end of the line, and doubtless excitements are too rare to be appreciated. They looked on with astonishment as the baggage and packages were being rapidly transferred from the *[train]* cars to the *[stage]* coach. The latter was entirely new and had not yet held a load of passengers. It very much resembled those heavy coaches which are used in New York to convey passengers between the steamboats, car depots, and the hotels, and appeared to be quite as expensively built. In large letters over the side was the following:

"OVERLAND MAIL COMPANY"

The time occupied in shifting the baggage and passengers was just nine minutes, at which time the cry of *"all aboard,"* and the merry crack of young John Butterfield's whip, denoted that we were off.

**at which time the cry of *"all aboard"*
the merry crack of young John Butterfield's whip
denoted that we were off**

I took a note of the *"following distinguished persons present,"* as worthy of a place in history: Mr. John Butterfield, president of the Overland Mail Company; John Butterfield, Jr., on the box; Judge Wheeler, lady, and two children, of Fort Smith; Mr. T. R. Corbin, of Washington; and the correspondent of the Herald.

John Butterfield Sr.(left), president of the Overland Mail Company, and his son John Jr. (right) sketched about the time they boarded the first Overland Mail Company stagecoach leaving Tipton, Missouri on September 16, 1858. John Jr. was the driver. John Sr. rode as far as Fort Smith, Arkansas, and returned to Tipton on an eastbound stage, then on to his hometown of Utica, New York. Image source: Frank Leslie's Illustrated Newspaper, November 27, 1858.

It had been decided to take no passengers but the last named gentleman *[the author of this diary, Waterman Ormsby]*, on the first trip, but Mr. Butterfield made an exception in favor of Judge Wheeler, agreeing to take him to Fort Smith, where he intended to go himself. You will perceive, therefore, that your correspondent was the only through passenger who started in the first overland coach for San Francisco, as all the rest of the party dropped off by the time we reached Fort Smith. Not a cheer was raised as the coach drove off, the only adieu being, *"Good bye, John,"* addressed to John, Jr., by one of the crowd. Had they have been wild Indians they could not have exhibited less emotion.

"The supply train" 1876 by E. Forbes
Ormsby calls these covered wagons "traveling hotels."

Our road for the first few miles was very fair, coursing through several small prairies, where for the first time I noticed those **traveling hotels** so commonly seen in the western country. These are large covered wagons, in which the owner and his family, sometimes numbering as high as a dozen, emigrate from place to place, traveling in the daytime, and camping near wood, water, and grass at night. All along the wildest western roads these hotels may be met in every direction, enlivening the way by their camp fires at night, and presenting pictures of domestic felicity which might well be emulated in certain quarters more comfortable and less homely.

We rode along at a somewhat rapid pace, because John, Jr., was determined that the overland mail should go through his section on time; and, though his father kept calling out, *"Be careful, John,"* he assured him that it was *"all right,"* and drove on.

The first stopping place was at "Shackleford's," about seven miles distant, and we seemed hardly to have become comfortably seated in the coach before our attention was attracted to the illumination of our destination — a recognition of the occasion which seemed quite cheering after the apparent previous neglect. The team wheeled up in fine style, and we found the change of horses ready harnessed and supper waiting. Mr. Shackleford assured us that he would have fired a gun for us, but he could not get it to go off. We took the will for the deed, however, and hustled in to supper, which was soon dispatched. After taking leave of Mr. Corbin and the others, we were off again to the next station, having been detained, in all, twenty minutes.

Bob Crossman standing by the historical marker in Syracuse, Missouri.

This locality is called Syracuse, and is principally owned by T. R. Brayton and Mr. Shackleford, who have done much to establish the route through this section. The Pacific Railroad Company is now building a depot here, and the western terminus will shortly be extended to it. I should have mentioned before that it is in Morgan County.

From this point I considered myself fairly under way in the coaches, and must confess that I felt quite as fatigued with the first few miles as with as many hundred which I have traveled since. The change from railroad to coach traveling is somewhat marked, though one of our party very justly observed that on the Pacific road the change is so gradual as to be hardly perceptible. I do think that road quite equal to that monument of human enterprise, the Long Island Railroad, though generally, I must admit, I found the western railroads very well managed.

As the road to the next station, though only thirteen miles, was nearly all up hill, we were one hour and forty five minutes in reaching it, which was considered pretty good time. Our horses were four in number, that being the allotment all along the line from Tipton to San Francisco. They were ready and harnessed at this point, and to change teams was the work of but a few minutes, and we were off again. This time we got a driver who was sick, and the road being somewhat bad made our progress slow, and the sixteen miles to Burns' occupied three hours.

**the driver did not know the road well
the night was dark, the roads very difficult,
and the coach lamps seemed to be of little use**

The driver from here did not know the road well, and we had to feel our way along, as the night was dark, the roads very difficult, and the coach lamps seemed to be of little use in the dim moonlight; and the sixteen miles to Warsaw on the Osage River occupied another three hours. Yet, though this might appear to be slow traveling, it was even faster than required by the time table. As we neared the stations we blew our horns to apprise them of our coming.

The original Warsaw station building is now being used as Reser Funeral Home (on right). In the lobby they have this photo (on left) of the same building when it was used as the Farmers Hotel in Warsaw, Missouri.

At Warsaw, though we arrived about three A.M., and ahead of time, we found our horses ready harnessed, and were soon on our way to the next station, eleven miles distant.

**the night was now dark as pitch
we had to be preceded by a man on horseback
with a light to show us the way through the ford**

The road led through a ford of the Osage River and a dense forest, full of rocky hills, and the night was now dark as pitch. As we left Warsaw we had to be preceded by a man on horseback, with a light to show us the way through the ford, but the river being rather low there was not much danger. I began to feel some fear of wet feet and mail bags when the water reached the hub, but we got over safely and pretty dry, as the water was not deeper than half the wheels. We made the eleven miles in two hours, and I must confess it was a matter of the utmost astonishment to me how the driver ever found his way in the wilderness. We went *"right along about east,"* as young John said, and much to the fear of the old gentleman *[John Sr.]* that we would upset.

The next ten miles was made in an hour and a half, bringing us to Quincy, where we took breakfast. Four-teen miles through the prairies brought us to Youst, in an hour and forty minutes; sixteen miles to Boli-var, in two hours and twenty minutes; eleven miles to Smith's, in one hour and four minutes; and twenty miles to Springfield, in three hours and five minutes — which made it just a quarter past three o'clock on Friday, when we were not required by the time table to leave the place until a quarter to eight on Saturday. The ride was, though rather fatiguing to a novitiate, rather pleasant on the whole. The views of the little prairies, the vast fields of corn, tobacco, and wild mus-tard seed, the picturesque encampment of the "travel-ers," the fields of Chinese sugar cane, droves of roving cattle, the sounding of merry horns as we approached the stations, the bustle of changing horses, and the en-tire novelty of the scenc, made an impression upon my mind which will never be effaced.

I can never forget the grotesque figures which my imagination conjured up out of the objects in the woods on our first night out. The stories I had read of bands of roving Indians, rambling through the forests but to kill and steal, all rushed to my mind, and transformed each decayed tree or stunted bush into a lurking foe. Then, the music of the forest, the moonlight struggling through the trees, the easy motion of the vehicle as it rocked to and fro on the rough road, like a vessel moving on the sea, all tended to make one thought-ful of the impressiveness of the occasion. Young John enlivened the road with his eagerness to get on and to make good time, and evinced the greatest anxiety that no accident should happen to interfere with the safe carriage of the mail. There seemed to be a sort of catching enthusiasm about the whole trip, which excited more interest — I know for myself — than I ever supposed could be mustered out of the bare fact of a common coach traveling over a common road, with a common mail bag and a few common people inside. But the occasion made them all uncommon, and I soon got so that I would willingly go without my dinner for the privilege of helping along that mail a quarter of an hour. Indeed, we did do this on our way to Springfield, when Mr. Butterfield got up a temporary lunch for us as the coach stopped alongside of a spring, and we took a nice social meal in its shade.

Springfield, Missouri with dirt streets and no power lines. ca 1870

I forget, now, what county Springfield is in, but you can easily find it by looking along the central part of western Missouri, and bringing your eye on the line of the source of her many small rivers. It is a flourishing town, of about two thousand inhabitants, and has been for twenty-five years the seat of the General Land Office. It has several churches, a branch of the State Bank of Missouri, and if somebody there had enterprise enough to build a lot of houses it would be a rapidly growing town. The passage through it of the overland mail, and the establishment of a daily line to connect with the railroad for St. Louis, have much increased its importance.

**As our team drove up
there was quite an excitement raised
people all gathered round to see the first overland mail**

As our team drove up to the door there was quite an excitement raised in the town, and the people all gathered round to see the first overland mail, congratulating both the Butterfields on the occasion. The time made from Tipton to Springfield was the quickest ever before made, owing to the promptness with which the relays of horses were procured; and had it not been for accidents, before spoke of, it would have been made in even quicker time. Every one conceded that the overland mail had done remarkably well, and pretty soon our arrival was honored with a salute of several guns.

"The Overland Mail – Changing Stage-Coach for Celerity Wagon"
Frank Leslie's Illustrated Newspaper, Oct. 23, 1858, pg. 325-328.
lithograph, hand colored ; 15 3/4 x 10 3/4 in.

Our stay was just long enough to change from the *[stage]* coach to one of the *[Celerity]* wagons, such as are used from this point to San Francisco. They are made much like the express wagons in your city which carry goods for transshipment, only they are heavier built, have tops made of canvass, and are set on leather straps instead of springs. Each one has three seats, which are arranged so that the backs let down and form one bed, capable of accommodating from four to ten persons, according to their size and how they lie. I found it a very agreeable bed for one, afterwards.

In the passage above, Waterman Ormsby is describing a Celerity wagon.
This is the only photograph in existence of a Butterfield owned Overland Mail Company Celerity wagon. This copy of a 1861 daguerreotype image is courtesy of the Nita Stewart Haley Memorial Library at Midland, Texas.

Mr. Ormsby relates: ... Each one has three seats, the backs of which can be let down to form one bed, capable of accommodating from four to ten people, according to their size and how they lie...

When the stage is full, passengers must take turns sleeping. Perhaps the jolting will be found disagreeable at first, but a few nights without sleeping will soon obviate that difficulty, and soon the jolting will be as little of a disturbance as the rocking cradle to a suckling baby. For my part I found no difficulty in sleeping over the roughest roads, and I have no doubt that anyone else will learn quite as quickly. A bounce of the wagon which makes one's head strike the top, bottom and sides will be equally disregarded, and 'Nature's sweet restorer' will be found as welcome on the hard bottom of the wagons as the downy beds of St. Nicholas...

White pants and kid gloves better be discarded by most passengers... the wagons and coaches can hardly be expected to equal the Fourth Avenue horse cars for comfortable riding.

Everything being in readiness, we got started again at four o'clock, having been detained at Springfield three-quarters of an hour. We drove off to the post office and took on a small through mail for San Francisco, and also the postmaster and another citizen, who wished to have it to say that they had ridden in the first coach from Springfield containing the overland mail. It was gratifying to me, as one of the few evidences of interest in the enterprise which we met. One thing struck me as creditable, and that was that the mail bag from Springfield was quite as large as that from St. Louis.

We kept traveling all day and night, of course, our way during Friday afternoon and evening being through an extremely dusty, hilly, and stony road, as will appear when I state the fact that the first fourteen miles took two hours; the next twenty miles three hours; the next fifteen miles two hours and forty-five minutes; the next seventeen miles three hours; and the next eighteen miles three hours and twenty minutes. This brought us to breakfast time on Saturday morning, at Callahan's, but about twelve miles from Fayetteville, Arkansas, very near the border line. Here we found Mr. Crocker, the superintendent of the line between St. Louis and Memphis and Fort Smith, Arkansas, where the two mails converge and proceed together.

We greased our wagon, changed horses, and got some breakfast

We greased our wagon, changed horses, and got some breakfast — all in an incredibly short space of time — after which we set out for Fayetteville.

The route leads over those steep and rugged hills which surround the Ozark range in this section of Arkansas, and we were just three hours going from Callahan's to Fayetteville. This town is located up among the hills, in a most inaccessible spot, in Franklin County, said by its inhabitants to be the star county of the state. It has two churches, the county court house, a number of fine stores and dwellings, and, I believe, about 1,800 inhabitants.

1870's North side of the Fayetteville Square, Post Office and New Drug Store.
Courtesy Shiloh Museum of Ozark History.
Peter Harkins Collection (S-90-194-172)

It is a flourishing little town, and its deficiency of a good hotel will, I understand, be supplied by Mr. Butterfield, who has bought some property for that purpose. He is the most energetic president of a company I ever saw. He appears to know every foot of the ground and to be known by everybody, while his son John has been very active in getting good stock on this end of the route, in which, I think, he has succeeded.

---

we were at this point

twenty-two hours and seventeen minutes ahead of time

We made a small addition to our mail here, and at just ten minutes to twelve started for Fort Smith, on the border line between Arkansas and Indian Territory, and about sixty-five miles distant. We started at ten minutes to twelve on Saturday, when the time table only required us to start at a quarter past ten on Sunday — so we were at this point twenty-two hours and seventeen minutes ahead of time as set down in the time table by which the Post Office Department required us to run — this too, in spite of the one or two little annoyances referred to, and a pretty heavy load of baggage and passengers which had not been expected. It could only have been accomplished by the most perfect arrangement for, and promptness in, the relays of horses and the excellence of the stock purchased. We had now gone two hundred and forty-three miles, through, I think, some of the roughest part of the country on the route, and yet gained time.

terrible pain in the back
which such incessant riding without sleep occasioned

I must confess that I began to get quite enthusiastic on the subject of the mail myself, and looked upon the mail bags and the horses with quite as much interest as I should have had in the Atlantic cable had I been on that world renowned expedition. I jumped out and got water for the horses, kept an eye on the mail bags, walked up the steep hills, and forgot the terrible pain in the back which such incessant riding without sleep occasioned.

We have now arrived at Colheet's [Colbert's] Ferry on the Red River, about eight miles below Preston, on the Texas border; we are just thirty-five hours ahead of the time table. An express is just leaving us for Fort Smith, and as I wish to send this I must cut off my letter without the most interesting portion — our reception at Fort Smith, meeting the Memphis mail, journey through the Indian Territory, and arrival here today at about ten o'clock. I must send this and take my chance to send the rest. I have one comfort, at any rate: the *Herald* will have the exclusive news, and I can wait with a better grace. We have the strongest hopes of reaching San Francisco in less than the twenty-five days. I find roughing it on the plains agrees with me, so that I guess I could go without eating or sleeping for a week. I hope I shan't have to try it, though.

Non-Butterfield - Concord Coach, Nederland CO 1914. John T. Carmack, driver

New York Herald, Sunday, October 24, 1858
Near Fort Belknap, Texas, Sept. 22, 1858

My LAST letter left the overland mail in route from Fayetteville, Arkansas, to Fort Smith, Arkansas. Since then we have passed through the Indian Territory, crossing the Red River at Colbert's Ferry, through Grayson, Cooke, Montague, Wise, and Young counties, Texas, to Fort Belknap, and are now on our way to Fort Chadbourne, from whence I expect to send this; and when we reach there we shall have gone 945 miles on our journey.

Fayetteville is in Franklin County *[Washington County in 1858]*, Arkansas, among the hills of the Ozark range of mountains. We left there on Saturday, the 18th inst., at two minutes before noon — just twenty-two hours and thirteen minutes ahead of the time required of us by the time table. Even among these hills you do not lose sight of the prairie nature of the West; for just after leaving Fayetteville you see a fine plain, surrounded with hills — in fact, a prairie in the mountains. After a rather rough ride of fourteen miles, which we accomplished with our excellent team in one hour and three-quarters, we took a team of four mules to cross the much dreaded Ozark range, including the Boston Mountain. I had thought before we reached this point that the rough roads of Missouri and Arkansas could not be equaled; but here Arkansas fairly beats itself.

**The wiry, light, little animals tugged and pulled
as if they would tear themselves to pieces, and
our heavy wagon bounded along the crags
as if it would be shaken in pieces**

I might say our road was steep, rugged, jagged, rough, and mountainous — and then wish for some more expressive words in the language. Had not Mr. Crocker provided a most extraordinary team I doubt whether we should have been able to cross in less than two days. The wiry, light, little animals tugged and pulled as if they would tear themselves to pieces, and our heavy wagon bounded along the crags as if it would be shaken in pieces every minute, and ourselves disemboweled on the spot.

For fifteen miles the road winds among these mountains at a height of nearly two thousand feet above the Gulf of Mexico. The approach to it from Fayetteville is through a pleasant and fertile valley; and I understand that these valleys comprise some of the best agricultural districts of Arkansas. The mountains abound in splendid white oak timber. As the road winds along the ridges you are afforded most magnificent views of the surrounding hills and valleys — especially in the winter, when the foliage is less an obstruction than it was when we passed over. But we had a clear day, and I can only say that our mountain views in the Highlands of the Hudson are but children's toys in comparison with these vast works of nature.

Connecticut hills and roads are mere pimples and sandpaper compared with the Ozark ranges

The term "Boston Mountain" is, I believe, derived from a prevailing western fashion of applying that name to anything which is considered very difficult. But Connecticut hills and roads are mere pimples and sandpaper compared with the Ozark ranges. By hard tugging we got up, and with the aid of brakes and drags we got down; and I can assure you we were by no means sorry when that herculean feat was accomplished. The mules which took us over the mountains carried us, in all, about nineteen miles, when we took another team of horses to carry us to Fort Smith.

"The Overland Mail Crossing a Stream at Night"
Frank Leslie's Illustrated Newspaper, Oct. 23, 1858, pg. 325-328.
Crossing the Arkansas River on schedule at 2 a.m. often a rider with a lantern would lead the stage from the ferry, across the mud flats, to the south bank.

We crossed the Arkansas in a flatboat much resembling a raft, at Van Buren, a flourishing little town on its banks. Our course through the soft bed of the flats (which were not covered, owing to the low state of the river) was somewhat hazardous, as our heavy load was liable to be sunk on the quicksands which abound here. But by the aid of a guide on horseback, with a lantern (for it was night), we crossed the flats, and up the steep sandy bank in safety.

Picking our way cautiously for five or six miles, we reached Fort Smith on the Arkansas River, just on the border of Arkansas and the Indian Territory, at five minutes after two o'clock A.M., having made the sixty-five miles from Fayetteville in fourteen hours and seven minutes, or three hours and seven minutes less than schedule time. We had anticipated beating the mail which left Memphis, Tenn., on the 16th to meet us at Fort Smith, several hours; but as soon as we entered the town, though at so unseasonable an hour, we found it in a great state of excitement on account of the arrival of the Memphis mail just fifteen minutes before us. But, though they had 700 miles to travel, five hundred of them were by steamboat, from Memphis to Little Rock, and it was said that they got their mails before we did.

**Horns were blown, houses were lit up
many flocked to the hotel to have a look at the wagons and
have a peep at the first mail bags**

Fort Smith is a thriving town of about 2,500 inhabitants, and they boast that every house is full. There are two newspapers, both of which were, I believe, started by Judge Wheeler, who was a passenger by the overland mail route from St. Louis. As several other routes over the plains pass through this place, and have contributed much to its growth, the people evinced much interest; and the news that both the St. Louis and Memphis stages had arrived spread like wildfire. Horns were blown, houses were lit up, and many flocked to the hotel *[John Rogers City Hotel]* to have a look at the wagons and talk over the exciting topic, and have a peep at the first mail bags. The general interest was so contagious that I, though I had but a few minutes to spare before the stage started again, actually employed the time in writing ten lines to my wife instead of the Herald. I must say, however, that I expected you would hear of the few facts I could then communicate, before a letter from me could reach you, by means of the telegraph.

An hour and twenty-five minutes was consumed in examining the way mails, arranging the way bill, joining the two mails from Memphis and St. Louis, and changing stages; and precisely at half-past three A.M. on Sunday, the 19th inst., the stage left Fort Smith, being exactly twenty-four hours ahead of the time required in the time table, which had been gained in the first four hundred and sixty-eight miles of our journey. I was the only person in the wagon which left Fort Smith — beside Mr. Fox, the mail agent, and the driver.

Mr. John Butterfield
though sixty-five years of age
borne the fatiguing sleepless journey as well
if not better, than any of the rest

Mr. John Butterfield, the president of the Overland Mail Company, had accompanied us thus far, and, though sixty-five years of age, had borne the fatiguing, sleepless journey as well, if not better, than any of the rest. Indeed, I felt ashamed to complain when I saw one of his years stand out so well. Certainly, if the overland mail does not succeed, it will not be for lack of his arduous personal exertions. He urged the men in changing horses at every station, often taking hold to help, and on one occasion driving for a short distance. He is, however, an old stager, and is in his element in carrying on this enterprise. I cannot be too grateful to him, on your behalf, as well as my own, for the kind facilities which he extended to me.

We forded the Arkansas at Fort Smith, and for the first time since our departure from St. Louis I had an opportunity to sleep in the wagon, wrapped up in blankets and stretched on the seats. It took some time to get accustomed to the jolting over the rough road, the rocks, and log bridges; but three days' steady riding without sleep helped me in getting used to it, and I was quite oblivious from the time of crossing the Arkansas to the first stopping place in the Indian Territory, about sixteen miles from the river, which we reached about daylight. Here is a large farm owned by an Indian and worked by a white man from the East. I here saw several friendly Choctaws on their way east.

The Choctaw reservation extends through the southeastern portion of the Indian Territory, and the Indians are to be met all along the road, either traveling or located in their log huts. Many of them are quite wealthy, their property consisting chiefly in cattle and Negroes. Their ownership of slaves is quite common, and many of them have large numbers. In their treatment of them they are generally more lenient than the white slaveholders, and appear to let them do pretty much as they please. I noticed in riding through the territory but little farming going on. The fact is, but little land is worked. Though the soil is well adapted for producing corn, tobacco, hemp, & c., they generally prefer to raise stock. They brand their cattle and let them run on the plains, which during nine months of the year yield excellent pasturage. During the remaining three months they generally get poor, having only the winter grass of the creeks to subsist upon.

Many of the Choctaws own large herds of cattle, and live well on the increase. Their habitations are mostly off the road. Those on the road appear to be the most miserable specimens of the western log hut, and many of them are deserted.

As we road along we could see them lazily basking in the sun or reclining in the cool porticos, *[see 'dogtrot' cabin photo below]* which are built, in most of the huts, so as to divide the house in the center, affording a very pleasant location for dining or sitting in warm weather.

What struck me forcibly was the squalid misery which seems to characterize most of them — which was only surpassed by the appearance of their Negroes, with whom, I am told, they often cohabit. They generally shrugged their shoulders as the stage passed, but seldom said anything beyond *"Good day"* — and only that when spoken to.

About seventeen miles from the crossing of the Arkansas we came to the residence of **Governor Wm. Walker**, the governor of the territory.

Governor Tandy Walker (1814–1877) and Walker's Station
The dogtrot, also known as a breezeway house, dog-run, or possum-trot, is a
style of house that was common throughout the Southeastern United States.

He looks like a full-blooded white man, though I understand he has some Indian blood in his veins. His wife is a half-breed Indian of the Choctaw Nation. He was elected at the last election and has held his office but about six months. The salary is one thousand dollars per year. He has a farm of several hundred acres, a very comfortable house, and owns several hundred head of cattle. The place is called Scullyville, and his house is made a station for changing horses. In personal appearance he looks like a well-to-do farmer. On this occasion he came out in his shirt sleeves and helped hitch the horses. He has considerable influence with the Nation, and is favorably disposed toward the Overland Mail Company.

Though, by the laws of the Nation, an Indian may procure a divorce at pleasure upon the payment of ten dollars, there is one provision which I think our strong minded women will approve of, and that is that the wife is entitled to half the property. This provision is rigidly adhered to, and husband and wife are quite as strict in their dealings with each other as with others. Most of the Choctaws speak our language, though for purposes of mere civility; they do not care much about using it. The bane of the Choctaws, as well as of many white nations, is the use of intoxicating liquors, which they will procure in spite of all precautions. The laws of the territory make it an offence, punishable by fine and imprisonment, to give or sell liquor to an Indian; but they will drink camphene, burning fluid, or "Perry Davis' Pain Killer," or the whole three mixed, for the purpose of getting drunk, and when in that state their performances are said to be not less remarkable than those of their white brethren in the same condition. They are generally quite averse to work, and it is with the greatest difficulty that they can be compelled to do their portion toward mending the road.

From the Arkansas River to Scullyville, there appeared to be considerable land under cultivation, but as we proceeded there was less to be seen. The land is well watered, and with little cultivation could be made to yield abundantly; but they prefer to let their stock grow and increase without their care, and draw their small pensions from the government. The Indians we saw along the road looked squalid and miserable generally, though occasionally we met some very fine specimens of the red men of the forest. These, however, were mostly half-breeds, who are by far the most enterprising and industrious, and avail themselves of the education fund to educate their children. This fund, I believe, amounts to $10,000, and is amply sufficient for its purpose. The Chickasaws, who occupy a more westerly reservation, are much more advanced in civilization than the Choctaws.

After leaving Gov. Walker's, the next station (sixteen miles distant) was reached in about two hours and a half, and two other stations, at about equal distances, in about the same time each. I took my breakfast and dinner out of a provision basket which had been kindly placed in the wagon by the forethought of Mr. Butterfield, who had not forgotten the needful with which to wash it down.

Though it consisted of but a few cold cuts, my memory still clings to it as the last civilized meal between Fort Smith and the barren plains where I now write. I have said nothing of the homely meals provided on the way from Tipton to Fort Smith, for I considered them as but the well known accompaniments of Hoosier life; but, ever since I left that last meal of cold ham, cakes, crackers, and cheese, fond recollection recalls it to view. Though I am no epicurean, I could not forbear writing its obituary.

About fifty miles from the Arkansas River, on our road, I noticed the first plain, or prairie, of consequence in the Indian Territory. It was a rolling plain, I should judge full twenty miles in circumference. The soil looked so black and rich that I was surprised to see so little verdure, but I soon learned that this color was caused by the grass having been set on fire. On the western border, Mr. McDonnell, the mail agent, pointed out to me a curious ledge of black sandstone rocks, which had very much the appearance of the ruins of a large building, so regularly were they laid.

The Edwards Store, Native Trading Post near Red Oak, Oklahoma
This is the only structure still standing in Indian Territory that witnessed
Butterfield's Overland Mail stagecoaches passing by. It may have been a flag
station, notifying the stage to stop to pick up mail or passengers.
The Edwards may also have occasionally provided meals for the stagecoaches.
Photo by and compliments of Susan Dragoo.

As we proceeded west, the country which had before — at least on our road — been of a forest nature, grew more open, and the rolling plains and smoother roads grew more frequent. We soon met many bands of Choctaw Indians in charge of large herds of cattle. They never took any more notice of us than to look pretty sharply at us and to say good day if spoken to. We also met many emigrants from Texas in their covered wagons containing their families and all their worldly possessions, camping at night and luxuriating on their dried beef, coffee, and perhaps corn from the nearest cornfield.

At Pussey [Pusley] (a station for changing horses, where an Indian of that name lives), about sixty-six miles from the river, I met an old Indian who owns seven hundred head of cattle, and a pretty daughter, and is willing to give the half of the one to the white man who will marry the other. Here I gave an Indian boy a paper of tobacco to give me water enough to wash my face, put on a blue flannel shirt, and considered myself pretty well on my way out West.

In the little plains which we passed, we frequently saw the tall posts which the Indians use in playing ball.

Native Americans Playing Ishtaboli or Lacrosse
Source: "History of Native American Lacrosse" By Thomas Vennum Jr
For a description of variations of this game mentioned above, called in Choctaw "Ishtaboli," see J. R. Swanton's "Source Material for the Social and Ceremonial Life of the Choctaw Indians," (Smithsonian Institution, Bureau of American Ethnology. Bulletin, No. 103; Washington, 1931). pp. 140-55.

The players divide themselves into two parties, one standing at each post. The throwers aim to hit the posts, and the catchers must capture the ball in little bowls with which each is provided, a penalty being inflicted for catching the ball with the hands. They become very much excited at this game, and gamble with it very often.

From the night of Thursday, the 16th, up to the night of Sunday, the 19th, I had traveled continuously without accident, both night and day, and at a pretty rapid rate. On Sunday night, when within a few miles of Blackburn's Station (which is about sixty miles from Red River), I thought all hopes of a quick trip for the first **Overland Mail** were at an end. We had taken a splendid team of horses at the last station, and had been spinning over the rolling prairies at a rapid rate; our route for some hours had been over these hills with their gradual elevations, and our driver had urged his team pretty well. We now came to a patch of woods through which the road was tortuous and stony. But our driver's ambition to make good time overcame his caution, and away we went, bounding over the stones at a fearful rate.

> **The moon shone brightly, but its light was obstructed by the trees, and the driver had to rely much on his knowledge of the road for a guide.**

The moon shone brightly, but its light was obstructed by the trees, and the driver had to rely much on his knowledge of the road for a guide. To see the heavy mail wagon whizzing and whirling over the jagged rock, through such a labyrinth, in comparative darkness, and to feel oneself bouncing — now on the hard seat, now against the roof, and now against the side of the wagon — was no joke, I assure you, though I can truthfully say that I rather liked the excitement of the thing.

> **Two heavy thumps and a bound of the wagon that unseated us all, and a crashing sound, denoted that something had broken.**

But it was too dangerous to be continued without accident, and soon two heavy thumps and a bound of the wagon that unseated us all, and a crashing sound, denoted that something had broken. We stopped and examined, but found no damage except a broken seat, and proceeded to the station.

Here a further examination, to our utter astonishment, disclosed the fact that the pole, or tongue, of the wagon was badly split. It was a mystery to me how we ever reached the station without completing its destruction. It took more time mend it than the ambitious driver saved. Moral — *"Make haste slowly."* After repairing damages we got starred again, and traveled the next 18 miles in two hours and a quarter.

The night was beautifully clear and bright, and I was tempted to stay up and enjoy it; but I had become too much fatigued with the journey to be able to withstand the demands of somnolence, and, wrapping myself up in my shawls, was soon obliviously snoring on the extended seats of the wagon. I awoke but once during the night, having been jolted into a position where my neck felt as if there was a knot in it.

They had stopped at a station *[Waddell's Station]* to change horses, and for the time not a sound could I hear. I had been dreaming of the Comanche Indians, and in the confusion of drowsiness first thought that the driver and the mail agent had been murdered, and that I, being covered up in the blankets, had been missed; then I recollected that I had a pistol and thought of feeling for it; but finally I thought I would not stir, for fear the Indians would see me — when I was brought to my senses by a familiar voice saying *"Get up there, old hoss,"* and found it was the driver hitching up a new team.

During the night we went eighteen miles in two hours and a half. The next thirteen miles took three hours, owing to the bad state of the roads, bringing us to Garey's [Geary's] station. Mr. Garey [Geary] has a hundred acres of corn, which is considered a pretty fair lot for this section of the country. Another ride of seventeen miles occupied but two hours and a half, bringing us to the **"Boggy Depot,"** where there are several painted houses and a few stores. I learned that near here, a few days since, an Indian got shot

Old Boggy Depot, 1837 by Vinson Lackey
Image courtesy of the Gilcrease Museum

while in a quarrel about politics — for you must know that the old Wigwam at Tammana is not the only spot where the braves settle political questions with hard knocks.

The Nation is divided on the question of forming a state government. The two parties wax strong on their respective sides, and frequent collisions are the consequence. I do not wish to be unfair on the subject, but I am given to understand that the half-breeds and whites and more intelligent full-bloods are in favor of the state government.

Fourteen miles from Boggy Depot we came to Blue River Station, *[Nail's Crossing]* where a very heavy bridge is building for the company. Here I saw a copy of the *Weekly Herald* — a distance of six hundred miles from St. Louis, and nearly seventeen hundred from New York overland, and twenty-five miles from any post office. I thought the *Herald* was appreciated there.

A ride of three hours *[although not mentioned, they passed Fisher's Station]* brought us to Colbert's Ferry on the Red River — the boundary between Texas and the Indian Territory. We arrived here on Monday, the 20th inst., at ten minutes to ten — being, altogether, thirty-four hours ahead of rime to this point. But here was a difficulty. There was no team to carry on the mail. Arrangements had been made to put it through in quick time on the regular day, but it was not expected a day and a half in advance. Indeed, there was nothing left to do but to put up with it. We had, by several mere accidents, been enabled to obtain our relays so far in advance, and now we could afford a little loss of time. We had a good dinner, and I took advantage of the opportunity to write to you — the first chance off the wagon since Thursday, the 16th.

Colbert's Ferry across Red River
Image from the set: "Stereoscopic Views of Texas and Indian Territory"
Source: Gerald T. Ahnert

Mr. Colbert, the owner of the station and of the ferry, is a half-breed Indian of great sagacity and business tact. He is a young man — not quite thirty, I should judge — and has a white wife — his third. He has owned and run this ferry five years, and has had excellent patronage, from its central location, being about midway between Preston and the one below.

Mr. Colbert evinces some enterprise in carrying the stages of the company across his ferry free of charge, in consideration of the increased travel which it will bring his way. He also stipulates to keep the neighboring roads in excellent order, and has already done much towards it. He has a large gang of slaves at work on the banks of the river, cutting away the sand, so as to make the ascent easy.

His boat is simply a sort of raft, pushed across the shallow stream by the aid of poles in the hands of sturdy slaves. The fare for a four-horse team is a dollar and a quarter, and the net revenue of the ferry about $1,000 per annum. He thinks of either buying a horse boat or having a stout cable drawn across the river, so that one man could manage the boat. I suggested to him to buy a piece of the Atlantic cable, but he was of the opinion that it would be too costly.

He owns about twenty-five slaves, and says he considers them about the best stock there is, as his increase is about four per year. He has a fine farm, and raises considerable corn — how much I do not know. At his table I saw sugar, butter, and pastry — the first two of which have been exceedingly rare articles since I left Fort Smith, and the last of which I have not seen anywhere else since I left Fort Smith. He is nearly white, very jovial and pleasant, and, altogether, a very good specimen of the halfbreed Indian.

We had determined, after giving our horses a brief rest, to proceed with them until we met the other team coming back from Sherman; but just as we were about starting with them the expected team rode up, and all haste was made for our departure over Colbert's Ferry into Texas. We crossed the wide, shallow, and muddy Red River on one of Mr. Colbert's boats, and saw quite a large number of his slaves busily engaged in lowering the present steep grade up the banks. He also undertakes to keep in order part of the road on the Texas side of the river. On our way to Sherman in Texas, we passed several large gullies, or beds of creeks, which are being bridged at the expense of Grayson County, in which Sherman is situated and of which it is the county seat.

Sherman is a pleasant little village of about six hundred inhabitants, and is noted for its enterprising citizens. We found Mr. Bates, the superintendent of this part of the line, ready with a team of mules to carry the mail on without a moment's delay. As soon as we drove up, our teams were unhitched and new ones put in their places at short notice. But Mr. Bates objected to a heavy load of ammunition which was in our wagon, as too much of an encumbrance for the mail, and in a twinkling another wagon was rolled out and we were started on our way. I had barely time to run a few steps to the post office to drop you a letter.

The time of our departure was twenty minutes to 5 P.M. on Monday, the 20th of September — four days, six hours, and twenty minutes from the time of our departure from St. Louis, a distance of six hundred and seventy-three miles, and we had traveled but one hundred and sixty by railroad, and were thirty-one hours and fifty minutes ahead of time.

The Non-Butterfield, Ouray Stage Line, Silverton, Colorado, ca 1890's

Near El Paso, Texas, Sept. 28, 1858

The Overland mail from St. Louis and Memphis to San Francisco met the mail from San Francisco to each of those places, this evening about half past eight, one hundred miles east of El Paso — eight hours ahead of time. The mail going west was due at El Paso (1,308 miles from St. Louis), on Tuesday, the 18th inst., at 11 A.M., and the mail going east was due at the same place (1,332 ½ miles from San Francisco) on the same day at 5:30 A.M. So you will perceive that the mail going east has rather beaten the mail going west, so far, though they may lose time in going over the remaining route.

I have already given you a hasty sketch of our progress from St. Louis, via the Pacific Railroad, to Tipton, Moniteau County, MO., thence to Springfield, MO., Fayetteville and Fort Smith, Arkansas, the Indian Territory to the Texas border, and our start from Sherman, Texas — having crossed the Red River at Colbert's Ferry about eight miles below Fort Preston. Since then we have passed through Gainesville, Forts Belknap and Chadbourne, along the Concho River — a branch of the little Colorado — to its source, across the great Llano Estacado or Staked Plain — a distance of eighty miles without water — to the Horsehead Crossing of the Pecos River, and up the east bank of that stream to Pope's Camp, crossing the Pecos about three miles above, and taking the line near the thirty second parallel for El Paso.

We travel night and day, and only stop long enough to change teams and eat. The stations are not all yet finished, and there are some very long drives — varying from thirty-five to seventy-five miles without an opportunity of procuring fresh trams. Many obstacles have been overcome, and I am sanguine of the ultimate success of the enterprise, however much I may now doubt its efficiency as an expeditious mail or available passenger route. I continue my narrative as far as possible. The following table will show the time table, time for leaving, the various time table stations which we have passed, and the time when we actually left:

Place	Time Table—Time of Leaving	Actual Time of Leaving
St. Louis, Mo., and Memphis, Tenn.	Sept. 16, 8 A.M.	Sept. 16, 8 A.M.
Springfield, Mo.	Sept. 18, 7:45 A.M.	Sept. 17, 4 P.M.
Fayetteville [Ark.]	Sept. 19, 10:15 A.M.	Sept. 18, 12 M.
Fort Smith, Ark.	Sept. 20, 3:30 A.M.	Sept. 19, 3:30 A.M.
Sherman, Texas	Sept. 22, 12:30 A.M.	Sept. 20, 4:40 P.M.
Fort Belknap, do.	Sept. 23, 9 A.M.	Sept. 22, 7 A.M.
Fort Chadbourn[e], do.	Sept. 24, 3:15 P.M.	Sept. 23, 7 P.M.
Pecos Riv., do. (Em. C.)	Sept. 26, 3:45 A.M.	

Source: The Butterfield Overland Mail

THE OVERLAND MAIL STARTING FROM SAN FRANCISCO FOR THE EAST.—[From a Photograph.]

by Waterman Lilly Ormsby, 1834-1908; Wright, Lyle Henry, 1903-1979 Bynum, Josephine M; Henry E. Huntington Library and Art Gallery, page 38

Butterfield's Overland Mail Co. stagecoach departing San Francisco, Sept. 1858

Image source: Harper's Weekly Dec. 11, 1858 from Bob Crossman's collection

Speech by Waterman Ormsby, Oct. 12, 1858
The Daily Alta California, October 12, 1858, page 1
Mass Meeting at Musical Hall

The Overland Mail Route: Narrative of a Passenger

In the journals of yesterday appeared a call, signed by hundreds of citizens, for a public meeting to be held at Musical Hall in the evening, for the purpose of expressing the sense entertained by the people of this city

[San Francisco] of the great benefits she is to receive from the establishment of the Overland Mail.

Pursuant to said call, the people assembled *en masse* as the time and place appointed... J. P. Haven, Esq., after a few appropriate preliminary remarks, stated that he took great pleasure in introducing to the audience **Mr. Waterman L. Ormsby**, special correspondent of the *New York Herald*, and the first and only through passenger by the overland mail route, in three hours less than twenty-four days. The moment this announcement was made, the most terrific applause accompanied Mr. Ormsby to the rostrum, who took matters very deliberately, behaving just as coolly as might be expected from an attache of a newspaper that has created no little of the excitement prevailing on this very subject of overland communication.

Mr. Ormsby, who is a young man, has endured his fatiguing trip remarkably well, and says himself, that he lost but little in flesh. The speaker, at the outset, stated that he came to San Francisco to write for the readers of the *New York Herald*, not to speak to the citizens of the former place, and he was not certain that he had a right so to use the property which rightfully belonged to another; but he found his excuse in the all-absorbing interest taken by the people of California in the enterprise which was of such vital importance to their future welfare and prosperity. He was not prepared to make a speech, and did not know but he would rather brave the dangers of another overland tour (if dangers there were) than to make an address before them.

The speaker cursorily glanced at the vast advantages to be derived from the inauguration of this enterprise to the territory along the route, as well as to California. New Mexico would be settled, and cities and towns would spring up at every available point. The advantages to our own agricultural, mineral and postal interests were also alluded to.

He (the speaker) had been told prior to starting on his tour, that dire difficulties would have to be encountered; that he must, pass over craggy peaks and waterless deserts; that he would meet rattlesnakes and grizzlies, and hostile Indians.

Instead of being in peril, he came across very comfortably. He got a meal whenever he wanted it, albeit not the most palatable. He often got beans to eat, and sometimes coffee, and sometimes not. They saw no Indians of consequence on the route. The distance from St. Louis to San Francisco he states to be 2,759 miles.

Mr. Ormsby then proceeded to give a brief narrative of his trip.

For the first one hundred and sixty miles from St. Louis he traveled on the Pacific Railway to Jefferson City; thence *[from Tipton, Missouri]* by Concord coach to Springfield, through the richest agricultural region in Missouri; thence to Fayetteville, Arkansas, through the Ozark Mountains. This part of the route is the roughest encountered.

He next went on to Fort Smith, the intersection of the Memphis route. Fifteen minutes after *[actually before]* they arrived at this point, the Memphis mail came in, which is the best evidence that the junction is at the proper place on the route. After leaving Fort Smith, passed through the Choctaw country to Red river. The Indians all perfectly quiet.

Sherman, Texas, was the next settlement; thence to Gainesville. The country in this section is very fine and well wooded. Phantom Hill, a deserted military station, was next stopped at, and successively Fort Belknap and Chadbourne. At both of these forts a few soldiers are stationed. From Fort Chadbourne to headwaters of Concha river, the southernmost point on the route and on the 32 degrees parallel; thence they struck over Liano Estacada, a barren plain, 75 miles in width.

Although in an uncovered wagon, *[actually in a covered*

Celerity wagon] Mr. Ormsby suffered little inconvenience in crossing this plain. He believes that very shortly, the trip over this plain will be made in a single day. Thence they journeyed to Pecos river, a tributary of the Rio Grande, and up that stream to Pope's camp, fifty miles below the old Emigrant road. This is on a line with Guadalupe Peak. Thence to Cornudas tanks and Tueco tanks, to Franklin, opposite El Paso; thence 113 miles up the Pecos river. On this section they had no animals except what they took along with them. Stations are needed here, and will soon be established.

The country between Red river and the Pecos is almost entirely uninhabited. Three miles an hour was the average time made on this section, but this delay was more than made up on this side of El Paso. Mr. Ormsby stated that the arrangements on the western half of the road are far more complete than on the eastern side. They then proceeded up on Col. Leach's road, through the Rio Grande and Mesilla valleys, crossing to Cook's Spring ; thence to Mimbres, in the Gadsden Purchase.

Provisions here have to be furnished by the company. The stations are from 16 to 20 miles apart. From Tucson, the route runs through the Pacheco Pass and Pimo villages, to Maricopas; thence through the valley of the Gila to Fort Yumas, on the borders of California. Midway on the sixty mile desert, there is a water station. The road up to Los Angeles, and thence to this city, is in fine condition.

Mr. Ormsby suffered none whatever from heat, and but little from cold, any where on the road. He deems the route a thoroughly feasible one, although there are still many obstacles to overcome. There is great need of military stations, and Mr. O. suggests that some of those in Texas be scattered along the route. The country abounds in many objects of novelty and interest, which it was impossible for him, considering the private relations he occupied towards the *New York Her-*

ald, to lay in detail before the audience.

At the conclusion of his narrative, which was listened to with deep and absorbing interest, the speaker was complimented with cheering — long, loud and enthusiastic. A resolution of thanks, offered by General Haven, and which will be found in the regular series, was adopted unanimously....

The Nevada Democrat
Wed. Oct. 20, 1858, page 1

Mr. Ormsby, the special correspondent of the New York Herald, was the only passenger by the Overland Mail which arrived on the 10th inst. He left New York Sept. 10th and arrived at San Francisco Oct. 10th. He laid over three days between New York and St. Louis, so his actual traveling time from New York to San Francisco was a little less than twenty-six days. He has made the quickest trip ever made across the American continent. Between St. Louis and San Francisco, the only halt made by Mr. O. was one of five hours, at Red River, where being ahead of schedule time, the stage was obliged to wait for horses. With this exception, and the few moments occupied at each station in changing horses, he traveled night and day for twenty-three days and twenty-three hours, sleeping in the coach, and eating as he could get it. We doubt if this feat has ever been excelled in the history of overland travel on the American continent. The entire distance from St. Louis is 2,729 miles.

1858 Scene on Broadway, St. Louis, Missouri. Wood engraving, English, 1858

Panorama of San Francisco
by Charles Magnus, Published by New York ca. 1860

CHAPTER EIGHT

Passenger/Employee Report, Oct. 10, 1858

as reported in the Daily Alta California, Oct. 10, 1858;
and as reprinted in The Daily Missouri Republican, Nov. 8, 1858, page 1

Upon arrival in San Francisco, new Daily Alta obtained from an
Overland Mail employee or passenger the following report:

San Francisco
Sunday, October 10, 1858
11 o'clock, P.M.

The Southern Overland Mail arrived in this city this morning at seven o'clock, in 24 days from St. Louis, by was of El Paso Tucson, Los Angeles and San Jose. The times of leaving the different points were as follows:

St. Louis, Sept. 16th, 8:30 A.M.

Fort Smith, Sept. 19th, 3:30 A.M.

Colbert's Ferry, Sept. 20th, 3, P.M.

Fort Belknap, Sept. 22d, 1, A.M.

El Paso, Sept. 30th. 5:50, P.M.

Tucson, Oct. 2d, 10, A.M.

Fort Yuma, Oct. 5th, 6:15, A.M.

Los Angeles, Oct. 7th, 2:20, P.M.

San Jose, Oct. 10th, 1, A.M.

From this it will be seen that the time to this city, *[San Francisco]* from San Jose, was six hours; from Los Angeles 66 hours, and from El Paso 9 days and 15 hours. El Paso is about half way between St. Louis and San Francisco, so that it took 15 days on the Eastern half and 9½ days on the Western half of the road. The Eastern half should be crossed at least as rapidly as the Western half, and at that rate the time would be but nineteen days.

The men at the different stations did not know when the mail would come, and were not prepared for it; so that considerable delay was caused in getting ready at most of the stations.

Upon arrival in St. Louis, a reported of the Daily Missouri Republican interviewed the arriving passengers on the Overland Mail Co. stage.

Daily Missouri Republican
Dec. 6, 1858, page 1

Sixteenth Overland Mail

The Overland Mail, the sixteenth since the inauguration of the great Southern Route, was delivered in this city about seven o'clock last evening. The time out is only twenty-five days, which, in the present desperate state of the roads over that portion of the line in Arkansas and Missouri, is better than could have been expected.

The passengers from San Francisco are MR. BREWSTER, H. R. MORTON, and a gentleman whose name was not learned; and from El Paso, MR. MOHRMAN and GEO. M. FULLER.

MR. BREWSTER is on his way to Memphis, expecting to reach that place one day sooner via St. Louis than he could on the Memphis branch of the Overland route.

Additional material on western end of the route:
The Glasgow Weekly interviewed two passengers. However their two column report on page two of the Dec. 9, 1858 issue does not mention Missouri, Arkansas or Indian Territory so it is not included here. However, it is a great resource for the western half of the Butterfield route.

– 124 –

To the Traveling Public.

GREAT WESTERN
Four Horse Stage Coach Line.

ARRIVES AND DEPARTS DAILY.

CHIBESTER, REESIDE & CO., PROPRIETORS.

Washington Telegraph, Washington AR, Dec 22 1858

CHAPTER NINE

John T. Chidester's Observations, Oct. 13 & 23, 1858

*John T. Chidester, of Camden Arkansas, was a frequent passenger
as well as a sub-contractor on Butterfield's Overland Mail Co. route
between Memphis and Fort Smith.
As recorded in the Sacramento Daily Union, Oct. 13, 1858
and The Memphis Daily Appeal, Oct. 23, 1858, page 2.
Appreciation is expressed to historian Gerald T, Ahnert
for discovering and sharing the Oct. 13th article below.*

Sacramento Daily Union
Oct. 13, 1858

The *Memphis Appeal*, of Sept. 6th, publishes the particulars of an **interview had with Mr. J. T. Chidester**, a member of the firm of Chidester, Reeside & Co., upon the western end of the route, between Memphis and Fort Smith, who came down to superintend the departure of the first train.

The *Appeal* says :

We learn from Mr. Chidester that all the preparations of the Overland California Mail Company are complete, and in perfect readiness for the commencement of the service. All the stations are prepared, and the last of the stock reached the ground a week ago.

The stations are ten miles apart, and through the Indian country, each station has a guard of twenty-five armed men - a force fully adequate, with the protection afforded by the manner of the construction of the stations, to successfully resist any number of Indians likely ever to be collected in one hostile body. Each train will be guarded from station to station, through the wilderness, by a squadron of twenty-five mounted men. *[Actually an occasional armed guard was used, but never 25 armed men]*

This is the only daguerreotype or photographic image of a Celerity wagon actually used by the Butterfield Overland Mail Co. The image of this Celerity Wagon was taken near El Paso, Texas, and Cottonwood Stage Station early 1861.
The driver in the 'ten gallon hat' was David McLaughlin.
Image courtesy of the Nita Stewart Haley Memorial Library at Midland, Texas.

The vehicles used upon the road beyond Fort Smith are of the description known as **Celerity wagons**. They are of the build of the common Troy coach, and the body is hung upon the same kind of springs, and in a similar manner. Instead, however, of the heavy wooden top, with iron railing round it in common use, they have a light canvas covering, supported by light uprights, after the manner of the Jersey wagon. This covering affords ample protection against the weather, while it greatly diminishes the weight of the vehicle, as well as its liability to upset. The Company have over one hundred of these coaches on the ground, and have been running them regularly and with very profitable results, for some time past, upon portions of the route.

Chidester also informs us of the means used to supply the stations in the Llanos Estacado, or Staked Plains, with water. This desert, by the route of the Company's road, is seventy-five miles wide. From streams on either side of the Plains the Company supplies water to the stations with regular water trains, fitted up expressly for the purpose.

No image exist of Butterfield's water wagons. The wagon shown here, typical of the water wagons used in the western deserts in the late 1800s, is mounted with a cylindrical sheet steel 450 gallon water tank. Image from the National Archives, offered royalty free by the Picture Collection of Historylink101.com

The wagons used for this purpose are constructed of large tin boilers, similar in shape to the boilers of a steamboat, and capable of holding as much water as a team of six mules can draw. These trains run regularly, conveying water to the different stations, where large reservoirs are prepared to receive and preserve it for the use of passengers and the employees and stock of the Company. This is, of course, a very expensive method of supplying the indispensable element, but, as thus far all efforts to obtain it by boring or otherwise have proved futile, the Company must submit to it for the present.

It will be seen that the Company has spared no expense to perfect such arrangements as will insure success to the enterprise. They have furnished the entire route with an ample supply of men, provisions, water, stock, vehicles, teamsters, and tools, and workshops, to keep their equipments in repair. It is a gigantic undertaking, but not beyond the compass of American courage and enterprise. The prudent foresight and judgment displayed by the Company in perfecting their arrangements, give assurance that every difficulty and danger will be surmounted, and that a rich harvest of honor and profit will soon reward the pioneers in this adventurous service.

Memphis Daily Appeal,
Saturday, Oct. 23, 1858, page 2

[This article contains the observations of John T. Chidester, of Camden Arkansas, a frequent passenger and sub-contractor of Butterfield's Overland Mail Co.]

California Overland Mail

It is due to the contractors and to the public, that we should state that the Memphis branch of the Overland Mail to California is now regularly received here semi-weekly. The last mail through arrived on Thursday last, and, it will hereafter reach here on Saturday and Wednesday each week, and will depart on Monday and Thursday. The first mail from California was some twenty-four hours behind time, on account of the expressman who bore it having been lost in Cache bottom, which is an almost impenetrable swamp.

At present, the mail is carried from the terminus of the Memphis and Little Beck railroad to Des Arc **in buggies,** *[The Sept. 25, 1858, Des Arc Citizen reported that a 'light wagon' was used from Madison to Des Arc, where it transferred to a stagecoach.]* it being impossible to get through the Mississippi bottom, especially "Lost Swamp," in consequence of the sloughs. By the first of December next, the iron will be laid down on the railroad to Madison *[Arkansas[,* on the St. Francis river, and the enterprising contractors, MESSRS. CHIDESTER, REESIDE & CO., will then commence running daily four-horse post coaches from Madison to Little Rock, making the time in twenty-four hours, thence a tri-weekly line of coaches from Little Rock to Fort Smith, and thence, the semi-weekly mail to California by the Overland Company.

The only drawback upon their operations, between this point *[Memphis]* and Little Rock, will be the Cache bottom, which, in extreme high water, they design to cross in skiffs, having coaches ready on either shore to receive the mails and passengers.

De Val's Bluff is the point of crossing on White river. *[Countless newspaper articles give the route as Madison - DesArc -Atlanta - Little Rock. Only here, and once in the Feb. 22, 1860 Des Arc Weekly (page 3) is this alternate route of Madison - Clarendon - DeVall's Bluff - Little Rock mentioned. It is not clear how often this alternate route was used by Butterfield.]*

We learn from high authority that it is designed by the Postmaster-General to establish a daily mail service, in coaches, to Little Rock, and that he is now making his arrangements to that end. This will inaugurate an entirely new era in that part of our sister State *[Arkansas]*, through which this route will pass, and will add another improvement to the others which have been added to this service by the present Intelligent, far-seeing and enterprising Postmaster-General.

News from Memphis at Little Rock and from Little Rock at Memphis, daily, in twenty-four hours, will arouse the dormant energies of some of our neighbors in our sister State *[Arkansas]*, giving them a foretaste of the "good time coming," when the two cities will be connected by the iron rail and the telegraph, and when a passenger may breakfast in Memphis and dine in Little Rock.

This movement of Postmaster- General Brown and of his efficient auxiliaries, Messrs. Chidester, Reeside & Co., is but the precursor of the extension of the railway and the telegraph.

The daily coaches are pioneers of the more rapid messengers — the locomotive and *[train]*, cars, which will ere long unite the two cities with bonds of iron.

It should stimulate our Arkansas friends, along the line of the road, to use every exertion for bringing about speedily the desired union of Tennessee and Arkansas, at the beautiful and hospitable metropolis of the latter State.

In connection with this subject, we deem it due to the contractors for carrying the California mail from

Memphis to Fort Smith, to correct a misrepresentation that has been extensively circulated, with reference to the time of departure of the first mail that left this city for the Pacific.

The correspondent of the *New York Herald*, who went through on the first coaches from St. Louis, stated in a letter to the *Herald*, that the Postmaster at Memphis delivered his mail some hours before time, thus leaving the impression that the mail actually left in advance of the schedule hour. The truth is, that the mail did not leave Hopefield, opposite this city, until ten o'clock, eight o'clock being the time of departure. This can be testified to, if necessary, by MR. ROBINSON, Secretary of the Memphis and Little Rock Railroad, and by the Superintendent of the road. There was a further detention on the road of two hours, and a detention, as we learn from MR. CHIDESTER, of two hours, at or near Little Rock, which caused the messenger to lose about six hours in all. But for these detentions, the Memphis mail would have arrived at Fort Smith some seven hours in advance of the mail from St. Louis. As it was, the St. Louis mail was behind the Memphis from fifteen to twenty minutes. We are confident from these facts, that when the Memphis coaches regularly run through, CHIDESTER, REESIDE & CO., can always land their passengers at Fort Smith in advance of passengers from St, Louis.

We are informed by the agent of the contractors here *[Memphis]*, that there are numerous applications now for passage on this route, but the company have been compelled to decline conveying them until the first of December next, when their coaches and stock will be upon the ground. *[Did not accept passengers Sept 18 -Nov. 30, 1858??]*

MR. CHIDESTER himself calculates that from ten to thirty passengers daily will be conveyed from Memphis to Little Rock, and we think his calculation is a safe one. Certain it is, that, with the greatly diminished fare and time, the route will be favored by travelers, and will come to be a great thorough fare. If necessary, any number of coaches, to supply the demand, will be added.

John T. Chidester, primary owner of Chidester, Reeside & Co.

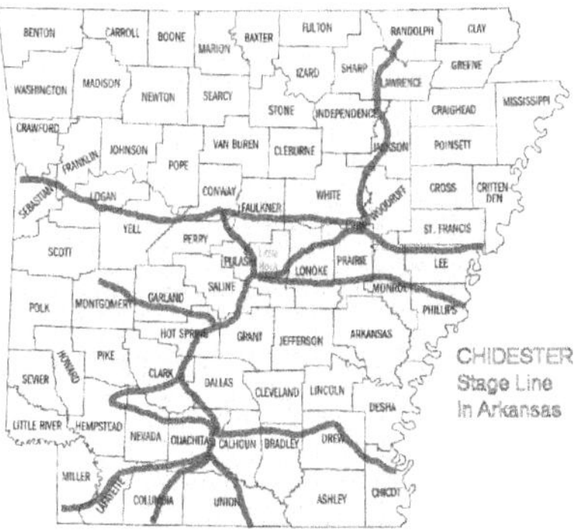

The beautiful Chidester home still survives in Camden Ark. The McCollum-Chidester Museum is open for tours Wed-Sat, 9-4.

Chidester had extensive passenger and mail stage coach routes across Arkansas.

When Butterfield realized the Arkansas River water levels were too low to use his steamboat in Sept. 1858, Butterfield hastily sub-contracted the Fort Smith to Memphis portion of the Overland Mail Route to Chidester.

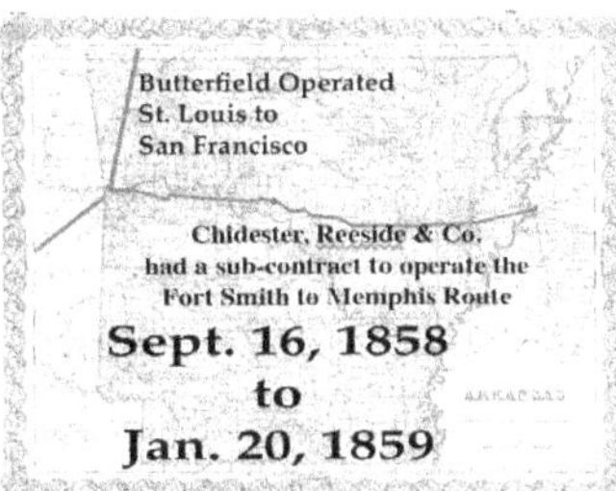

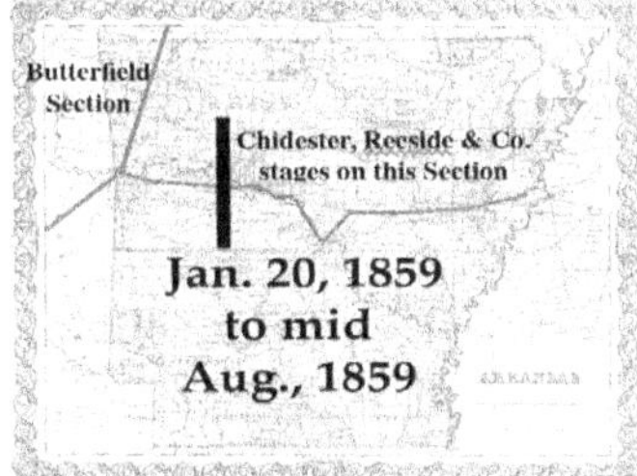

Chidester's sub-contract ended in August of 1859. Thereafter the entire route was under the direct control of Butterfield's Overland Mail Co. until March, 1861 when this southern ox-bow Overland route was closed down, and route moved north to avoid the Confederate states.

CHAPTER TEN
George S. Dana, Oct. 15, 1858
*as reported in the Daily Alta California, Oct. 16, 1858, page 1 and 2;
and also in The Sacramento Daily Bee, Oct. 18, 1858; and
also reprinted in The First Overland Mail: Butterfield Trail –
St. Louis to San Francisco, 1858-1861,
edited by Walter B. Lang, page 128*

ARRIVED OVERLAND
Daily Alta California, Oct. 16, 1858 page 1

The only passenger who came through by the overland stage which arrived yesterday, was Mr. George S. Dana, from Rochester, New York. Mr. Dana is an old Californian, having first crossed the Plains in 1849.

In speaking of him and his experience, the *Rochester Democrat and American* [Rochester, New York] of Sept. 14th, says, in alluding to his first trip across the plains:

"The Indians attacked the party, and stampeded or killed their animals, so they were compelled to travel on foot 2,276 miles, embarrassed by four feet depth of snow at the South Pass. In the Mariposa mines he encountered his first experience as a gold digger, and was somewhat successful. On returning, he came via Panama, and was on the Isthmus at the same time of the fearful riot there, a witness of the dreadful slaughter of American citizens. His hair-breadth escapes, have not, it seems, quelled his adventurous spirit. He expects now to enter the service of the U.S. Mail Co., which transports the mails across the Plains from St. Louis to San

Francisco. Mr. Dana's experience and hardihood fits him for such a service, and he has the highest recommendations from prominent citizens here. He is a native of this city, having been born in the village of Rochester in 1825. The best hopes and wishes of his friends will follow him in his western journeyings."

And we may add, that it affords us especial pleasure to welcome all such old Californians back again to their adopted home.

NOTES OF A TRIP ACROSS THE PLAIN
Daily Alta California, Oct. 16, 1858 page 2

Mr. George S. Dana, who came across the continent with the mail which arrived yesterday overland by the southern route, has given us some information in regard to his trip.

The route may be divided into the following main divisions: from St. Louis to Tipton, on the Missouri road, 160 miles by railroad. Tipton is the point where the stage route really commences.

The First Butterfield Overland Mail Run in 1858
In 1858 the Pacific Railroad from St. Louis arrived at Tipton, Missouri and John Butterfield personally carried the first mail bag, boarding an Overland Stagecoach headed through Fort Smith and on to San Francisco.
Painted by Frank Nuderscher (1880 – 1959) for the Missouri Pacific Museum.

From Tipton to the Arkansas river 468 miles. The

greater portion of this distance is over rich grassy plains, with abundant timber and water.

Near the Arkansas are some mountains, which are, perhaps, the roughest portions of the road.

The Boston Mountains, Arkansas' Ozark National Forest
The Boston Mountains portion of the Ozarks extends north of the Arkansas River Valley as a rectangle twenty to thirty-five miles wide and 200 miles long.
Image source: Devil's Den, Ark. by Springfield Daily Citizen

From the Arkansas to the Rio Grande, at El Paso is a distance of 898 miles; partly over a grassy plain, and partly over a desert of sand, with mountains here and there. There are places where water is scarce, particularly over the sand hills, where the wheels of the coach sink almost to the hubs for a distance of about fifty miles.

From the Rio Grande to Fort Tejon, via Tucson, is 1,040 miles, most of the distance over a desert, with occasional mountains to cross, and here and there fertile little valleys. From the Tejon to San Francisco 372 miles, via Visalia.

The stations where horses are changed are all kept by Americans, and are on an average about fifteen miles apart, except on the deserts. Concord coaches are used from San Francisco to Tipton, the coaches being changed about once in sixty miles. The draft animals are all horses except for about 400 miles the other side of El Paso, where mules are used. The number of men employed on the road and at the stations amounts to more than 500. Meals are provided for at the stations where the stages stop in the morning, noon and evening. Sleep is shy for the first week, but after that the passengers get used to the thing and could sleep if the coach were tumbling a precipice.

This drawing from the Tombstone Epitaph in 1886 was part of an advertisement promoting the stagecoach service from Tucson, Arizona to Tombstone, Arizona.

Mr. Dana had not been in a bed for a month when he arrived here. He gained eight pounds on the road, and ways it is a pleasure trip as compared by the trip across the Isthmus by steamers.

Fort Smith, 1890's, banks of the Arkansas river, image source: Butler Center for Arkansas Studies

First Stage Arrives at Fort Smith From San Francisco

ARRIVAL OF THE OVERLAND MAIL.—The Overland Mail arrived here yesterday morning ½ past 7 o'clock, being 21 days from San Francisco, and having four through passengers from that city. The Anvil Battery was brought forth by the Young Men of our city, and 350 rounds were fired, in honor of the event, and while the Anvils were playing in full tide, Lts. Steen and Bell, of the Fort, brought out two six pounders, and a detachment of U. S. Troops, and fired 32 rounds, which caused the valley of the Arkansas to reverberate with the joyful news of the *Safe Arrival* of the *first* Overland Mail *from California.* Three Cheers for Hon. A. V. Brown P. M. General; three cheers for John Butterfield, and the Overland Mail Company.

Maj. Hicken and Mr. Eberle, of this city, for whose safety so much interest was felt, on the arrival of the news of the loss of the Austria, arrived here this morning in the Memphis branch of the Overland Mail, well and hearty, without the smell of fire on their garments. We congratulate them and their friends on their safe arrival and welcome them home.

Weekly Arkansas Gazette, Oct. 16, 1858, page 2

Closeup of a sketch by passenger Wm H, Hilton. See below for full image.

CHAPTER ELEVEN
Observations of Wm Hayes Hilton, Oct. 23, 1858
as reported in the Nashville Patriot, Oct. 28, 1858

The St. Louis Democrat sent a reporter to meet the arriving
Butterfield's Overland Mail Co. stagecoach.
The reporter interviewed passenger W. H. Hilton for this article.

St. Louis Democrat, 25th inst.
The Overland Mail — Fourth of the Series

The Overland Mail which left San Francisco on the 28th ult, arrived in this city Saturday night. No papers were brought by the mail, and but few letters. The few papers in possession of the passengers when the stage left San Francisco were distributed along the route.

In conversation with **Mr. W. H. Hilton**, a passenger by this mail, we learned some particulars which may not be uninteresting to our readers. Mr. Hilton left San Francisco on the 18th of September, and arrived at Los Angeles September 23d. At this point Mr. Hilton remained until this stage arrived, which was on the thirtieth. On that day Mr. Hilton left Los Angeles, and arrived here as above stated.

Through California and Arkansas the arrangements are complete, and the stage glides over the country as swiftly as in all probability it ever will. But on the plains the arrangements are as yet incomplete.

— The company, however are rapidly filling up every deficiency in the way of men and mules. Mr. Hilton thinks that the trip will be made inside of twenty days, with great ease, when once the company gets everything fairly under the way. He considers the route decidedly favorable, and in all respects safe and pleasant.

Some of the stations are sixty-five miles apart; but most of them are from eight to ten miles. On the plains are the corrals — either of logs or stone — and occupied, some by a dozen men and some by no more than four or five. The stage was detained fourteen hours by a sand storm in the California Desert and two days by reason of high water in Kern river, at the point of crossing which the ferryboat was out of repair, which was supplied as speedily as possible.

The company are making preparations to bridge the various streams that cross the road, and have already engaged a large number of men for instant work.

Adobes, or Mexican brick, are used in the construction of station houses along the route and in many places workmen are engaged in making roads.

Mr. Hilton was provided with a canteen (as also were the other passengers) filled with water, from the want of which he was thus preserved.

The mails from St. Louis bound westward were far enough advanced to justify a belief that they would reach San Francisco in due time.

William Hayes Hilton
Image courtesy of Gerald T. Ahnert

Mr. Hilton was an artist. He made several sketches of his various trips as shown below.

Gerald T. Ahnert writes,

In October 1858, William Hayes Hilton was a Butterfield passenger. His original drawings of a Butterfield stage wagon are in the Huntington Library collection. My discussions with the archivist confirmed my suspicions that Hilton's drawings were made sometime after his trip. He left no description. The only identification was on the drawings. One of the drawings was of a San Antonio and San Diego (Jackass Mail) "ambulance" and its passengers sleeping along the trail. In October 1858, Farwell, a correspondent on a Butterfield stage wagon, was at Arizona's San Simon Stage Station. He mentions seeing the Jackass Mail wagon near the station. Hilton may have drawn this Jackass Mail wagon as he was there about the same time as Farwell. Because Hilton made his drawings of the Butterfield stage wagon from memory, he appears to have represented them as the same as the "ambulance" shown in his Jackass Mail drawing. A key ambulance feature is the extended roof over the driver-conductor as shown in all of Hilton's drawings for both Butterfield and the Jackass Mail. Butterfield's Stage (Celerity) Wagons did not have this feature.

Sketch Books of Mr. William Hays Hilton
Sketch Book 1, in the order they appear

[Below, only sketches of Wm Hilton's with stagecoaches in them are shown.]

"Coast Range, Marysville Butte from West, Cherokee, Nevada Co."
by Wm H. Hilton

Cherokee, California (60 miles north of Placerville) was not a Butterfield Route, but may have been on a Pioneer Stage Line route. Its unclear what mountains the artist is referring to.

Source: Huntington Library, call number mssHilton Book 3,San Marino, CA

Volante, 1858, Initial "W" in upper left

The Volante is a Spanish one- or two-passenger carriage, having two wheels and an open, hooded body. The body was set in front of the wheels and attached to the long shafts. The carriage was usually pulled by one horse, which was ridden by the coachman, although two or three horses were also used. Volantes were popular in Spain, Cuba, Mexico, and Louisiana. From about 1830 to 1870, great numbers were manufactured in New York City.

Sketches of Mr. William Hays Hilton
Sketch Book 3, in the order they appear

"Overland Stage Route - Comet, Arizona, 1858" by William Hayes Hilton
Gerald T. Ahnert notes: While crossing Arizona as a Butterfield passenger, Wm Hilton saw the Jackass Mail stage camped for the night and made this sketch.

This is no doubt that this is Donati's Comet, observed from June to November, 1858 with the naked eye. This comet will not be seen on Earth again for another 1,600 years. The artist of this sketch [and several others reproduced in this book] was a passenger in 1858 on Butterfield's Overland Mail Co. stages across California, Arizona, Nevada, and Mexico. His nine sketchbooks, from 1850 to 1870, are at The Huntington Library. Source: Huntington Library

"Alamo Mucho Station" by William Hayes Hilton
Note the Celerity wagon headed down a steep embankment on left side of sketch. The artist entitled this sketch 'Alamo Mucho Station.' He misspelled name of Alamo Mocho Station, which was one of the original Butterfield Overland Mail stations. The Alamo Mocho Station is located south of the Mexican border, in Baja California.
Source: Huntington Library, call number mssHilton Book 3, San Marino, CA

"Tucson Desert and the 'Picacho' - view from the south" by William H. Hilton
Picacho Peak is located in Arizona between the cities of Phoenix and Tucson.
Source: Huntington Library, call number mssHilton Book 3, San Marino, CA

"Guadalupe Pass, 3rd View" by William Hayes Hilton
Guadalupe Pass is a mountain pass in Culberson County, Texas.
Source: Huntington Library, Book 3, San Marino, California

"Celerity Stage Passenger Shooting Antelope for Pleasure" by William Hilton
Legend has it that Wells Fargo Co. rules for stagecoach passengers in the 1870's included: "... Firearms may be kept on your person for use in emergencies. Do not shoot them for pleasure or at wild animals as the sound riles the horses. In the event of runaway horses, remain calm. Leaping from the coach in panic will leave you injured, at the mercy of the elements, hostile Indians, and hungry wolves. Forbidden topics of discussion are stagecoach robberies, Indian uprisings, politics, and religion..."
Source: Huntington Library, call number mssHilton Book 3, San Marino, CA.

"Crossing Boggy River, Texas, 1859" signed by William Hayes Hilton
This sketch by William Hays Hilton that he entitled, "Crossing Boggy River, Texas, 1859" clearly shows that there were times that fording a creek or river was difficult. The title of this sketch may be referring to the Boggy Creek about 15 miles northwest of the Butterfield Route that passes through Fort Belknap, Texas. The other possibility is that he was sketching one of the three sites that actually are on the Butterfield Route: North Boggy Creek, Middle (Muddy) Boggy, or Clear Boggy in Indian Territory (Oklahoma).
Source: Huntington Library, call number mssHilton Book 3, San Marino, CA.

"Overland Mail Stage, Arizona, 1858" signed by William Hayes Hilton
In 1858, passenger Waterman Ormsby wrote, "The mules reared, pitched, twisted, whirled, wheeled, ran, stool still, and cut up all sorts of capers. The wagon performed so many evolutions that I, in fear of my life, abandoned it and took to my heels, fully confident that I could make more progress in a straight line, with much less risk of breaking my neck."
Source: Huntington Library, call number mssHilton Book 3, San Marino, CA

"*The Overland Mail Coach from Arizona as it is Crossing the Country*"
Published by Hiram C. Hodge, 1877, etching artist unknown

CHAPTER TWELVE
To the Editor of the *Herald*, October, 1858
as reprinted in The Press Argus, Van Buren, Arkansas
September 19, 1958, Section A, page 23
Passenger is actually Waterman Ormsby, although not acknowledged in paper.

... We are still, however, about twenty-seven hours ahead of the time table, having traversed the hardest roads on the route, and making about one third the entire distance. We have traveled night and day. The relays of horses being ready at most all the stations promptly.

We have suffered but one detention of consequence, and that was of five hours, at Colbert's ferry, over the Red river, where I managed to write you while the express waited. **I had expected to be able to write in the wagons when we reached the prairies, but I found them too uneven,** and the creek crossings and routes too frequent to admit of my carrying out my purpose.

We are doing finely, and astonish the natives with the facility of our progress. Slow as it has been, compared with what it will be when the route is fully established, and horses put where they should be in the place of the mules, between Sherman and Fort Belknap certainly, and I do not know but further.

We have been favored thus far with excellent weather though I felt the extreme warm days and cold nights of this country rather uncomfortable. As night comes on I have to keep putting on clothes, and as morning comes I gradually take them off, to a certain extent.

I have not seen a bed or had time to get a comfortable meal since we left St. Louis.

This place is the regular military station of the Second Regiment Cavalry, Major Thomas, and now has ten companies stationed here.

I will, as soon as possible, give you an account of our journey from Fayetteville, Ark., where my last letter left us. I have many expectations of going through to. San Francisco safely and in time.

West side of the square in Fayetteville, Arkansas, looking southwest along Block Street, circa 1872. Includes City Hotel, Henry Wayland's General Store and the Morning Saloon. Credit: Courtesy of Shiloh Museum of Ozark History / Washington County Historical Society Collection (P-499)

East side of the square in Fayetteville Arkansas, Left to right: Baum Brothers, Cravens Smith Bakery, Dr. Paddock, Hitching Post on the east side of the Fayetteville Square, 1870s. Credit: Courtesy of Shiloh Museum of Ozark History / Peter Harkins Collection (S-90-194-165)

Daily Alta California.

SAN FRANCISCO, SATURDAY MORNING, NOVEMBER 6, 1858

CHAPTER THIRTEEN

Mr. J. M. Farwell, Nov. 6, 1858
*as published in the Daily Alta Cal., Dec. 7, 1858 San Francisco;
also as reprinted in "The First Overland Mail: Butterfield Trail"
by Walter B. Lang, excerpts from pages 126-127.*

Fort Smith, Nov. 6, 1858

...To Red river is now 13 miles and a half, the road being fair, but a little rough, until within about half a mile of the river, when we find The Choctaw Nation.

The Choctaw Nation

We were taken across the river in a ferry-boat and are now in the Choctaw Nation.

*"Butterfield Run Through the Ozarks" by Phillip W. Steele, 1966
Arrow added to highlight location of Colbert's Ferry.*

Here we took dinner and then rode to Carriage Point, 13 miles, a good road. From this to Blue river is

13 miles, the road being rough, intersected by gullies. At about 8 o'clock P.M., we were at Boggy Depot, where are some 50 inhabitants of the Choctaw people. It was formerly a depot for Government supplies. This is 16 miles; thence to Little Boggy Bridge is 17 miles, over a rough and stony road. To Water's *[Waddell's]* station is 13 miles, very stony road and uncomfortable riding. To Blackburn's is 16 miles, where we took breakfast. Benley's *[Pusley's]* is 18 miles; Riddle's 17; Holloway's 18. All this road is rough, and is run through oak groves. Trahem's *[Trahern's Station]* is 16 miles, and Gov. Walker's is 16 miles further, where we arrived at about 11 o'clock P. M. This is the residence of the Governor of the Choctaw nation. We were provided with coffee, and set out for our next station.

Fort Smith

We arrived at the Poto ferry *[Poteau ferry]* about 3 o'clock A. M., which we crossed, and soon stopped at Fort Smith to breakfast.

Fort Smith's City Hotel, Site of Butterfield Offices where Employee Boarded Image source: U. A. Little Rock Center for Arkansas History and Culture. The Roberts Library / Butler Center collection dates this photo as ca. 1870.

Here found the agent of this section of the road, Mr. Crocker, who treated us with every kindness. The relay was soon in readiness and we were again on our way. We now look forward to the end of our journey.

Mr. J. M. Farwell
Daily Alta Correspondent

Daily Alta Californian
Dec. 11, 1858, page 2

We are in receipt of a letter from our overland correspondent, completing a description of his trip across the country, from Fort Smith to St. Louis. The crowded state of our columns prevents its publication this evening.

Daily Alta Californian
Sunday Morning, Dec. 12, 1858, page 1

The following letter should have reached us by last mail stage, but was in some way delayed on the road, and was not received until yesterday. It completes the chain of description of the overland route from Fort Smith to St. Louis.

Daily Alta Californian
St. Louis, Mo., Nov. 10, 1858

The section of the route from Fort Smith to this city *[St. Louis]* was traversed with little difficulty, when the state of the roads, as we found them, are to be considered. At the former point *[Fort Smith]* we arrived at dawn, and remained until the sun appeared. Once more on our way, four miles travel brought us to the western banks of the broad Arkansas *[river]*. Here, the horn of the coachman was in requisition, but more blasts were sounded than — I opine — were ever blown to wake the warder, who was wrapped in morning slumber on the inner side of castle moat, to bring the lazy boatman, who finally appeared *[Van Buren Ferry]*, and transported us to the opposite shore.

The method of boating deserves notice. A fleet

boat is constructed with wide wheels, like an ordinary steamboat. Then a treadmill is attached to each, upon which a horse is placed, taught to commence walking at the tinkle of a bell, and to stop at the same signal.

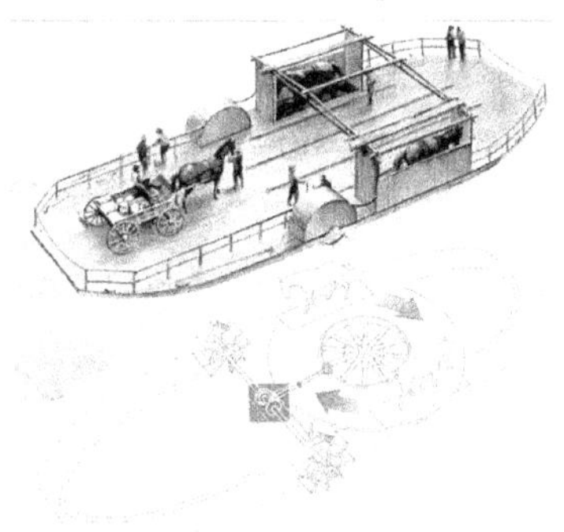

J. M. Farwell is describing a ferry similar to the 63' length x 18' beam 'Superior Horse Boat Eagle' that was operating in 1841 out of Westport, New York seen in this sketch. This New York ferry was featured in the October 1989 issue of The National Geographic. John Russell Young, in August of 1859 described this same Van Buren ferry in his report to Philadephia's The Press. William Tallack also described this same ferry in his 1865 book "The California overland express: the longest stage-ride in the world"

The boat is headed up stream, and the horses commence their arduous task. The direction of the boat is so continued, and so strong was the current, that we barely reached the point of destination on the other shore. The river at this time, we were told, was unusually high for this season.

Here is situated the flourishing town of Van Buren, containing some 4,000 inhabitants. No stop was made here, and we were soon ascending a hill on its outskirts, the commencement of what are termed the Boston Mountains.

The first station was Ousley's, [Woosley's station] a 13 mile drive, and the next Brody's 12. It was about 11½ o'clock when we reached the latter, and here we procured an excellent dinner, and treated with great kindness by the family, and were soon on our way again.

We next came to Parker's [*Park's Station*], 20 miles, and thence to Fayetteville, 16 miles. Mr. Chas. E. Butterfield, the son of the contractor, has accompanied us from Fort Smith, and here he left us. He is the Superintendent Road Agent on this section of the route. Every attention was shown us by him while in company, and I left him with regret. [*At Fayetteville, the Overland Mail Co. established a major stable and wagon works, and constructed the Butterfield House Hotel, operated by Charles Butterfield, a son of John Butterfield, owner and manager of the line.*]

The Fayetteville Female Seminary, originally on the second story of a store on the downtown square, moved in 1841 to this newly built site on Mountain Street. An 1841 issue of 'The Witness' (Fayetteville's first newspaper) described the new location as a "retired part of town which offers every convenience for the young ladies to take exercise without exposure."
Image source: "Fayetteville History," Facebook

The latter portion of this road had been stony, and, in consequence, the riding unpleasant in the extreme.

Night has come on, and to add to this, the rain had commenced falling. Our horses were good, and with an expert driver, we made good speed.

Fitzgerald Stone Barn used by Butterfield is still standing in Springdale, AR. Photo by Susan Young.

The next station is called Fitzgerald's, the distance

13 miles. Snow, mingled with rain, filled the air, but the stout canvas covering of the carriage *[Celerity wagon]* protected us, and alike from the weather. When we reached Callahan's, 10 miles on, the road became smooth, and at Harlan's, *[Harbin's]* 18 miles further, it was good and nearly level.

At Crouche's 15 miles further, ever a perfectly level road, we breakfasted, having made 56 miles during the night, for the most part over a rough road. At 11½ o'clock we came to Smith's, 17 miles, and one o'clock and 40 minutes were at Ashmore's, 21 miles further. Here the road is stony and muddy, which continued until we arrived at Springfield, 14 miles from the last station.

The Town of Springfield, Missouri

Springfield is a large town, containing some 5000 inhabitants, and is situated in an agricultural and mining district. Our delay here was short, and we were soon off for Evan's, where we soon arrived, having added 8 miles to our journey.

We now come to a kind of rolling prairie land, being well adapted for cultivation but poorly for roads. The wheels were sinking deep in the mud, which appeared to become worse as we advanced. The horses soon weary, but they still labored on, and we miles further, at Smith's we changed, and came to Bolivar, a distance of 10 more.

On the following morning, the 8th of November, at 7 o'clock, we arrived at Gray's station, where we breakfasted. Thence we came to Quincy, 15 miles, a small town, and changed team at 10½ o'clock. To Bailey's is ten miles, the roads still muddy, and bad traveling. A short distance from the last station we cross the Pomme du Terre, the passengers footing it over an incomplete bridge, and the carriage and horses being ferried.

Covered Bridge Spanning Pomme de Terre River south of Warsaw, MO ca. 1910
Source: postcard image, penciled on back: "Fairfield Mill in July 1910"
This may be the bridge referred to in the paragraph above.
The enslaved of Judge George Alexander built this covered bridge spanning the
Pomme de Terre River south of Warsaw, MO. The judge Alexander arrived in
this area in 1832 and purchased an Indian village for $60. Near the bridge was
a mill and a small manufacturing complex at the hamlet of Fairfield, Missouri
At the time of this photograph in 1910, the bridge was quite dilapidated.

We now come to the town of Warsaw, 10 miles situated on the eastern side of the Osage river. Here is another ferry. Burns' is the next station, where a relay is obtained, 15 miles, and thence to Mulholland's, we passed over a very muddy road, 20 miles. The next relay is the last to be performed with animals. We had been anxious for some days to see this portion of our journey, and we are not sorry to be again seated in the coach, and driving our last twenty miles.

Arrival at Tipton:

At Tipton we found ourselves soon after dawn, where we were allowed a short respite. Here we found Mr. John Butterfield, another son of the famed contractor, who superintends this portion of the road. On the 1st trip of the mail from San Francisco, this gentleman came over the road, and by the knowledge thus obtained, is at once acquainted with all its necessaries.

At 9 o'clock we took the *[train]* cars, and behind the iron horse were whirled along at a more rapid rate than we had yet succeeded in at-

Tipton to St. Louis, Engine #152,
Missouri Pacific Railroad, 1872

taining with the animals, during the 2500 miles of travel. This road *[railroad track]* is to be extended to Springfield, and eventually may be the eastern link binding St. Louis to our Queen of the Pacific. Mr. McKissock, the Superintendent of the road, informs me that it is the intention to extend it still farther west than the present terminus.

I send you a copy of the time table from Tipton to St. Louis, by which you may leave all the way-stations.

It was dark when we arrived in the city *[of St. Louis]*, and the only knowledge that we had of it was, the lights, as they appeared to glance past us, and as our speed was slackened, we found that we had completed our long journey. Several friends were waiting our arrival, and among them I desire to mention the Agent of the Stage line in this city and also of the American Express. For his kindness I shall ever be grateful.

We were soon provided with quarters at the Planter's House; a good night's sleep refreshed us, Comanches and Apaches were forgotten, and this morning I arose, and so far from being fatigued by the journey, I was in as good physical condition to commence by return, as when I left San Francisco for St. Louis.

Mr. J. M. Farwell
Daily Alta Correspondent

St. Louis, Mo., Nov. 14, 1858.
Snow, Rain, Mud, etc.

The snow and rain are falling thick around us, completing the twenty-first day of continued rain and stormy weather. Cold, damp and disagreeable it has been since my arrival, the sun having scarcely shown his cheering face. On Friday he *[the sun]* made an attempt, which was a decided failure, and yesterday, another, which perhaps, might be pronounced more successful; muddy, in the extreme, besides — and the mud, too, of a peculiar nature, which seems to be adverse to the standing of individuals, not socially or morally, but in the street. One is obliged to walk with considerable care and attention to his footing, or be liable to disastrous consequences. Observable, also, is a want of bustle and stir, which usually characterizes large cities; this is attributable to the weather in a great measure, few persons caring to expose themselves to its inclemency, unless forced to do so. I am told that such weather is very unusual here, even in mid-winter. Now I am here, I am perforce [inevitability] in the position in which Touchstone was, and perhaps, sometimes inclined to admit the force of his exclamation:

"Ah! Now I am in Arden, the more fool I.
When I was at home, I was in a better place,
But travelers must be content."

The mail, which should have followed us from San Francisco, was due here last evening but has not yet arrived. We are at a loss to account for the delay.

Subjoined, I present a summary of the events that have transpired with departure of the last mail stage from this city for San Francisco.　*Mr. J. M. Farwell*
Daily Alta Correspondent

St. Louis, Nov. 10th, 1858.

I arrived in this city *[St. Louis]* last evening, having accomplished the trip in little less than twenty-five days. My notes along the road have been written under very embarrassing circumstances, six persons having been crowded into a coach intended for one-half the number, and the jolting and jamming being decidedly troublesome to either physical or mental exertion, especially when combined in the effort at letter writing.

Our trip might have been completed in much less time, had it been necessary. The route is an excellent one, and the distance through can be made, in my opinion, in eighteen days if necessary, as it will be eventually, when the stations are all located and the company's arrangements are fully perfected. The company are pushing matters along with surprising rapidity, and are deserving of every encouragement. I shall forward a complete itinerary of the route soon, so that the public of California may be fully posted concerning it.

Popularity of the Overland Route in St. Louis.

There is scarcely less enthusiasm in St. Louis, regarding the overland mail route, than in San Francisco. I have met with a very cordial reception here, and find quite as much excitement existing among the people, upon the question of the overland communication, as there was in San Francisco, when I left there some weeks ago. I have been literally besieged with queries in regard to the route, and from the very general interest manifested among all classes, it may be set down that there is every thing to hope for in the way of aid and assistance from the people of Missouri at least, for the future perfection of overland communication with the Pacific Coast. *Mr. J. M. Farwell*
Correspondent

Daily Missouri Republican, St. Louis
J. W. Farwell's Observations Nov. 10, 1858, p. 2

Upon his arrival in St. Louis, J. M. Farwell was interviewed by the local newspaper, The Daily Missouri Republican, and published Farwell's observations in the November 10, 1858 issue.

Mr. J. W. FARWELL, of the *Alta California*, Mr. SKILL-MAN, and four other passengers, left San Francisco on the morning of the 15th of October. Two of the passengers liking the appearance of El Paso, stopped there, another one stopped at Pagas river, while Mr. FARWELL and Mr. SKILLMAN came to this city *[St. Louis]*. To the kindness of Mr. FARWELL we are indebted for the following notes of the journey.

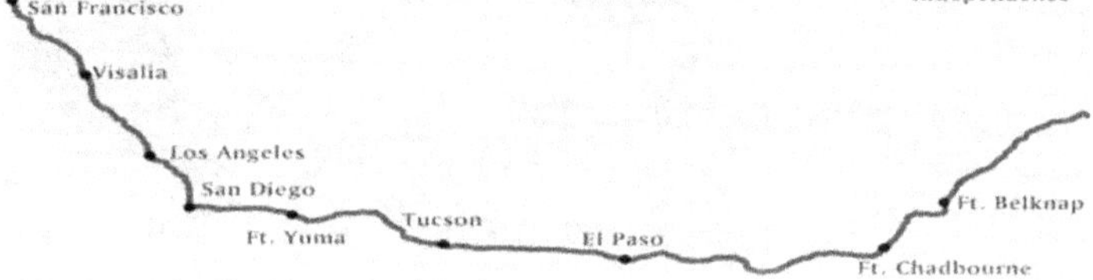

Southwestern part of Butterfield's Overland Mail Route

The road up to within fifteen miles of Los Angeles was very good. On the pass here, which is about two and a half miles in length, the people of Los Angeles expended about eight thousand dollars in improving it, to induce the mail company to adopt that route. At Kern river the road was bad for a short distance; again at Temecula the road began to grow bad and continues so until San Felipe or Devil's Canyon is reached. Ten miles from the latter place the road enters the Desert; 18 miles further on is a new station, called Palm Springs, from the fact that until recently palm trees grew in the vicinity. The next station is at Carissacrick, a small stream of water strongly impregnated with sulfur. Indian Wells is the next station. Along this portion of the road the dust is very bad, being strongly of an alkaline nature, it is offensive to the smell, and very irritating to the skin.

– 156 –

**a tornado overtook them
sand was so thick that they were unable to see
lost on the desert for three days and three nights
discovered a bullock - killing the animal – he drank its blood
by which means he saved his own life**

At Almo, the succeeding station, a few days before our traveler arrived there, the men having charge of a mail, left the wagon and undertook to get it through on horseback to the next station. In a tornado which overtook them on the road, one of the men lost his hat, on getting down to get which, his horse took fright and ran away. His companion dropped his blankets, and in endeavoring to get them lost his horse likewise, but succeeded in saving the mails, which he carried on foot to the next station, the Indian Wells on the Yuma. Although but a few years distant from each other in the storm, the sand was so thick that they were unable to see and thus became separated The one who was left behind remained lost on the desert for three days and three nights, and would have perished with thirst had he not discovered a broken down bullock which some emigrants had left by the wayside. He succeeded in killing the animal with his knife; he drank its blood by which means he saved his life He was rescued by men sent out from the station in search of him.

Passing several unimportant stations, Mr. FARWELL arrived at Fort Yuma. Seventeen miles from this Fort are the newly discovered gold miles of Arizona. From inquiries made here, he ascertained that miners, of whom there were about a hundred a work, were making from seven to forty dollars per day. It was reported that the diggings were much richer in the hills above the present miles, but a large band of hostile Indians of the Tonto Apaches tribe were encamped there, and it was not deemed prudent to prospect in that direction until the Indians were ran off, which they hoped to be able to do in a short time. The next station worthy of *mentioning* about fifty miles from the diggings. It is thus named from the fact that HENRY CRABBE and his companions, who were supposed to have designs on Sonora, were killed by the Mexicans. The next place is Tucson, a Spanish town of some four hundred inhabitants. At this place they were warned to look out for the Apaches encamped some distance ahead. About one hundred and seventy miles from Tucson found four hundred Apaches encamped for the winter. The Indians showed no signs of hostility.

Tho hundred miles from this place is the Mimbres River, a little branch of the Gila. Leaving this they came on to the Mesilla Valley, where they first struck the Rio Del Norte.

Passing El Paso, the next place of note reached was Sierra Guccho. — At this point are several large natural tanks in the solid rock, which were supposed to contain sufficient water for the mail trains passing this point. On the arrival of the mail here, it was discovered that the tanks had gone dry, and water had to be hauled a distance of thirty miles for the mules. It was found on examining the tanks, that they could be made to contain sufficient water to supply the trains. If, however, water sufficient can not be provided here, the route will be changed to that of the old San Antonio trail, fifty miles longer than the present route, but more level and affording more water.

At the next station, thirty six miles further on, there are natural reservoirs which have also gone dry, and to which water had been hauled a distance of thirty miles. Several Indian signs were seen in this vicinity. The road is very bad, being sandy and rocky, alternately. Next station Guadalupe, eighteen miles distant. Four miles beyond this is the Pinery, where a grove of pine trees, the only ones to be met with on the road, is found. Next stopping place is the Pagos river, sixty miles from the Pinery. From this place there is a stretch of fifty-four miles without a change of teams. Leaving Horsehead, the route stretches across the Llano Estacado, or Staked Plain, the most beautiful portion of the route, the road being as hard and level as a barn floor. They traveled over this place a distance of eighty miles without water, except what was carried in a keg for the use of the passengers — the mules having none. The large herds of deer and antelope and flocks of fowls led to the inference that there must be water on the Llano in opposition to the generally received idea in respect thereto. The first water reached on the Llano is at the head of the Little Concho river. Between this place and about thirty miles west of Fort Chadbourne, is Grape Creek, where seven mules and one horse had been sto-len by a strolling band of seven Comanches a few days prior to the arrival of the mail, in open day, and under the eyes of three men engaged in building a station house. The men said they would have offered resistance but had no arms.

Mr. Farwell says they were well armed but lacked courage. From this place the road continued good until they reached Red River, where they

Early Scene of Springfield, Missouri Public Square. Arrow points to Butterfield Station at Nicholas Smith's Union Hotel
Source: E. P. Rose, The Ozark Mountaineer, March 1955, page11

met with the effects of recent rains in that section. After crossing the Big Boggy and Little Boggy the roads continued to grow worse, until they arrive at Springdale, in some places being almost impassable.

Account of the Pony Express and Stages on the Central Route, Spring 1859

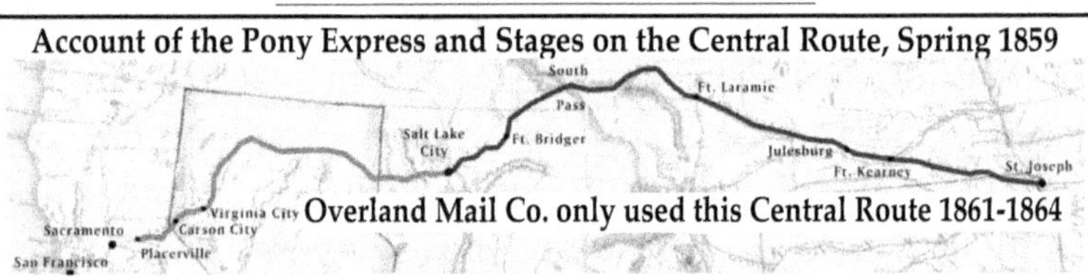

Overland Mail Co. only used this Central Route 1861-1864

Harlow Chittenden Thompson, in a wagon train along the Central Route in the spring of 1859, two years BEFORE Butterfield started using that route:

*"We saw something of the **Pony Express** riders also the **overland stages**.*

*The **Pony Express** had been put on that spring as an experiment, those in charge claiming that the distance from Sacramento, California, to Omaha could be made with a light letter mail and important dispatches in ten days time. Think of it! Nearly two thousand miles to be covered in two hundred and forty hours.*

It was interesting to see those wiry, daring fellows ride. You would see them away in the distance a mere speck, but on they came, rushing like the wind, stopping for nothing except to mount a fresh horse and perhaps swallow a cup of coffee. Their horses were natives of the plains, small in size and hardy. The riders were of slight build, weighing less than one hundred pounds, thinly clad, with hat often hanging down their backs; with bright colored handkerchiefs tied around their foreheads; belts around their waist; and their package of letters fastened to the saddle tree behind. As they came upon you like a flash, with a yell or cheery laugh, passing you at full speed, one could not help admiring them.

*The **overland stage** was an older enterprise, and carried the mail for Uncle Sam and passengers when there were any to carry. From what I saw, I should say there was but little passenger business. The ride was long and tiresome and people feared the Indians. These stages were four-wheeled vehicles with two seats inside, facing each other with seating capacity for three. The mail pouches were piled on the bottom in between the seats. The wagon was covered, and what is known as a 'thorough-braced wagon.' It was drawn by four good mules. The driver's seat was outside, considerably higher than those inside. Accompanying each coach was a man riding a mule, called 'the whipper.' When upon level plains the team always went at full gallop, the whipper riding by their side plying a blacksnake whip almost constantly.*

While they were willing to take mail from emigrants, they would not stop or slack up at all. The mail must be securely tied in a snug package, and when we saw the stage coming someone must be in readiness on horseback and galloping by his side, pass the package to the whipper. Oftentimes they would pass our camp at night with a rush, the whipper cursing the mules and plying the whip at the same time. It was a wild rough sort of a life..."

Source: "Across he Continent on Foot in 1859" by Harlow Thompson,
74 typed pages, on-line files of the Oregon California Trails Association

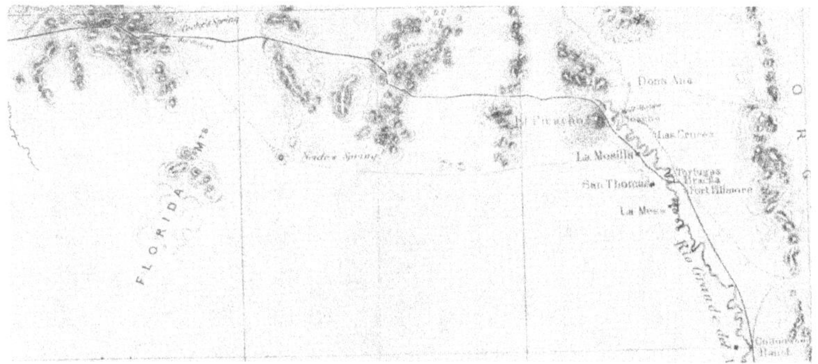

Leach's 1858 Wagon Road Map - Cottonwood Station to Cooks Spring Station [showing a small section] Image Source: N.Y. Public Library, Digital Collection

CHAPTER FOURTEEN

Passenger Observations, *Fort Smith Times*, Nov. 9, 1858
as reprinted in The Memphis Daily Appeal, Nov. 14, 1858, page 2

Los Angeles, Nov. 14, 1858
Arrival of the Sixth Overland Mail

The stage came in with the mail from San Francisco, on Saturday last, 22 days out, bringing dates from Los Angeles to the 9th of October. There were five through passengers, to wit: H. B. LINDSLEY, D. HARTMAN, J. D. HARTMAN, T. LONGHEAD AND J. LONGHEAD.

The *Los Angeles Star*, of the 9th, gives the following account of the arrival at that place of the first overland stage :

"On Thursday, at 1 o'clock P.M., the first through stage of the Overland Mail Company arrived here *[Los Angeles]* from Memphis in twenty-one days.

"Mr. Ormsby, a reporter of the New York Herald, was the only passenger. He speaks in the highest terms of the road and all the appointments. He left New York on the 10th, and St. Louis on the 16th; he has private dispatches to the 17th ult.

"There was no mail for this city. No papers were received by this arrival.

"No inconvenience was felt from the heat during the journey. Passengers easily became accustomed to sleeping in the stages, and are subject to no fatigue for want of steep.

"The stage from here, with six passengers, was met on the other side of El Paso — all well.

"The report of the murder of the Americans by the Mexicans at St. John's station is confirmed. Mr. St. John is alive. The Company have offered a reward of $500 for the apprehension of each of the murderers.

"The prescribed time for running is 27 days, but the first trip will be made in 24 days, being two days less than schedule time. Mr. Ormsby is of opinion that the trip can be made in twenty days.

The joyful and important event of the arrival of the first through stage from Memphis was hailed with great satisfaction by our citizens, and a salute of a hundred guns were fired, in honor of the event, during the afternoon." — *Fort Smith Times*

Passengers on the Sept. 21, 1858 Eastbound Stage
LEWIS LONE, for Memphis Tennessee
GEORGE W. FIDLER, for Memphis Tennessee
SAMUEL GAY, for St. Louis, Missouri
VIRGIN ODEN, for St. Louis, Missouri
JEFFERSON LAKE, for Memphis Tennessee
WILLIAM H. HILTON, for St. Louis, Mo.*
WILLIAM ROSE, for Los Angeles
JOSEPH WALES, for Los Angeles

The next stage for Memphis leaves Friday, 25th inst.; for Los Angeles, Wednesday, 23d instant. The regular trips for Memphis from this city take place, for the future, without fail, on Mondays and Fridays. *San Francisco Herald, Sept. 21 as reprinted in Memphis Daily Appeal, Nov., 4, 1858, page 3; and True Democrat of Oct. 27, 1858, page 2.*

---

*sketches made by William Hilton on his trip are printed in an earlier chapter in this book.

CHAPTER FIFTEEN

J. B. Nichols' Report, Nov. 24, 1858
*as reported in the Nov. 24, 1858 issue of the Fort Smith Times;
and as reprinted in the Saturday, November, 27, 1858 issue of the
Des Arc Citizen of Des Arc, Arkansas, on page 2.*

OVERLAND MAIL – **Mr. J. B. Nichols**, of the O. M. Co. arrived in our city on Sunday last, from El Paso, having left there on the 3rd inst. He reports the line clear through, from this place [Fort Smith] to San Francisco, in perfect order. Mails to and from making time at all the Stations.

Mr. N. reports late sign of hostile Indians, but met none on the trip in, and found no difficulty whatever on the route, no depredations having been committed on any of the *[Butterfield Overland Mail]* Company's property, save the stealing of some 6 mules from the Station at Grape Creek about the 1st inst.

Fears are now entertained as winter approaches, that the Indians will be quite troublesome.

The health of all the men in employ of the [Butterfield Overland Mail] Company, is generally, very good, and all being in good spirits, enjoying themselves 'between times' hunting, as the country abounds in game, such as Deer, Elk, Antelope, Turkeys, Prairie Hens & c.

The road from Red River out is in fine order, the road cleared and streams bridged from Red River. Here the road is not so good, those being improved some, and in places are well worked. One the whole, he says, that the [Butterfield Overland Mail] Company do not [does not] anticipate difficulty, sufficiently great to prevent them from making contract time throughout the year. – *Fort Smith Times*, 24th inst.

***

J. B. Nichols, Agent
as reported in the Memphis Daily Appeal, June 10, 1859, page 3.
based on an interview with OMC agent, J. B. Nichols.

THE CALIFORNIA MAILS

Mr. **J. B. Nichols**, the popular agent at this city of the Overland Mail Company to California, shipped twenty-five horses for Helena yesterday, by the steamer *J. C. Swon*, for the Overland Mail service. The service in the State of Arkansas has been greatly embarrassed by the prevailing floods, but the waters have receded sufficiently, it is thought, to render it practicable to transport the mails again over the Memphis and Little Rock Railroad, the superintendent having signified to the agent here his willingness to receive the mails at Hopefield in future. The regular trains have not yet commenced running upon the road, but the mails will be transmitted through the medium of **hand-cars**. *[see image below]* The labor will be tedious, but the route, even in its present precarious condition, is a more practicable one, perhaps, than that by way of Helena.

***

Memphis Daily Avalanche, Jan. 15, 1859, page 4

Due to flooding, the track bed was too soft for trains to pass, so light weight hand-cars were used to deliver the Overland Mail between the Mississippi River and Madison,

CHAPTER SIXTEEN

Milo June, Tipton Butterfield Agent, Nov. 6, 1858

as reported in the Nov. 6, 1858 issue of the
Weekly Jefferson Inquirer, Jefferson, Missouri, page 2

On Wednesday last we were favored by **MR. JUNE**, Agent of the California Overland Mail, with copies of California papers up to date of Oct. 9th. The latest dates that our friends have, who live in such out of the way places as New York or Philadelphia, is Oct. 5th. Four days behind time, and the poor fellows call that 'news.' We suggest to them, that if they want to get late news from California, so subscribe for the *Inquirer*.

MR. JUNE, in writing to us, says: *"This mail left San Francisco October 8th, and reached here 7 o'clock, A.M., to-day, 3rd. Five passengers came through. They were detained by high water at Red River, Texas, and all the way this side, more or less, but you will see that it is only twenty-six days this morning since they left San Francisco.*

Two Passengers are here that came by the way of New York. They left San Francisco on the 5th ult., and reached here last evening, having come through without an hour's delay on the road. The passengers by the Overland Mail have best them nearly three days to this point."

As this route will be receiving much attention, we refer all those desirous of obtaining information concerning it to MR. JUNE. His address is Tipton, the point where the Overland Mail Coaches connect with the Pacific Railroad.

SAN FRANCISCO, MONDAY EVENING, DECEMBER 6, 1858

CHAPTER SEVENTEEN
Warren Baer, *Nov. 25, 1858*
*as printed in the Dec. 6, 1858 issue of the Evening Bulletin; and
as reprinted in "The First Overland Mail: Butterfield Trail,
San Francisco to Memphis"by William B. Lang, pages 43 to 51; and
also as reprinted in "The Butterfield Overland Mail"
edited by Lyle H., Wright and Josephine M. Bynum
The Huntington Library, San Marino, California*

Fort Smith, November 25, 1858
...There were twelve hats lost by us during this trip, which caused any amount of naughty words to be issued against the Company for placing six men in a stage only intended for four. With four persons in a coach, the trip would be pleasant, provided horses were substituted for the miserable little worn-out mules that are made to drag the coaches through nearly the whole route, almost from El Paso to within 200 miles of this place *[Fort Smith]*. The horse-teams are expected to make up the time lost by the mules. The horses are in as good condition, as the mules are out of condition. When the horses are attached to the stage, they dash along at the rate of eight miles an hour, and the wearied passengers feel inspired with new life.

Ever since leaving Guadalupe Pass, the weather has been freezing cold at night, and during the day overcoats were in constant demand. The snow-storm that met us on the Pass extended to this place *[Fort Smith]*, for snow in detached and isolated beds was visible during our whole journey to Fort Smith. We crossed the Red River in a ferry boat at night. The water looked cold and currentless.

About $150 has paid or will pay the whole expenses (fare, provisions, & c.) of travel of passengers to this place *[Fort Smith]*. The eating is mostly at the stations, the fare consisting of bread, coffee, meat, and sometimes beans, for which is charged 50 cents. Were I to travel the road over again, I would take but one pair of large warm blankets, a revolver or shot-gun, and the stoutest suit of clothes I could get, with a strong *loose* pair of boots, as several have had swelled feet owing to the tightness of their boots. Some cans of preserved fruit will prove a great luxury on the route.

I have much more to say, but as the mail will close within the next hour, I must bid the readers of the *Bulletin* adieu. Though weary from the late journey, I am thankful, that after so long a trip, I have safely arrived, having met with no accident, and not suffered from any serious sickness. *Warren Baer*, Correspondent
San Francisco *Evening Bulletin*

Fort Smith, Ark., November 26, 1858

I wrote the *Bulletin* at considerable length by last mail. Before leaving for Memphis this evening, I find time to indite *[compose]* a few sentences in a friendly social way — of things in general — with due regard to substance and not to order.

This town *[Fort Smith]* is located on the site occupied by the Fort, or rather the land pertaining to the fortification. The houses are most substantial structures, being built of brick and of comfortable dimensions.

The Arkansas river flows conveniently along its suburbs; and the town being built at the head of navigation renders this point one of great importance in the eyes of traders and merchants. It is supposed that the number of its inhabitants exceeds 2,500, with a rapid influx of emigrants. Every house is occupied that can possibly be had, and others, now used for stores, are in great demand for family residences. This being the dividing terminus of the Overland Stage Co.'s route, has attracted the attention of land speculators and horse drovers in any quantity. Gambling flourishes to some small extent, but the faro table is not exposed to public view. It is at this place and Van Buren that the Choctaw, Chickasaw, and other neighboring Indian tribes spend their annual receipts from Government; and it is here also that the Overland Mail Co. spends large sums in repairing their stages, feed for horses, and other incidental charges pertaining to the carrying on of such a gigantic line of stage travel.

The fashion of carrying revolvers is recognized here; but a more hospitable and obliging set of inhabitants, I have seldom seen. Seeing brick houses, struck me with a most pleasurable relief from adobe buildings and Mexican serapes. *[a long colorful blanket with fringe]*

The stage stops at the City Hotel, where most of the persons connected with the O. L. M. Co. board. On landing at this comfortable abode, I was most kindly welcomed by Mr. J. K. McKenzie the proprietor. Californians could not well fall into better hands, enjoy more pleasant quarters, or obtain choicer fare than they will find here.

Yesterday the weather was quite warm and the sun sent down cheering beams of light to gladden the hearts of all sojourners, but today it has been raining and a gloomy mist hangs over the chimney tops.

City Hotel, Fort Smith hosts offices of Overland Mail Co.
The Roberts Library collection dates this photo as ca. 1870
Image source: U. A. Little Rock Center for Arkansas History and Culture.

All of us who came in the stage have the twitches at night, or what is called by stage-drivers the "starts." This, I hope, will soon wear off. It is occasioned by being so long confined in a sitting position, and constantly tossed up and down by the jolting of the stage.

I have sometimes thought, when tired out — almost worried to despair — while sitting in the [stage] coach, dragged by four weak and puny mules across the plains, that I would be the first to censure most loudly the Company for placing their fastest teams at the extremities of the route; but now, all feelings of anger, and all desire to complain, have vanished with the conscious blessing that has been conferred upon us, in permitting us to reach this post of destination, over so wild and desolate regions as we have traversed, without suffering one hour from thirst or hunger, and without one mishap or accident.

**I feel truly grateful; and shall ever cherish
the warmest feelings of friendship towards the kind friends
who toil and endure on the distant regions of the desert and
who so kindly & cheerfully administered to the travelers' comfort.**

For my own safety, I feel truly grateful; and shall ever cherish the warmest feelings of friendship towards the kind friends who toil and endure on the distant regions of the desert and the plains, and who so kindly and cheerfully administered to the travelers' comfort.

We little know the trials and dangers to which the drivers and the men of the various stations along the central portion of the route are exposed. It is almost certain that scarcely a man leaves the confines of these stations, who is not watched by some lurking savage; and some of the drivers are two nights and days in the box, urging their teams along these wilds; yet, be they ever so fatigued, cold, hungry, or annoyed, they always have a cheerful reply to the inquiries of the passengers, and a kind and ready promise that the station is not far ahead when a better team will be had to hasten the long journey to its end. These drivers, agents and conductors are noble fellows, every one of them — save one; but let him slide. His faults are known, which is more than can be said of his merits.

I have had many calls on me today, and the greatest interest is manifested in all pertaining to the Gila river mines and Indians. The specimens of the Gila gold I brought from the mines on that river, and also my specimens of silver from the mines near Tucson, have excited much interest; and many persons have called to see them.

Had I the journey to go over again, the first examination I would make, would be as to who were to be my companions. A good humored, considerate set of fellows can render the trip most agreeable; but a single bore will mar the pleasure of the whole company. I have traveled with three different sets of passengers, and found the foreign portion of them the first and the last to complain. Probably the French population would prove excellent comrades on such a long journey.

Warren Baer, Correspondent

San Francisco *Evening Bulletin*

Memphis, December 6, 1858.
Delays at Fort Smith and Des Arc

On my arrival at Fort Smith, on the 24th of last month, I then and there wrote concerning matters and things that I thought would be of interest to the readers of *The Bulletin*. After being detained there for want of conveyance, for two days, until the morning of the 27th, I started in Reesides & Co.'s tri-weekly coaches for the small town of Des Arc, situated on the White river, Arkansas, being 210 miles from Fort Smith.

[In Sept. 1858 when the Arkansas River did not allow Butterfield to use his steamboat, The Jenny Whipple, to deliver the mail between Fort Smith & Memphis. Butterfield had to hastily engage Chidester, Reeside & Co. as subcontractors to operate the Overland between Fort Smith and Memphis for the first year.]

I reached Des Arc on the morning of the 29th, and was delayed there three days more, waiting for a steamer bound for Memphis, which I was fortunate enough to obtain on the evening of December 1st. I arrived at Memphis on the evening of the 4th.

Personal Adventure
Our Correspondent Drenched at Dardanelles

The only place of any slight importance bearing the semblance of a village, was Dardanelles, which is nearly equidistant between Fort Smith and Des Arc — located on the Arkansas river. When we reached Dardanelles, it was late at night, and raining in an old fashioned way, worthy of '49 memory.

[The University of Winnipeg's Dr. Danny Blair and Dr. W. F. Rannie, have determined that 1849 was unusually cold and wet, with heavy rainfall that summer causing unusual and protracted flooding.]

We were most unceremoniously turned out of the coach by the driver, and delivered into the charge of the ferryman, who took the mailbags on his shoulder, and, his lantern in hand, told us to follow him to his boat at the ferry landing, about one mile distant up the river. There was no remedy for this unexpected tramp; so, placing our blanket on our backs, and va-lise in hand, the passengers proceeded to accompany him through a torrent of rain, up the river bank, and across the stream in his small boat. It was well for the coachman that he could not be found when we started on after the ferryman; he certainly would have been roughly handled. We all got soaking wet by the time we reached the coach on the opposite bank, and three of our party were considerably used up next day from the effects of the drenching.

Nine Miles East of Dardanelle Ferry - Potts Stage Station
Kirkbride Potts, postmaster and station agent, built this home in 1858 for his
family. This building also served as an official Butterfield Overland Mail Co.
home station. This magnificent structure is open for tours Thus.-Sat. 10-3pm
in Pottsville, Arkansas. Image: "Potts Tavern" by Gloria McHahen, 1984
Print 83 of 500 in Bob Crossman's collection.

Delay in Reaching Memphis

On arriving at Des Arc, one of the passengers — that's myself — waited for a Memphis boat, while three of them took a passing steamer for New Orleans. The mail for Memphis was sent from Des Arc for Mem-phis on horseback over the country — being a distance of some 80 miles — while we were left to shift for ourselves in the way of getting to Memphis. The company paid our fare through. This was all right and according to agreement, but I am certain that the department at Washington never contemplated that a delay of five days would take place owing to a want of means of conveyance — being two days at Fort Smith and three at Des Arc.

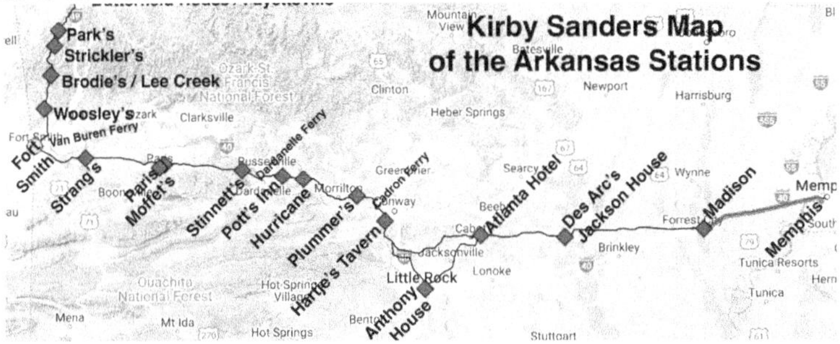

The Butterfield Overland National Historic Trail from Fort Smith to Des Arc
Map by Kirby Sanders

The road from Fort Smith to Des Arc passes over a very even country, and through forests of oak. The soil looks cold, and much of the country is subject to over-flow. We passed many farm-houses, and many fields were under cultivation — producing corn and cotton, but not, I should think, judging from appearances, in any great quantity. At many houses where we took our meals along the route, very little inquiry was made of us as to the nature and character of the route through, but there were always plenty of men and women to inquire about some Jones, Smith, or Thompson who had — many days, or rather years, ago — proceeded to California, and been absent, *"so, so long-very long-ago, and never been heard of more."*

The fare on this portion of the road was of a very ordinary, but the sweetest dish that cheered our hearts was a roast opossum — though we saw nary coon — which I know is not the case with you San Franciscans, who, I suppose, see one daily in your walks along Montgomery Street.

The White River

It is about 300 miles from Memphis to Des Arc by water, and about 80 or 90 by land. White River is a very beautiful stream, free from snags, and resembles in size and appearance the Sacramento. I enclose a card of landings and distances. <This has not come to hand. It was probably overlooked in sealing our correspondent's package.> The stream abounds in trout, perch, and cat-fish, and the passengers amused themselves in shooting geese and ducks from the steamer's deck. It has been raining every day since we left Des Arc — sometimes nearly all day, and then a slight sprinkle the next.

Steamboats at Des Arc (Prairie County); 1860s.
Image source: Courtesy of the Arkansas State Archives

The steamer *"Return,"* on which I came, brought any quantity of game — such as deer, ducks, geese, turkeys, prairie hens*, wild pigeons*, and partridges, all of which appeared in fine condition. *[* The Greater Prairie-Chicken is now extirpated from Arkansas, and the Passenger Pigeon is now extinct.]*

1872 Sketch of Memphis from the shore at Hopefield, Arkansas

Entering the Mississippi
Thoughts Suggested by It

It was near night when we entered the Mississippi River. Its muddy waters rolled quietly along as though ten thousand skeletons, the victims of steamboat accidents, lay not beneath its surface. No one, after a long absence from the shores of the Mississippi, can contemplate its mighty stream without feelings of awe, amounting almost to trepidation. On each side stand the tall, slender cottonwood trees and the buoyant willows, high up on the trunks of which are the watermarks of the late overflow. Steamers of giant proportions and costly decoration float on its muddy tide, while below the surface of its waters the alligator rattles in his toils the bones of the dead. It may be said with truth that this river has cost more lives than ever it has made fortunes. We passed the wreck of the steamer *"Pennsylvania,"* on our way up, lying between this city and the mouth of White River — in the blowing up of which 250 lives were lost I think it would take many days to make two hundred and fifty fortunes. When we take into consideration the number of steamboats constantly running up and down the Mississippi, the wonder is, not that so many lives are lost, but that more human beings are not destroyed through accident.

Nearly nine years ago, I left the mouth of this famous river, on a journey round the Horn for California, and after so long an interval of time I have returned to its banks, a wiser, I hope, if not a richer man. One knows not whether the flight of Time is the same through all space and over all lands and seas, but it seems to me that his minutes to me, since I left California, have grown into hours, and that he lags in his speed and moves not with such velocity as he was wont in the bracing air of the Pacific.

Early Memphis to Hopefield Ferry, perhaps the ferry "Nashoba"
When steamboats were not available, the Overland Mail crossed from Memphis to Hopefield, Arkansas by ferry, then boarded the train for a short 24 mile trip, where stages carried the mail and passengers the next 2,700 miles to San Francisco.
Image from Gene Gill, www.historic-memphis.com

Description of Memphis

Memphis is, as most of the readers of *The Bulletin* are doubtless aware, located on the east bank of the Mississippi River, 900 miles from the Gulf of Mexico, by the course of the river. Its population is about 30,000, with a daily floating population of some 2,500. The city is about two miles long and one mile wide, with a suburban belt quite closely settled. Besides its river commerce, it has four railroads diverging from its center to the north, south, east and west, viz: Memphis and Ohio — completed 100 miles, intended to connect Memphis and Louisville; Memphis and Charleston — completed through to Charleston, 500 miles; Mississippi and Tennessee — connecting Memphis with the Mississippi Central Railroad at Granada, Mississippi; and the Little Rock Railroad — connecting Memphis with Little Rock, Arkansas, completed to St. Francis river, 40 miles.

Steamboat Loaded with Cotton on the Mississippi River

About 370,000 bales of cotton are shipped from this port to all other ports of the United States, being an increase of 60,000 bales over last year.

The soil in the immediate vicinity is peculiarly adapted for brick-making, being of a pure yellow clay, very sticky and tough. As a consequence of this element of city structure, the houses are mostly built of brick, being of large and capacious dimensions, and with great architectural beauty in their structure.

The city *[of Memphis]* itself is placed on a ridge of high bluffs, far above high water, and presents quite an imposing aspect from the *[Mississippi]* river. Steamers are constantly passing and stopping at the levee, which is generally covered with cotton bales and other merchandise. All night long the bells of the departing and coming steamers are sounding their approach or departure.

The greatest ornament, in the way of buildings, in the city, is the Gayoso Hotel, a very handsome edifice, standing out in bold relief, fronting the river, with a prominent portico in front. It is usually crowded with travelers, and its great hall presents a scene of constant confusion, caused by the arrival and departure of passengers.

Image Source: "Memphis Moment: The Gayoso House," by Steve Pike

The Gayoso Hotel

The dining-room is very large, but the cooking and attendance at table is scarcely more than ordinary. The chambers are lighted with gas, and the servants are mostly slaves, very obedient but very stupid. Its floors are covered with carpet from top to bottom. The furniture is mostly of burnished mahogany. It is a most superb structure, but is only fitted to accommodate travelers whose purses are well filled with the precious dust *[gold dust]*. Liquor sells at the bar for 12½ cents per glass, but, on Sunday, all liquor must be purchased by the bottle, as it cannot be had at this hotel.

Serious Sunday Visages of the People — The Ladies

Last Sunday I walked through the city and all the people whom I met wore most sanctimonious faces, as though under the observance of the vigilant eye of the church. I always allow a certain amount of hypocrisy to all men, but really the individuals I met last Sabbath put me to blush. I should take it, that the collections taken up at the churches afford a comfortable living to the preachers. All the people here dress in black, and look as though they were going to a funeral. Probably, after all, I met nothing but cotton operators, absorbed in deep study.

The ladies here do not dress with that stylish elegance that adds so much to the superb figures of our Pacific belles The faces of the women have not that healthy glow that distinguishes the promenaders on Montgomery and Stockton streets, yet they are of robust figure and no doubt make excellent wives.

The Theaters - Miss Avonia Jones

There are two theaters here — Vy Crisp's Gaiety and the Washington Street Theatre. They are both open at the present time and doing an excellent business.

Miss Avonia Jones is performing at the Gaiety. I saw

her as "Juliet" to Mrs. Jones (her mother) as "Romeo." Miss Avonia is rather handsome, with a strong, masculine voice. She has considerable grace in her carriage, and steps across the stage with some majesty; yet, I think, she would appear to better advantage in some tragic character requiring more masculine qualities than Juliet is supposed to possess. However, I saw her but for a night, and may be

wikipedia.org" Avonia

wrongly impressed by her acting. One of the theaters (the Gaiety) is surely the worst conductor of sound in the United States. Both these seats of the muses are much inferior to the American, in your Sansome street. Court Square, located in the center of the city, is about 450 feet square, in which a variety of trees are planted. It is quite an ornament to the city.

Approaching Home For New Orleans!

Tomorrow I take a berth in some passing steamer for New Orleans, and, I trust, may be as prosperous in the final close of my journey, as I have been favored throughout the long tramp to this place.

The river is rising, and so is my expectation and desire to reach the home of earlier days.

That some, whose faces were, once, more than familiar, and whose voices could be recognized amid the darkest hours of night, have faded from existence, is painfully true; but that many of my former friends still live in the enjoyment of health, is also true. These I trust to find as dear to me as ever; and as faithful in their friendship, kind and indulgent as they were wont to be in my youth, my wayward boyhood.

Warren Baer, Correspondent
San Francisco *Evening Bulletin*

New Orleans Daily Picayune
December 11, 1858

Mr. Baer, of the San Francisco Bulletin, arrived at Memphis the other day via the overland mail route, and gave the *Memphis Bulletin*, of the 5th inst., a sketch of his trip. The *Bulletin* says:

The party encountered a severe snow storm on Guadalupe Mountain, and were compelled to walk nearly the whole distance between Crow Springs and Pinery Stations, a distance of twenty-six miles. The Comanche had driven off six mules from the Conchos station, and burned the grass in the neighborhood of the station. Beyond this malicious feat no other act of a hostile nature had been committed.

The snow storm that set in at the Guadalupe Pass reached Fort Smith. The deer and antelopes were most plentiful, while the wolves were constantly loitering along the track.

The passengers do not speak in a very favorable manner of the mule trains. They are too slow and too feeble to render the services required of them.

There is no guard to protect the passengers against the attacks of the Indians. The coaches are very easy, when in motion, but that they are too narrow in the seats, which are, as at present placed, fit only to accommodate four persons, but are occupied by six, rendering the trip extremely crowded and unpleasant.

The weather was very cold, and they *[passengers]* were compelled frequently to alight, and run with the mules to keep their blood in circulation. The long rolling prairies of Texas were the worst part of the road, the sticky nature of the soil rendering it heavy both to mules and horses.

The passengers were detained five days on the route — two at Fort Smith, waiting for the *[sub contractors of Butterfield's Overland Mail Co.]* Reeside coaches — and three days at Des Arc awaiting the return of the steamer *Return*. The alkali water affected all the passengers more or less as a purgative, but its effects soon wore off, and the passengers suffered but a few days from its use.

Nearly all the water, on striking the desert, is of a brackish flavor, and in many of the streams, such as the Gila and Pecos, it is almost brackish. The only sulfur spring on the route is found on the Pacheco Pass. It is strongly scented, tasting of sulfur and being cathartic in its effects, the passengers did not drink it with impunity.

The passengers complain of the great delay occasioned by there not being a stage ready to convey them from Fort Smith to Des Arc, and there being no way supplied to transmit them on their journey when arriving at the latter place. Three of them embarked on a small steamer for the mouth of White river, but were extremely disappointed at not being able to proceed direct to Memphis, for which city they were booked in San Francisco.

The Apaches and Pimas Indians had been engaged in a severe contest, which resulted in the death of the Pimas chief. The chiefs being hereditary in this tribe, there was great mourning for his loss, and his son was declared future chief. The Pimas Indians supply many of the stations with corn and wheat sell on the most reasonable terms to the emigrants and station keepers. These half-civilized savages complain bitterly against the Great Father at Washington, because of his neglect of them. They say that they fight the Apaches, the white man's enemy, but they never receive any kind of assistance from the whites, who accept their services against the Apaches.

The Gila mines, which are situated 18 miles above Fort Yuma, on the Gila river, are represented as developing in a most satisfactory manner, it being stated that those who work average some $4 or $5 per day.

Mr. Baer had beautiful specimens of silver ore taken from the Cerro Colorado silver mine, now under the charge of Major Heintzelman, situated near Tubae, Arizona Territory. The wealth of the above named Territory in mineral resources is represented as immense.

Warren Baer, author of these observations as a special correspondent to the San Francisco daily Evening Bulletin, MAY BE the same Warren Baer, who was founder and editor of the Mariposa Democrat in 1856-1857. He was replaced as editor by Wm. Godfrey in 1858, and the paper ceased publication that year. Warren Baer is renown for publishing the first detailed and extensive account of the Yosemite Valley in 1856. He expressed sorrow over the desire of the American who travels overseas to catch a glimpse of the Alps of Switzerland or valleys of Italy, many of which "possess no wonderful attributes of greatness, save in the mind of the traveler, that will compare with the scenery, separately or in whole, of the Yosemite Valley."

Fort Smith, 1860
Postcard displaying an artist rendering of the fort buildings at Fort Smith, Arkansas during the time the Butterfield Overland Mail Co. The Butterfield offices were just a couple of blocks east of the fort, at the John Roger's City Hotel, and later St. Charles Hotel within sight of the fort. One of these Fort buildings is still standing in 2023, preserved by the National Parks System.

CHAPTER EIGHTEEN

Eastern Conductor Speaks Up
For Red River to Tipton Route

as reported in the Daily Alta California, Monday, Dec. 20, 1858

The Overland Mail

In the *Alta* of the 29th of October, we had occasion to speak of the delay in the eastern half of the Overland route, and that the time lost from St. Louis to El Paso had to be made up by the California half running faster than the schedule called for. In reply to that article, we have the following letter from the conductors of that portion of the route from Fort Smith to St. Louis, which relieves them of the responsibility and throws it upon somebody else's shoulder. Where shall the blame for the delays be placed? Who shall answer?

Fort Smith, Nov. 21, 1858

Editors *Alta*: — In your paper of, the 29th, you mention some fast time that has been made on the western end of the Overland Mail route, and also that the time is not made on the eastern end of the route, and if eastern conductors and drivers do not do better than they have done, the route will have to be run by Californians. Now for the eastern end of the route, as far as Red river, which is about 660 miles, we will say that the time is made, and west of that we cannot say how the time is made, only that the mail from California always comes to Red river behind time, and may have to make it up and arrive in St. Louis in time. We also say that the eastern conductors and drivers take just as much interest in the running of the mails as our California friends; and you will see by this that the time is lost west of Red river, therefore they must speak for themselves.   Yours Respectfully,

EASTERN CONDUCTOR OVERLAND MAIL

Unknown Image

CHAPTER NINETEEN

Pursuit of a Husband, Dec. 23, 1858
as reported in the Jan. 26, 1859 issue of The Nevada Democrat, Nevada, California, page 1

The St. Louis correspondent of the *San Francisco Bulletin*, in his letter of Dec. 23rd says:

Among the passengers by the twenty-first Overland Mail who reached St. Louis last evening, was Mrs. Hall or Hale, an English lady.

Her husband left England several years since, and came to the New World — she knew not whither. Being desirous of rejoining him, she took ship at Liverpool for one of our Eastern ports, and came over. Learning that he was probably in Australia, she went thither on a long and perilous passage, arriving there only to learn that no such person was a dweller at that end of the earth. With hope still in her heart, she sailed from Melbourne to San Francisco. Failing there to hear of her truant spouse, she despaired of success, and reluctantly decided to abandon him for lost, and return by way of the **Overland Route** and the west to her former home in England.

On alighting from the *[train]* cars in this city *[St. Louis]*, last evening, almost the first person she encountered was her long absent lord.

Your readers may imagine the joy of the poor woman at meeting the object of her long and wearisome search over far off lands and oceans, and amid countless hardships and dangers, at a place where she had never expected it, and when hope itself had ceased to guide her pathway.

ARKANSAS STATE GAZETTE AND DEMOCRAT.

C. C. DANLEY, Editor.   "ERROR ceases to be dangerous, when REASON is free to combat it."   W. F. HOLTZMAN, Publisher.

LITTLE ROCK, ARKANSAS, SATURDAY MORNING, DECEMBER 25, 1858.

CHAPTER TWENTY

D. Jones, December 25, 1858

as reported in the Dec. 25, 1858 issue of the Weekly Arkansas Gazette, page 3

LATER DATES FROM CALIFORNIA – Two passengers came through from San Francisco, **D. Jones** and Christian Krause. They left that place [San Francisco] early on the morning of the 22d of last month, and have made the trip within twenty-five days, being some twelve hours ahead of the regular time. Four of the passengers who started in the same mail came on as far as the new gold diggings in Arizona.

Mr. Jones reports the road along the entire distance is in admirable condition for travel. No unnecessary detentions occurred to the mail, during the journey, which fact is highly commendatory of the well systematized plan under which affairs of the road are conducted, and the invariable efficiency of its operation.

In reference to the Gila River gold miles, our informant states that comparatively little excitement exists in San Francisco concerning them, although from along the road for hundreds of miles, on both sides of the mines, there is an immense emigration pouring into them, and the emigrants are eager to test their productiveness...

None of the regular employees of the Overland Company have deserted the stations for the mines, but some of them are very sick with the gold fever. Quite a number of the supernumeraries, such as grooms and side-drivers, have left for the diggings...

Colbert's Ferry across Red River
Image from the set: "Stereoscopic Views of Texas and Indian Territory"
Source: Gerald T. Ahnert

DAILY MISSOURI REPUBLICAN.
ST. LOUIS, MONDAY MORNING, JANUARY 3, 1859

CHAPTER TWENTY ONE
Major Emery, Jan. 3, 1859

The Daily Missouri Republican frequently sent a reporter to meet the Butterfield's Overland Mail Co. stagecoach to obtain a list of arriving passengers and in hopes of obtaining an interview of interest.

Daily Missouri Republican
St. Louis, Missouri
Monday, Jan. 3, 1859, page 2

We are in receipt by the twenty fourth Overland Mail of California papers to the 6th of December. The mail left San Francisco at 12 o'clock, P.M., on that day. The stages brought six passengers. Of these, MAJOR EMERY was from San Francisco, MR. MORGAN, WM. BURKE, and WM. WILCOXSON, from Oregon, MR. HARDIE from Tucson, and DR. THOMPSON from Manilla Valley.

Maj. Emery had remained over two weeks at Fort Yuma. While there, he learned some particulars about the Gila *[gold]* diggings, which he has politely communicated to us... The number of persons employed in the diggings, is about 250... The gold is found in gulches, and the dirt is carried to the river for washing. The miners have generally nothing but picks and pans to work with. The gold is fine scale gold, and is reckoned to be worth $18 to the ounce... some four or five hundred ounces have been taken out... in only about a month...

Mr. Emery saw on the way at least one hundred thousand... sheep...

In Arizona... silver mining.. now being worked near Tucson... There is work going on at the great copper mine, the ore of which yields 50 per cent of metal. This ore is waggoned to Fort Yuma, and thence sent down the Colorado by steamers, which navigate the river...

The mail station at the Concha river (Texas) was visited by some Comanche Indians on the 21st. Eighteen of them, part of a larger number who kept at considerable distance, came down upon the corral which enclosed the mules, and ran off thirty-one of them. One of them was recovered. There were five Americans at the station, who were taken by surprise, but who fired upon the Indians as they were making off with their booty.

On the 23d the stage met Sheriff Jones, formerly of Kansas, with his wife and small party, going to Arizona.

The road was excellent as far as Red river; *[at the Texas and Indian Territory border]* but this side the recent rains had made traveling very heavy. The only wonder is that, with the roads in such condition, the conductors on this line are able to make the time as they do. It is Mr. Emery's observation, as it is the testimony of all who have traveled over this route, that the Butterfield Company's agents and employees are doing all in their power to make dispatch and give satisfaction to passengers.

ARKANSAS TRUE DEMOCRAT.
Volume 16   LITTLE ROCK, ARKANSAS, WEDNESDAY MORNING, JANUARY 5, 1859.   Number 12

CHAPTER TWENTY TWO
Passenger, Jan. 5, 1859
as printed in the Jan. 5, 1859 issue of the
Arkansas True Democrat, Little Rock, Arkansas, page 2

TRAVEL BY OVERLAND MAIL COACHES –
Speaking of the arrival of the eighteenth Overland Mail from San Francisco, the St. Louis Republican says:

Since the **Overland Mail** has indubitably proven itself a cheap, speedy, and secure means of travel, the rush at San Francisco, Los Angeles and other places, to obtain seats in the coaches has become tremendous.

When our informant left San Francisco no less than one hundred persons had made application at the office of Mr. McLean, the agent there, for passage. So eager and importunate were they to secure passage that they had adopted the course of deciding by lot who has to stay over. To facilitate this, and be as impartial as possible, the agent would not accept engagements for seats more than two stages ahead. Every few days, therefore, there were places in a third *[stagecoach]* to be drawn.

About half way over the route a passenger was found at a way station, where he had stopped to lay over for a few days nearly a month previously. As all the succeeding stages came by so filled with passengers he had been unable to get on again to complete his journey on to St. Louis. At the time the late mail arrived there he was so well worn out with his long resting spell that he offered a large bonus for his seat, but failed to get it.

Buffalo Bill's Wild West Show, Deadwood Stage, 1890

CHAPTER TWENTY THREE
J. P. Myers, Jan. 7, 1859
The Daily Missouri Republican frequently sent a reporter to meet Butterfield's Overland Mail Co. stagecoach to obtain a list of arriving passengers and in hopes of obtaining an interview of interest.

Daily Missouri Republican, St. Louis, Missouri
Friday, Jan. 7, 1859, page 2
Twenty-Sixth Overland Mail

The mail from California and the Pacific Coast, via the Overland Route, was delivered in this city *[St. Louis]* last night, being the twenty-sixth mail received since the organization of this great postal thoroughfare...

The present mail is twenty-four days out, and incurred delays at Tucson, Fort Smith and other places, that reduced the time expended in travel to twenty-three. The passengers who have arrived here, are Messrs. J. B. Hutchinson and J. M. Stowe from Texas, and J. P. Myers of Mansfield, Ohio, who is returning to that State from California. **From the latter (Mr. J. P. Myers) we have received the following interesting information concerning the trip.**

Mr. Pardee, who left here *[St. Louis]* on the 6th December, with the President's Message, was taken sick on his arrival in El Paso, and compelled to stop at that place. Beyond that point the message was Expressed horseback from station to station, at the rate of two hundred miles for every twenty-four hours. The person bearing it when met by Mr. Myers, on the 19th ult., was twenty miles East of Fort Yuma, and about seven hundred and eighty miles out from San Francisco. The message would be delivered in that city, it was thought, in less than seventeen days...

Three companies of United States Dragoons had gone out from Los Angeles with a train of eighteen wagons, to establish a post in the Navajo country, three hundred miles above Fort Yuma, on the Colorado river. The Navajoes, after driving back the mail, which was returning from Stockton to Kansas City, Missouri, had declared that no more mail parties should pass through their Territory, and that they would massacre the next one which came in their way.

Along the Butterfield Route, the one over which Mr. M. came, the employees of the Mail Company and the Comanches were virtually at war. The former are sturdy, hardy fellows, and seemed more anxious to fight than their Indian enemies. They were building strong station houses of adobe or stone, and had from ten to twenty guns at each of them. The Comanches had gone to a station, believed to be Pope's, beyond the Llano Estacado, and run off twenty-seven mules. When the stage arrived there, the station men were all out hunting for their lost stock and the coach was compelled to keep on forty miles further with the same team for want of a relay...

Mail Count From the *Daily Alta*, Dec. 11. 1859
Overland Mail.. for St Louis distribution 410, city 43, total, 453 *[letters]*. Little Rock distribution, 31; Memphis distribution 145, city 4; total 149. New York distribution 240, city 127; total 367. Other offices... 10. California...133. Grand total, 1,143. *[letters]*

Anthony House, Little Rock, Arkansas' Home Station
To enter Little Rock, Butterfield's Overland Mail stage crossed on the
Arkansas River ferry and stopped at the Anthony House on the southwest
corner of Markham and Scott streets for mail and passengers.
The three story Anthony House was a famous landmark in Little Rock.
Following a fire in 1840 the three story hotel was rebuilt with red brick.
Photo courtesy of The Arkansas State Archives (Image #ASA 5300.36)

CHAPTER TWENTY FOUR
Passenger Letter, January 8, 1859
as printed in the January 12, 1859 issue of the Arkansas True Democrat,
Little Rock, Arkansas, on page 2.
Written from the Anthony House, the Butterfield Home Station in Little Rock.

Anthony House, Little Rock
January 8th, 1859

Mr. Editor: Having business in your town we availed ourselves of the facilities offered to us by the new line of *[Butterfield's Overland]* mail coaches just put into operation between Madison, the termination of the Memphis and Little Rock railroad, and this place *[Little Rock]* by those enterprising and energetic men, Chidester, Rapley & Co., and although owing to the heavy rains which has just fallen, the roads were in the worst possible condition. We with the mail, were safely landed at our destination *[Little Rock]* yesterday afternoon, making the time from Madison, our starting point, in about twenty-seven hours, and the connection between Memphis and this place in about thirty hours.

After the journey was safely accomplished we could not refrain from contrasting our speedy trip in comfortable coaches with the slow, wearisome tugging and plodding through mud and mire we have heretofore endured in passing over the same on horseback.

When first informed of the great enterprise of making the mail connection between Memphis and this place *[Little Rock]* in but little more than one day's time by means of coaches, we were inclined to doubt the possibility of effecting so desirable an object; but now we know that in the worst of weather and most unfavorable condition of the road, there has not, since the line went into operation, been a single failure to deliver the mails in due time, and to carry passengers with safety and comparative comfort.

Indeed, those who know Mr. Chidester well, also know that there is no such word as "fail" in his vocabulary. From an acquaintance with him, and from witnessing the energy which has been infused into all the employees connected with this line we are fully assured that the contractors will not only be successful in carrying the mail in schedule time, but that they will also be able to transport any number of passengers in comfortable coaches, drawn by fleet horses, and driven by experienced, careful and accommodating drivers. We feel no hesitation in saying that the citizens of the state ought to consider themselves fortunate, that this and all the other lines of coach mail transportation in their midst have fallen into the hands of such a company of enterprising and thorough-going men as Chidester, Rapley & Co.

The line from Memphis to this place *[Little Rock]* is more important than any other in the state because it is the pioneer which marks out a route to be followed by the great Pacific railroad, which must sooner or later be built by the general government or by private enterprise. The protection of immense territory and the urgent demands of the commerce of the world require it, and render it a work of necessity. Its construction is sure, being now only a question of time. In this point of view the immense importance of this line to the state, to the south and to the whole Union is too apparent to need comment.

Now it may be safely said that the days of old fogyism *[fogyism: an adherence to old-fashioned or conservative ideas and intolerance of change, often coupled with dullness or slowness of personality]* are waning, and days of advancement and improvement are beginning to dawn even upon Arkansas which has hitherto made so little progress in developing the might resources of wealth and greatness, so long concealed and unknown within her borders. And may we not hope that the citizens will arouse to press forward every movement which will promote our progress and improvement.

It is understood that Col. Butterfield, who is now here, is engaged in supervising the transportation of the Overland Mail to California, thus showing that at least one arm of the great Pacific railroad must pass through our midst.

In wishing success to Chidester, Rapley & Co., we cannot refrain from congratulating our most excellent Post Master General, Aaron V. Brown, for his success in establishing and putting in operation by means of such active and go ahead agents, the important mail connection by Overland with California, thus binding with another cord the golden state of the Pacific coast with her older sisters of the east.

*Chidester's Home
in Camden, Arkansas
- artist unknown*

CHAPTER TWENTY FIVE
John T. Chidester, Jan. 12, 1859
*Interview of John T. Chidester as it appeared in the Jan. 12, 1859 issue
of the Memphis Daily Appeal, Memphis, Tennessee.*

The Overland Mail from California arrived *[in Memphis]* last evening, in schedule time, bringing us San Francisco dates to the 17th of December.

Mr. Chidester, who has the mail contract from this city *[Memphis]* to Little Rock, came with the mail from Fort Smith. He informs us that the line, is now well stocked with four horse coaches, and that he will hereafter put both the mail and passengers through to Little Rock, in from twenty-six to thirty hours, and to Fort Smith in three days.

This it the second mail brought through from California in schedule time, and we may very reasonably hope that Mr. Butterfield has redeemed his pledge to this community, and that the mail will in future arrive and depart regularly. When this is the case, then will the country know how properly to appreciate the laudable enterprise and commendable zeal of our public spirited Postmaster-General, in opening up this great pioneer highway between the Pacific and the Mississippi valley. After years will vindicate both the wisdom and vitality of the enterprise.

Mr. Chidester at present in the city, and will in a few days open an office at the Gayoso *[hotel]*, when he will be prepared to ticket passengers through to California and all Intermediate points.

Early Memphis to Hopefield Ferry, perhaps the ferry "Nashoba"
The Overland Mail crossed from Memphis to Hopefield, Arkansas by ferry,
then boarded the train for a short 24 mile trip, where stage carried the mail
and passengers the next 2,700 miles to San Francisco.
Image compliments of Gene Gill, www.historic-memphis.com

CHAPTER TWENTY SIX

Passengers Observations, Jan. 1859

ANOTHER OVERLAND MAIL
as reported in the Daily Jefferson Inquirer, Jan. 6, 1859, page 2

... we are indebted to the courtesy of the Agent, Mr. June... The roads were in such excellent order that the stage made seven miles an hour, until it entered Texas.

NEWS BY OVERLAND MAIL
as reported in the Memphis Daily Appeal, Jan. 26, 1859, page 3;

St. Louis, January 25. The Overland Mail of the 31st ult. arrived yesterday...

A large fire was raging in the woods near Fayetteville, Arkansas. It was feared that it would extend many miles and destroy much property...

Contractor Butterfield had abandoned the project of conveying the mail from Fort Smith to Memphis by the river, on account of low water. *[Originally Butterfield intended to use his steamboat, Jennie Whipple, to carry mail & passengers between Fort Smith and Memphis, but the water was too low in September of 1858.]*

THE OVERLAND MAIL
as reported in the Memphis Daily Appeal, Jan. 27, 1859, page 3

The Overland Mail from San Francisco of 30th ult., reached this city *[Memphis]* last evening. The news brought by this arrival had been anticipated by telegraph, published in our paper yesterday morning. The delay in the arrival at this city was caused by the bad conditions of the roads in Arkansas — the ice in the White river bottom almost precluding travel. We are indebted to Mr. W. H. Walton, of the Memphis and Little Rock Railroad, for full files of California papers to the 30th ult.

MR. WALTON'S OBSERVATIONS   *page 2*

... **Mr. Walton**, the *[Butterfield]* agent, informs us that the mail reached Fort Smith in due season, the weather and roads to that point being fine, but that the roads between Arkansas and White rivers, owing to the recent rains and heavy frosts, were almost impassable. In many places the sloughs were covered with ice two inches thick, which broke under the weight of the *[stagecoach]* coach and seriously impeded its progress...

JAMES GLOVER'S OBSERVATIONS
as reported in the Memphis Daily Appeal, Jan. 28, 1859, page 2

The Overland Mail, which left San Francisco on the 3rd instant at noon, reached this city *[Memphis]* yesterday at 5 o'clock — twenty-four days and five hours from San Francisco. There were four through passengers to St. Louis.

Mr. James Glover, the Superintendent between Fort Chadbourne and El Paso, came through to this city. He reports the road in excellent order beyond Fort Smith, and that there had been no recent Indian depredations along the route. From Fort Smith to Little Rock there is some very bad road, and the White river bottom is almost impassable.

Mr. Glover informs us that the mails come into Fort Smith with perfect regularity in nineteen to twenty days. This, considering the length of the line and the difficulties to be overcome, is a most wonderful performance. Between these points the average speed is one hundred and twenty miles in twenty four hours,

There were no through passengers to this city, *[Memphis]* owing, we suppose, to the fact that under the arrangements of Contractor Butterfield, through tickets to St. Louis from San Francisco cost the Eastward-bound passenger one hundred dollars, while if he comes to Memphis he must pay the sub-contractors thirty dollars more for passage from Fort Smith to Memphis, a difference of thirty per cent, against Memphis. *[This is the only source that mentions a $30 fee.]* From Fort Smith to Memphis the roads are better than to St. Louis, and there are sixty-five miles less travel by railroad, but this difference in distance, is not sufficient to counterbalance the difference in the fare.

Mr. Glover expressed great surprise in learning, on his arrival at Fort Smith, that the mails between Memphis and that point were not carried regularly in schedule time. He says that sixty hours is ample time, and that Butterfield & Co., have the sub-contractors, Chidester, Rapley & Co. obligated in a bond, with a heavy penalty affixed, to perform the service in the time specified. But we infer that if the failure of Butterfield & Co. to perform the service they have contracted with the Post Office Department to perform is overlooked, they are willing to extend the same leniency to Chidester, Rapley & Co., the more so as the delinquencies of the latter cost them nothing.

"Corn Exchange Hotel in Mesilla" mural by local artist Cliff Donaldson

CHAPTER TWENTY SEVEN

Passenger Reports, *Sacramento Union*, Jan.-May,1859

{dates: January 1,3,11,17,20,26,28 and 29, 1859;
February 9, 12, March 2, May 2, 1859]

The Sacramento Daily Union newspaper apparently sent a reporter to meet each
Butterfield's Overland Mail stage in hopes of interviewing passengers for news.]

Sacramento Daily Union

Sacramento, California, Jan. 1, 1859

The Southern Overland Mail.

A correspondent of the *Bulletin*, writing from St. Louis, after his overland journey, complains of the crowding of the stages with more passengers than they are capable of conveying. He says some six or seven were taken when only four could be conveniently accommodated. He adds:

Now this, because of the nature of the trip (incessant traveling night and day for so long a time), and from a company receiving so liberally from the National Treasury for a nominal service with a prospective good, is mean treatment. The point I wish to suggest to passengers is this — to know before starting what *"four through passengers"* signifies, and then rely upon themselves for protection against these self-sufficient, autocratic way-agents.

Sacramento Daily Union, Jan. 3, 1859

Southern Overland Mail.— This mail left San Francisco, Dec. 80th, with three through passengers — JO-SEPH WHITELEY, for Fort Smith ; H. A. HANSON and HENRY FOOS for St. Louis. It carried 1,00l letters — 567 of which were for the Atlantic States.

Sacramento Daily Union, Jan. 11, 1859

Overland Routes. — On the 10th of December the *St. Louis Democrat* published the following **statement of a passenger** by the Southern Overland route from San Francisco :

The party met with considerable delay, by reason of the miserable condition of the roads in Arkansas and Missouri.

An accident occurred by the breaking of the stage pole on the "Desert." On this account the driver had to put back to the station last passed, which occasioned a delay of some eight or ten hours. Rumors were rife of Indian depredations. It was reported that Lieut. Beale's party had been attacked by Comanches. There was also a report that the Indians had attacked the mail stage on the overland route which passes through Stockton. At one of the stations between El Paso and Tucson the Company had employed two or three Mexicans to assist their own hands in building a station. The Mexicans watched their opportunity, and attacked the Americans, who, taken by surprise, were unable to make any resistance. Two of the latter were murdered, and the others fled The Mexicans then seized upon the horses and escaped. The number is not mentioned. It was said that the horses had been recovered.

Sacramento Daily Union, Jan. 17. 1859
Letter from St. Louis by the Southern Overland Mail
St. Louis, Dec. 20, 1858

ARRIVAL OF THE OVERLAND MAIL. On Friday evening, Dec. 17th, the telegraph from Jefferson City unexpectedly announced the arrival of the twentieth overland mail from San Francisco, in twenty-four and one-half days. We had not looked for it before Saturday.

At half past six o'clock, the omnibus brought the through passengers to the Planters' House, and on stepping into one of the sitting-rooms, I saw a hearty, weather-beaten man sitting between two of the reporters of the press — the latter busily engaged in taking notes. It would not have taken a Californian to have placed his finger upon the new arrival, so unmistakably did he bear evidences of his long journey. Very little was gleaned from him, as the trip was made without any unusual incidents to mark it.

The names of the two passengers are D. JONES and C. KRAUSS. I know neither of them...

Sacramento Daily Union, Jan. 20, 1859
Letter from St. Louis by Southern Overland Mail
St. Louis
Thursday, Dec. 23rd, 1858

... The mail by the Southern route arrives here *[St. Louis]* pretty much like clock work. Since I have been here it has come in to the hour, with one exception, and then it was ahead of time. The twenty-first Overland Mail arrived last night. The **passengers report** an earthquake halt an hour after they had left San Francisco. They bring news from Arizona, and encountered a good deal of snow, but met with no particular adventures that I could hear of last night. All were well, and got through safely. I enclose the following items...

Snow on the Southern Route

The roads were in very good condition from San Francisco to Gila river. At the latter place they encountered the effects of recent rains in that region, and the roads continued in a wretched state the remainder of the route, but particularly bad east from Fort Belknap.

The coach was overturned three times, once three miles this side of Van Buren, Arkansas, and twice the other side of Fort Yuma, California, but, fortunately, no one was injured.

Twenty-five hours were consumed in coming the first seventy-five miles from Tucson. Through Apache canyon the snow was fifteen inches in depth. At Apache they were forced to leave the coach and walk a distance of twelve miles in the night, through snow two and a half feet in depth. By this operation, BEARDSLY had his feet badly frozen. He says he never before experienced such a night of suffering.

Along this portion of the route it required twenty-four hours to travel a distance of fifty-eight lies.

A severe sand storm was encountered on the Colorado river, which, however, did not materially impede progress, as it came from the west; otherwise it would have been the occasion of much lost time.

A company of United States troops were quartered at Tucson, which had lately left Fort Buchanan. Another, a relief company, was met at Apache Pass, on the way to the latter Fort. The condition of the soldiers was truly pitiable; many of them having their hands and feet badly frozen, and all undergoing the greatest hardships.

A Lady Passenger. — MRS. HALE, who lately arrived from San Francisco, overland, and previously from Australia, found her husband here most unexpectedly.

Sacramento Daily Union, Jan. 26, 1859
Making Himself Comfortable
BUTTERFIELD, one of the contractors on the Southern Overland Mail route, has purchased a large farm and beautiful residence, in the vicinity of Fayetteville, Arkansas, where he designs taking up his future abode.

Sacramento Daily Union, Jan. 28, 1859
Since my last, we *[St. Louis]* have had two arrivals of the mail, overland — those of the 3d and 6th of December. The first got in on the 30th, with two through passengers — A. H. CURTIS and W. W. WALLS — the other three having been left at Fort Smith. From San Francisco to the Colorado, the roads are reported good, but from the latter point until the passengers struck the Pacific Railroad, they were in a wretched condition.

The mail which left San Francisco on the 6th arrived here on Saturday night last.

Sacramento Daily Union, Jan. 29, 1859, page 2
The number of letters sent by the Overland mail to and from California, is still quite small, though gradually increasing. The highest number that has yet gone into the bag for St. Louis and Memphis is 1,068. Since the first of the year, the contents of the mail have been 800 and 1000 letters, each time. A month since, a little rising of 500 letters were sent. This shows that our Overland mail facilities are gradually coming into use, and we are advised that a good portion of the correspondence of mercantile classes in San Francisco is forwarded by the Southern route. The proportion of letters sent to western cities in the Overland bag is about five per cent, of the whole number, and the number of letters dispatched under three cent stamps is about one in five, or twenty per cent, of the entire mail. The people of the East do not seem to have yet awakened

to an appreciation of the advantages of more frequent communication with the Pacific. About two-thirds as many letters as leave California by the Overland mail are received by that route, at San Francisco. A few letters are sent and received by the Central or Placerville mail every week. The bag by this route is made up every Thursday at San Francisco.

Sacramento Daily Union, Feb. 9, 185, page 4
Letter By The Southern Overland Mail.

From Our Special Correspondent. St Louis, Thursday, Jan. 13, 1859. ...On Thursday evening, the 11th January, the twenty-seventh Overland Mail arrived here *[St. Louis]*, having left San Francisco at noon on the 17th of December. On the same day of its arrival in St. Louis, as we were informed by telegraph, but at an earlier hour, the mail reached Memphis. This was owing to the fact that the line through Arkansas has been improved, by the addition of stock.

Sacramento Daily Union, Feb. 12, 1859, page 2

The following account of a fatal affray at Fort Yuma is from the *Bulletin:*

"A shooting affray occurred at Fort Yuma on the 2d instant. The parties were EDWARD GEORGE, formerly of Adams & Co.'s, and subsequently of the Pacific Express Company, of San Francisco, and ALEXANDER BUCHANAN, an employee of the Overland Mail Company; WILLIAM TWILLEY, stage driver, and a fourth, whose name I do not know. They were playing cards for a can of sardines. George accused Buchanan of showing his hand to his partner. The lie passed, and both broke for their revolvers. As Buchanan reached behind him to draw, George fired, and hit him below the right arm, the ball passing through him. Buchanan now drew and shot George near the right nipple, the ball passing through him to lodge in the side of Bill Twilley. George fired again and so did Buchanan, missing him however. Buchanan fell dead about twelve feet from the spot where he first fired. George fell and is supposed to be mortally wounded. Bill Twilley is not dangerously hurt. Buchanan was a Walker man; he went from Calaveras county with a company."

Sacramento Daily Union, March 2, 1859, page 4
The last Overland mail, from San Francisco Jan. 7th, arrived here *[St. Louis]* on the _1st. The trip was a good one, weather fine, and roads in fair condition. One upset occurred, without injuring any one. It was laid over one night at Fort Smith, which delayed its delivery here fifteen hours.

Sacramento Daily Union, May 2, 1859, page 4
St. Louis Correspondent, April 7, 185
Quite unexpectedly the Southern Overland Mail of the 14th of March came in *[St. Louis]* on Tuesday night last— the __th inst.— making the trip in twenty-two days and a quarter. It had not been looked for, and was not telegraphed from Jefferson City, as usual, and consequently took every one by surprise. There appears to have been no through passengers, at least none have reported themselves, and consequently there is no way news.

The news from your State *[California]* is quite as devoid of interest us that on this side of the continent. The last mail out of which we have any information made the trip in twenty-two days and twenty-one hours. Putting that trip and this together, it would appear that the Overland Mail is making about the same time as the steamers from New York and Panama. It would appear, therefore, that with an even start, you are likely to receive the news as quickly by one route- as the other.

*Commercial Hotel
Butterfield Memphis Offices
[building on the right]
The hotel was built in 1848 and
survived until about 1891.*

CHAPTER TWENTY EIGHT
Correspondent, *Memphis Avalanche*, Feb. 17,1859

The Memphis Daily Avalanche newspaper apparently made an arrangement with a reporter to make a trip over Butterfield's Overland Mail Co. stagecoach route traveling from Memphis to San Francisco.

The Memphis Daily Avalanche
Memphis, Tennessee
Thursday, Feb. 17, 1859, page 2

Little Rock, February 11th 1859

DEAR AVALANCHE: Holy Moses! Did you ever ride a fiery, hard-trotting horse, bare-backed, with a rope-halter for a bridle, twenty miles over a rough road? If you did, you can form some idea of my trip from Madison here *[Little Rock]* in the stage.

[Leaving Memphis by ferry across the Mississippi River, the Overland Mail boarded the train at Hopefield, Arkansas for a 24 mile ride to the end of the tracks 12 miles east of Madison, where it transferred to a light wagon or buggy bound for Des Arc, Little Rock and Fort Smith.]

Over roots, through mud and water for miles, across Arkansas railroads, *i.e.* white-oak rails a foot thick laid cross-wise *[description of a corduroy road over soft or swampy areas]* — in ferry boats at night, and lastly through miles upon miles of ice. I started from Madison at twelve o'clock P.M. on Wednesday. The stage was built to carry four persons, but there were six to go, and go we must, so they seated the corner men and drove the middle ones in with a maul. Once seated (or drove in) we started at a staving pace, otherwise called a walk.

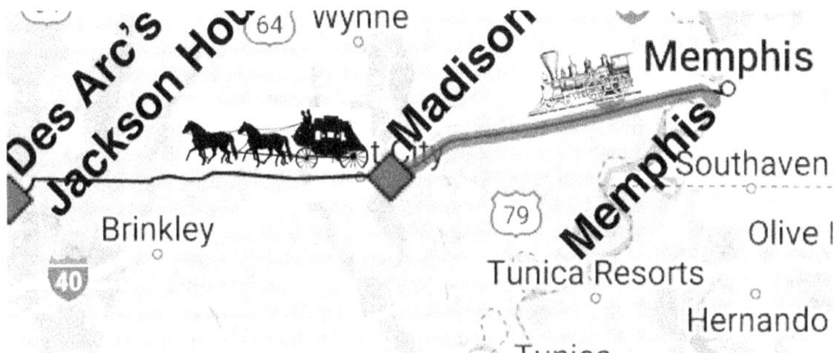

Butterfield Overland National Historic Trail, Des Arc to Memphis

I soon found all my companions were North Carolinians, and were a good, jovial set. They had been out from the old North State some six weeks, and were beginning to *pine* for the sight of a pine, and to long for some good, long sandy roads. I assured them that as to the first they should be gratified, and directly, when we had reached the summit of Crowley's Ridge, I pointed out a good-sized pine tree. What was my surprise when they called a halt, and, dismounting, took a good cry around the tree, embracing it, and declaring that — *"Boo hoo — it minded them of old Carliner and the light — goo-hoo-hoo—boo-hoo-hoo!"* Seated again, one of them commenced *"drawing the long-bow"* and bragging on the old North State [of North Carolina]. He assured me that they only planted one turnip seed in the middle of a patch, and that when it grew, they had to set the fences back! Now it wouldn't do to be beaten, so I immediately told him of that famous turnip which was planted in St. Francis county, and which was pulled through the world by the Antipodes! I assured him that if he'd go about a half a mile off, to the right of the road, he could see the hole it made — (he sat on my seat) but he wouldn't bite.

Steamboat on the L'Anguille River ca 1908
Courtesy of the Butler Center for Ark. Studies, Central Ark. Library System

After a while we came to L'Anguille River, *[the Butterfield route crossed here about five miles west of Forrest City, and about twenty-four miles west of the end of the train tracks]* and here, by some mishap, the *[ferry]* boat got loose and went floating down the river. I thought the safest place was on the bank, so, as she started, I jumped off. The ferryman brought her back, however, and we started off and got along finely for about twenty miles, when we left the Carolinians swearing that they *"would like Arkansas very well if they could only see a little sand."*

An old ferry crossing the White River at Des Arc.
Butterfield's Overland Mail crossed the White River by ferry at this point.
The dates of this particular ferry's operation at Des Arc are unknown.
Image courtesy of Lower White River State Park Museum of Des Arc

We crossed the White River at night, and went afloat again, our two funny men (negroes) quarreling as to which was the best landing, the upper or lower, and nearly floated past both, so I hushed the matter up by knocking upper landing down, and directing the other to land where he pleased. *[Des Arc landing, where the Butterfield station was at the Jackson House]*

Jackson House Hotel
The old Jackson House, later known as the Des Arc Hotel, on 4th and Main in Des Arc was demolished about 2011. Staff at the Des Arc Public Library identify this as the original structure.

Next day (Thursday) we arrived at this place *[Little Rock]* about six o'clock P.M., having been thirty hours in the stage. I find this place very lively; every one seems to be trying to amuse himself, at the theatre, the legislative halls, or some other place of amusement... *[at Little Rock, the Butterfield station was at the Anthony House]*

To enter Little Rock, Butterfield's Overland Mail stage crossed on the Arkansas River ferry and stopped at the Anthony House on the southwest corner of Markham and Scott streets for mail and passengers.

Memphis Avalanche, Feb. 17, 1859, page 2
El Paso, Texas, January 25, 1859

Dear Avalanche: — In accordance with my promise, I resume my seat to give you a hurried sketch of things as they are along the Southern overland mail route to California. I arrived here *[El Paso]* but recently, having stopped for some time at Fort Smith, Fort Belknap and

Fort Chadbourne.

After quitting the valley of the Arkansas, I found the country mostly destitute of timber though the lands are generally very good...

I noticed, a short time since, over the signature of the President of the Overland Mail Company, as appeal to the citizens and Legislature of Arkansas for a turnpike road from Memphis to Little Rock. It is my opinion that that gentleman had not at that time traveled over the country lying between the two places, as there is scarcely a rock to be found on any part of the road from one place to the other, while the grade that would necessarily have to be made for a turnpike would answer every purpose for a Railroad.

According to the Nashville Union & American issue of Aug. 30, 1857 the first locomotive out of Hopefield was the "Little Rock." This Memphis and Little Rock Railroad engine #1 used in the Little Rock Division may be the "Little Rock."

Why, then, shall not the people of Arkansas continue to push ahead the *"Iron Horse,"* and let every day carry him a little farther West. I am candidly of the opinion that it would cost more to build a turnpike, even after the grading is done, than it would be to lay the ties and iron for a railroad, especially through the White river, St. Francis and Mississippi bottoms.

If I mistake not, the [train] cars are now running on the Memphis and Little Rock Road to the East bank of the St. Francis [river]. Let those, then, interested in the early prosperity of that State, continue to battle with every obstacle that may be thrown in their way, and I will venture to suggest that ere the term of the Overland Mail Company expires, the locomotive will be heard to whistle on the *Llano Estacado* of Western Texas, directly from Memphis to the El Dorado of the Pacific State. But, as I have already made this communication too long, I will lay down my pen. I shall probably write you again from San Antonio, as it is my intention to go there soon. Till then, adieu.   INGOMAR.

Leaving Memphis by ferry to cross the Mississippi and board a train for a short 24 mile trip to the end of the tracks near Madison, Arkansas. Much of the railroad track across the "great Swamp" between the Mississippi and Madison, Arkansas was elevated on trestles. No period photo exist of this stretch of track, however this particular image of similar trestle is near Rogers, Arkansas.

Brigadier-General Benjamin McCulloch
(November 11, 1811 – March 7, 1862)

CHAPTER TWENTY NINE
Major Ben McCulloch, Texas Ranger, February 1859

The route from Memphis to Little Rock continued to shift due to river wa-ter dropping too low, or excessive rains turning the roads through the eastern swamps into quagmire. In mid-February 1859, Texas Ranger Major Ben Mc-Cullough traveled from Fort Smith to Memphis. He reports that the route still had problems, and it was his impression that there was a Yankee plot to kill the Memphis branch by making service intolerable.

In February of 1859 Major McCulloch traveled north from Guaymas, Mexico to Los Angeles where he boarded Butterfield's Overland Mail Co. stagecoach bound for Memphis, Tennessee, and then on to Washington D.C.

Major McCulloch made his impressions of the Butterfield well known through a series of interviews with several newspapers, as reproduced below.

Newspapers of the day often spelt his name "McCollough."

The Sacramento Bee, Sacramento, California
Thursday, February 10, 1859, page 3

TELEGRAPHIC — Col. Ben McCullough, has arrived on the 10th January, overland, at Guaymas.

[NOTE: Guaymas, Mexico is 600 miles southeast of San Diego, California.]

Memphis Daily Avalanche, Memphis, Tennessee
February 16, 1859, page 3

PERSONAL. — Major Ben. McCullough, the gallant pi-oneer, is at the Gayso House.

[NOTE: The two newspaper notices above help to determine that Maj. McCol-loch's trip on Butterfield's Overland stagecoaches took place sometime between January 10th and February 16th, 1859.]

Memphis Daily Avalanche, Memphis, Tennessee
February 18, 1859, page 2
The Overland Mail Establishment
Cheat and a Humbug

Butterfield & Co. contracted with the Post Office Department to carry a semi-weekly mail overland, in four-horse post coaches, from the city of San Francisco, California, to St. Louis, Missouri, and Memphis, Tennessee. For this service they are to receive the neat little sum of $600,000 per annum — a sum amply remunerative, and for which the public have a right to expect a full and complete compliance with the aforesaid contract. In this reasonable expectation, however, the citizens of Memphis, at least, have been most egregiously disappointed. So far as this city is concerned, the overland mail route establishment has proven a humbug and a cheat; and for this Butterfield & Co. are responsible, as we think the facts will abundantly show.

The overland mail route branches at Fort Smith, Arkansas — one branch leading to St. Louis and the other to this point *[Memphis]*. The St. Louis branch, we understand, is under the direct ownership and control of BUTTERFIELD & CO. We further understand that it is well stocked and well managed; that it is provided with every facility for the safe and rapid transportation of the mails and passengers; that every encouragement is held out to travelers to go over it in preference to all other routes, and that, in fact, there is, as to it a full and entire compliance with the requirements of the contract.

The Memphis branch, however, is managed very differently. With the exception of about eighty miles – the distance from Fort Smith to Dardanelle – the Company have let this route to other parties. From the latter point to Little Rock, the sub-contractors have stocked it with considerable little two and three-horse coaches into which they often cram two or three persons more than they can comfortably contain, and with which they creep rather than travel along their Journey. Delays too, are continually occurring upon the route.

MAJ. BEN MCCULLOUGH, who has just passed over it, informed us while in this city *[Memphis]*, two days ago, that he was delayed three hours at Fort Smith *after St. Louis stage had left;* that he was also delayed five hours at Dardanelle, and seven hours between the latter point and Little Rock. At Dardanelle the mail was put upon horses, and the passengers compelled to crawl along in two three-horse coaches, at the rate of little more than three miles per hour.

These facts explain why it is that the passengers and mails for Memphis, upon a better road, and a shorter distance of nearly two hundred and fifty miles less travel than those for St. Louis, are some times twenty-four hours behind the other in reaching their destination, when they should be thirty hours in advance.

MAJ. MCCULLOUGH further states that at Fort Smith, and every point, the impression is sought to be that the St. Louis line is the main route, while the one to Memphis is spoke of as a mere branch, and every means and power of the agents and employees of the Company used to induce passengers to take the former instead of the latter. Such open and flagrant violations of the terms of their contract, and such marked and barefaced favoritism should not and must not be tolerated.

MESSRS. BUTTERFIELD & CO. are public agents in the employment and service of the Government, and they have no right to use their position — as it is evident they are doing — to benefit one portion of the country to the prejudice of another.

Memphis and the Southern Stages are as much entitled to the advantages growing out of the establishment of the overland mail route as St. Louis and the Northern States, and if MESSRS. BUTTERFIELD & CO. cannot or will not do us justice, it is the duty of the Department at Washington to cancel their contract, and place some more capable, more honest and more equitably disposed persons in their stead. There must be a change, and that quickly, for the whole thing, as at present arranged and conducted, is a fraud upon the Government, and an insult to the Southern people.

Weekly Arkansas Gazette
Little Rock, Arkansas, Sat., Feb. 19, 1859
Maj. McCullough informs us, further, that instead of being forwarded by the stages of Butterfield & Co. immediately, as were the St. Louis passengers, the Arkansas and Memphis passengers were detained at Fort Smith from twelve till half past three o'clock; and on the route, that they were detained at Dardanelle from eight o'clock in the forenoon until one o'clock in the afternoon; that they were **detained at Mr. Plummer's in Conway County,** *[see images on following page]* from ten o'clock at night until five o'clock next morning.

It took the stages from five o'clock in the morning until six o'clock in the evening to reach Little Rock — a distance of only forty-three miles; and they were detained at Little Rock from six o'clock Saturday evening until the next Monday at four o'clock in the morning — making, in all a detention of more than forty-eight hours from the time of the arrival of the stages at Fort Smith, until their departure from Little Rock for Memphis.

Signature of Confederate Brig. General Ben McCulloch.

Samuel Plummer's Station
Maj. McCullough was delayed at Plummer's station for 7 hours overnight.

Plummer's Station House & Leather Shop were both standing in 2021.

The leather shop is still standing but the Station collapsed in Dec. 2022.

Quarters for enslaved at Plummer's Station were still standing in 1987.

The barn at Plummer's Station was still standing in 1987.

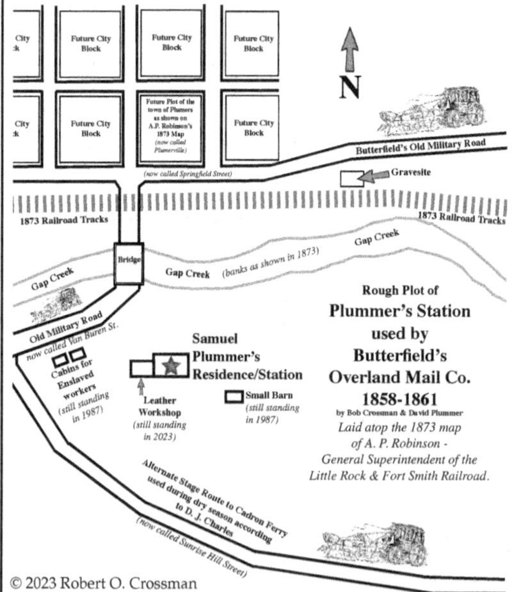

Samuel Plummer purchased 160 acres and built his home in 1830 along with an adjoining leather shop on the Old Military Road.

In 1858 until 1861 it served as a swing station for Butterfield's Overland Mail Co.

Photos of the enslaved cabins, and assistance in drawing this rough plot, compliments of David Plummer.

Major Ben McCullough
as reported in the Weekly Arkansas Gazette, Little Rock, Arkansas
Saturday, February 19, 1859, page 2

Among the distinguished arrivals of the week, we note that of **Major Ben McCullough**, of Texas. We have known Major McCullough for several years, and in many respects, he is a man of decided mark. His participation in the frontier scenes of Texas, and his long service, and many daring deeds, as a Texas Ranger, are matters belonging to the history of the times; and, if future historians do him justice, he will rank among the first, and most prominent, of the early Texans.

He came to this place *[Little Rock]* from Sonora, Mexico, a great part of the way by the overland California stages. From him we received much valuable information in regard to the route, and the manner in which it is conducted; and on him we place great reliance, in having many of the abuses of the contractors remedied or abated – for he promised to see the Postmaster General, and confer with him fully on the subject.

Major Ben McCullough's Memphis Route Complaints
as reported in the Weekly Arkansas Gazette, Little Rock, Arkansas
February 19, 1859, Saturday, page 2

The Overland California Mail – The South Sold Out – Some weeks since we expressed the belief that it was the purpose of Butterfield & Co. to throw Arkansas and Memphis off, and favor St. Louis, and a more Northern terminus of the California overland mail. We had, last Sunday, the pleasure of meeting **Major Ben McCullough**, of Texas, who came a passenger, by this route, from the Plains, and from a conversation with him, we regret to say that our previous fears were confirmed, and we have now so doubt of the fact that it is the deliberate intention of Butterfield & Co. to divert the travel from the Arkansas route and turn it to St. Louis, the distance to which point is greater, and the road rougher, than by the Arkansas and Memphis route.

MAJOR MCCULLOUGH says that the agents and strikers over the whole line west of Fort Smith, speak of St. Louis as the route for travelers – no allusion is made to the Arkansas [Fort Smith to Memphis] route, and if passengers persist in making inquiries as to it, they speak of it only as a branch, and as subordinate and inferior, in every respect, to the St. Louis route.

MAJOR MCCULLOUGH informs us, further, that instead of being forwarded by the stages of BUTTERFIELD & Co. immediately, as were the St. Louis passengers, the Arkansas and Memphis passengers were detained at Fort Smith from twelve till half past three o'clock; and on the route, that they were detained at Dardanelle from eight o'clock in the forenoon until one o'clock in the afternoon.

That they were detained at MR. PLUMMER'S in Conway County, from ten o'clock at night until five o'clock next morning; that it took the stages from five o'clock in the morning until six o'clock in the evening to reach Little Rock – a distance of only forty-three miles; and they were detained at Little Rock from six o'clock Saturday evening until the next Monday at four o'clock in the morning – making, in all a detention of more than forty-eight hours from the time of the arrival of the stages at Fort Smith, until their departure from Little Rock for Memphis.

It is true that the contractors in this route forward the mails which are sent by it, so as to reach Little Rock and Memphis within or perhaps, before, the schedule time; and in response to our inquiry why the mail was not forwarded in four-horse stages as BUTTERFIELD &

Co. have contracted to do, we have been answered – because there were no passengers to make stages necessary. It does not matter whether there are passengers or not, the contract required that the service should be done – and the contract should be complied with. But has it not occurred to those apologists why no passengers come by this route! The reason is plain: it is because there are not stage facilities on it to convey them to Memphis as soon as Butterfield & Co. convey them to St. Louis on the other route. The grade of service is below that required by the contract, and the detention, on this route, enables passengers to get through sooner by taking the St. Louis branch. It is but fair to presume, if things continue as they are now, that passengers never will come by way of the Memphis and Arkansas route. This too in the face of the known fact that it is the nearest route, that the road is not so rough, and that the climate is milder, than on the St. Louis route.

Messers. Butterfield & Co. have sub-let their line from Fort Smith to Memphis, to a company of very worthy gentlemen residing at this place; and we are informed and believe that they comply with their contract with Butterfield & Co. to the letter; We say this in justice to them, because they are men who are in the habit of making no contracts which they do not comply with. We wish them the greatest amount of pecuniary [financial] success in their contract, to which we have but a single objection: which is, that they are not the principals instead of sub-contractors. As principals, they would comply faithfully with their contract with the government; as sub-contractors, they only have to comply with their contract with Butterfield & Co., which may be a very different thing from a contract with the government.

There is also an objection to sub-letting a mail contract, to contractors who already have a contract to carry another mail over the same route. It is that their duties, on their own contract, are paramount to, and must take precedence of, all other duties – and it might frequently happen that the faithful discharge of those duties would occupy all of their time and means, and prevent them from doing duty at all as sub-contractors.

If we intended that this line should be the fore-runner of the Pacific railroad, and mark out its way. Hence the Northern contractors, with their Northern interests and feelings, favor a Northern route. Hence BUTTERFIELD & CO., Northern men, prefer the Northern route and throw obstacles in the way of the Southern, which they know to be the nearest, best, and most practicable. Hence they sub-let their contract from Fort Smith to Memphis, and make special drummers of all their agents for the St. Louis route – thus paying the contractors pecuniarily *[financially]* as well as politically.

We are in the minority, and speak only for ourself – and we can stand the oppression and injustice of the government, and the bad acts of BUTTERFIELD & CO., as well, and as long, as any one. But we are anxious to see the majority, for once unite with the minority, on a question which all admit to be right and contend for their right as Southern men, all of which are embraced in the simple word – justice.

GOV. BROWN, the Post Master General, is a Southern man, and his letting of the overland mail was heralded as a great measure for the benefit of the South. Now that the South is about to have its benefits wrested from her, will he do her justice, by compelling BUTTERFIELD & CO. to do their duty, or procure some contractor who will comply faithfully with his contract! Or, as the Governor is said to have cast a longing eye towards the

White House, will he desert the South and "crook the pregnant hinges of the knee" *[quote from Hamlet, Act 3, scene 2]* to the North, the seat of power and of votes! "We shall see what we shall see."

Maj. Ben McCullough and the Overland Mail
as reported in the Nashville Union and American, Nashville, Tennessee
Sunday, February 20, 1859, page 2
and the True Democrat, Little Rock, Arkansas, Wed., March 16, 1859, page 2

Memphis Appeal of Feb. 17:

We had the pleasure of a visit yesterday from Maj. Ben McCullough, of Texas, who was *en route* for Washington City, from Sonora, and who came through Arizona on the overland mail coaches. Maj. McCullough states that the branch of the overland mail from this city *[Memphis]* to Fort Smith is most shamefully managed, so as to detain passengers at least twenty-four hours behind the mail, which is pressed forward on horseback, leaving the passengers behind.

There can be no doubt, from the statement of Maj. McCullough, that the branch from here *[Memphis]* to Fort Smith is a complete sham and imposition upon the people of this section, and that the favoritism of Butterfield & Co. has been carried just far enough.

We now call upon the Postmaster General to hold Butterfield & Co. to a strict compliance with their contract, or enforce upon them the penalties which the law and contract empower him to do. We have relied upon their promises long enough, and it would be criminal connivance in this wrong longer to indulge their impositions upon this section.

Source of Chart below: adapted from Postmaster's report of March 3, 1859, p.12

[NOTE: During the first three months of operation, after leaving Fort Smith, it took the mail to Memphis 3½ more days - always more than the 25 days required by the contract. If passengers were occasionally left behind while the mail sped forward by horse express, then the travel time for passengers would have been significantly longer.

Other sources place responsibility on the condition of the poor roads between Des Arc and Memphis, along with the sub-contractor's obligations to his other overlapping mail contracts that required different departure days and times from Fort Smith. The truth may be somewhere in between.]

A table showing the time in carrying the MAIL between San Francisco and St. Louis & Memphis, from September 16 to December 31, 1858		
Date Departure from San Francisco	Number of days to St Louis	Number of days to Memphis
September 16, 1858	23	27
September 20, 1858	26	28
September 24, 1858	24	27
September 27, 1858	26	31
October 1, 1858	25	28
October 4, 1858	26	28
October 8, 1858	26	30
October 11, 1858	26	29
October 15, 1858	25	28
October 18, 1858	27	31
October 22, 1858	25	
October 25, 1858	26	29
October 29, 1858	26	27
November 1, 1858	27	30
November 5, 1858	27	30
November 8, 1858	26	28
November 12, 1858	27	29
November 15, 1858	26	26
November 19, 1858	26	28
November 22, 1858	25	36
November 26, 1858	26	32
November 29, 1858	26	29
December 3, 1858	27	31
December 6, 1858	26	31
Average number of days	25.8	29.2

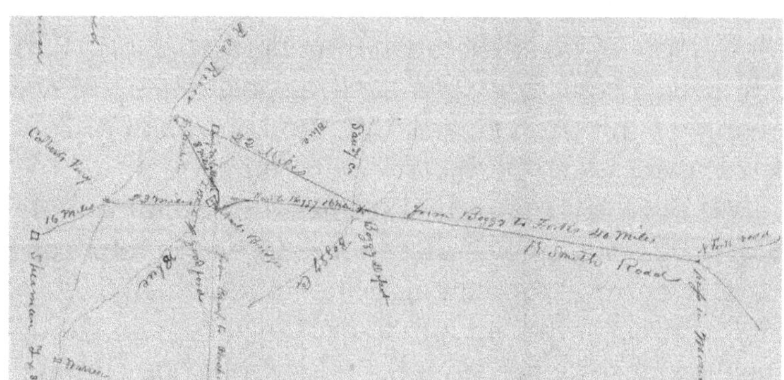

1862 Sketch of Camp McCulloch, by an unknown Confederate officer. Built near the Nail's Station on The Butterfield Overland National Historic Trail, about 25 miles north of Colbert's Ferry on the Texas - Oklahoma border. Fort McCulloch was the main Confederate fortification in southern Indian Territory during the Civil War. Built by troops under the command of Brig. Gen. Albert Pike. North is at the right.

In response to frequent criticism appearing in the newspapers, Superintendent James Glover answered:

James Glover Responds to Criticism, May 28, 1859
as printed in the May 28, 1959 issue of The Arkansian,
Fayetteville, Arkansas.

From the *Memphis Avalanche* – THE OVERLAND MAIL NO HUMBUG – Grayso House, April 28, 1859 – Editors Avalanche – Sirs: In your paper of this morning is a communication headed, "The Overland Mail a Humbug," which contains so many errors, that I cannot permit it to pass without correction....

Each of the mails that arrived there [Memphis] this week came in inside of twenty-three days, while their contract gives the company twenty-five days. Permit me to say to your many readers, and the community generally, that the [Overland Mail] Company have become satisfied that they cannot depend on other contractors to carry their mails and passengers and have notified them that they will put on their stock as soon as they can procure enough to stock the road.

Your readers should remember that the Mississippi bottom has been overflowed for two months, and the [Overland Mail] company have had to send their mails by boats, at heavy expense to Helena and from there to Little Rock, on horse's back, or wagons, or any other way they could to get through.

You have had as regular mail in your State [of Arkansas]. Your mails fail oftener on your railroads than they do by this route. Such staging has never been done on this, or any other continent, as is being done by Butterfield & Co.

Yours respectfully, James Glover
Superintendent of Overland Mail Co.

*Skiffs were used to deliver the mail during high water across Arkansas.
Image source: 1859, The Book of the Thames from its Rise to its Fall, p. 393*

CHAPTER THIRTY
W. H. WALTON, March 28, 1859

*The Daily Missouri Avalanche frequently sent a reporter to meet Butterfield's
Overland Mail Co. stagecoach to obtain a list of arriving passengers and in hopes
of obtaining an interview of interest.*

The Memphis Daily Avalanche
Friday, Feb. 25, 1859, page 3

... the mail containing the same dates reached our post office at eleven o'clock last night, through the almost superhuman efforts of the agent, Mr. W. H. Walton...

Mr. Wm. H. Walton, the indefatigable mail agent on the Overland route to California, in the service hence to Madison, Ark., had a mail to ship yesterday morning, and his troubles, incident to the effort, were most grievous. The mail is due at Hopefield, opposite this city, at eight o'clock, but the fogs were so thick that the ferry-boat dare not attempt to make the crossing, and, not to be thwarted, our friend Walton fed the proprietor of a **skiff** with a good round sum to make the trip with the mail. The mail bags were deposited in the skiff, and the oarsman struck out for Hopefield. He rowed lustily for a full half hour, and brought up at the bow of the steamer Belfast, a few hundred yards below the starting-point, on the same side of the river.

Hoping for better luck next time, the party braved the river and the mist again, and eventually found a safe harbor at Fort Pickering about two miles below this city *[Memphis]*.

The third and last effort was more successful, and Mr. Walton was finally moored at Hopefield, Arkansas, at ten o'clock. But his troubles were not altogether aquatic, for during the run to Madison the train met with an accident which delayed its arrival at Madison until half-past three yesterday afternoon. Mr. Walton did not reach this city with the overland mail until eleven o'clock last night; and when we saw him he seemed somewhat depressed with the trials and vexations incident to an Arkansas mail agency.

The Memphis Avalanche, March 1, 1859, page 3
...Owing to the injuries to the track of the Memphis and Little Rock Railroad, caused by the high water, which has effectually barred the passage of trains, the mail was brought to this city *[Memphis]* by hand-car.

Source: History and Use of the Railroad Handcar, railroadhandcar.com

The Memphis Avalanche
Wednesday, March 23, 1859, page 3
Flooding Inhibits Overland Mail Co. Delivery
THE OVERLAND MAIL — The overland mail from California, with San Francisco dates to the 25th ult., reached this city *[Memphis]*, by the *[steamboat]* Kate Frisbee, from Helena, at 2 o'clock yesterday morning. The railroad route

hence to Little Rock is so obstructed by the waters at present as to preclude the possibility of the passage of the mail over that route, and thence it is brought, for the time, overland from Little Rock to Helena, at which point it is met by the agent, Mr. W. H. Walton, and transported to this city *[Memphis]* by boat.

The last mail lay at Helena twenty-six hours, awaiting the arrival of the *[steamboat]* Frisbee. **Mr. Walton** will leave with the return mail by the first boat tomorrow for Helena, and will meet the forthcoming mail at Helena, Sunday next. Mr. Walton informs us that in many localities in Arkansas it is found absolutely necessary to transport the mails, for miles, in skiffs.

Normal Route When Floods Were Not Covering the Train Tracks

When floods were not covering the train tracks, the normal route began when bags of transcontinental mail were transferred from the Memphis Post Office to the Butterfield offices at the Commercial Hotel. Mail bags and passengers were then carried to the docks to board a ferry across the Mississippi River. Arriving at the train station in Hopefield, Arkansas mail bags and passengers boarded the train for a short 24 mile ride over the 'great swamp' of eastern Arkansas, arriving at the end of the tracks. A light wagon carried Overland mail and passengers to Des Arc, Arkansas where transfer was made to a stagecoach for the balance of the trip to Fort Smith. At Fort Smith, merging with the St. Louis stage, and on to San Francisco.

This is an 1858 map of Memphis, Tennessee by E.W. Rucker with bold text and arrows added. The location of the ferry shown here is from a map of Memphis printed in the May 14, 1862 issue of the New York Times

*Rev. Thomas McConnell Johnston, Eleanor Steele Johnston
and one of their sons, James Richard Johnston. ca. 1865
Photo courtesy of Janet J. Johnston*

CHAPTER THIRTY ONE
Rev. Thomas McConnell Johnston's Diary, March 1859

*The Travel Diary of passenger Rev. Thomas M. Johnston
on the Butterfield Stage from Missouri to San Francisco*

In 1859, Rev. Thomas M. Johnston headed for California from Missouri on the Butterfield stage. He became one of the first Cumberland Presbyterian ministers in California, founded a church at Alamo, Contra County, California and he printed "The Pacific Cumberland Presbyterian," a weekly newspaper.

His diary was transcribed verbatim by his great-granddaughter, Janet J. Johnston, retaining original spelling and grammar. Below is an excerpt of his diary, March 10, 1859 to April 2, 1859.

MARCH 1859

Thursday, 10 Morning cloudy & likely for rain. Stage from Cal. Passed this morning for St. Louis. Faired off in the evening & turned cool. Feel better today than I have since I left home. Very anxious to be traveling. Stage for the west, not yet arrived. Hope the Lord will protect me, & be glorified by me whether it be by my life or by my death. My heart is sad.

Friday, 11 Morning cloudy & cool but soon faired off. Stage arrived at 9 last night but had to wait for the Memphis stage *[at Fort Smith]*. Left at 10 A.M. Made a fine days travel over a good country through Chocktaw Nation. Stage crowded. A dreary day to me. I may be buried on the plains. Thy will be done O God.

Saturday, 12 Morning fair & frosty. Made a good nights travel, but I did not sleep much. Wind S. E. & very chilly. Feel badly. Met Eastern bound stage. Felt a little like turning back. Country not so good today. A good deal of Pine timber. No one any company to me.

Sunday, 13 Day cloudy & very chilly. Wind S. Crossed Red River last night. Reached Sherman at 4 A.M. Took breakfast at Gainsville a vilage in the prairie. Quite unwell. Feel like giving out. Country level. Praire country not much timber. Range good. Saw fields planted with corn.

Monday, 14 Sick all night. Too sick all day to notice the country much. Took pills. Traveled through Jacksville & Ft. Bellknap during the night. Range giving out. Though very sick, I feel calm & clear, & do not regret having started. God be praised for his mercy unto me.

Tuesday, 15 Day fair & quite windy. Making good speed. Passed Ft. Chadburn last night. Entered the Staked plains this morning. Feel much better today. Country level but poor. Green grass give out. No timber. Some Muskeet brush. Cannot think of home, but tears flow from my eyes.

Wednesday, 16 A very pleasant day. Feel calm & serene. Healthe stil better. Traveling on finely. Reached the Pecos River. Scenery dull & monotonous. Saw large herds of Antelope today. Traveled over a barren sandy plain. My mind constantly wandering to my poor distressed wife & children. Oh God take care of them & bless them.

Thursday, 17 Day unpleasant. Wind from the North. Traveled up the Pecos all last night & all day today. Not very well today. Did not sleep much last night, the road was so rough. Pecos is an ugly stream. Narrow deep channel runs swiftly & is muddy.

Friday, 18 Day fine. Crossed the Pecos last night. Took breakfast at a station where there are some fine springs & some pine timber, where we met a Surveying party. Crossed the Guadalupe Mountains. Feel tolerably well today. Wonder how my poor family are.

Saturday, 19 Day pleasant except high winds. I feel like I was recruiting some. Reached El Paso on the Rio Grande at 2 P.M. Stoped to spend the Sabbath. A Mexican town built of Adobies on both side of the River. Crossed the River into Mexico. Some find land in the Valley & fine vineyards.

Sunday, 20 A beautiful clear morning. The birds singing like Spring. Met with Claud Jones here. Had preaching here today. The first Protestant preaching every done. Preaching at 11 & at night. Had an interesting meeting & was very kindly treated. O God water the seed sown.

Monday, 21 Morning clear & beautiful. Day windy. Feel that I am recruiting some. Spent the day in writing. Wrote home & to St. Louis Observer. Left at 8 P.M. Had some flattering offers to remain at El Paso. A fine field for Missionary labors.

Tuesday, 22 Morning Clear & calm, but day windy. Passed Ft. Fillmore last night. Crossed the Rio Grande, & passed the town of Mesilla in the valley of the same name. A very pretty & rich valley of land mostly settled by Spaniards. Made a good days travel over a poor rough country.

Wednesday, 23 Day pleasant. Made a good days travel, mostly over a level somewhat sandy plain. Passed in sight of snow caped mountains. Writing every chance to Letitia. Health improving. Wish my family was along.

Thursday, 24 Morning fine. Day warm. Crossed San Pedro last night. In sight of snowy mountains this morning. Passed Tucson about 5 o'clock P.M. Situated in the valley of the Santa Cruz. Some good land & fine prospects of wheat crops.

Friday, 25 Day very fine, rather too warm. Traveling down the Gila River. Passed the Peg More vilages *[Pimo Indian Villages]* this morning. Some good land. Indians farming in their rude way. A good deal of Alkali. Wonder how all are at home.

Saturday, 26 Morning fair & pleasant. Feel tolerably well only. Day very warm. Suffered with heat & Alkali dust. Not much country today. Met the Eastern bound Stage. Feel very lonesome. Wish I was home.

Sunday, 27 Morning fair but windy. Passed Gila City last night & arrived a Ft. Yuma this morning. Not very well. Could get no breakfast. Had an awful time with dust. Caught in sand storm. Poor days travel. Lay be nearly all night.

Fort Yuma (on hill in upper right) ca. 1852
According to Gerald T. Ahnert, "Fort Yuma (top right), Jaeger's camp & ferry (top left), ferry (on river left), and trail on south bank (bottom center left)"

Monday, 28 Sand storm stil raging furiously. Dared not leave camp. Wind abated about 11. Left camp but had a pretty hard gale all day. Very unpleasant. Traveled slowly over a sandy plain. Not very well, & quite gloomy in mind. Dont know whats to become of me.

Tuesday, 29 Day fair but cool. Traveling in the Coast, or rather Gulf Mountains where there are some cove with fine Springs & some Spanish Rancharies, & herds of Goats, Sheep, & Cattle, & plenty green grass, the first for a long time. Made a good days travel.

Wednesday, 30 Morning fair & frosty. Traveling in a beautiful valley covered with rich green sward. Some fine buildings & farms. Appearance of wealth & civilization. Large herds of beautiful stock grazing. Scenery romantic & delightful. Passed Los Angeles at 10 A.M.

Thursday, 31 Last night rather cold. Passed Ft. Tejon at 2 last night. Morning cloudy & spitting snow. Sun broke out occasionally through the day. Traveled all day in sight of snowstorm on Mountains. Another month gone, & such a one I never spent before. Feel that my health has improved. God be praised.

APRIL 1859

Friday, 1 Day clear with cool chilly wind from N.W. Passed Visalia last night, & crossed Kings River. Traveling in the beautiful Valley of San Joaquin. Crossed Coast Mountains at Pacheco pass. Entered upon another month, but what will be the result. God only knows but he will do right.

Saturday, 2 Day fair, with frost this morning. In sight of San Francisco Bay at day light. Arrived at the City at 9 & stoped at the What Cheer House. Feel that God has been very kind to me. Feel a little sore & tired. Gained 7 lb. Since I left home.

In early 1860, Rev. Johnston sent for his family.
His daughter, Rebecca Johnston Yoakum's account of her trip
on the Overland is reproduced in a later chapter of this book.

Printed with permission of his great-granddaughter, Janet J. Johnston

CHAPTER THIRTY TWO

Jennie Whipple Passenger, March 23, 1859
as reported in the Saturday, April 16, 1859 issue of
The Arkansian of Fayetteville, Arkansas, page 2

Philadelphia, March 23, 1859

...I write and will give a hasty account of our trip to this city and of some of the things of interest I have seen.

After staying at Van Buren four days we took passage on the steamer Mary Cook for Napoleon, The accommodating Captain concluded that he would go no further than Little Rock, where we remained one day and shipped on the *[Butterfield's]* **Overland Mail steamer, Jennie Whipple** for Napoleon, thence on the fine passenger mail packet Kate Frisbee for Memphis. The Mississippi river at Napoleon was very high, only lacked seven inches of being to the high water mark of last spring.

Memphis is beautifully situated, entirely above overflow and seems to be rapidly improving, and will - doubtless, ere many years – be one of the most important cities in the Southwest, on account of its situation, commerce and manufactures, and being accessible from all parts of the United States by the Mississippi river and tributaries and numerous railroads converging from every direction. It is to be hoped that the citizens of Arkansas will awake to their interest, and particularly those immediately interested in the Memphis and Little Rock railroad, and second the generous efforts of Memphis in their behalf and complete, this road to Little Rock. That done, and half the battle is won. Such an impetus will then be given to internal improvement as will make Arkansas what nature designed her to be, the garden spot of the Union...

CHAPTER THIRTY THREE
Jennie Whipple Passenger, Mar. 26, 1859
as reported in the April 6, 1859 issue of the
Arkansas True Democrat, Little Rock, Arkansas, page 3

ARRIVALS – MARCH 29 JENNIE WHIPPLE FROM MEMPHIS

DEPARTURES – MARCH 29 JENNIE WHIPPLE FOR MEMPHIS

Notes by the Way From Pine Bluff, March 26, 1859

Mr. Editor: Your readers who have honored my notes with a purusal, will, I am thinking, conclude that I lead a rambling life – since no two numbers have hailed from the same locality.

One week ago, I left Memphis for Monticello, per *[the Butterfield Overland Mail Co. owned}* steamer **'Jennie Whipple,'** and ascended the Arkansas River to this place [Pine Bluff], and made the residue of the way in a hack chartered especially for the trip.

And here, let me remark by the way, that the **Jennie Whipple** is a beautiful little craft, with a gentlemanly captain and an obliging clerk, whose endeavors to render their passengers safe and satisfied, were unremitting. Speed, comfort, and safety seem to be their watch-words.

Pine Bluff has improved very much since your correspondent was first here, twenty-seven years ago. It was then a very small place. Now, it ranks among the best towns in Arkansas, with an intelligent and enterprising population. I notice several churches, an elegant court house, and there is here, as I am told, one of the best schools, both male and female, to be found in this latitude. It is under the charge of Geo. D. Alexander, A. M., assisted by a corps of able teachers. Mr. Alexander's name is sufficient guaranty that the school ranks the best in the State *[of Arkansas]*. I hear it spoken in terms of great commendation...

Sketch on the Jack-Ass Mail Route by Morgan Wolfe Merrick
"Overland Mail Party sighting Indians in the distance"
From left to right: Freman Tomas; J. Cook; T. Rife; Garner known as Clown,
J. Hettler; and a passenger. Source: "From Desert to Bayou: The Civil War
Journal and Sketches of Morgan Wolfe Merrick"

CHAPTER THIRTY FOUR

Passengers Report, March 30, 1859

as reported in the March 30, 1859 issue of the Washington Telegraph
Washington, Arkansas, , page 2

THE OVERLAND MAIL — The passengers by the last overland mail from California, complain of a great want of the commonest articles of food at several of the stations. For some 400 miles they report that a pound of flour cannot be obtained, and at many of the stations corn laid in for the mules was the only article of food they could obtain. This they *[the station employees]* pounded into meal, and with such provender were made to satisfy the appetite rendered keener by travel.

Persons going to California by land, we doubt not, would find it more agreeable and safer to go by the San Antonio and San Diego *['Jack Ass']* route. The mail *[on the 'Jack Ass' route]* is now carried in good coaches from San Antonio to San Diego in fifteen days, and there is a direct line of stages from this place, via Austin, to San Antonio.

1860 Fort Smith Downtown Businesses
The Fort Smith Post Office was located in Clines Drug Store

CHAPTER THIRTY FIVE

A. G. Mayers, Fort Smith Postmaster, July 5, 1859

Letter to the editor from Postmaster A. G. Mayers
as it appears in the Daily Missouri Republican
newspaper issue of Tuesday, July 12, 1859, page 2.

Daily Missouri Republican
Tuesday, July 12, 1859, page 2
Post-office, Fort Smith, Arkansas, July 5th, 1859

MR. EDITOR: My attention has been called to an editorial in the *St. Louis Democrat* of the 30th ultimo, reflecting severely upon myself, as Postmaster at this place, in regard to the performance of my duties in connection with the Overland Mail.

This editor exhibits not only ignorance in regard to the duties of our office, but mistakes or misrepresents the facts of the case. Let me enlighten him a little, then, as to the *modus operandi* of the Overland Mail, and as to what is expected and required at the Fort Smith Post-office, both of which are probably of more importance than the *Democrat* appears to suppose.

The eastern end of the Overland Mail route is formed by two branches, starting, one each, from St. Louis and Memphis. These branches meet at this point [Fort Smith] and unite in one line to proceed directly to

San Francisco. When I first took charge of this office, we were not permitted to use, nor was the office in possession of a **key for opening brass mail locks**. In a short time afterwards, the Department, in view of the great convenience that would arise from putting both mails (coming from Memphis and St. Louis) into one bag — forwarded to this office a **brass key**, thereby giving us authority, and, in fact, making it imperative that we should open the through mail at this point. This we have done, and shall continue to do until otherwise ordered by the Postmaster General. So much for our *right* to open the St. Louis through mail. *[This paragraph confirms that the Overland Mail bags were locked while in transit.]*

The Democrat also asserts that we have been acting contrary to the protest of the St. Louis Postmaster. Such is not the fact, for we have never received any communication from him upon the subject, and though we are always willing to be corrected when we are wrong or receive the suggestions of other postmasters, we must reserve the privilege of obtaining our instructions from headquarters. The gentlemanly Postmaster of your city*[St. Louis]* appears to understand this better than the *Democrat.*

Mistakes can and do occur with everybody, and we acknowledge that some mistakes might have been made by us when we first took charge of the post office, before we had become accustomed to the routes and changes of the different mails; but we object most strenuously to having the burden of all the mischief and mismanagement that may occur upon the Overland Mail Route cast upon our shoulders.

We do not know where all the fault is, yet we know of at least one mistake which occurred in the St. Louis office, when part of the letter mail for this place *[Fort Smith]* was put in the through bag, and part in the way bag.*["Through mail" was to be carried all the way-through the entire 2,800 miles route. "Way mail" was to be delivered to one of the 100s of postoffices along the way.]*

Might naught such a mistake have occurred with the Los Angeles mail? If there is any derangement in the Overland Mail, the fault is *not* the Fort Smith office, nor will the mere assertion of the *'Democrat'* prove it so.

Let this editor, before he again attempts to take us to task, be sure he is right, then go ahead.

Very respectfully,
A. G. Mayers
Post-master at Fort Smith, Ark.

1896 Fort Smith, Arkansas
The building on the right is the federal courthouse in Fort Smith (Sebastian County), completed in 1890. From 1890 to 1896, Judge Isaac Parker heard cases in this building. On the left is the original 1887 county courthouse.
Source: Encyclopedia of Arkansas, "Fort Smith Courthouses, 1896"

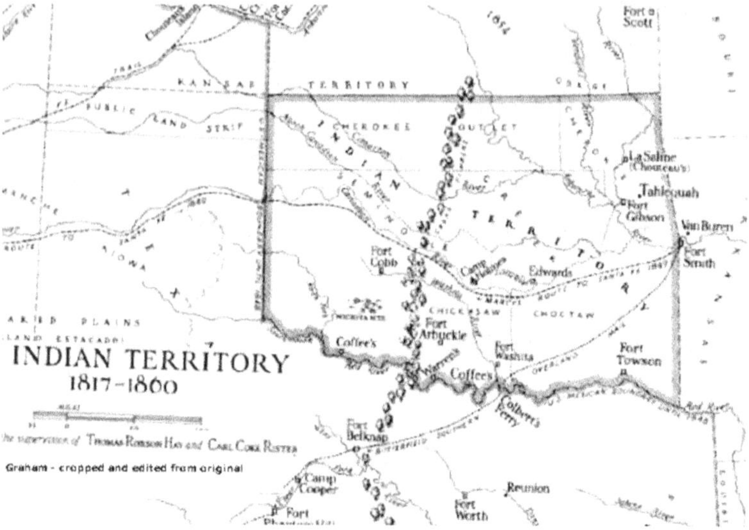

Indian Territory Map 1860
Image source: OKGenWeb

CHAPTER THIRTY SIX

"Authentic Source," *Daily Missouri Republican* July 11, 1859

It was the custom of the Daily Missouri Republican to report the arrival of the Overland Mail Co. stage from San Francisco, and for a reporter to interview arriving passengers who had a story to tell.

Daily Missouri Republican
Monday, July 11, 1859, page 2

An explosion of powder on the 19th ult., at Blue, in the Chickasaw Nation, killed two negroes and wounded six or eight others. About five pounds of powder had been mixed in a keg with some sugar and coffee, and MR. NAIL, who has charge of one of the stands *[stations]* of the Overland Mail Company, set a negro at work to separate them. A crowd of negroes, little and big, gathered around. One of them procured a coal of fire, took some of the contents in his hand, and put the coal to it. It exploded, and was communicated to the keg, around which the negroes were standing, with the fatal result already stated.

[The "statements below derived from an 'authentic source'"…]

The Overland Mail.

The friends of this great enterprise have watched its progress with much solicitude. At first, as is well known, it was thought to be altogether in advance of the time for the establishment of such a mail line, and Eastern people interested in the steamships, everywhere discouraged and ridiculed it. But, luckily, the then Postmaster General was a man of enlarged views, and was disposed to do justice to the West, and to give the contractors on this route a fair trial. They have done wonders. From the time of the reception of the first mail, now nine months ago, it has been carried with more regularity than the mail between St. Louis and New York. This fact of itself is sufficient to show what can be done on the line; but it is also a fact, that the line is beginning to be appreciated, both in California and the Eastern States of the Union, as the statements below, **derived from an authentic source**, will show:

*Whole number of letters sent and received by the **Great Overland California Mail via Los Angeles**, for the quarter ending June 30, 1859, from the St. Louis Post-office.*

Sent during mo.	April .. 10,647	Amount postage ......$ 907.01
" "	May 13,824	" " 1,057.28
" "	June 15,196	" " 1,063.33
Total number	 39,667	.... $ 3,027.62

Red'd during mo.	April... 7,960	Amount postage......... $606.30
" "	May 10,524	" " 781.95
" "	June.... 14,742	" " 1,233.49
Total number	 33,226	.... $ 2,621.74

There were 742 direct packages received, which were mailed direct to other offices, estimated to contain about 7,000 letters; and an English and German mail is also sent to San Francisco, of which no account is taken, but it is very large and the foreign postage swells up the amount. Two such bags were received yesterday to be forwarded this morning.

*Whole number of letters sent and received from and to this office by **steamers via New York and Panama**, for the quarter ending June 30, 1859, from the St. Louis Post-office.*

Sent during mo.	April .. 3,913	Amount postage ......$ 410.90
" "	May 2,066	" " 211.78
" "	June 1,767	" " 180.70
Total number	 7,746	................$ 802.48

Red'd during mo.	April... 3,012	Amount postage........$ 341.53
" "	May 2,580	" " 304.14
" "	June 2,040	" " 252.98
Total number	 7,632	................$ 898.65

It will thus be seen that, while the Overland Mail is rapidly increasing, that by the ocean steamers is diminishing; and this will continue to be the case. The Overland Mail will soon be the great mail for the country.

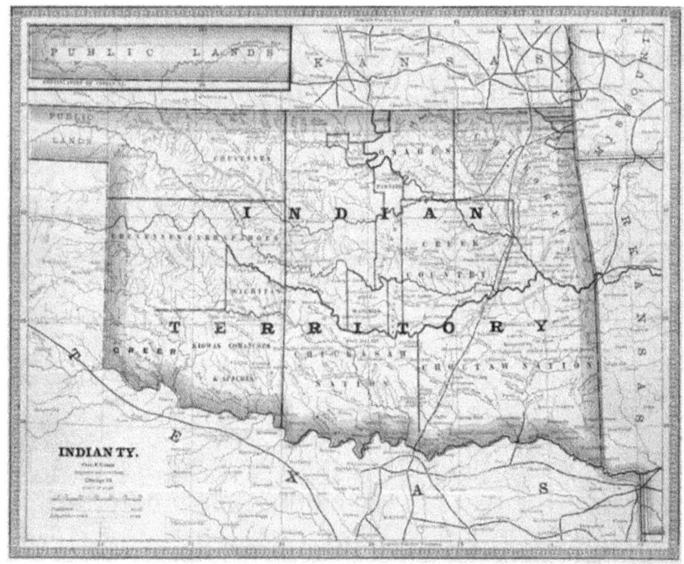

1883 Indian Territory (Oklahoma) Map

C H A P T E R 37

John Russell Young (1840-1899)
the 7th Librarian of Congress 1897-1899

CHAPTER THIRTY SEVEN
John Russell Young, August, 1859

I must express my appreciation to Dr. C. J. Messer for directing me to this 1859 series of articles by "The Wanderer." Dr. Messer, after a year of research, was able to determine that the anonymous author of the "Wanderer" letters was indeed John Russell Young. At the age of 18, in August of 1859 John R. Young boarded Butterfield's Overland Mail Co. stagecoach at Syracuse, Missouri.

Young was born on Nov. 20, 1840, in County Tyrone, Ireland, the son of George and Eliza Rankin Young. Brought to the United States when he was less than a year old, he began his formal schooling in Philadelphia, then became a ward of an uncle in New Orleans, where he continued his public schooling. In August 1857, he secured a position as copy boy on the Philadelphia Press, beginning a long and fruitful association with its editor John W. Forney. He later served as the 7th Librarian of Congress from 1897-1899 in Washington D.C.

The Press, Philadelphia, Monday, Aug. 2, 1859

St. Louis, July 27, 1859

A restless desire to get somewhere in the far West has prompted my present trip to the Indian Territory, which adjoins Arkansas upon the west....

The Press, Philadelphia, Monday, Aug. 15, 1859
"Wanderer In the Choctaw Region"
Correspondence of The Press
Camp, Indian Territory
Aug. 4, 1859

I am at last arrived within the bounds of the Choctaw Country west of Arkansas, after many knockings up and down, through weeks of travel upon railway cars, steamboats, and stages, and I propose to take up the account of my wanderings...

The trip from Chicago to St. Louis takes from 9 o'clock in the morning until midnight; and it is so tedious and dusty that the traveler is thankful when the *[train]* cars reach Alton, Illinois upon the Mississippi River, some 27 miles above St. Louis, and he can take the boat...

Visitors to Cape May know the corduroy road *[a road paved with hundreds of parallel logs over swampy or soft spots]* out to Cold Springs... You are tortured with an agony of doubt as the coach bounces and leans now to this side and then to that side, that you will be hurled into the opposite lady's bandbox, or have hustling down upon you with crushing effect the burly old gentleman weighing near three hundred, who sits close by with a malicious grin upon his rubicund phis...

Corduroy Road Fairfax, VA

St. Louis is a larger place than Chicago. It is a much older settlement. Chicago wharves are crowded with large ships and steamboats like those upon the Atlantic seaboard. It concentrates the commerce of the lakes.

St. Louis, on the contrary, lives upon the river trade. Her levee is lined with the peculiarly shaped, pugnosed, flat bottomed steamboats. When the water is high, everybody is busy as a bee, and when the water is low the levee is almost deserted, and gangs of men linger about or perambulate the river front, as heartily wishing for "a rise" as the fire boys upon a winter night wish for "an alarm."

There are Chestnut and Walnut, and Market streets, and Second, Third, Fourth, and so on, as in Philadelphia. Fourth street is the great business thoroughfare. Horse cars *[horse drawn trolley]* are run, as well as in Chicago. The hotels are as bad as bad can be.

Boat runners, runners for railroad companies, and agents for thousands of things, pester you every hour, and if you depend upon them without looking for yourself you are sure to be misled. When you find half a dozen agents, each publishing his route as this or that number of miles nearer than the others, the conclusion is that at least five of them are incorrect.

The people are in general not very civil, and when they answer you a question, you are impressed with the belief that, like the inhabitants of a certain part of England, they want to be paid for the information.

St. Louis is fast becoming a German city; as is the State of Missouri a German State. German emigrants are constantly arriving. Many pass through and continue on to Texas. I heard a say that they were damned Abolitionists, and should not be permitted to touch a slave State, for they would to make it a free State in a little while. Texas, it is constantly stated, if fast becoming a free State, because of the influx of the German element. If the vote were taken, it is believed that slavery would be abolished there, remunerate the slave-owners, at the same time for their property. These things I learn way out here near the Texas frontier, but cannot vouch for them from personal observation. This I do know, that in passing through Missouri the cleanest, neatest, thrifticat *[well managed]* settlements are those of the Germans. Already their vineyards have given a great staple, and a source of profit to that State. They are industrious and careful, and make the best of citizens. I should expect, from what I saw, that they would be welcome acquisition to any State.

Republicans favor Sunday theaters, Sunday dancing, and Sunday drinking, and the Democrats are for their prohibition

The same kind of a contest in reference to Sunday celebrations is going in St. Louis that you have in Philadelphia, with this difference, that the Republicans favor Sunday theaters, Sunday dancing, and Sunday drinking, and that the Democrats are for their prohibition. The Germans are mostly Republicans. Upon the outskirts of the city they have immense lager-beer gardens, and dance-halls, and theaters, which are crowded on Sundays. Sometimes a singing society will march on a Sunday through the streets, with flags and banners, and of course with the loudest kind of brass band. The fight waxed warm when I was there. The election may have taken place since my departure. If it has, you can tell which carried the day - Hon. Frank P. Blair's party or its opponents. *[NOTE: Frank P. Blair, a Republican congressman from Missouri (1857-58, 1861, 1864) at the outset of the war, he organized pro-Union military units among German-Americans which were instrumental in keeping Missouri in Union.]*

There is a goodly number of Irish in St. Louis. As one strolls through the city, he sees upon signboards, upon meeting calls, upon lawyers' shingles, and everywhere else, a noticeable proportion of Macs *[people with last names such as McDonald]* and euphonious jingle belonging most usually to the descendants of bright-eyed Erin. *[Erin is an archaic name for Ireland.]* The Irish emigrants are found in hotels, upon the levee, in steamboats, and along the line of the railways, as well as in the various business vocations. I was struck with one peculiar fact: For three or four squares at the upper end of Fourth Street, there is scarce a house not occupied as a drinking shop. Upon one side they are all German, and upon the other all Irish. In the evenings the lodgers upon the one side are seated upon the benches outside upon the pavement, smoking all sorts of pipes, and discussing politics apathetically in the language of their fatherland, and opposite the benches are equally crowded with excited Hibernians, *[NOTE: Hibernia is the Classical Latin name for the island of Ireland.]* constantly getting fire for their pipes, which go out in the moments when venting their opinions in rich eloquence and richer brogue.

Steamboat, "City of Muskogee" on the Arkansas River

I designed taking the boat for Memphis, then for Napoleon, then for Little Rock, and then for Fort Smith; but *"the best-laid schemes of mice and men gang aft agley"* [often go astray] My baggage was upon the boat, and I was about to start when I ascertained that there was no navigation above Little Rock, and that the boat was stuck in the mud between there and Napoleon.

If I had gone that route, I might, by good luck, have arrived at Fort Smith in a month. *[NOTE: Instead he bought a ticket for Butterfield's Overland Mail Co. stagecoach.]*

I took the Pacific railroad, and came to Syracuse in

Missouri. This Pacific railroad is to run west through Missouri to Kansas City. Not long ago it stopped at Tipton, over a hundred miles out, and instantly a wooden town was erected, with stores and drinking shops, etc., etc. It has gone since six or seven miles further, and Tipton is picking itself up and journeying upon the railroad to squat at Syracuse, the new stopping place.

New towns have sprung up as the road has progressed. You see it published that the fare is only five dollars to Sonora, or six dollars to California, and you at once look to see by what route you can get so cheaply to the new El Dorado; when you learn that both places are in Missouri. The road runs close to the Missouri River, as turbid and muddy a steam as ever existed. It has a color and is altogether in appearance like a thick mixture of potter's clay and water. They drink it freely out here, but I would not dare try it.

At Syracuse, after supper, I get ready my weapons and blankets, and was tumbled into one of the **overland mail coaches**, there to endure for an uncomfortable number of days and nights — to be shaken, and bounced, and rushed on the great **overland route** to California. The regular Missouri stage was crowded, and three of the passengers were taken in with me, as I was the only overland passenger.

**mud flew, wheels rattled,
and the heads and sides of the passengers were
continually in contact with the sharp edges of the coach**

The guard mounted the box, the driver gathered up the reins, the boot was looked to, the way-bill and the one passenger compared, then the agent cried out *"are you ready?"* The guard replied affirmatively, after which came the order *"off,"* and instantly we were whirled along the road at a furious speed. The mud flew, the wheels rattled, and the heads and sides of the inmates were continually in contact with the sharp edges of the coach.

These coaches are wagons, with light bodies fastened to the axletrees by thorough braces. The covering is simple canvas, upon a light framework. There is no padding inside, except the seat. They are made as light, and as uncomfortable, and as cheap, and as strong, as a New England builder could devise.

In this article, the author is describing one of the "Celerity" wagons, that Butterfield ordered from the J. S. & E. A. Abbot Company of Concord, New Hampshire. This is the only photograph in existence of a Butterfield owned Overland Mail Company Celerity wagon. Butterfield used two types of stages: a Concord Mail Stage and this lighter Celerity wagon. The driver of this Celerity shown above in the 'ten gallon hat' was David McLaughlin. This copy of a 1861 daguerreotype image, courtesy of the Nita Stewart Haley Memorial Library at Midland, Texas.

It is impossible to sleep or to sit in them in an easy position. But they make good time, never being behind, but always ahead of their schedule.

Every ten or eleven or fifteen miles, accordingly, as stations can be secured, horses and drivers are changed. Not a moment is lost; it being the business of the guard or conductor, who is changed only every hundred miles, to save all the time he can. Not a bit of care is taken of the mail or packages that come through. The bags and packages are thrown anywhere, under the seats, tread upon, and left generally to take care of themselves. A mail came to Fort Smith so wet that few papers were readable.

This ought to be looked to. The Government subsidy is excessively large, and it would seem from what I saw that the company only cares to make time so as to secure it without forfeit, and carry a small bundle of papers through from one side to the other to insure puffs and notices from the newspapers.

With all the drawbacks this is a grand undertaking, and **Mr. Butterfield** and his associates deserve praise for what they have done. It is the longest stage-route in the world, and runs through a new and wild country, inhabited mostly by hostile Indians.

Ferry at Warsaw, Missouri
"The first ferry was established on the Osage River in 1831 by Lewis Bledsoe, located where the site of Bledsoe Ferry Park, near Truman Dam, is located today. Bledsoe's Osage Ferry served the Boonville-Springfield Road, parts of which were also called the Old Military Road or Wire Road, east of town. Another ferry was later established by Mark Fristoe to the west." Source: Legends of America. com "Warsaw, Missouri-Rich History on the Osage River"

Swollen streams and deserts have to be crossed, bad roads have to be run over, and mountains have to be surmounted. I know the difficulties, for I experienced them for four days and three nights, going at a break-neck speed. Once our four horses, coach and all, came near being precipitated into the Osage River. We came thundering down a hill into the ferry flat boat; the breaks were tried to be put down when we got aboard, but they would not work, and we would have had an ugly bath if a little fellow in immense red-top boots had not caught the leaders and swung them about.

In Chicago and St. Louis everything is half dime - a *Press* is five cents, a New York *Herald* is five cents, and any Chicago paper is five cents. So in St. Louis. It is the procrustean bed down to which everything is cut, or up to which everything is stretched. *[NOTE: The "bed of Procrustes," is the arbitrarily and ruthless forcing someone or something to fit into an unnatural scheme or pattern.]*

It is in like manner traveling through Missouri and Arkansas. Everything is four bits, or fifty cents. If you get a corn dodger *[a fried, baked or boiled cornmeal dumpling served with greens]* and a piece of bacon - four bits, although the original cost of the articles did not exceed a half dime.

The station at Warsaw has been added onto and serves as a Funeral home today.

At Warsaw, in Missouri, where we broke our fast after a fearful night's travel, it was only after exhausting my lungs I got milk for a cup of liquid, by courtesy called coffee, and that the slave girl, half dressed, obtained from Sukey, who stood out near the hall door. The keeper of the tavern sat down and took good care of himself, and didn't care a tinker's anathema how his guests fared. If you were not ravenously hungry, you could not stand a dirty canvas shirt-sleeve in your coffee, or a dirty negro girl wiping a plate for you with her *hands*. The other stopping-places, with one or two bright exceptions, were similar in character. The supper I had at the last stage to Springfield in Missouri, I hold in grateful remembrance. It was more than **Apician** in its luxury of white bread and a glass of milk, and good coffee. *[NOTE: Marcus Gavius **Apicius** (14-37 AD), was a wealthy Roman merchant and gourmet, after whom was named one of the earliest cookbooks in recorded history.]*

At Springfield, my three fellow-passengers got out, and their places were taken by four others, bound for Arizona. I have seen **Pike's Peakers**, and I know to what utter wretchedness they have been driven to get into the settlements.

Pike's Peakers Crossing the Plains by Albert Bierstadt, 1859

I have told them Horace Greeley's accounts, and they utterly deny that they are true. All speak alike. One has just left our camp with a bundle as large as a good-sized loaf of bread, a stick, and a slim pocket-book, to walk to Sherman in Texas on his way to California. He said he could not make fifty cents a day, and he is able-bodied, and from proof yesterday willing to work. If only fifty cents a day can be made at Pike's Peak, the emigration had better start for the sand of the

Arkansas, for fifty cents a day can be made washing them.

I hope the *Arizona Travelers*, who go out to dig silver, will have better luck.

In Arkansas and Missouri, I was rather astonished to find so many settlements. Both States are more settled than is Ohio or Indiana along the route of the Fort Wayne road *[Fort Wayne, Indiana]*. But I must say that the farming is not so good, as it is in either of those States, nor do the people live one-third as well. They depend too much on their warm climate and fertile soil. They plant, and then let the seed take care of itself.

"The Arkansas Traveler"
"The Arkansas Traveler" was a popular comedy sketch on the vaudeville circuit. It revolved around the encounter of a (usually lost) traveling city person with a local, wise-cracking fiddle player. Various jokes at the expense of the "city slicker" were interspersed with instrumental versions of the song. To hear several version of it, go to YouTube.com and search for "Arkansas Traveler song"]

If you have heard the ***"Arkansas Traveler,"*** it is not a bad fit at some of the northern districts of Arkansas.

Sunday morning I was delighted, at daybreak, to see the Boston Mountain. I knew that in five or six hours I would be in Fort Smith, where I could get a night's rest. The road was soon traveled. We were ferried across the Arkansas.

The ferry was a flat boat, and the engine — two blind horses, working upon a turn-table which turned the paddle wheels. The captain was a fine, intelligent black fellow. He rang a bell, and the engines started; he rang, and they stopped. He rang yet again, and they started again. To put on more steam only required some blows of a stick. The rudder was a long oar.

[The painting below by Marjorie Reed depicts a Concord Mail stage headed down a sharp hill to the ferry at Van Buren. In fact, the hill was so steep, it is said that the stage would drag several logs behind it to slow their descent.]

"Down Main Street to the Van Buren Ferry" (circa 1981)
by Marjorie Reed (1915-1997)
Oil on canvas, 24 × 36 inches, signed lower right.
Sold at Auction: $5,750 at the 2009 Coeur d'Alene Art Auction.
[Actually a "Celerity" wagon, not a stage, was used on this part of the route.]

Of Fort Smith and the rest of my trip I will write soon. It was once a large military outpost. Troops wintered here, and during the summer have gone out to the Antelope Hills, where the Comanches are troublesome. Now it is one of the prettiest towns west of the Mississippi.

Mr. Cline, a Pennsylvanian, has upon Walnut Street one of the largest and best-stocked stores I ever saw. It was an agreeable surprise to know there was out here such a place where one could get some of the little comforts that we needed. *Wanderer*

1860 Fort Smith Downtown Businesses
The Fort Smith Post Office was located in Clines Drug Store

[NOTE: *The news reporter, John Russell Young, ended his ride on But-terfield's stagecoaches at Fort Smith. He spent the next few months ex-ploring each of the nations residing in Indian Territory, writing five ad-ditional letters to Philadelphia's The Press to report on this experience. He may have taken passage on the Butterfield to return to St. Louis on his way back to Philadelphia, but as of now no record of that has surfaced.*

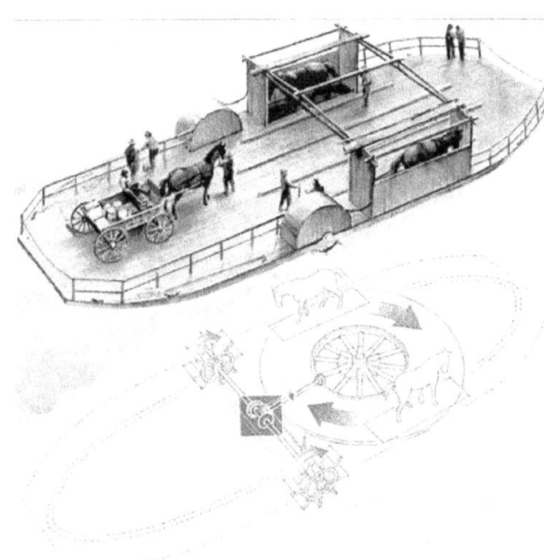

High-Tech Ferry at Van Buren, Arkansas John Russell Young seems to be describing a ferry similar to the 63' length x18' beam 'Superior Horse Boat Eagle' that was operating in 1841 out of Westport, New York seen in this sketch. This New York ferry was featured in the October 1989 issue of The National Geographic. William Tallack, in July of 1860 described this same Van Buren ferry in his journal.

Van Buren's "High-Tech" Ferry Operator
William Francis Hayman, operated the horse powered ferry at Van Buren that
was used by Butterfield's Overland Mail Company to cross the Arkansas River.
William F. Hayman is pictured here with is grandchildren.
From left to right: Abbie Hayman, John Hayman, and Will Hayman.
Source: The Press Argus, September 19, 1958, Section B, page 4

1870 Fort Smith store fronts include: Drug Store, Dentist, Stoves & Tinware,
Buckley & Welch Hardware & Dry Goods, and Apothecaries/Druggists

A Second Letter from "Wanderer"

as reported in the Nov. 7, 1859 issue of The Press, Pittsburgh, PA, page 1

Fort Smith, Ark., Oct. 9, 1859

This brave, enterprising little town *[of Fort Smith]*, far out upon the further edge of the frontier settlements of the United States, deserves especial notice. Its importance is not generally known in the East or North.

The first impression is that it is a military post, and occupied solely by troops and camp-followers. This is not so. It is more than a military post. Located at the point where the Poteau *[river]* intermingles its waters with the hurrying Arkansas *[river]*, upon high ground and in a genial climate, with a population of some two thousand souls, and standing as the chief source of supply to the traders and people of the surrounding Indian nations, it holds commercially the principal position in the State. As the eastern terminus of Lieut. Beal's wagon road to the Pacific, so near completion that but one or two streams remain to be bridged, it looks out upon the west as it is the most direct route to New Mexico and California. Herculean exertions are making, and have been made, by northern Missouri to prevent the profitable Santa Fe trade which it has heretofore enjoyed, pouring, as it promises to, into the nearer channel, which touches Fort Smith.

Fort Smith – the technical Fort Smith – was abolished last month, and Fort Cobb established further west *[250 miles due west]*. I presume that the buildings and enclosure, one part of which is in Ar-

Fort Smith Commissary Building Built 1822, still standing in 2023.
Image: Library of Congress ca: 1936

kansas and the other in the Choctaw country, will be used in the future as a depot of military stores.

In no part of the United States have I found more attractive society than that of this place. Every profession and occupation of life is represented. There are army officers, leaders of Government expeditions, intelligent Indian agents, good lawyers, skillful physicians, admirable dentists, energetic merchants, and excellent handicraftsmen. I state this fact, because it is not expected to find all these things so far West. If I had the pen of a Jenkins I would tell how beautiful are the ladies, how well dressed and accomplished, how sociable and delightful are the parties, and how New York and Philadelphia are ignored for remembrances of the entrancing gaiety of New Orleans.

"The overland mail - view of Fort Smith, Arkansas." Engraving depicting the Arkansas river, two boats, and buildings of Fort Smith on far side of river.

The warehouses of the merchants are capacious – so large, indeed, that they would challenge attention even in our large cities. There are many of them, and I will give a description of one for all. Bostick, Griffith, Pennywit, & Co. fronts upon Garrison Avenue, and faces the fort. In the trading houses at Hong Kong, China, one can find anything from a needle to an anchor, from a pap-spoon, to a coffin. *[NOTE: a pap-spoon is a spoon for feeding infants.]* So you can here — saving, perhaps, the anchor. Let us look in after the United States Government has paid Indian annuities.

As you approach Fort Smith, you find the trails lined with horsemen and horsewomen, and the roads covered with ox-wagons, like the old Conestoga of Pennsylvania. The scene in and about the store is animated to a noisy degree. Here is Bostick, Griffith, Pennywit, & Co's wagons are crowded around it; ponies, oxen, and mules are intermingled in apparently inextricable confusion; men and boys, pale faces, Africans and aborigines, ply long whips mercilessly, and jerk out deep-sounding oaths in half a dozen languages; the women and children, squaws and papooses if you will, are huddled up in corners, in wagons and under them; upon the edge of the sidewalks — anywhere in fact — and as a drunken Indian rushes in all directions with a fascinating eccentricity, you involuntarily get ready to count how many have been trampled to death, and are disappointed in finding that nobody has been hurt but the Indian himself. Everybody is *gee-upping* and *wo haking*; earnest and pathetic appeals are made to bovine Toms, Neds, Musics, Brandies, and Bucks, varied occasionally with objurgations *[harsh reprimands]* of great violence and stinging sarcasm. The whips, called Pike County revolvers, are wriggling everywhere their vast length and going off like the sharp, rapid discharges of a rifle regiment in action. One clerk is trafficking with a party of Creeks in their own language, others with Choctaws and Cherokees. Young Roberts, of Philadelphia, who has won golden opinions here, drives a pen in tho counting room that would astonish a Government reporter with the rapidity with which it covers paper; Mr. Dunne, a true gallant-hearted son of Erin, is everywhere, as if we were all aboard a sinking steamboat, and there were only five minutes to get everything ashore, which task he intended to accomplish, and over all this din and bustle presides, with clear head, quick eye and affable manners, Mr. S. L. Griffith, one of the foremost merchants and influential men of Arkansas.

**There are no bank notes
all trade is in gold and silver**

There are no bank notes, and all trade is carried on in the Jackson currency of gold and silver. I met one trader in the Indian country with $29,000 in gold. He was mounted upon a mule, had a twine bridle and a willow fixing over the old bag, in which he carried his money, for a saddle. He was on his way to pay his debts in Fort Smith. One would imagine, judging from his appearance, that he had hardly enough to feed himself on the way.

Another season, when the water is too low for navigation in the river, and the Indian country has been pretty well supplied, a silence broods over the town, unbroken, unless by some town-customer or a stray red-skin after firewater, or a Government train starting out with stores for the troops at the outposts, or the arrival of the **overland mail**, whether from California or the East, or the unexpected whistle of a steamboat that, during the hot months of summer, and when the sand has absorbed the water of the river like a sponge, has rolled along, one might think, upon the dew drops of the night before, for certainly a four-inch rule would sound the channel anywhere. At all times it seems to be an acknowledged religious duty on the part of whites, blacks, and copper-colored to get drunk immediately after they have reached town. I can attest that this is a duty unswervingly discharged.

Tho post office is at the store of A. H. CLINE. This,

beside being the largest drug store in Western Arkansas, is the chief news emporium, and the exchange for all the editors, merchants, lawyers, physicians, and principal men of the town, such as Captain Rogers, an old Pennsylvanian, and the founder of the town; Major Page, who understands well the resources of this section; Captain Montgomery, of the U.S. Army, and the efficient quartermaster at the Fort; the successful Mayers Brothers; Dotson, the first lawyer, and counsel of the Choctaws; Rudd Crocker, a young man in charge of this division of the **California overland mail**, and prominent for his energy of character; Mr. Stoddart, a merchant, formerly of Philadelphia; and the mayor, Mr. Wolfe, also formerly of Philadelphia, and so on. There are many others I would like to name.

There is no tannery. Hides are sent to St. Louis, from which all leather wanted is obtained. Mr. J. R. Kennedy has a grist mill, and an immense coach and wagon factory. He is popular as a public-spirited citizen.

There are two hotels worthy of notice: the City Hotel, the best, kept by Mr. Mackenzie, and the St. Charles, by Mr. Flemming.

There are three newspapers, all Democratic in politics. The *Fort Smith Times*, conducted by Judge Wheeler with notable ability, the *Fort Smith Herald*, a good paper, and *The Thirty-fifth Parallel*, ably edited by General A G. Mayers, postmaster, and a prominent politician. It is named in compliment to, and as advocating the superior claims of the thirty-fifth parallel route of Beale to the Pacific.

Van Buren, five miles distant from Fort Smith, and upon the other bank of the river, is the older town, though with scarce one half the population. It has a fine courthouse, large stores, and some elegant private residences, which, with much good taste, are environed with extensive flower gardens. It was here General Sam Houston, the hero of San Jacinto, and present Governor of Texas, flourished previous to the Texan revolution. It is not far off where he lived when he had a Cherokee wife, and was citizen of the Cherokee nation, savaged in Oriental turban, fancy hunting shirt, leggings and moccasins, leading a wandering life, and altogether as gloriously acting *"Big Injun"* as ever was seen.

Wanderer

*Built in 1851, the old U.S. courthouse and jail in Fort Smith, **was already standing at the time Butterfield's offices were just a few blocks away at the City Hotel.** The National Park System maintains, for tourist, the courthouse, "Hanging" Judge Parker's courtroom, and reconstructed gallows.*

Two Hundred and Fifty miles west of Fort Smith, near Lawton, Oklahoma — Fort Sill was established to guard against the Plains Indians' raids into Texas and Oklahoma. After the end of the Indian wars, it became the center of missionary activity in Southwestern Oklahoma. (Oklahoma Historical Society)

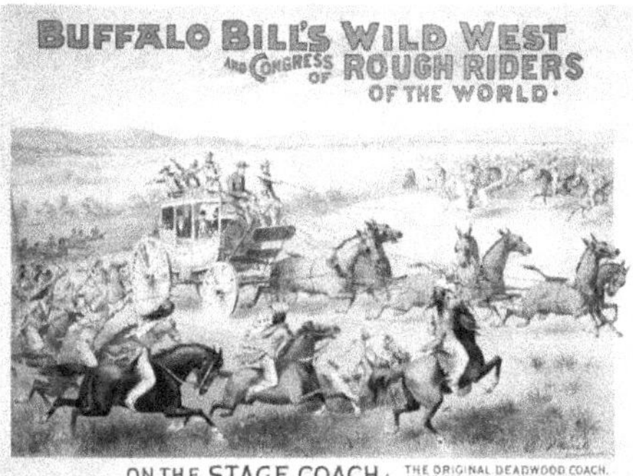

Authentic Poster for "Buffalo Bill's Wild West"

CHAPTER THIRTY EIGHT
Henry Everett, Esq., September 19, 1859
*as reported in the Oct. 29, 1859 issue of The Hydraulic Press,
North San Juan, California, page 4*
A Trip Overland

The following interesting account of an overland journey to the Eastern States, by the southern route, was written by **Henry Everett, Esq.**, an old and well known citizen of Nevada county, in a letter to one of his friends here, who has kindly permitted its publication. Mr Everett had just rejoined his friends of his youth after a separation of sixteen years. He writes from Metamora, Illinois, under date of September 19th, as follows:

"I found my way to San Francisco and on board the coach, without any accidents or incidents worth relating. We left the Stage Office at 12 PM., in a beautiful Concord coach, myself being the only passenger booked through to St. Louis; we had, however, a full load of way passengers — two ladies for Visalia, one from the ladies school at Benecia. We passed through the beautiful valleys of Santa Clara and San Jose, arriving at Gilroy in the evening, where we left the coach and took the wagon — similar to those used in the winter by the Cal. Stage Co.

Before day-light, on the morning of August 20th, we crossed the mountains by what is called the Pacheco Pass, and were invited to walk one mile.

"Tucson Desert and the 'Picacho' - view from the south" by William H. Hilton
Picacho Peak is located in Arizona between the cities of Phoenix and Tucson.
Source: Huntington Library, call number mssHilton Book 3, San Marino, CA

This brought us into the great Tulare Valley, which is an immense plain, without a tree in sight and almost barren. I thought it a very hard looking country, but have seen worse since. The dust and heat were almost intolerable; and I set this down as the hottest day's ride on the whole trip. At Visalia we left all of our passengers, and took on four bound through *[to St. Louis]* and one for Fort Yuma.

Next day, we passed around Tulare Lake, left the valley and crossed a spur of mountains running down to the coast.

A group of unidentified men camping along with their dog. Tulare Lake, 1880.
Image source: Wikipedia, "Tulare Lake"

Passed Fort Tejon in the night, south of the Tejon Pass. On descending the mountain, we found a fine country, good grazing and plenty of stock.

Tejon Pass, California

Arrived at Los Angeles, at 12 PM., three days from San Francisco. This is really a delightful country — the finest vineyards and the most extensive that I have ever seen — grapes in abundance but peaches and apples scarce. The hills are apparently swept as clean as a house floor, yet stock look finely.

We left in one hour, with six passengers from this point a conductor is sent with the mails, who usually travels about two hundred miles, when his place is taken by another. The driver's route is about eighty miles. *[Other sources say conductors change about every 120 miles, and drivers every 60.]*

As we leave Los Angeles, going east, the country grows more barren, and occasionally a belt of deep sand is met. Wherever we find a spot of arable land, it is generally occupied. On the second day from Los Angeles, we entered the Desert in San Diego county. Here we changed wagons, taking a lighter one with but two seats for six passengers. This rendered our journey very uncomfortable, and was the worse part of the whole arrangement. It was the fault of the agents in sending too many passengers, and ours in not being *posted,* and raising an insurrection at Los Angeles. As it was, we, who were first on the way-bill, had not the conscience to turn a fellow passenger out to starve on the desert, so we endured the inconvenience.

As we enter the desert, we pass between high barren mountains, through a deep canyon. We had been traveling at the rate of eight miles an hour, but now could make only four or five. The ground is entirely barren, except occasionally a sage bush. Fortunately for us, as we entered the desert, a shower had just passed, effectually laying the dust, though rather impeding travel.

Fort Yuma on Colorado River, 1875

We arrived at Fort Yuma in three days from Los Angeles; here we crossed the Colorado by ferry into Arizona Territory. The descriptions of this country that I had seen, were not verified at first sight. We traveled twenty miles over a dry, barren country, and through a suffocating dust, to the first station on the Gila River.

This is the field of the gold excitement, now passed away. They said white men could not work on the living they got there — Arizona straight, and beans three times a day. A few months ago, a great many people were at this point. I saw the ravine in which gold was found; every-body has left and the Gila mines are a hum-bug. As we traveled up the Gila, we found, instead of dust, mud which greatly impeded our progress, and from this point we lost time.

Gold Rush Miners using a 'Long Tom'
Image source: westernmining.com

The valley of Gila is quite narrow. The mountains on either side are high masses of barren rock, without a vestige of vegetable life visible —the road passing up within a few yards of its banks. The land on either side with irrigation perhaps might be made productive, but the people there say that water cannot be made to run in ditches, the soil being of so loose a character that water will sink and disappear — I do not vouch for this.

As we leave the Gila, the country improves; we find a good grazing country, but for the want of water. In this vicinity I noticed a very small *lizard*, apparently in the last stage of starvation, and remarked it as the first specimen of animal life that I had seen in traveling five hundred miles. Scarcity of water is the great difficulty under which this country labors.

The Indians are cultivating land in this vicinity,

and raise a great deal of corn. On the 28th, we arrived at Tucson, three days from Fort Yuma. This is a small place, built of *mud*, and inhabited by a mixed population of Americans and Spanish. The only thing attractive, that I saw, was a plate of *fried eggs*, and *I didn't see that long.*

As we leave Tucson, we find a splendid region for prairie dogs and rattlesnakes — coyotes won't live there. The country is rough, and our road, in passing through the canyons, was merely the channel of the water. The rains which had fallen before us had washed them badly, and in passing through one of them in the night, we drew into a deep hole and turned a complete somersault — *Douglas Democrats and all.* No damage was done, however, and we all came out right side up.

In this section some fear appears to betray itself in regard to the Indians. The stations are built of stone, with walls three feet thick, and stocked with rifles and shot guns, as though an attack was hourly expected.

On the 31st, we arrived at Mesilla Valley, on the Rio Grande. This is principally settled with Mexicans, but presented really a flourishing appearance. Water from the Rio Grande is carried through it by means of ditches, and excellent crops of corn bear witness to the fertility of the soil. Leaving the city, we cross the Rio Grande, travel down the east bank and come into Texas. In eight hours ride we were at El Paso, 48 hours behind time. We then followed the river down ninety miles, for a portion of which distance the soil is good, and in the hands of Americans would be a perfect paradise. Leaving the river and turning our course eastward, we found the country a little more mountainous, but by dodging through canyons we avoided most of the hills.

Water is the great want of this country, and I do

not see how it ever can be supplied. Some of the stations are forty miles from each other, and even then water has to be carried 25 miles. At one of the stations, we found the stock all stolen by the Indians, and one hundred miles further, at another station, the savages had, the day before, surrounded the house, firing some two hundred arrows into it, thus frightening the station keepers while they tore down the corral, took away the mules, slaughtered the cattle on the ground and left them.

We passed this station in the evening, and were warned that an attack would be made on us from a slough through which we had to go. Our six shooters and Sharpe's rifle were all ready for them, but we passed quietly through. Of course we were greatly disappointed in not having an opportunity for displaying our *fighting qualities.*

Antelope and deer abound in this section, also coyotes and prairie dogs. On the 7th, we arrived at Sherman, Texas, and again got wagons with three seats.

The country is much improved here, and is generally cultivated. Sixteen miles from Sherman, we crossed the Red River and entered the Indian Territory.

Choctaw Indians, Indian Territory, ca. 1860

This is a fine country *[Oklahoma / Indian Territory]*, well wooded and watered. Forty hours travel brought us to Fort Smith, in Arkansas.

Fort at Fort Smith as seen from Arkansas River banks ca. 1860
Image purchased from a dealer in St. Cyprien, France by Bob Crossman

The country through Arkansas and Missouri is much more hilly than any other through which we passed. We saw hardly anything growing but corn, and a portion of that was quite poor. The people through there are lazy — the country shows it. I did not see a man at work in the whole State *[of Arkansas]*. As we get north into Missouri, the country looks better, and has the appearance of better cultivation.

We arrived at Syracuse *[Missouri]*, the terminus of the Pacific Railroad, in 23 days and 3 hours from San Francisco. As the *[train]* cars had left at nine o'clock, we had to lay over; and, taking a berth, I did some fast sleeping, I assure you.

Next day, I took the *[train]* cars and arrived safely at St. Louis in the evening. — Our fare on the whole has been *hard* — bacon, bread and coffee includes the whole *[coffee bean]*. No *champagne*, no oysters. I got as 'poor as a shad' *[sickly]* at first, but gained on the last quarter and came in two pounds heavier than when I started.

only $35 for 23 days of food

The expense was only $35 *[for 23 days of food]*. Two meals a day was all that we wanted of the kind. At each end of the route the company use fine American horses; on the plains — mustangs and mules.

I learned to sleep very well in the stage, in a sitting position. The coaches are designed for passengers to lie down, by turning down the backs of the seats, but we were too full to admit of this.

Our trip was some two days longer than usual, but perhaps it was as well for us, for we got comparatively no dust, getting mud instead.

Butterfield's Overland Mail Route from San Francisco to Memphis & St. Louis

On the whole, I consider the Overland Mail coach a great institution.

I consider the Overland Mail a great institution

I am satisfied that the trip can be made regularly in sixteen days, by putting on more stock and making more stations. A great many of the stations are now thirty-five and forty miles apart.

I think less of the country than when I came through it. But a small portion of it will ever tempt white men to settle on it. As a practical route for a railroad, I think it possesses great advantages. There are really no great impediments or obstacles, no mountains of any magnitude, and as a general thing, a perfect plain.

I do not think we were required to walk more than three miles on account of hills. This seems almost improbable on a journey of 2,700 miles, when it is considered that we were loaded heavily all the way over the worst part of the road — having nine and ten passengers. One gentleman, sixty years of age, took passage at Los Angeles and came through without resting —still it is a hard journey — let no man take it for pleasure. For myself, I am not sorry that I have taken it. I have gratified an old curiosity to travel over "the plains." The expense of the journey is about two hundred dollars from San Francisco to St. Louis."

[Note: The October 19th article above from The Hydraulic Press reprints a letter of Mr. Everett dated September 19th. On Oct. 15th, the same paper printed a shorter account of Mr. Everett's same account, as shown below/]

Henry Everett, Esq., Letter of September 15, 1859
as printed in the Oct. 15, 1859 issue of The Hydraulic Press, page 1

The St. Louis correspondent of the Union, writing from that city under date of September 15th, notices the arrival overland of **Mr. Everett**, of French Corral, and as he has many friends hereabouts, we publish that portion of the letter relating to his trip and the incidents connected with it:

Among the passengers who arrived on Monday night were J. H. RAY, of Los Angeles, and a **MR. EVERETT**, of Nevada. The account of the trip, furnished by the *Democrat*, is interesting:

"The passage was rather unpleasant, and the mail was delayed about three days behind its usual time by incessant rains. — When but a short distance from the Colorado river the stage mired, and, in the effort to extricate it, partially overturned. No injury was done, however, to any of the passengers.

Another incident of a similar kind occurred when near the West Mesilla Valley. One portion of the stage sunk almost two feet, owing to the extreme softness of the ground over which they were traveling.

While passing through the Rio Valley, an attack was made by the Apache and Comanche Indians upon one of the stations, and ten or eleven valuable mules were stolen. About two days after that, the Comanches stole from another station nine mules, one horse and eight or nine beef cattle. They slaughtered the latter at a short distance from the scene of their depredations, and left the dead animals untouched, but took the horse and mules away. This shows very conclusively that the robbery was not committed because they wanted food, but merely to carry out malicious designs.

At one place they shot at the station houses with their arrows very frequently, but fortunately no person was wounded thereby.

Nothing of any importance occurred from the time they left El Paso till they reached the Arkansas river. When opposite Van Buren the stage mired, and by some it was thought almost impossible to move it. In endeavoring to extricate it the tongue of the mail coach was broken, to remedy which it was found necessary to go back about four miles to Fort Smith, where another stage was procured, in which the passengers were safely conveyed to Tipton *[Missouri]*.

The robberies committed by the Indians, depriving them of their mules, caused considerable delay, as they were obliged to drive one train 60 miles without changing, which was about four times the distance they should have traveled, considering the state of the roads."

Albert D. Richardson, 1865
Image by Brady

CHAPTER THIRTY NINE
Albert D. Richardson, Sept. - Oct. 1859

Beyond the Mississippi: From the Great River to the Great Ocean, 1857-67, by Albert D. Richardson, American Publishing Co. 1867, pages 214-238.

From pages 206 to 209:

On the fifteenth of August I again started for the far frontier. At Syracuse, one hundred and sixty-eight miles west of St. Louis, and then terminus of the Missouri Pacific Railway, I left the *[train]* cars for a *[stage]* coach of the Butterfield Mail Company. *[Note: Actually the official name was the 'Overland Mail Company.']*

Our coach, leaving Syracuse after dark, jolted along for fifty miles during the night, and at sunrise stopped for breakfast in Warsaw, Benton county *[Missouri]*— a genuine southern town, surrounding a hollow square with court-house in the center; streets gullied by water and overgrown with weeds; frame houses, log houses and stucco houses, with deep porticoes and shade trees; negroes trudging with burdens upon their heads; deserted buildings; tumbling fences and a general tendency to 'the demnition bow wows.' *[from Charles Dickens, means 'going to the dogs']* While washing on the hotel porch we asked the host for soap.

Landlord (imperious and tobacco-stained) — *"Soap for the gentlemen."*

Clerk (obsequious and flippant) — *"Soap for the gentlemen."*

Porter (white and Celtic) — *"Soap for the jintilmin."*

Waiter (white-eyed and Ethiopic) — *"Cook, bring soap for de genmen and be quick about it!"*

The cross-eyed cook, from Afrie's sunny fountain, at last appeared with the longed-for article; but the incident was a shining illustration of the Institution.

We forded the Osage though it is navigable above Warsaw for half the year. The region was hilly and rocky, intersected by many streams and timbered with a dozen varieties of oak; the houses long and low with outside chimneys; corn the principal crop; great numbers of cattle raised chiefly for the California market; and not more than one farmer in ten owning slaves.

After passing some beautiful prairies and enduring another night of uneasy slumber, we woke in Springfield *[Missouri]*, on the summit of the Ozark Mountains — the leading town of southwestern Missouri. Here was the office for the sale of Government land in that quarter of the State, amounting to three millions of acres. Some of this was subject to entry at twenty-five cents per acre; but settlers had secured the fertile tracts years before, and the residue was rough and sterile.

Springfield *[Missouri]* has pleasant, vine-trellised dwellings, and two thousand five hundred people. The low struggling hotel with high belfry, was on the rural southern model: dining-room full of flies, with a long paper-covered frame swinging to and fro over the table to keep them from the food; the bill of fare, bacon corn bread and coffee; the rooms ill-furnished, towels missing, pitchers empty, and the bed and table linen seeming to have been dragged through the nearest pond, and dried upon gridirons.

During my stay a half-witted negro was arrested for outraging a lady. In the fierce excitement it aroused, some hot-heads proposed collecting all the slaves from the adjacent farms, and burning them on the public square. Two years earlier, two negroes had been burnt at the stake in Jasper, the second county to the west, for a similar crime, aggravated by the murder of their victim and her family. Now, Springfield *[Missouri]* would have no burning, declaring it too barbarous. But on the second day a mob broke into the hall where the negro was confined, took him from the officers, who did not attempt resistance, and hooting and yelling ran with him to the outskirts of the village and hung him upon a locust tree. He seemed to die of fright, for he never struggled after he was drawn up over the limb. Leading citizens assured me that for the same offense a white man would have received the same punishment; but how terribly unjust the system which, denying light and education to these poor creatures, still held them to a strict criminal responsibility!

Many immigrants were passing through the town. I was told of eight North Carolinians bound for Arkansas, who stopped a few hours on the public square, and were asked innumerable questions. One communicative fellow replied that they were going to found a town; the pursuit of each person was already marked out, and there were no drones among them.

What was this man to do? He was to open a store.

And that? Start a blacksmith's shop.

And the other, standing behind him? Engage in sheep raising.

So they were nearly all classified, when a decrepid, white-haired octogenarian, venerable enough for old Time himself, was observed sitting in one of the wagons.

– 274 –

'Why, who is that?' asked the eager questioner.

'That's my grandfather.'

'What is *he* going to do? He can't be of any use to your settlement.'

'O yes,' replied the North Carolinian promptly, 'we are taking the old man along to start a graveyard with!'

Missouri with her unequaled resources of timber, coal, iron, lead, stone, and farming lands — with an area larger than New England, a genial climate, central position, and the grandest rivers of the world bounding her on two sides — was now prosperous and flourishing. Two years later I passed over the same route from St. Louis, to find the country blazing with civil war which swept away many fruits of the labor of twenty years. But it extirpated the poison that embittered her springs of life; removed forever the mammoth stumbling-block from her path of progress; cut loose the fetters that bound the young giantess hand and foot.

From Springfield *[Missouri]* I continued by coach sixty-five miles to the little, dilapidated settlement of Cassville, were I left the coach for the great Lead Region. *[Note: At this point, he gave up his seat on the Butterfield stagecoach, and spent several days exploring the lead mining region of Missouri. Lead was first mined in Missouri's Greene, Webster and Christian counties in the 1850s. The periods of highest production were from 1858 to 1918 and during World War I.]*

From pages 214 to 224:

...Returning to Cassville *[Note: Cassville was a station of the Butterfield Overland Mail Co.]* I journeyed on by the mail coaches, which over mountainous roads accomplished more than a hundred miles every twenty-four hours. Great pride was felt in this *'Overland'* line, and an old local mail stage still lumbering over the same track was derisively known as *'the underland.'*

Our first point was Keetsville - a dozen shanties which looked like a funeral procession in honor of Keets, whoever he may have been. The neighbors called the place 'Chicken-Thief.' Another hamlet a few miles to the southward was known as 'Scarce-o'Grease!' Near most of the farm dwellings were spring-houses where the matrons kept their milk and butter. Cellars were little known through Missouri and Arkansas because reputed damp and unhealthy — justly in a few sections, but unjustly in most.

After crossing the *[Arkansas]* state line we were jolted over the rough Boston Mountains, and obtained a moonlight view of Fayetteville, a pleasant county town with several churches, the United States land office for northeastern Arkansas, and pleasant dwellings. A rough village beyond is named 'Hog-Eye.' If not euphonious the nomenclature hereabout is at least original. The generous log house where the passengers breakfasted was kept by a widow, whose worldly condition a local clergyman on board thus described: *'She's got lots of niggers and a heap of truck.'* *[property]*

All day we were among mountains with farm houses few and far between; and at evening we looked down upon a pleasant picture. At our feet the village of Van Buren nestled among shade trees; immediately beyond, the shining waters of the Arkansas river wound through a rich green valley; still further, the deep many hued foliage of the Indian Territory dotted with blue mountain peaks melted into the deeper blue of the sky.

Crossing the stream *[Arkansas River]* by a ferry of two-pole power, and riding five miles along its deeply-shaded valley, we reached Fort Smith, in western Arkansas, on the border of the Indian Territory.

Chapter XVIII
Life at Fort Smith, Arkansas 1859

FORT SMITH is an abandoned military post, nominally head of navigation on the Arkansas, (Indian: smoky, bow-shaped river,) though steamers *[Steamboats]* ascend to it only half the year. At high water they run one hundred and sixty miles above to Fort Gibson.

The pleasant town *[of Fort Smith]* now contained three thousand people. Its chief trade was with the neighboring Cherokees and Choctaws. By law, debts contracted by the Indians out of their own Territory could not be collected; but the Fort Smith merchants trusted them freely and were faithfully paid.

Every day scores of Aborigines added picturesqueness to the streets. The men wore gay, fringed frocks instead of coats, and red kerchiefs or turbans for hats; but otherwise dressed like whites. The petticoats and frocks of the women displayed as many colors of the rainbow as their purses would permit.

Though more civilized than any other tribes the males scorned labor. Often one trudged empty-handed up from the ferry, while behind toiled his squaw with a heavy keg or other burden upon her shoulders, and one of their negro slaves also unencumbered brought up the rear. He came as interpreter; the negroes all spoke English while many of their Indian masters did not.

According to my voluble landlord there were many slaves about Fort Smith. In winter especially, field hands had a far easier time than their masters. They were well supplied with spending money and went to a frolic almost every night:

'I overseed for three years on a Louisiana cotton plantation. There the niggers have to work right on through the winter, for that's the picking season. They begin at daylight and keep at it till dark; an overseer follows them with a big whip, and you'd think at first that they had a powerful hard

time. But no matter how tight they are worked, just let them get together at night with a fiddle, and Lord, — how they will frolic! Keep it up till morning too, dancing and singing. That's the place for niggers; put them in the South and they are just happy.

'The man I overseed for was a mighty fine master — kind, but right strict. He kept them well clothed, for half of them are too careless to look out for the future. Growing cotton is the most profitable business in the world; the planters don't raise any thing else except a few sweet potatoes, but buy all their provisions. Picking cotton is the great thing. A woman will pick faster than a man, but a child twelve years old will frequently beat them both. It can't be learned — it's a kind of sleight[matter of dexterity]. *Those planters think nothing of paying twenty-five hundred dollars for a good picker.'*

'Are there many slaves among the Indians, across the river?'

'Yes sir. John Ross governor of the Cherokees has over a hundred; and there's a right smart sprinkling through the whole nation.'

'How are they treated?'

'Badly. The Cherokees and Choctaws don't govern them; in fact, the niggers are masters and do about as they please.'

The negroes of Fort Smith had Methodist and Baptist churches. Like the temples of the whites, these places of worship had no bells; and the Sunday morning congregations were called together by the tooting of a dozen horns — a ludicrous form of the church-going bell.

Many negroes had bought their freedom, and some had

THE CHURCH-GOING BELL.
Image by Stephens, Engraving by Richardson

acquired considerable property. Several laundresses and nurses first redeemed themselves, and then their husbands and children. But the Arkansas legislature had passed a stringent law requiring every free negro remaining in the State after January 1860, to be sold as a slave, and have his property confiscated to the county. He was graciously permitted to choose a master, who after paying his appraised value would own him absolutely. In western Arkansas schools are very rare, and many children grow up incredibly ignorant. At the time of my visit several of the State legislators were unable to write their own names.

Outside of the few large towns, the epicurean tourist endures many tribulations. In rich stock-growing regions he finds sweet milk for his tea and coffee a rarity, and for drinking a myth. Butter seldom visits his table, but sometimes confronts him laden with odors never wafted from Araby the Blest. *[reference to Paradise Lost by John Milton, 'winds blow Sabean odours from the spicy shore Of Araby the blest..']* Of strong coffee, sour milk as a beverage, molasses, hot heavy biscuit with saleratus *[baking powder]* visible to the naked eye, and fat pork floating in gravy, he will find in abundance. Pastry may haunt his dreams, but seldom his repasts. Even the inevitable corn-bread, though of richest meal, comes in such a questionable shape as to have no temptation for his palate.

One waggish old settler told me this story:

'I have been living down here for twenty years. The desk in my office is at the head of a long flight of stairs; and in the haste of business my inkstand is often knocked off and rolled down. For a long time I could get no material that would stand this usage. Glass was out of the question. Stone broke like crockery. The hardest wood soon gave way. Finally a lucky thought struck me. I sent up to one of my neighbors — the widow B. — for a piece of her corn-bread. After ruin-

ing several fine tools I succeeded in hollowing it out into an inkstand. That was ten years ago; and, stranger, I've used that inkstand ever since and I reckon it's good for two generations longer!'

Banks were unknown; and gold and silver the only currency. The State contained just forty miles of railroad — from Memphis toward Little Rock. The speed of regular passenger trains by the time-table was seven miles an hour.

A pioneer who settled in Fort Smith when there were only five houses, and before the military post was established, told me stirring tales of the early days. The town was a rendezvous for adventurers and desperadoes. By crossing the Arkansas *[River]* on the north side, or the Oporto *[Note: actually spelled Poteau River]* on the west, criminals reached the Indian country beyond the reach of civil process. Deadly affrays were common; and the most trivial quarrels settled by pistol and bowie knife.

During my stay a lad of fourteen became angry with a gentleman who taught a girls' singing school; and while the teacher was surrounded by pupils, twice snapped a pistol at him. The caps failing he flung a boulder which knocked the teacher down senseless and bleeding, among his terrified little singers. The young would-be murderer was held to bail. Two planters quarreled about a real estate trade, and the lie was passed. Two days later, one lay *[hid]* in the woods several hours and while his enemy was passing *[by]*, killed him with a shot gun. He was held to bail.

In a drinking saloon, a youth of eighteen wantonly murdered a Cherokee Indian. The city council offered two hundred dollars for his capture, and when taken he also was held to bail. For years no one had been punished for homicide. The carrying of concealed weapons was common; and a citizen assured me that he had seen a clergyman in the pulpit on Sunday with the handle of a bowie knife protruding from his pocket.

My chief personal experience at Fort Smith came in the form of a typhoid fever, prostrating me for weeks. In that climate the disease often clings to a patient for five months. Producing a dull stupor with little perceptible pain, it is accompanied by malignant inflammation of the bowels. But nature provides a remedy. The green leaves of the bene plant, maturing at just the right season, after soaking in cold water, produce an agreeable glutinous syrup which rapidly replaces the lining of the intestines carried away by the dangerous disease. This tropical plant, grows in profusion, and is said to be identical with the *Sesamum Orientale.* Who knows but that it was the mysterious 'open sesame' of the Arabian robbers?

I was among strangers and they ministered unto me. Good fortune threw me under the roof of a Maine family who nursed me with patient tenderness. After weary days, I escaped from the sick chamber to breathe again the blessed open air. The stifling cloud upon my brain passed away, and left me like one just awakened from a heavy slumber. In that humid climate I convalesced but slowly, and longed for the inspiring air of the mountains. At last in open rebellion to my physician I parted from the new friends to whom I owed my life, rolling away in the *[Butterfield]* overland stage which by a shaky ferry crossed the Oporto *[NOTE: actually spelled Poteau River]* into the Indian Territory.

On the rich bottom-lands, oak, cottonwood, sycamore and pecan were festooned by vines burdened with delicious grapes, and enclosed by dense canebrakes. The small canes are shipped North for pipe stems, the larger ones for fishing rods. Three soft blue mountains melted into the southern horizon.

Fourteen miles out, I left the coach at the **residence of Governor Walker**, executive of the Choctaw nation. He was educated in Kentucky, intelligent and agreeable; nearly as white as myself, and with no betrayal of Indian origin in speech or features. His wife, a very dusky half-breed, did the honors of his table gracefully. His farm of one hundred acres was all enclosed and under high cultivation. His log house, long low and hospitable with broad portico in front, was surrounded by stately oaks and graceful locusts. Several out-buildings served for kitchen, executive office and negro quarters.

GOVERNOR WALKER'S RESIDENCE, CHOCTAW NATION, INDIAN TERRITORY. Page 219.

Image by William Waud, Engraving by David & Speer

Little darkeys were ubiquitous, decorating every niche and perch with nimble cupids in bronze; performing gum-elastic feats unequaled; visible suddenly from behind corners, over fences, through windows, and under one's feet; dropping down from every point of the compass as if scattered by some genie from his overflowing pockets; gathering themselves together with whoop and somersault; displaying rows of ivory, and wooly curls; then miraculously vanishing again.

The Indian Territory contains a hundred and fifty

thousand inhabitants: Cherokees, Choctaws, Creeks, and Chickasaws. Each tribe resides on a separate tract, and has courts, legislatures schools and universities.

Their physicians are great botanists, knowing the virtues of every green thing from the cedar of Lebanon to the hyssop upon the wall. They use a large horn for cupping, exhausting the air from it with the mouth through a little aperture, and piercing the spot with a sharp, neat lance, of ingeniously-ground glass. They are firm believers in the **counter-irritant** principle, and for every internal inflammation press a burning brand against the body.

The Cherokees lead in civilization. They are largely tinctured with white blood. In their most populous sections one may travel all day without seeing a person of unmixed Indian extraction.

A COUNTER-IRRITANT.
Image by W. Fish, Engraving by Fay & Cox

Slavery among them was farcical rather than tragical. The negroes, far more intelligent than their masters, did much as they pleased, owning money, cattle and ponies; and as they made all purchases for the family, often feathering their own nests. John Ross, head chief of the Cherokees, was a very wealthy land and slave owner. He was nearly white, and had married a lady from Philadelphia. I was interested in a volume of Choctaw laws, a curious grafting of the forms of civilization upon a stock of barbarism. Each statute began:

*'Be it enacted by the Warriors and chiefs
in National Council assembled.'*

One was authenticated by the signatures of 'Black Fox, Principal Chief; Path Killer, Secretary.' Another was signed 'Turtle-at-Home, Speaker of Council;' and a third 'Ennautanaueh, Speaker.'

One legislator bore the name of 'BIG RATTLING GOURD' — appropriate for many a white Solon. Another was called 'THE DARK;' I fancy he was full-blooded. One act was 'for the relief of BETSEY BROOM,' doubtless a good housewife — while she was new. Among other names in the volume were: GOING SNAKE, THE HAIR, SLEEPING RABBIT, SPIRIT, THE BARK, DEER-IN-WATER, BRIDGE MAKER, WOMAN KILLER (unquestionably a dandy,) WALKING STICK, OLD' FEATHER, THE TURKEY, SOUR JOHN, THE TOUGH, FLYING BUFFALO, SPRING FROG, BIG HEAD, JOHN JOLLY, and SOFT-SHELL TURTLE.

The Creeks are less advanced in civilization. In summer after working part of a day they often seek some cool shallow spot in the river and lie in the water for hours. Thus old travelers relate that dwellers on the Isle of Ormus *[Hormuz Island in the Persian Gulf]* were wont to sleep in wooden cisterns immersed in water up to their heads.

They are famous pedestrians, often walking sixty or seventy miles a day. With a little sack of dried meat suspended from his neck, and his pockets filled with cakes of pulverized potatoes and beans, carefully wrapped in husks, the Creek starts on a tour of two or three hundred miles, and leaves the hardiest horse behind.

The Choctaws used to flatten their foreheads artificially. From the extreme of barbarism they have advanced steadily in civilization since 1831, when they removed from Alabama to this region. They are honest faithful and peaceable, owning all lands in common, but permitting any one of their tribe to remain undisturbed on the tract which he cultivates. Most are of unmixed Indian blood, though whites who have married Choctaw wives and been adopted into the tribe, enjoy all the privileges of citizenship save eligibility to the three highest offices. Where the father is of pure white blood and the mother an Indian or half-breed, or vice versa, five of the children may be entirely white, with Saxon features, and a sixth will have unmixed Indian lineaments, with a skin dusky as the darkest Comanche or Pueblo.

The Choctaws produce much cotton in their rich valleys. Stock raising is the most lucrative employment. I found oxen selling at fifty dollars per yoke, cows at ten dollars each, and horses at twenty dollars apiece. Calves and colts branded with the owner's mark run at large, require no feeding in winter, and in two or three years are ready for the market. Every citizen's brand is registered in the public records, so that stray animals are easily reclaimed. According to Marco Polo the same system existed among the Tartars in the thirteenth century: '*Every man who owns oxen or other cattle marks them with his seal and then turns them out upon the plains or among the mountains; and whoever finds one straying brings it to him whose mark is upon it.*"

The Choctaw language though rude and rudimentary is often poetic. Fingers are 'sons of the hand,' and leaves 'tree-hair.' A river is a 'water-road,' and the moon, 'the night-traveling sun.' Arrows are 'cane-bullets,' and bows 'wooden guns.'

In sharp contrast to their white Arkansas neighbors the Choctaws appropriated money freely for the education of their children. At ten large mission boarding schools six hundred pupils were studying. After graduating here promising boys were sent to eastern colleges at the public expense. In a girls' school super-intended by a Methodist clergyman, the sixty pupils all slept in a long hall. Sometimes at the dead of night one would strike up a sacred hymn; one by one all the little sleepers would wake and join her, until the building rang with their voices. Next some little copper-hued girl in night-gown would mount a chair for a religious exhortation. Others would follow, till the little devotees with their groans, sobs and shrieks, rivaled a camp meeting.

At other times a single girl would wake and begin some low weird song. One after another all would rouse and join her, the chant swelling until all these little throats roared forth the old war whoop of the Choctaw tribe! The teachers could not prevent these midnight entertainments even by whipping. The girls acquired language readily, were intelligent and in average capacity equaled white children.

The constitution of the Choctaws contained this provision: 'The tenure of all

A CHARMED LINE.

Image by F. Beard, Engraving by David & Speer

offices shall be for some limited period of time, if the person appointed or elected thereto so long behave well!'

Elections were by ballot. The legislative debates were in Choctaw but the records in English. Neither atheists nor *'persons not believing in future rewards and punishments'* could hold office. Murderers were almost invariably caught, and publicly shot ten days after conviction. The penalty for stealing *'negroes, horses, mules, or jackasses'* was *'one hundred lashes well laid on the bare back'* for the first offense, and death for the second. Kidnappers were branded with the letter T (thief) on the forehead, and received a hundred lashes, also *'well laid on.'* Excessive cruelty to animals was punishable by fine and thirty-nine lashes; treason, by death ; manslaughter by one hundred lashes; grand larceny by one hundred lashes, and the second offense by death; libel, by: *'Such number of lashes on the bare back, well laid on, as the court in its discretion may adjudge, having regard to ·the nature and enormity of the offense.'*

Obviously this was no place for a roving journalist; and I took the coach *[Overland Mail Stagecoach]* going west. It was filled with passengers, including a loquacious Californian who introduced himself as General ___, without stating upon what bloody fields he won the title.

Our road led among wooded hills and park-like forests and across rich prairie openings, alive with hundreds of grazing cattle often white as snow. Men women and children of all hues between alabaster and ebony, lounged upon the long porticoes or on the grass under the tall trees. Some Indian girls wore the latest city modes with enormous crinolines *[hooped petticoats]*. How absolute the sway of that gentle empress whose silent commands from her silken chambers go forth over sea and land, even penetrating the primeval forest and ruling the dusky daughters of an unknown race!

Many farmers had superb corn-fields. In early days the untamed Choctaws raised only grain enough for their subsistence. The first night after planting a corn patch, the hunter's wife walked around it trailing her night-gown upon the ground, thus encircling it with a charmed line which neither voracious worm noxious insect could cross. The brave fancied that, Byron-like, the destroyers, of his grain venerated a petticoat: *'A garment of a mystical sublimity, no matter whether russet silk or dimity!'*

The second day, we had left the mountains behind and were among beautiful prairies. Boggy Depot, capital of the Choctaw nation, contained two trading houses and half a dozen dwellings. It is near the country of the Chickasaws who have a separate government. A few years ago their legislature abrogated all existing laws and passed a fresh code. They sent the new manuscript laws into Texas to be printed, without retaining a copy. The messenger lost them while fording a river; and they were never recovered. The courts were in a muddle which would have surprised Stephen Blackpool *[a character in 'Hard Times' by Charles Dickens]* himself, until a new legislature supplied the deficiency.

Approaching Texas we sang with the jolly German travelers: *'Nut-brown maids and bread that's white,*
These shall be our lot to-night;
Maids of white and bread of brown,
Shall greet us in to-morrow's town.'

The Indian Territory, nine time times larger than Massachusetts, is better watered and timbered than Kansas or Illinois; has a delightful climate, a soil unsurpassed in the world, and enormous fields of coal. Adapted to every product from cotton to Indian corn, it is the most beautiful farming country under our flag, and when the railroad shall penetrate it, will leap into the condition of a populous and powerful State.

Before seeing its inhabitants I was skeptical about the possibility of civilizing Indians. But these once cruel and barbarous tribes were now governing themselves, educating their children, protecting life and property far better than adjacent Arkansas and Texas, and rapidly assuming the habits of enlightened man.

At Preston we crossed the Red River into Texas. Light draught steamers have sometimes ascended to Preston; but the river is really navigable only to Shreveport, Louisiana. Thirty miles above Shreveport begins the great 'Raft'— an immense collection of trees and drift-wood half embedded in the earth and firmly wedged together. It extends for seventy miles up the channel, sometimes spreading out to a width of thirty miles, and dividing the stream into many branches which do not all reunite for a hundred miles.

One authority derives 'Texas' from *Teha,* (happy hunting ground) applied by the Aztecs who fled thither after the subjugation of their country by Cortez. According to another tradition it is an Indian word signifying 'friend.'

Before daylight on the first morning we met the California mail *[the eastbound Overland Mail stagecoach]*, with six smoking horses on a swift run through drenching rain, and the passengers lustily singing, "Down upon the Swanee River."

Every day thereafter we encountered a stage from San Francisco, always stopping a moment to exchange gossip and newspapers... Our first Texas town was Sherman, capital of Grayson county...

From pages 237-238:

El Paso, twelve hundred miles from St. Louis and from San Francisco, was the half-way point on the great

Overland route. This was the first rapid line across the continent. **John Butterfield** and his associates were paid six hundred thousand dollars a year for carrying tri-weekly *[it was actually twice a week]* mails between St. Louis and San Francisco. Ruling influences in Congress and the White House compelled them to adopt a far southern route through the Indian Territory, Texas and Arizona; while a branch line from Memphis also joined the main stem at Fort Smith, Arkansas. The coaches ran day and night, ordinarily going from St. Louis to San Francisco in twenty-one days, though the law allowed twenty-five. It was the longest stage route in the world.

To establish this line three thousand miles across mountains, deserts, dangerous rivers and the territory of hostile Indians, was a gigantic enterprise. The stages ran by a time-table, and with so much regularity that during twelve months there had not been a single failure to deliver the mail on schedule time. Every day for two winter months, near the middle of the long route, the coaches from St. Louis met those from San Francisco within three hundred yards of the same spot. The through fare was a hundred and fifty dollars, exclusive of meals, which cost from forty cents to one dollar. The line continued in operation till the war broke out in 1861, when the Texans and Arkansans seized most of the mules and coaches. It was then removed to the central route. The Wells-Fargo company, composed of the same stockholders, now carry mails and passengers from the western termini of the Kansas and Nebraska railways, via Denver Salt Lake and Nevada, to California.
Albert D. Richardson, Sept. - Oct. 1859

———————————————————

A teamster leads wagons used for hauling ore in this 1868 photo by Timothy O'Sullivan of the Savage Works in Virginia City, Nevada, which depicts the mill workings for processing Comstock ore during the Bonanza era.
– Courtesy Library of Congress –

CHAPTER FORTY

Capt. Smith transported silver bullion, Oct. 13, 1859
First Silver Bullion to be Shipped on Butterfield
Through Texas, Indian Territory, Arkansas & Missouri

To discourage robberies along the route, Butterfield Stages were not allowed to carry shipments of gold, silver, bullion, money, bank notes, or valuables of any nature. In fact, #8 among the *"Special Instructions to Conductors, Agents, Drivers and Employees"* included: *"No money, jewelry, bank notes, or valuables of any nature, will be allowed to be carried under any circumstances whatever."*

However, it appears on this one trip in mid-October of 1859 an employee of the Butterfield intentionally violated special instruction #8.

*Glasgow Weekly Times,*Glasgow, Missouri
Thursday, Oct, 13, 1859, page 1
Consignment of Arizona Silver

Messrs. Wm. S. McKnight & Co., No. 27 N. Main Street, [St. Louis] have received a consignment of about two hundred pounds of Arizona silver, in the form of what is termed bullion. The silver is in small plates of irregular shape, as it comes from the smelting furnace, which weigh probably three pounds each. The metal in this state contains about ten percent of gold, and the whole consignment is valued at $4,600.

This silver is from the famous Arizona mines, and was shipped by MR. CUNIFEE — a merchant of El Paso, Texas. It came by the **Overland California Mail Coach,** in charge of Capt. Smith, Superintendent of the Mail on the El Paso division. This silver is the first shipment of any article other than mail matter by the Overland coach, and its transportation was an exception to a general rule, made by the courtesy of Capt. Smith, who, as he was about to visit this section on business, took charge of the valuable packages.

We learn that there are nearly two tons of silver bullion awaiting shipment at El Paso, which would come forward immediately, if there were any means of transporting it safely. A special Express, for the purpose of carrying bullion and other heavy articles, is now needed on this route, and the Overland Mail contractors will doubtless soon put one into operation. — Silver in bullion and in bars is almost the only medium of exchange in Arizona and Northern Texas, and the proper facilities should be afforded merchants in that region to conduct their mercantile operations, which are of rapidly increasing importance in the wide field of their Territory, and also to St. Louis merchants. — [*Republican, 6th.*]

Entrance to the Tough Nut Silver Mine in Tombstone, Arizona Territory.
Note two men standing on the upper right.
Source: Wikipedia, "Silver Mining in Arizona"

*Lady Traveler from
"Stagecoach" (1939)
Staring John Wayne*

CHAPTER FORTY ONE
Goodrich, October 15, 1859
*as reported in The Hydraulic Press, North San Juan, California
Sat. Oct. 15, 1859, page 1*

THE RULING PASSION.

Mr. Goodrich, late proprietor of the Alameda County Gazette, *[the Alameda County Gazette, San Leandro, California in operation 1856-1876]* gives a very interesting account in that journal of his trip overland to the " States," and in descanting upon the merits and demerits of his fellow passengers, says that one of them was a "rat" printer, who owns an interest in a paper published at Cincinnati. He shows up the points of the file-tailed gentleman in a very unenviable manner.

In speaking of the trials of the lady passengers, he says — *"Poor lady travelers! How they are to be pitied! They have to sit upright; they cannot sprangle* [to sprawl with limbs spread out wide] *themselves out over two or three seats at a time, as the men can, or at least if they can, they won't, or if they would, they don't. And then they look so demure and consider every little fright of the team as a precursor of a runaway or a general smash-up."*

Sarah Ann Harlan, photographs taken about 1880, and 1890.
Source: The Chronicles of Oklahoma, Summer 1961, and Autumn 1961

CHAPTER FORTY TWO

Sarah Ann Harlan, January 13, 1860(?)
as reported in the Autumn 1961 issue of The Chronicles of Oklahoma,
by Muriel H. Wright, page 311-315.

Note: Sarah Ann Harlan dictated this account at the age of eighty-four in 1913 and is included in the WPA Indian Pioneer Oral History Project. Mrs. Harlan tells the story of her Butterfield's Overland Mail Co. stage trip from Fort Smith westward through Indian Territory. Her story mentions Skullyville and Boggy Depot.

[Her story begins:] "ON THE BUTTERFIELD OVERLAND MAIL STAGE ...About this time the Government of the United States made a contract with a company by the name of Butterfield, to run a stage line carrying U.S. mail, and passengers from Rockford, Illinois, to San Francisco, California, *[actually it was St. Louis & Memphis to San Francisco]* running direct through the Indian Territory. We thought this a grand thing that now we could get mail, and it would come through so much faster. We considered it a well equipped road...

[From Fort Smith, I] took the stage for home. The *[Butterfield]*conductor told me that they were loaded and that the company was not compelled to take extra passengers, advising me to go over to Skullyville *[Walker's Station]*. That would be the next stand. I went out late in the evening, hiring a buggy to take me out *[to Walker's station].*

I knew I would have to stay all night in Skullyville and eat breakfast there. This was in January and very cold weather.

Next morning I heard the [Butterfield Conductor's} horn just about daybreak. I began to dress...

Colonel Leflore, a lawyer and friend of mine... said, *"I must fix a rock for you today, it is so cold."* He prepared the rock and put it in the stage. When the conductor yelled *"all aboard,"* she [Miss Clark, a fellow passenger] ran and jumped into the stage, pulled the rock over by her and put her feet on it. Colonel Leflore remarked what a hard trip it would be on me, and asked if the rock would keep hot until we got dinner. I turned to her, pulled the rock from under her feet and said, *"This rock was put here for my special benefit. If you can derive any benefit from its being under my feet, all right."*

...We traveled all day, did not stop for dinner but stopped the next one for supper. We changed horses every ten or twelve miles, and drivers, too, but not conductors — the conductor called out supper for those in the stage. I knew this place, and knew they never had decent meals.

When we went in I saw a half dozen eggs lying on the bed, and put those eggs in the fireplace to cook. When I came back in I pulled them out, dropped them in a pan of water and then put them in my hand satchel. She [a fellow passenger] ran off and forgot to pay for her supper. I called to her and said, *"Come back and pay for your supper, even if you are a Yankee. It's only twenty-five cents."* I wanted to catch her.

Well, we traveled on, miring down and prizing out, miring down and prizing out. She [a fellow passenger] had traveled all the way from Rockford, Illinois, and finally got awfully sleepy. I said, *"If you want to sleep, lie down on my lap and I will let you sleep."* That was the first word I had said to her after calling her down. She thanked me very kindly, and told me she was on her way from Rockford. When day was just breaking I said, *"I am very sleepy; wish you would get up."* She asked me to lay my head in her lap, which I did, and went to sleep.

We soon came to a creek. Campers along the creek said to the driver, *"The creek is swimming,"* but they drove in. I was asleep when the water splashed all over the stage. We were immersed in water. I jumped up and said, *"What does all this mean?"* I soon saw that we were in great danger, and the curtains were all keyed down with iron rods. I heard voices on the bank.

There was a gentleman on the stage going to Texas. I asked him if he could swim. He said he could, a little, and I asked him if he could not save us ladies. He said he was afraid we might drown him. I said, *"You haven't any heart, or you would risk that."* Death was staring us in the face. I asked him if he had a knife.

He said, *"Yes, do you want to kill me?"*

I said, *"No, do you think I would send my soul to hell for such a little pea looking object as you? Give me your knife quick."*

He opened it and handed it to me.

I ripped the curtain open from top to bottom. Then I said, *"Oh! Is there not a man who can save us?"*

One of the campers [on the shore] said, *"I'll try."*

He plunged in. He was on a very small gray mule. Getting up as near the stage as he could, he turned the mule loose and said, *"Now, I am a good swimmer, but can't get any closer. You leap. If you don't catch anything, you shall not drown."*

I said, *"I am going first, I have got too much to live for."* I believe in protecting self first. I made a leap. I grabbed him by the neck and we both went under. He then carried me out until we struck bottom, and led me on to where the water was about knee deep.

"Now," I said, *"do save the other lady."*

She was almost frozen when he got her out and so was I. But I had been used to these things, living in a pioneer country.

I said to this man, *"I have no money here, but if you will give me your name. I will leave it in a merchant's store in Boggy Depot."* I wrote his name on a piece of paper with a piece of rotten wood. These depots, in that day and time, were just places used for rations. The conductor went to the next station to get harness. He thought that by evening the water would be down so he might get the stage out.

We stayed all day on this bleak prairie. Toward the middle of the day, I saw a wagon coming which I knew was a freight wagon. There was an old Negro driving it that I knew well. He belonged to the Indians. I called to him to know if he could make us a fire. He got some wood and built us one, then took his ax and cut some poles, went to his wagon and took out some blankets and stretched them around to protect us from the wind.

The conductor got back late in the evening and pulled the stage out. Everything was wet. The old Negro had some coffee and eggs. He made us coffee in an old black kettle, and had an old cup to drink from. He boiled the eggs in the coffee. I was glad to get something hot. But Miss Clark refused to drink the coffee because she thought it wasn't clean.

Then we had about eleven miles to drive to the next station. I knew the lady who kept the stage stand. She had just moved there. Her son had a small store. The conductor told her she would have to provide dry clothes for us; then he went to the store and got a bottle of liniment, brought it to her and told her to rub us with that. He also brought two glasses of stuff called pain killer, and told her to have us drink that so we would not get sick. We drank it, but I thought it would burn me up.

By this time, I began to get pretty well acquainted with Miss Clark, and found I had a heart for her. She told me she was from Vermont, having been educated at Port Edwards. There they educated poor girls, found positions for them, and sent them wherever they could find a place for them. Then the girls were to send back one half their monthly wages until their education was paid for.

Well, I was in need of a governess, at that time, and in talking to her, I saw she was the teacher I wanted, so begged her to go home with me. She was on her way to Bonham, Texas, to teach in an academy. I told her what I would give her, which was fifteen dollars more than she was to get at this academy. But she said she had a written contract, and could not think of going back on it. She asked me why I could not send my children to Bonham. I told her I would write my husband. I jokingly said: *"You know we have been baptised all our sins are washed away."*

She said: *"I know, I love you now where I hated you before."* I said: *"Ditto, Sister."* That was the thirtieth day of January, my birthday.

[Sarah Ann's passage on the Overland Mail may have occurred in early January 1860, based on Miss Clark's teaching contract, and that the founding of the first educational academy near Bonham, Fannin County. Texas occurred in 1860 – the Ladonia Male and Female Institute.]

I wrote to my husband about my great adventure and asked him what he thought about sending my little daughter and his little daughter to Bonham. He told me to do as I pleased. My third stepdaughter was still in Fort Smith. She came home; so I made arrangements to take them all to Bonham to school that fall.

Source: Appreciation is express to Oklahoma historian, Susan Dragoo for finding this first person passenger story in the Autumn 1961 issue of The Chronicles of Oklahoma, by Muriel H. Wright, page 311-315.

"1862 Memphis Post Office"

The Overland Mail began its 2,700 mile journey to San Francisco at the Memphis Post Office

CHAPTER FORTY THREE

Passenger, Overland Mail stage, April 6 & 12, 1860
as reported in the April 6 and 19, 1860 issues, Memphis Daily Appeal, on p.2

The Great Overland Mail, Letter From Fort Smith

Fort Smith, Apr 6, 1860

EDITORS APPEAL: Feeling a deep interest in this *[The Overland Mail Company]*, one of the great enterprises of the age, I have thought it would perhaps tend to promote the growing interests of your important city to direct renewed attention, on the part of your real estate owners, bankers, merchants, hotel keepers, railroad stockholders and citizens, to the present and prospective advantages of this mode of travel and means of keeping up an active correspondence with our Pacific sister States and territory.

The demonstration that a mail could be safely carried between St. Louis and Memphis, as points of departure and arrival, to and from San Francisco within twenty-five days, was, twelve months since, actually doubted; and experience has shown that even with the deviations from a more direct course, the trip is generally made in an average of twenty days and nights.

From inquiry and clear observation, it is found there is a want of general information among your citizens of the existence of such a means of communication with our Pacific coast, whereas it comes home to every

© 2024 Robert O. Crossman

individual feeling any interest in the promoting, sustaining of legitimate avenues of inter-communication, to be thoroughly posted in relation to so great an undertaking as this Overland Mail for and from California. Strangers visiting your city, a center already from its position, find even the hotel proprietors, merchants and others, ignorant of the days, hours of departure, name of the local agent, where the office is located; and one would suppose that the stockholders of the Little Rock Railroad would feel sufficient interest to have a sign put up over the ferryboat landing at their crossing, to let the multitude passing know the fact of such a connection.

It would be a subject of interest to the Chamber of Commerce of your city to submit to *an efficient committee* the advantages at present, and prospective, to the city of Memphis, to encourage and sustain the great Overland Mail to and from California. The same body in the city of San Francisco have had their attention directed to a similar branch of the subject, and its president made a report giving statistics, etc., a short time since.

Why is it that upon arrival of a mail within twenty days, Tuesday afternoon last, NO NOTICE is made of such event? Is it of no importance to a city like Memphis? Are her real estate owners, merchants, hotel keepers, railroad stockholders, citizens, about to allow one of her *arteries* to be cut lose? It may not be generally known, that strong efforts are being made to discontinue this portion of so great a route.

Memphis has decided claims for less distance, better travel, hence to Fort Smith, than from St. Louis. This writer contends that it is just as practicable for the traveler to make the trip hence to San Francisco, as it was to do so by stage from Portland to this point twenty years since.

For general information, the office of the Overland Mail is for the present at the Commercial Hotel, Jefferson Street, B. F. Candy local agent. Days of departure, Wednesday and Saturday, at 8 A.M. Ferry boat for Little Rock Railroad, foot of Jefferson Street *[to cross the Mississippi River to the Hopefield, Arkansas train station.]*

An Old Californian

Overland Mail, Letter From Fort Smith
Fort Smith, Ark., April 12, 1860

Leaving your city *[Memphis]* on the morning of Saturday, April 7, '60, *[with an Overland Mail Co. ticket]* to connect with the Little Rock railroad at half past eight o'clock, by skiff, the very punctual ferryboat leaving quarter before the hour (8 A.M.)(and at the north it is considered punctuality to keep the time fixed) to take the overland stage at Madison, we reached this point, (after a very pleasant trip, excepting one upset Monday night, but no one hurt) Tuesday at 8:30 A.M., giving about two days and nights respite for the balance of this interesting route to travelers. We had a good steamer Tuesday night here.

[It appears that this passenger rode a Butterfield stage from Madison to Des Arc and perhaps on to Little Rock. Then from Des Arc or Little Rock rode a Butterfield arranged steamboat to Fort Smith. This however was not on the Butterfield owned steamboat Jennie Whipple. The Whipple was still hard aground in Indian Territory, stuck on a sandbar between March 27, 1860 and until some days after Feb. 20, 1861.]

If the citizens of Arkansas had any public spirit, and would justly appreciate the present and prospective advantages to their State, and take vigorous measures to improve a portion of the road now traveled, they would soon feel the return in the increased travel and opening up of settlements. But such is the crude short-sightedness view some take of this great overland route, binding together the Western, South-western and Middle States with our Pacific sister territo-

– 301 –

ry that not comprehending the growing interests the present opens to the observing mind, and not seeing the immediate results, they decry the great undertaking which reflects credit upon the energetic, indomitable individuals who have so successfully demonstrated the entire practicability of the route.

The trip from Memphis to this point *[Fort Smith]* is as practicable as any portion of travel in the western part of New York was twenty-five or thirty years since; and if the parties offering refreshments to travelers would prepare the food with more care in cooking, seek a little more variety, which the preserved vegetables and fruits in cans of the present day permits, and really wake up, and not sleep away a growing harvest, and observe cleanliness shown in the clean towels and washing arrangements in the rooms, table-cloths, etc., they would have the hearty approval of travelers.

This place, Fort Smith, is sometimes alluded to as the residence of a desperate community. Hearing the sound of the church-going bell last evening, upon inquiry found a weekly prayer meeting was the occasion, and as a stranger I always like to feel the religious pulse of any place I may be visiting in my travels, I found a respectable gathering of old, middle aged and young — indicative of an interest in religious matters — and was interested and instructed by the exercises of the evening.

St. Patrick Catholic Church, Fort Smith, 1848 The first church for Fort Smith's Catholic congregation was a small log building constructed in 1848. The little log church of Saint Patrick at the corner of what is now 3rd and North "D" Streets. The total cost for the structure was $258.[50].It was followed in ca. 1870 by a frame church. Image source: icchurch.com

From the temporary sojourn in the city I am very favorably impressed with the place — there are signs of prosperity, and domestic comfort, and attractive society. The City Hotel affords very creditable accommodations for travelers, and I would recommend Memphis as a point of departure — affording a respite here *[Fort Smith]* — to meet the St. Louis division.

Taking your title *[title of the newspaper, Memphis Daily Appeal]*, I, as a stranger, *"appeal"* to your public spirit to adopt a more sensible course, and to notice the arrival and departure of each and every overland mail, and not credit that to St. Louis which belongs to your own growing city.

You will find in Daniel L. Kandy, the local agent, a ready co-operator in placing at your disposal late papers — and I was pleased to hear, Saturday last, that the Little Rock Railroad and the Overland Mail Company have taken a front office in the Commercial Hotel *[in downtown Memphis]*; and now let your citizens awake to the growing importance of this artery from your flourishing city.

The Chamber of Commerce of your city, I hope, will act promptly upon the suggestion in my first letter: of appointing an efficient committee to report upon the present and prospective advantages of the great Overland Mail to your city.

It would be a great convenience to travelers if some time was fixed upon a governing departures of railroads, steamboats, etc., in your city.

An Old Californian

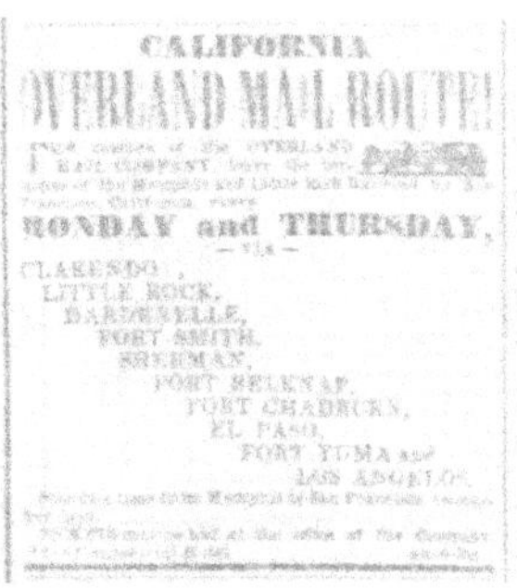

*Overland Mail Company advertisement
from the Memphis Daily Appeal,
Thursday, Nov. 3, 1859, Page 4*

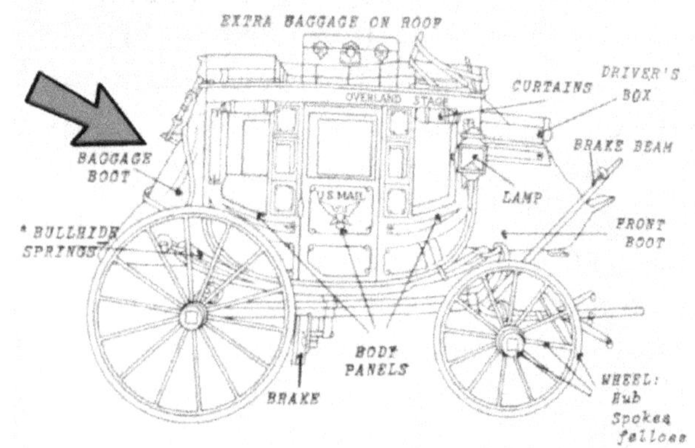

Passenger rode in the rear baggage boot the entire trip.

CHAPTER FORTY FOUR
Passenger in the 'Boot,' April 27, 1860
as reported in the Friday, April 27, 1860 issue of The Arkansian,
Fayetteville, Arkansas, page 3

Passenger Rides in Boot All The Way

We learn that a passenger recently arrived in Fort Smith from California, who made the entire journey in the boot of the Stage coach; the stage was crowded with passengers, without trunks, and the enterprising traveler, rather than wait, took passage in the boot. "He'll do to travel." — *This quote is an apparent reference to a joke of the day, referencing fitting 'into such narrow arrangements.' The joke is found in the 1852 publication, Yankee Notions: or Whittlings of Jonathan's Jack Knife," Volume One, September, page 267.*

*"Annibal, what is Cupid?" "One of the boys. He is said to be as blind as a bat, but if he is blind **he'll do to travel.** He found his way into Aunt Man's affections, and **I wouldn't have thought any critter could have worked his way into such narrow arrangements with its eyes open."***

Passengers on the Over Land Mail route report considerable trouble with the Comanches on the line of late; about one week ago the Indians made a descent upon a station, killed three of the employees and drove off the stock. This is the report and we have no doubt of its correctness.

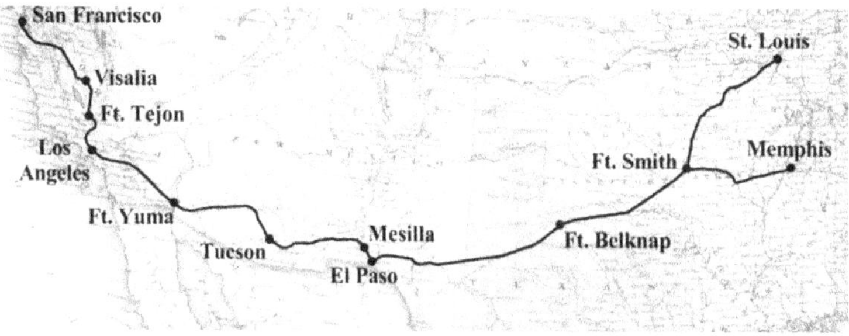

SOUTHERN OX-BOW ROUTE 1858-1861
Image Source: "Mails of the Westward Expansion, 1803 to 1861"
by Steven C. Walske & Richard C. Frajola, Western Cover Society, 2015, p. 161

CHAPTER FORTY FIVE

Rebecca Johnston Yoakum, Spring 1860

In 1934 at the age of 89, the daughter of Rev. Thomas M. Johnston, Rebecca Johnston Yoakum of Merced, California, told her story of being a passenger on Butterfield's Overland Mail Co. stagecoach.

Eleanor Steele Johnston, known as the first woman to journey to California on the Butterfield stagecoach, traveled with her children Finis age 17, Rebecca age 15, John age 7 and William age 3. They were passengers on the westbound Butterfield stage in 1860 which departed from near Hurley, Stone County, Missouri to reach San Francisco.

[Source: "Adventure of the Butterfield State" by Ralph L. Mulliken, The Los Banos Enterprise, Thursday, June 30, 1966, Section A-1]

Mrs. Rebecca Yokum, a delightful old lady who lived long, long ago in Merced, came to California in 1860 on the Overland stage. If you will listen to her story you will have a deeper feeling for this little bit of the Overland road that passes through Los Banos.

Mrs. Yokum told me in January 1934, of her trip seventy-four years before over this very piece of road. By the way it was through the San Joaquin Valley that the **Butterfield Overland** stages made their fastest time. Here is Mrs. Rebecca Yokum herself to tell you her story in her own words:

"We felt just terrible when our little negro girl refused to come with us to California. When I was a baby Grandfather Steel who owned lots of slaves, gave her to my mother to help take care of me. I suppose her name really was Frances but we always called her France. I was born in Missouri in 1845 and was the baby of the family for nine years. France and I grew up together. When I was old enough I was sent to school, but of course France couldn't go because she was just a negro. But I wanted her to know something too, and so when I would get home from school I always taught France all that I had learned for the day. She got so she could read and write as well as I could. I don't remember of my mother giving France a licking. If there was anyone to get a whipping I was always the one that got it.

Father was a Cumberland Presbyterian minister. He went by *[Butterfield's Overland Mail]* stage to California in 1859. At first he wrote us that we were to come to California by water by way of the Isthmus of Panama. *'Don't come by stage under any circumstances,'* he wrote us.

Later he sent word that he was coming back to Missouri. Mother had made up her mind that she was coming to California. She was a very determined woman and without waiting for father to get back she prepared to set out without delay for California on the Butterfield Overland Stages.

France positively refused to go with us. She declared she was afraid the Indians would get her. Shortly before we were ready to start, she was taken sick and we sent for Dr. Wills. While she was sick she and mother had a long talk.

"Well, if you don't want to come to California with us," said mother, *"I will free you and you can stay here in Missouri."*

"Oh, no, no." begged France. *"I don't want to be no free nigger! Look at Winnie,"* she pleaded.

Winnie was an old negro woman who had been freed years before. She lived all alone in a little shack on the edge of town. She scarcely eked out a living and was an object of pity by all.

"Then," said mother, *"you can pick out who ever you want for your master."*

France was just getting over her sickness and she quite naturally picked out Dr. Wills. Everything was all agreeable with the Doctor and mother arranged to leave France with him.

It was April, 1860 Mother wrote that we were coming. Our tickets were bought several days in advance and called for our trip to begin at Springfield, Missouri and end at Santa Clara, California. Grandfather Steel lived five miles this side of Springfield, and as the **Overland stages** passed right beside his plantation, where we were staying at the time, it was arranged that the stage should stop at the plantation and take us on board.

On the appointed day the stage coach drawn by six horses came to a sudden stop at my grandfather's gate. All of us children were filled with glee at the prospect of our great adventure. With mother and the older ones it was different. Their eyes were filled with tears now that the time for parting had arrived. Our trunk was hastily stowed away in the boot at the end of the stage.

Deadwood Stage, 1889 - Image in the public domain.
*It is generally thought that passengers never road atop Butterfield's mail stage-coaches. However, in her old age, this Missouri passenger below told a reporter that "the **top** of the stage was covered with men sitting back to back..." However, it was not possible to set atop the Celerity wagon because of its soft canvas top.*

The top of the stage was covered with men sitting back to back. Inside the coach were still more men. There were three wide seats and one of these had been reserved for my mother and us children. On a high seat in front sat the conductor and the driver.

We were five that set out that Friday morning, my mother, my three brothers and myself. My oldest brother was seventeen. He had a belt buckled around his waste and a pistol stuck in it. Wasn't he going out West where the Indians were and wouldn't he need a gun!

I was fifteen and had a very beautiful hat, of which I was very proud. It had a wide brim and lots of flowers on it.

My youngest brother was three and was all decked out with the cutest pair of little red topped boots. The stage was so crowded that mother had to hold him on her lap. Between mother and I sat my younger brother, John, who was seven. Everything on the stage was so shiny and new that we felt we were in a palace. The driver kicked off the brake and we were off for California with the horses on the run.

We had a large lunch basket filled with provisions to last us until we got well along on our way. In our trunk we had enough clothing to last us for the entire trip. The only person we knew on the stage was a neighbor man.

He was about to set out for California by water, but had decided to come by stage instead and be of assistance to mother with us children.

We soon found that the stage made no stops whatever except to change horses. It ran continuously day and night. About every fourteen miles there was a stage station. At these stations there was generally only men. The moment we rolled into the station the tired horses were dragged away and fresh ones put in their places.

Speed seemed to be the one and only thing the stage people desired. As soon as the horses were securely fastened to the stage, away we would go on the run. Usually the two horses in the lead were unbroken mustangs and the faster they ran the better satisfied the driver seemed to be.

Of course we didn't sleep any the first night. But the second night out I was that tired that I just had to sleep. When I awoke I found that I had fallen over in my sleep and had been lying with my head in a young man's lap. He was the meanest man in the world, I thought, to let me sleep that way. He tried to be nice to me but I was so mortified that I wouldn't even look at him.

I think it was at Fort Smith that we lost our lunch basket. There were large steps on the side of the coach for the passengers to enter the stage. It was about ten o'clock at night and we happened to set our basket on the step for a minute. Some dog or something must have grabbed it in the darkness, for when we looked for it, our lunch was gone.

Sunday morning we passed through an Indian reservation and saw our first Indians. These were the only good Indians we saw on the whole trip. As we galloped along that morning I remember in particular seeing a cabin where an old Indian was sitting outside and playing away to himself on his fiddle. He was serenely happy.

After the loss of our lunch basket we had to buy our meals at the stage stations. But I would just like to see you eat what they served. Beans! Black bread! Often mother would pay a dollar for bread only to find it was spoiled. At the stage stations there were generally only men. Usually they would bring it right to the stage and hand it to us. There were only a very few times that we got to eat at a table.

When we had been about a week on our journey the stage company took off the Concord coach we had been riding in and put us on board a two seated mud wagon. There wasn't near room enough for all the passengers and some of the men were forced to wait behind for the next stage.

The Indians were simply terrible. When we got into the real Indian country we would see them at every stage station. They would come swarming around us as soon as the stage drove up.

They were regular thieves and would have stolen the clothes right off of our backs if they could. Somewhere at one of these stops my beautiful hat disappeared and mother had to fish out a sunbonnet out of our trunk for me to wear the rest of the way to California.

That older brother of mine, who really meant to be so brave, was sitting in the stage at one stop watching the Indians. They were surging all around us. No doubt some clever Indian brave saw the pistol he was wearing and schemed how he could get it. In all probability he slipped up behind my brother with a sharp knife and so skillfully did he slit the belt that my brother never once missed his gun until the station was miles behind.

The little red topped boots my baby brother was wearing were the envy of every Indian squaw and the conductor told mother emphatically that on no occasion whatever was she to leave the little boy alone for a single minute or the Indians would steal boots, little boy and all.

The same conductor and driver went with us for a day or so at a time. We never changed conductors and drivers at the same station. One of the men was always fresh. They were very stoical about things. It was just a part of their business to take risks. When we arrived at a station one of them always stayed on the stage with the passengers.

The other tended to the stage business. Fresh horses were always ready for us the minute we drove up. The horses were given no rest on the road between stations but were rested for days at the stations. The horses always went on the run. We would never have gotten through it they hadn't.

We came to a stage station where the Indians a day or two before had massacred not only the stage station keepers but the passengers on the incoming stage as well. The only persons to escape were a white woman and child and two men, one of them a negro.

The man himself was wounded and the party remained at the station until he died. Then the woman and child and the negro man set out on foot to go the fourteen miles or so to the next station.

The refugees reached the station in safety but when we arrived the Indians were swarming around this station and apparently getting ready for another massacre. Besides this woman and her little girl there was also another woman and two children at the station. Although our stage was filled to over flowing the station keepers piled these five people right in with us.

They wanted to get them away before the Indian attack on the station could commence. We were piled two and three deep in the seats. They road with us until sometime the next day when we came to a fort and the stage people put them off.

While the horses were being changed I said to the negro who was being left behind:

"Aren't you afraid the Indians will kill you?"

"No mam," he replied. "Not while there are any white men around. The Indians never take a black man if there are any white men."

Oatman Flat is where an emigrant train was massacred. There is a high mountain on one side. On the other side there is a flat *[prairie]* and beyond that another mountain. Here the Oatman people were massacred. A while flag was flying when we went by. We saw what was left of the wagons and the place on the mountain where the people are buried.

The wreckage was all heaped up in a pile. The canvas was gone off the wagons and the bows *[of the wagons]* were all bare. The Oatman children that got away were Olive and Lorenzo. We saw them afterwards in California. Olive was a pretty little girl but the Indians had tattooed her face something terrible and cut lines in her cheeks.

Three or four times on the way we changed stages. One time was at the river. The water was high and the stage couldn't get across. The stage drove up to the river bank and we all got out. A great mass of drift wood had been washed down by the flood. We had to walk across the stream on this drift wood. On the opposite bank another stage was waiting for us. Two men were helping me keep my footing on the drift wood.

I got smart and jumped ahead. As I did so, I slipped and fell into the water up to my waist. As they pulled me out they said sternly: "Now you stay where we put you after this!' To add to my discomfort, our trunk with all our extra clothes had been left behind several days before by the stage company. They had put it off in order to lighten the stage one place where the Indians were so bad.

One dark night we were traveling without lights. We were not even allowed to talk out loud for fear of an Indian attack. We had to cross a stream and as we plunged down the bank the two horses in the lead broke away in the darkness. There was great excitement. Everyone had to get out as the stage was unable to haul the passengers through the stream.

The stage men were endeavoring to recover the horses and we could hear them calling out, "Catch the leaders!" Mother and the boys had to wade through the water. But someone, I don't know who, grabbed me in the darkness and carried me across the stream in his arms.

Of course at first we didn't sleep much at night, but we soon got so we could sleep sitting up in the seat while the stage rocked back and forth over the road. I can still go sound asleep sitting bolt upright in a chair. I learned to do so the three weeks we traveled in those overland stages.

Several times we saw Indians dancing around their camp fires at night. Mother would wake me up to look. The naked warriors would dance around in a circle in the firelight, imitating with their leaping and prancing the darting and shooting of the flames.

One time we saw the Indians dancing as we passed down by the bank of a river. Another time we saw a wild band dancing in the woods right near our road. We could see them perfectly plain as we went past. They were leaping and yelling like fiends. Our conductor and driver were very worried that night. The Indians were having a war dance and the stage men felt sure that the Indians were getting ready for a massacre.

Oh, the Indians were terrible. They made us stay right in the stage while they changed horses at the stations. I felt so bad I began to cry. Mother heard me. "Brace up, Rebecca," whispered my mother bravely, "you're going to California."

One day we thought the Indians were chasing us. We could see a large band of horsemen gradually gaining on us in the distance. The stage men were very uneasy. When finally the band overtook us, it turned out to be a lot of Mexicans who were running down some Indians that had been on a raid.

We had only alkali water to drink much of the way and when we would come to a place where it had rained the stage driver would stop the stage and let us scoop the water off the rocks to drink.

I never knew there were so many buffaloes in the world. We saw thousands and thousands of them. In going through one herd they were so thick in front of us that the stage horses had to slow down and go on the walk. Two of the men on the stage jumped out and caught one of the little baby buffaloes. They wanted to take it right along with us and were going to put it in the boot with the baggage. But the conductor wouldn't let them.

Somewhere after we got into California we were all, one forenoon, going through mountains. The road was very narrow and every few minutes the conductor would play a little tune on a bugle to warn any other travelers that the stage was coming. The long notes of his bugle, echoing through the mountains, sounded very romantic. Before we got out of the mountains we met another stage coming up the grade.

There had been a mistake in the signals and the two stages met in a narrow part of the road where it was impossible for the two to pass. The stage men took off four horses from the upcoming stage and tied them to a tree while the men on both stages got out and piled up rocks beside the grade. Then with the two horses they pulled the stage over on the rocks and let us get past.

Father had no way of knowing whether we were on our way to California or not and he was at the point of starting back to Missouri. There was a telegraph line that followed the stage road over the Pacheco Pass and ran part way down into the San Joaquin Valley. He telegraphed ahead as

Rebecca's Father

far as he could to see if we were on the stage that was coming from the East. The report came back that the stage had gone by on the run but that they could see a woman and some children on board. Father felt sure that it was us and proceeded at once to get a house in readiness for us.

I was so tired I don't remember how many days it was, but sometime after we got into California we reached a town called San Jose. I know it was half past seven in the evening on the third of May, 1860. It was dark and cold. The lamp inside the coach was lit and the curtains all fastened down to make it as warm as possible. We were again in a Concord coach and were sitting four in a seat. The coach was crowded.

My little brother was sitting in my mother's lap. She had held him the entire twenty-one days of our trip. The only sleep we had had was what we could catch while the stage coaches traveled along with the horses on the run. For three weeks we had no change of clothing. We were little short of dead!

There seemed to be some sort of difficulty. The stage people came over to the stage and inquired if there wasn't a woman and some children to get off at San Jose. Mother replied: *"No. Our tickets call for Santa Clara."*

While the stage was still waiting, a tall strange look-ing man with whiskers all over his face stepped out of the darkness. He poked his head through the curtains and peered into the coach. He looked us over carefully in the dim light and then said firmly: *"I guess you will get off right here!"* Then he smiled. It was father!!

Arising from her easy chair, Mrs. Yokum, the little girl of long ago, made her way over to the mantle where an old fashioned clock was ticking boisterously. *"This is the same clock that was sitting on the mantle piece when father took us that night to our new home in California. It has been running ever since."*

She placed her hand on the sturdy wooden case and peered carefully into its face - a face stained like her own with the tears and joys of a long life-time. *"I can't hear you tick any more,"* she said to the clock, *"but I can see your hands go round and so I know that you are still running."*

Then turning to me: *"Stage coach days weren't so awfully long ago, after all. They tell me that I have been seventy-four years here in California. But our journey across the plains"* — she paused and I knew she was gazing far back into the past — *"it seems like only yesterday."*

<hr>

[Source: "Adventure of the Butterfield State" by Ralph L. Mulliken, The Los Banos Enterprise, Thursday, June 30, 1966, Section A-1]
The travel diary of her father, on his trip to California, is reproduced in an earlier chapter in this book.

<hr>

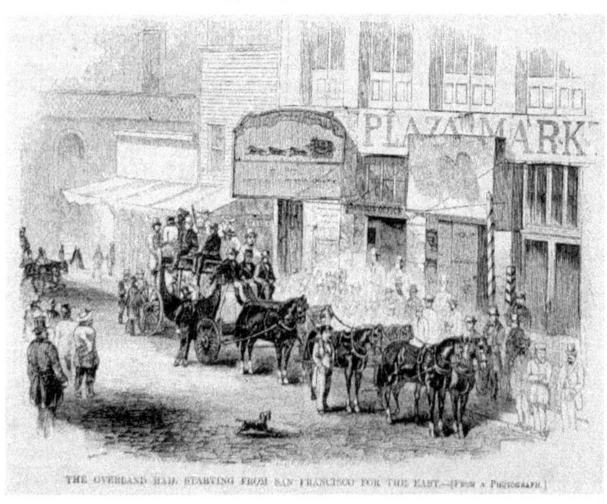

"The Overland Mail Starting from San Francisco for the East" [FROM A PHOTOGRAPH]

Published in Harper's Weekly, December 11, 1858

*Envelope from
the collection of
Bob Crossman.*

*Envelope from Hiram S. Rumfield addressed to his wife on March 5.
Probably originally contained Hiram's letter of March 5, 1863 reprinted in the
1928 issue of the American Antiquarian Society, pages 270-288.*

CHAPTER FORTY SIX
Hiram Rumfield's letters

found in "LETTERS *of an Overland Mail Agent in Utah*" *edited by Archer Butler Hubert* also reprinted in The Press Argus, Sept. 19, 1959, Section D, p.1 *and unpublished letters from the Huntington Library. Hiram S. Rumfield was assistant treasurer of the Overland Mail Company. Before he took up his duties in Salt Lake City in January, 1861 he served a tour of duty as local road agent. Hiram wrote a series of letters to his wife, "Frank" back home in Tiffin, Ohio. Marilyn Heifner researched his genealogy to discover Hiram had a sister Elizabeth (1827-1910) and a brother Areus (1822-1888). Hiram married Francis B Ray. They had 4 children: Mary F. (born 1854), Elizabeth (was listed as Lizzy in 1880 census, born1857) , John P.(born 1858), and Janis B. (born 1860)*

Fort Smith, Arkansas
June 22, 1860

Dear Frank, *[Frank is Hiram's nickname for his wife.]*

As soon as possible after my arrival here on Tuesday morning I wrote you, and wrote somewhat hurriedly as the Overland Mall for Saint Louis was then about due, and I did not wish to lose the opportunity by any means.

I have thought that it might be of interest to you to learn something of the character of the country through which I passed after leaving the western terminus of the Pacific Rail Road, from which place I wrote you the evening before my departure for this remote region.

From Syracuse to Springfield, a distance of one hundred and thirty miles, a vast stretch of prairie, interspersed with occasional patches of hazel, shumach

[Sumac] and scrub oak, intervenes.

The road is firm and smooth and but few hills are met with of sufficient height to interrupt rapid driving. The surface of the ground is somewhat undulating and the soil generally harsh and gravelly and in many places of considerable extent, absolutely barren. If brought under the influence of proper cultivation much of it would doubtless prove highly productive.

But of this I cannot speak advisedly, as throughout the entire portion of the State of Missouri, lying between the points named above, few improvements, amongst the many to be met with, will compare favorably even with the worst class of farms in any of the older portions of Ohio.

A general and almost unvarying aspect of indolence, ignorance and shiftlessness characterizes the country throughout. The farm houses are constructed of the rudest materials and the most barbarous styles of architecture. Dwelling houses, out buildings and fences, that have long since reached a chronic stage of dilapidation, do not seem to suggest to their respective owners the necessity of timely repairs to save them from utter demolition. Farming implements are of the most antiquated kinds and are permitted to rust and rot at the places they were last used.

The space by the road side in front of each house is generally filled up with the ruins of old wagons, sleds and harrows scattered about in promiscuous confusion, and a profusion of empty whiskey barrels too — plainly indicates the true cause of the miserable slothfulness which is everywhere so plainly apparent.

Fruit and shade trees which are reared and cherished with such tender care by the thrifty and intelligent husbandman, are but seldom met with in this region of poverty and indolence. The growing of wheat is generally neglected; whilst corn is to the lazy Missourian, what the camel is to the wild Bedouin of the dessert. Towns are few and far between, but whenever met with they exhibit the same indications of prevailing sloth, inactivity and negligence, which are so prominently displayed throughout the country.

On every hand an indifference to personal comfort is seemingly manifest. Streets are laid out with the least regard to regularity or convenience, and are more or less obstructed with the accumulated filth and debris of years. The public houses are execrable beyond conception. Everything in and about them is calculated to excite a feeling of unutterable disgust. A moderately good meal is not to be had at any of them; and indeed would seem beyond the resources and capacity of the country to provide. The nigger cooks are greasy and filthy in the extreme, and appear to display a diabolical ingenuity in making every dish they serve up inexpressibly distasteful to the palate of the traveler. No one not accustomed to such fare, unprovided with the stomach of a mountain trapper, or a California gold hunter, can make much progress in disposing of such unsavory viands, *[an item of food]* yet for each accommodation of the kind — the victimized stranger is obliged to disburse fifty cents, whether he eats anything or not.

Along the entire route north of Springfield *[Missouri]* we found an extreme scarcity of water. Throughout the entire state of Missouri but little rain had fallen since the opening of spring. Creeks were almost everywhere dry, and the few wells the country affords, exhausted by the extraordinary drains upon the liquid stores. At each station where the horses were changed, the thirsty passengers would sally on ahead in search of a sip of nature's beverage, but in many instances they would meet with but indifferent success. Water we seldom failed to find in these periodical rambles, but none that I could have partaken of at home. And then the utensils we were compelled to drink it from! Frequently from a gourd, but that would do very well. Sometimes from a pan lathered over with clots of sour milk; several times from the buckets which had served to supply the horses; once from an old rusty tin wash bowl which was thus brought into double service by the frugal housewife.

On another occasion a long walk at night following a devious path that led far into the wilderness brought us to a spring of muddy water, to drink of which the only available thing at hand was a portion of an article of crockery *[broken chamber pot]* which shall be nameless — but which many years ago, when entire, may have occupied a place beneath the bridal bed of the obliging matron who directed us to this refreshing spot.

Some miles north of Springfield *[Missouri]* the road leaves the plain and winds it way along the Ozark Mountains upon the summit of which the town is situated. The location is a beautiful one and the surroundings such as are calculated to inspire the enthusiastic lover of rugged natural scenery with feelings of sublimity. But unfortunately the town adds nothing to the charm, and a breakfast at the only hotel it contains will certainly dissipate any romantic notions that may have previously found their way into the head of the journalist.

Pursuing our way over the mountains we found the road extremely rough and circuitous. No open plain meets the eye and a succession of steep and rocky hills render traveling dangerous and wearisome. Woods on either hand so thickly studded with vines and spread oak as to be almost impenetrable to a rabbit, imparts a gloomy aspect to the highway.

For 556 miles after leaving the last named points, no town and but few settlements are met with. The Mail Company's stations are built by the road side and afford accommodations alone for the drivers, station men and horses.

Springs abound in these mountains. The water boils up through a mass of broken white flint stone and is incomparably excellent. No filtered rain water cooled with northern ice would I prefer to a draught fresh from these pure sparkling springs of the wild Ozarks, when drank beneath the impenetrable canopy of foliage that shields them from the rays of the southern sun.

Fayetteville, Arkansas Square, 1870

**at length come to Fayetteville
a lovely town in Arkansas,
handsomely shaded by deep files of trees
that line the streets on either hand**

Traveling along day and night through this solitary region we at length come to Fayetteville, a lovely town in Arkansas, 110 miles from Springfield, and 60 miles from this place *[Fort Smith]*. The town reposes upon the mountain tops, and is handsomely shaded by deep files of trees that line the streets on either hand. It contains a court house, several churches and many fine private residences, and is the seat of the University of Arkansas. *[Marilyn Heifner points out that although Hiram's letter states "University of Arkansas" actually at the time the name was "Arkansas College" founded in Fayetteville in late 1850. The U of A was founded as "Arkansas Industrial University" in 1871. Classes were first held in 1872, and the name "University of Arkansas" name was not officially adopted until 1899.]*

From the steps of the court house I there witnessed the sale of a slave boy — a spectacle that was indeed grating to my feelings.

Fayetteville, Arkansas Public Square, 1860

From Fayetteville to Van Buren, the point where the Arkansas river is first reached. The road lies through high and rugged mountains, the wild scenery of which is occasionally diversified by valleys covered with corn, many of which are in the form of an oblong circle and of one or two thousand acres in extent.

No one who has never passed over this road can form any idea of its bold and rugged aspect. It winds along the mountain sides over a surface with masses of broken rock, and frequently runs in fearful proximity to precipitous ravines of unknown depth. Over such a route as this the coaches of the mail company are driven with fearful rapidity. The horses are seldom permitted to walk even when traversing the steepest and most tortuous hills, and when drove at their utmost speed, which is generally the case, the stage reels from side to side like a storm tossed bark, and the din of the heavily ironed wheels in constant contact with the flinty rock, is truly appalling. The man who can pass over this route a passenger in one of the Overland Mail Coaches, without experiencing feelings of mingled terror and astonishment must certainly be oblivious to every consideration of personal safety. Yet with all these indications — of danger and recklessness — accidents rarely occur, and since the Mail Company has been established, not a single life has been lost on this part of the route.

The coaches are built expressly with reference to rough service — and none but the most reliable and experienced drivers are placed upon the mountain districts. The horses are of the most powerful descriptions to be found, and when once thoroughly trained to the service perform the laborious run with apparent pleasure and delight.

Although my letter is already extended beyond the limits originally intended I must not conclude without saying something more in relation to this place *[Fort Smith]*. I must say that I have been very agreeably disappointed in whatever pertains to the town and the inhabitants thereof. Stores well stocked with goods of every quality and description to be found in the older towns of the northern states, are numerous. One establishment in the large three story brick block across the street *[probably across the street from the City Hotel]* contains more goods than can be found at Sullivan's.

Drug stores, there are two; one of which is as handsomely fitted and furnished, and contains as large a stock as any concern of the kind I have yet seen in Cleveland.

There is a bonnet and dress making establishment where everything in that line of business is got up agreeably to the latest eastern styles and patterns.

The general appearance of the town is rather prepossessing *[attractive]* to the stranger, than otherwise.

There are three churches of moderate architectural pretensions, and a female seminary of fine external appearance and which is said to be well conducted and liberally sustained.

There are several hotels in the place. That at which we board *[John Roger's City Hotel]* is said to be the best kept, and affords accommodations with which I am tolerably well satisfied. The only drawback consists in the fact that the rooms being large contain two or more beds each and accordingly no one can get a room for his exclusive use. The servants of which there is a large number for a house no larger than the City Hotel, are all slaves. They seem to perform their respective duties with alacrity, and are not so importunate for an occasional quarter as their brothers of the north.

Slaves are numerously held in and about the town and are universally full blooded blacks. Indeed I do not remember, having seen a single mulatto since I came into Arkansas. As free "niggers," are not permitted to live in this State every colored person met with is presumptively a slave.

[NOTE: "In an effort to keep all Black Arkansans enslaved, the Arkansas General Assembly passed a bill February 12, 1859, banning anyone with Black ancestry from living as a free person in Arkansas. At the time the bill was passed there were 700 free Black people residing in Arkansas. The bill stated that if they did not leave the state by January 1, 1860, they would be enslaved once more. Arkansas was the only state to pass such a law, though similar bills were considered in other slave-holding states. There are no reports of this law being enforced. However, the law did work to divide people by race rather than by free or enslaved status and forced over 500 people to flee their homes in Arkansas." 'Slavery in Arkansas' by the Arkansas State Archives, arkansasheritage.com]

Indians of various tribes, (or nations as they are

here called) are seen in large numbers about the streets every day. They come into town from the Territory usually at an early hour in the morning, and spend the day loafing among the various whiskey shops fronting on the river. At night they return home as peaceably as they came and no one but themselves seems the worse of their coming — the rum sellers certainly not. They generally ride good horses, and many of them are men of property, and hold slaves.

Every where in the Territory the sale of ardent spirits is peremptorily prohibited which accounts for the regularity of their visits to this place *[Fort Smith].* All along the western border of this state *[Arkansas]* the whites drive a lucrative business at the expense of the "poor Indian" whose proverbial appetite for strong drink leads him into the wildest excesses.

I came into possession of the keys of the office yesterday the duties are neither arduous nor perplexing so far as I can judge from the brief experience I have had.

[The offices of Butterfield's Overland Mail Company were at the City Hotel, where most of the employees were also boarded. The stables behind the hotel typically boarded about 100 horses belonging to the mail company. When the City Hotel was lost due to fire, Sept. 1860, the offices were relocated to the St. Charles Hotel about two blocks away.]

A word or two in relation to the climate. We have had pretty warm weather since my arrival here, but it does not enervate *[cause someone to feel drained of energy]* the system to the extent that the same degree of heat in the north causes us to feel. Owing to some atmosphere peculiarity it is almost impossible to contract a cold. I have slept with the windows open in a strong current of air without experiencing the slightest ill effects therefrom. This you know, I could never do in Ohio, without endangering my health.

I have heard nothing from you since I left home. I

shall be grievously disappointed if I do not get a letter by Sunday mail. Do not fail to write to me as often as you can, as you can readily imagine how anxious I am to hear from you.

I hope that you will soon become reconciled to our brief separation and if things go on as I now have reason to expect, we will try our fortune for a time at least — if providence has so ordered — in this handsome and social little city *[Fort Smith]*, situated upon the border of civilization.

In the meantime be of good courage. I meant to say a word or two to the dear little children but feel much fatigued with the labor of writing this long letter.

Say to Mary that I will write her a nice little letter by the next mail. Kiss the children one and all for me.

My respects to Mr. & Mrs. Beilhartz and the girls; also to Mrs. Craig and all others who may inquire concerning my welfare. Remember me to Angaline and the little Anny.

Very truly your loving husband,
Hiram

P. S. Should you have any trouble in reading this letter get Mr. Beilhartz to read it for you, but show it to no one else, that is, to no person out of his family.

Fort Smith, Aug. 9th, 1860
Thursday afternoon

Dear Frank — *[Frank is Hiram's nickname for his wife.]*

Your kind letter of Wednesday night came to hand this morning about 8 o'clock. You must have had a busy time of it on the 1st on the occasion of the "Grand Republican Rally." I hope you did not exert yourself beyond your strength in attending to your numerous guests.

I was happy to hear that the children had all regained their usual health.

Yesterday was the regular mail day but as I did not expect the Overland on time owing to the almost starved condition of the stock between this place and Fort Chadbourne. I thought I could safely defer my semi-weekly task until today. Robinson has gone to the Red River Valley in Texas for the same object that induced the sons of Jacob to go down into Egypt to buy corn. *[Genesis 42:1-9]* A supply is wanted to distribute along that portion of the route above named, a distance of about 500 miles. Such is the scarcity of grain that in order to obtain a supply and distribute it at the points needed it will have to be waggoned hundreds of miles at an average cost, including transportation, of at least five dollar per bushel.

From this you will be able to appreciate some of the difficulties encountered in keeping the "Overland" in a state of efficiency. There is not one bushel of grain to be had on the line between this point and Fort Chadbourne.

The drought has absolutely destroyed everything. The grasshoppers have even perished from want of sustenance.

Robinson expected to be absent about three weeks. He will have a laborious time of it, but I hope will get around in good condition. He said he expected to start for Ohio soon after his return from the South West.

So far my duties have always been the most arduous and perplexing in the absence of Mr. Robinson. I do not mean that such is the case as it regards the ordinary routine of business, as that is easily attended to.

He was away when the accident happened to the Stage Coach, of which I wrote you an account some time since. Last Monday night, Old Sol, as we familiarly called him, my principal assistant in the office, was shot by a Cherokee Indian, in front of the Saint Charles Hotel. The pistol ball entered near the navel and penetrated the abdominal cavity. The unhappy affair occurred about 11 o'clock. I was asleep in bed when one of the conductors aroused me, and informed me of the melancholy event. As soon as possible I hurried to the office where I found the wounded man lying on a cot, surrounded by a crowd of sympathizing friends, and a doctor engaged in probing the wound. At first sight I was convinced that the injury was mortal, though the doctor assured him that it was not necessarily so. I had him removed to the City Hotel as soon as possible where he lingered in intense agony until Tuesday evening when death kindly interposed and his sufferings were at an end. The duty of preparing for his funeral mainly devolved upon myself. Everything was done decently and in order. The funeral was appointed to take place at 11 o'clock yesterday morning. The Rev. Mr. Sample of the Presbyterian Church who, at my request had been with Sol some hours before his death, conducted the services in the great-hall of the Hotel. He preached a short but impressive discourse, and denounced the practice of carrying fire arms in the most emphatic manner. After the services the corpse was borne to the cemetery. Four large 4 horse coaches belonging to the Mail Company were first in the procession after the hearse, and were followed by many carriages and buggies belonging to the citizens and kindly tendered for the occasion. It afforded me a melancholy pleasure to witness so numerous an attendance, and the degree of sympathy that seemed to pervade the community in behalf of the unfortunate man.

Sol was formerly from Utica, New York, and came out here with the parties by whom the Mail Company was established, about two years ago. He was unmarried as far as we can ascertain. He was of a wealthy family, but had long since squandered his patrimony in riotous living. We informed his friends east of the circumstances attending his death. I have always found him a useful and reliable man, and am fearful that we will not find another soon who can discharge the duties that pertained to his position with the same degree of energy and efficiency. I enclose you one of the notices I had prepared for the funeral.

The Indian was arrested soon after the occurrence that terminated so fatally. Today I have mainly devoted in preparing for his examination which is set for tomorrow.

The mail has just arrived at the door and I must stop. I will write again on Saturday. My health continues good. You must not be alarmed on my account as it regards the "Injuns" shooting one as I have nothing to say to them and keep "o' nights" like a good boy. You know that I am afraid of nothing, but I have always thought that prudence was the better part of valor and this principal I act upon.

My love to the children and yourself.

In haste truly your affectionate husband,

Hiram

Fort Smith, Arkansas

September 25, 1860

Your letter of the 13th inst., informing me of the painful and dangerous illness of our beloved little son came to hand on Thursday morning the 20th. This sad intelligence reached me at an hour of excitement and alarm.

A disastrous fire was then raging on the opposite side of the street, and the devouring element threatened all that was valuable in the city. Fortunately —

I might say providentially — the morning was calm, otherwise the scene of destruction would have been fearful to contemplate.

As it was, the principal buildings destroyed were the Garrison block and City Hotel, the latter being the house at which we boarded. The Garrison block was the pride and glory of the city.

It was erected some years since at a cost of seventy four thousand dollars, and was exclusively devoted to business. In a room on the second story of this massive pile, the fire originated and so rapid was the progress of the flames that every effort to save the building was utterly unavailing. But few goods were saved from the numerous stores the building contained.

The Cline drug stores — the owners of which are cousins to the Yerks of Tiffin — was completely destroyed. The misfortune of these worthy young men is peculiarly sad and deplorable. They were engaged in the business some seven years and at the time of the disaster their drug store was one of the largest and best arranged establishments of the kind to be met with anywhere.

Originating in a room immediately above, the fire soon found its way through the intervening floor, and, in an instant the entire concern was enveloped in a sheet of flame. They had no insurance whatever, and thus in the brief space of a few minutes they were reduced from comparative wealth to a state of *[extreme poverty]* penury.

The post office was in Clines store; and not a single letter out of some four thousand, exclusive of the Overland Mail from Memphis, was saved. Among this mass of ill fated letters was one for your own dear self, which I had written and mailed the day before in expectation of the Overland mail the ensuing night. This letter embraced one and a half sheets of cap paper and was worded in my best style. At a later hour, the same day, I mailed two others, one which was directed to our good friend, Doctor B. and the other to Mr. Robinson at New York.

The furniture of the City Hotel was mostly saved. The alarm was about the hour of four in the morning. As soon as I could get down stairs, I aroused the "Overland boys" and ordered a large baggage wagon to the door with all possible expedition. Everything in and about the room I occupied, on which I had any claim, was saved — except my "night shirt" and the coat I wore away with me from Tiffin. These, owing to some cause or other — not very clear to me — could not be found.

After arranging for the removal of the effects of this office, in case of necessity, I returned to the Hotel, and remained upstairs aiding in the preservation of the property of the kind hearted McKensie until the advancing flames drove us from the house.

The part I performed consisted in removing the furniture, bedding, etc. from the various rooms, and depositing the same at the head of the "great stair way." In this perilous service I was mainly aided by three young ladies — of position in society — where coolness during that trying hour did not forsake them.

Various theories prevail as to the origin of this disastrous fire; but the generally received opinion is, that it was the work of design, and this opinion is strengthened by the force of concurrent circumstances to which I have neither space nor time to allude at present.

It was under the circumstances thus briefly detailed that the dangerous condition of our fair haired boy was announced to me. You may readily imagine that this announcement was in no way calculated to dispel the gloomy feelings that then oppressed my mind. I at once had recourse to the telegraph — and at a seasonable hour the following morning received the gratifying response that the little fellow had fully recovered from his late malady. In the "burned letter" I alluded to the "great bile" with which you were so sorely afflicted when you wrote me on the 8th inst. I was much distressed to hear of your sad condition, though I cherished the reasonable hope that during the time occupied in the transmission of the letter your painfully troublesome visitor had disappeared from your seat of horror!

I was favored with a letter from Robinson, by the last mail but one, written at Mansfield. He therein stated that he found his family all well except his wife who was very lame. For this reason she could not go to Tiffin, and therefore he concluded to defer his promised visit until on his return from New York. I have heard from him by telegraph since he reached the city and shall expect a letter on Thursday next. I hope he may arrange his matters satisfactorily and return here as speedily as possible as I assure you I am extremely anxious to get back to Ohio once more. I am comparatively indifferent as to whether I retain my position here or not; and certainly will have no desire to remain in the service of the Mail Company in any position whatever, unless the controlling parties in New York concede to Robinson the several reforms in management and the enlarged authority he demands. The matter will doubtless be determined on at an early day — perhaps in time to advise you of the result by the next mail but one. For the sake of our friend Mr. R. I fondly hope that he may succeed in the object of his mission east.

Among the numerous officials in the service of the Company with whom I have been brought in contact since my arrival here there is none so eminently qualified for a high and responsible position as himself. And yet under the present system of mismanagement, this man has been obliged to be subordinate to a set of ignorant and brutish road-agents — who, years ago graduated from the stables of the Ohio Stage Company, and are now, in morals, better fitted for the depraved associations of Mott and Mulbury Streets *["Mott and Mulbury Streets" refers to lower Manhattan's notorious slum neighborhood in the 1800's called 'Chinatown.']* than for the companionship of men of moderate decency. Should the Directory in New York so far ignore the true interests of the Company as to compel Robinson to give way to these insolent and bombastic interlopers, they will discover, at no very remote day, that they have committed an error fraught with incalculable damage to the prospects of this "great enterprise."

In your letter of the 8th written under the inspiration of your "bile," you briefly referred to an exciting event that lately transpired at the house of Mr. P. At the time said letter came to hand, I had not received yours of the 5th and therefore was oppressed with uncertainty as to what all this meant. I was at first fearful that Mr. P. himself was compromised in the matter by aiding in, or conniving at, the attempt made to conceal the evidence of degradation in which the fair fame of his unhappy daughter was so unexpectedly involved. As you made no mention of this fact in your succeeding letters I charitably concluded that he was in no wise connected with so foolish and desperate an undertaking. This sad occurrence overwhelmed me in pain and heartfelt sorrow. It has fixed a stain upon the escutcheon of a worthy and high minded family that the tears and sympathies of generous friends can never efface; and has left a wound in the heart of a kind and indulgent father which time will fail to heal; and which will bleed anew at each remembrance of his daughter's waywardness.

But what has become of the pusillanimous — whose villainy has caused all this scandal at the expense of the good name and peace of mind of this hitherto happy family? Is he permitted to run at large and gloat with devilish pleasure at the great ruin he has accomplished? If the infamous wretch were here in Arkansaw his miserable carcass would furnish the material for a public pastime.

The other day I looked upon the body of a horse thief who was shot down in the street during an effort to escape from his captors who had kindly tendered him a rope. I cannot say that I was wanting in sympathy for this unfortunate man as I saw him covered with dust and blood and writhing in the agonies of approaching death; but I could have looked upon the bloody spectacle with comparative composure if this victim of popular fury had met his fate for conspiring against the virtue of an artless girl.

I wish you would take pains to write me more fully in relation to this matter as whatever you may have to say upon the subject will be interesting to me.

I was glad to hear that little Mary had re-commenced her studies. You must be careful and not let her over task her mind by undertaking tasks unsuited to so young a child. She is ambitious to learn — and in this she could be encouraged to an extent consistent with her tender years, and not beyond.

It seems that our neighbor Craig has concluded to abandon the service of Smith Barnes & Co., and return to his old avocation. You may well ask, what is to become of them? I am really sorry for his family, but it is out of my power to afford them any permanent aid. If he cannot retain a place in Tiffin how is he to secure one abroad? Some months ago I gave you my views at length touching his proposition to aid you in moving hither in consideration of a situation, secured to him on my part. — Of all the places in the world this is the last one he should ever think of coming to in the hope of mending his unfortunate habits. The "Injun" rifle whiskey — sure to kill at forty rods — would soon do the business for him. I do not know that he has ever seriously entertained the thought that I might be pre-vailed on to use my influence in his behalf; but if he does, you must give him no encouragement whatever.

I have heard nothing from you on the subject of peaches this many a week. Have you made arrange-ments for a supply? It is needless to inform you that the cans put up through my agency will go into a very small space without much crowding. The truth of the matter is that there was nothing of the kind to be had here — during the season — except clings, and this de-scription, if I am correctly informed are unfit for that purpose. I could have had plenty of grapes by paying 25c a pound for them, if I had thought they would justify so high a figure. If you cannot get a supply of peaches there, have Mrs. Patterson order you what you may want through Patterson Brothers & Co., from Cin-cinnati and I will settle for them on my way home next month.

Say to Mary that if nothing happens, she may give her birthday party whether I succeed in getting home or not by the 17th of October. The poor little thing has had her heart fixed so long on the pleasure to be derived from a birthday festival that you must not disappoint her if you can avoid doing so. I need not admonish you that her childish expectations can be fully grati-fied without going to any great expense in the matter.

I was pleased to hear that you had at length succeeded in finding another girl. I hope she may continue to give you reason to regard her as a useful acquisition to your household, though I would not like to vouch for that on so short an acquaintance. You must try to keep her and Laney from getting into any of their jars. Laney had better stay with you until it is determined whether we will move this fall or not.

I have not heard from Mr. Bill as yet in reply to my letter. I wish you would ascertain whether it reached him or not. It was written some five or six weeks ago. Mr. B. is doubtless so busy with his grain operations that he cannot find time to write.

Have you heard from the folks at home lately? I have had nothing from them for a month or more, and I am at a loss to comprehend the cause of their pro-tracted silence. I have not had a letter from Arens(?) for two months or more.

Since the fire we *[the offices of the Overland Mail Co.]* have moved our quarters to the Saint Charles Hotel — one square *[block]* below — this office, towards the river. The fare does not come up to the standard of the late City Hotel, though it is quite passable. I have secured a very comfortable single room — nearly as large as our bedroom at home. It contains a sofa bed, mahogany bureau, and other conveniences to correspond. Take it altogether, and I am much more comfortably situated than before the fire. The weather continues dry and warm. We had several fine showers some three weeks ago but their effects have long since ceased to be dis-cernible.

On the 19th we were favored with a cool wind from the north west, but the change of temperature was of short duration. There is no immediate prospect of a necessity for putting up stoves or refitting fire places;

these comforts you have doubtless enjoyed for some time in that cold region. Frost seldom makes its appearance here before the middle of November. The foliage is beginning to look sear and yellow but this is solely attributable to a want of moisture.

I am sorry that my letter to Mr. B. was lost as I am fearful that I will not find time to write another for some days if at all before my return home. You must inform him of this circumstance and express my regrets upon the subject. They have all been so kind to us that I know not how to reward them sufficiently. You can let them see my letters to you whenever you think they contain anything of interest.

Miss Rumsey's bill I think was quite moderate for the amount of service performed. Did you show her any remarks in relation to herself contained in my letter of the 19th of August? But I must write a short letter to Robinson and therefore will not have time to say more at present.

Remember me to Laney.

Hoping that through the goodness of God you are all in the enjoyment of health.

I am as ever Truly your affectionate Husband,

Hiram

P. S. My love to Mr. and Mrs. B. & family and earnest thanks for their kind attentions to you & the children.

I will send my draft on Tomb, Huss & Co. to W. M. Johnson, by this mail in payment of rent due first of October and request him to hand receipt to you. So you need give yourself no trouble about this matter.

[The following is a previously unpublished letter of Hiram to his wife, from the files of Huntington Library.]
In the process of making the transcript below, I appreciate the assistance of the president of the Butterfield Overland National Historic Trail Association, Marilyn Heifner.

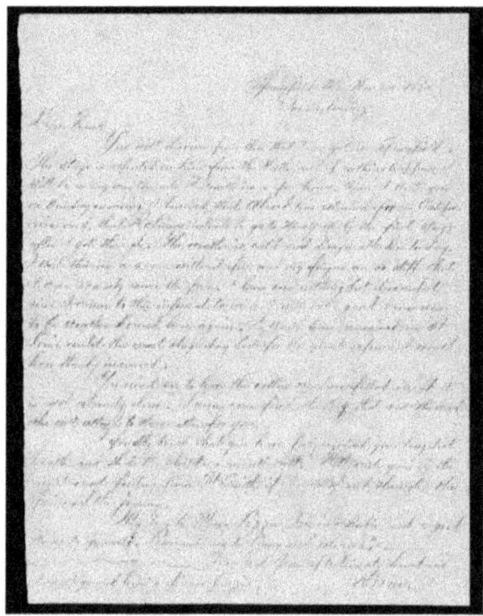

Springfield, MO
Nov. 20, 1860
Tuesday Evening

Dear Frank,

You will discover from this that I am yet in Springfield. The stage is reported on time from the North, and if nothing happens I will be on my way towards Fort Smith in a few hours. Since I wrote you on Sunday morning, I learned that Alvord(?) has returned from California and that Robinson intends to go to New York by the first stage after I get through.

The weather is cold and disagreeable here today. I write this in a snow without fire and my fingers are so stiff I can scarcely move the fingers. I have seen nothing but discomfort since I came to this infernal town and will take good care never to be weather bound here again. I would have remained in St. Louis until the next stage day, but for the great expense I would have thereby incurred.

You must see to have the cellar windows filled in if it is not already done. Laney can find the boy that cut the wood and will attend to the matter for you.

I fondly trust that you have fully regained your long lost health and that the children are well. Will write you by the mail route Friday from Fort Smith if I am spared through the perils of the journey.

My love to Mary Lizzie Janice & Babie and a good ___ to yourself. Remember me to Laney and Johanna.

Very Truly Your Affectionate Husband,

Hiram

I must go and hunt a fire or freeze.

[The following is a previously unpublished letter of Hiram to his wife, from the files of Huntington Library.]
In the process of making the transcript below, I appreciate the assistance of Erin Glassman, Joe Huck and the president of the Butterfield Overland National Historic Trail Association, Marilyn Heifner.

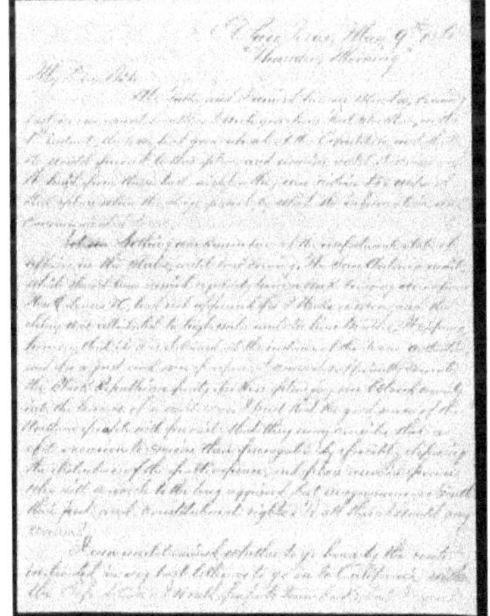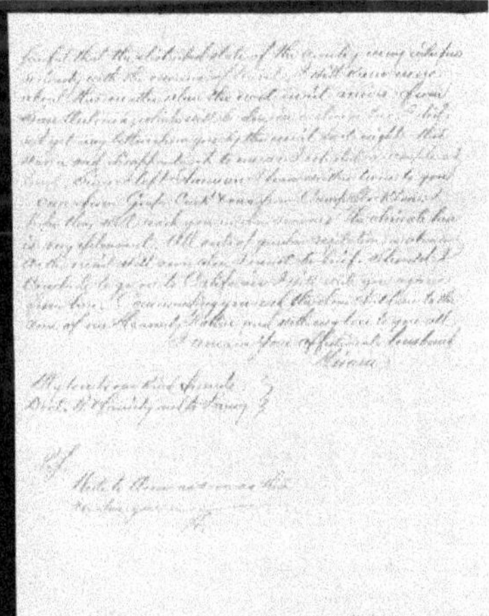

El Paso, Texas
Thursday Morning, May 9, 1861

My Dear Wife,

Mr. Talber and I arrived here on Monday Evening last in our usual health. I wrote you from Fort Stockton, on the 1st instant, that we had gone ahead of the

Expedition, and that we would proceed to this place and remain until it comes up. We heard from them last night — they are within 150 miles of this place when the stage passed, by which the information was communicated to us.

Nothing was known here of the unfortunate state of affairs in the States, until last evening. The San Antonio mail, which should have arrived regularly twice a week bringing news from New Orleans, had not appeared for 3 weeks or more and the delay attributed to high water and Indian troubles. It appears, however, that it was detained at the insistence of the Texan Authorities, and for a just and wise purpose. I cannot sufficiently excoriate the Black Republican Party for their plunging our beloved country into the horrors of civil war. I trust that the good sense of the Northern people will prevail — that they may consider this a fit occasion to exercise their prerogative by forcibly deposing the disturbers of the public peace and place men in power who will concede to the long aggrieved but magnanimous South their just and constitutional rights: to all this I would say amen!

I am undetermined whether to go home by the route indicated in my last letter or go on to California with the Expedition. I would prefer to turn back, but I am fearful that the disturbed state of the country may interfere seriously with the means of travel. I will know more about this matter when the next mail arrives from San Antonio, which will be due in a day or two.

I did not get any letters from you by the mail last night — this was a sad disappointment to me as I expected a couple at least. Since I left Sherman I have written twice to you — once from Grape Creek & once from Camp Stockton. I hope they will reach you in due season.

The climate here is very pleasant. All sorts of garden vegetation is abundant.

As the mail will soon close I must be brief. Should I conclude to go on to California I will write you again from there. Commending you and the dear children to the care of our Heavenly Father, and with my love to you all.   I remain your affectionate husband

My love to our kind friends
Doct. B. & family and to Laney
P. S. Write to Areus as soon as this reaches you. H.

[During the dismantling of Butterfield's presence on the Southern route in preparation for moving north to the Central Route for the completion of their Postal Contract, the following previously unpublished letter by Hiram was written to his wife.]

The context for the following letter:

On June 30, 1857, Giddings' contract to carry the mail between San Antonio and Santa Fé ended. On the next day, a new contract to carry the mail on through to San Diego, California, was scheduled to begin. James E. Birch, from Swansea, Massachusetts received the contract for route number 8076 for $149,800 to provide semimonthly service to San Diego with connections to the Lower Road from San Antonio. After Birch's death, George Giddings received a new 3½ year contract for Route number 8076 for twice a month (semi-monthly) service paying $149,800 per year beginning on January 1, 1858. On June 1, 1859, the new Postmaster General Holt ordered Giddings to reduce his weekly service to 24 trips per year at a contract price of $120,000. April 1860 the route was reduced to San Antonio to Fort Yuma only.

In March/April, 1861 when the Butterfield's Southern route ended and relocated north to the Central Route, the new Postmaster General offered Giddings a new four-year mail contract. It was for a route to run from San Antonio to Los Angeles, beginning on April 1, 1861. At that time, most Americans thought that the conflict between the Federal government and the Southern States would be settled peacefully and that the mail service would be allowed to continue as before until the Union and the Confederacy could agree to a treaty.

*On April 1, 1861, George Giddings and his brother James were on board the westbound stage when it left San Antonio. **George was on his way to meet with Butterfield representatives at Fort Stockton to buy their remaining stock and equipment.** James Giddings was headed to California to organize men and material for the resumption of the mail contract to Los Angeles. It ap-*

pears that George was attempting to buy all the equipment from Fort Stockton to California, belonging to the Butterfield Company. THIS APRIL 1861 BUYING TRIP OF GEORGE GIDDINGS IS THE CONTEXT FOR THE FOLLOWING LETTER OF HIRAM RUMFIELD.

Historically, it appears the transaction referred to in this letter may not have been completed. An encounter with Indians resulting in the death of George Gidding's brother, and the newspapers report that 18 stagecoaches were transported north to the Central Route to begin running between Salt Lake City and Carson City July 1, 1861.

In the process of making the transcript below, I appreciate the assistance of the president of the Butterfield Overland National Historic Trail Association, Marilyn Heifner.

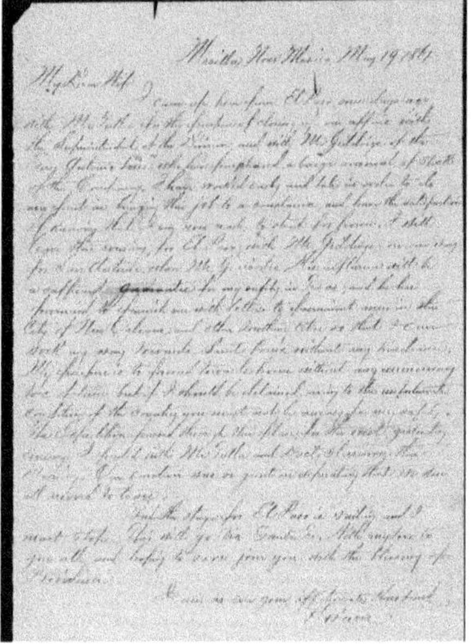

Mesilla, New Mexico
May 19, 1861

My Dear Wife,

I came up here from El Paso, some days ago with Mr. Tuller, for the purpose of closing up our affairs with the Superintendent of the Division, and with Mr. *[George]* Giddings of the San Antonio line, who has purchased a large amount of stock of the Company. I have worked early and late in order to do my part in bringing this job to a conclusion, and have the satisfaction of knowing that I am now ready to start for home.

I will leave this evening for El Paso with Mr. Gid-

© 2024 Robert O. Crossman

dings — on our way for San Antonio, where Mr. G. resides. His influence will be a sufficient guarantee for my safety in Texas, and he has promised to furnish me with letters to prominent men in the City of New Orleans and other Southern Cities so that I can work my way towards Saint Louis without any hindrance.

My purpose is to proceed towards home without any unnecessary loss of time, but if I should be detained owing to the unfortunate condition of the country, you must not be uneasy for my safety. The expedition passed through this place, for the west, yesterday Evening. I parted with Mr. Tuller and Doct. Stevenson this Morning. Our emotion was so great on separating that we were all moved to tears!

But the stage for El Paso is waiting and I must stop. This will go via Santa Fe. With my love to you all and hoping to soon join you with the blessing of Providence.   I am ever your affectionate Husband

Concerning Hiram Rumfield's letter above sent from Mesilla, New Mexico, postal historian Jody Cody (in a letter to Bob Crossman) writes:

Mesilla, New Mexico Post Office

The Mesilla, New Mexico Post Office was established 21 January 1858 and was still operating at the time Rumfield wrote his letter. The Mesilla Post Office was effectively and forcibly closed two months after Rumfield's letter on 25 July 1861 following the Union defeat and Confederate Army occupation during the First Battle of Mesilla.

A peculiar form of regional self-government was in place at Mesilla, and across southern New Mexico Territory, when Rumfield mailed his letter in May 1861. The Provisional Government of Arizona Territory was formed by a vote of a convention of delegates held at Tucson, New Mexico on 03 April 1860. The Provisional Government of Arizona Territory encompassed the area of the US New Mexico Territory south of 33.40" north latitude, including Mesilla. Later, on 16 March 1861 this Arizona provisional government seceded from the Union. Rumfield would have been aware that Mesilla was locally under the control of a hostile Arizona Territorial government located in Tucson. The United States did not recognize the provisional or seceded government at Arizona and considered Mesilla to still be under federal control and located within the US Territory of New Mexico. The pending war would change all previous territorial borders and provisional and seceded governments thereby leading directly to the creation of the Territory and State of Arizona.

The earliest recorded surviving postmark from Mesilla, New Mexico is dated 03 November 1861. No postmarks from Mesilla are known from the period of the Butterfield Overland Mails. If the original envelope from the Hiram Rumfield letter survives, it would be a significant item of postal history with a postmark from Mesilla six-months earlier than currently known."   *Source: Joe Cody, Postal Historian*

1855 Saint Louis, MO (partial close up of wider panoramic scene)
Stone engraving by Leopold Gast and Brother, 1855
Courtesy of Missouri History Museum
Photograph and Print Collection, St. Louis Lithographs and Engravings

LETTERS OF REFERENCE

Three of the letters of reference mentioned above by Hiram above have survived in the archives of the Huntington Library. Images and transcript of the originals are below.

In the process of making this transcript, I appreciate the assistance of the president of the Butterfield Overland National Historic Trail Association, Marilyn Heifner.

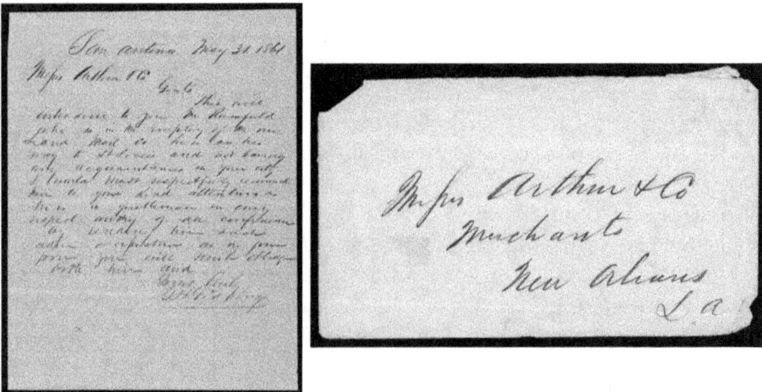

Mfrs. Arthur & Co.
Merchants
New Orleans, LA

San Antonio
May 31, 1861

Mfrs Arthur & Co.
Gents

This will introduce to you Mr. Rumfield who is in the employ of the Over Land Mail Co. He is on his way to St Louis and not having any acquaintances in your city I ___ must respectfully recommend him to your kind attention as he is a gentleman in every respect worthy of all conveniences by making him such ___ ____ as in your ___ you will much oblige both him and

Yours Truly. G. Giddings

[Giddings also wrote a similar note to "Gen. E. B. Nichols" both Galveston, Texas. That brief note was published in the American Antiquarian Society journal on page 252 in its 1928 issue.]

El Paso, Tex.
May 20th 1861

Mess. Cross & Hensley
Gents

The bearer of this Mr. H. S. Rumfield of the O. L M. Co. at this place & whom we take pleasure in introducing to you visits your city on business for the company and attention shown him will be appreciated by

Yours Truly
Mc Knight & Richardson
per Aylmer

[McKnight also wrote similar notes to "H. Meyer & Co., and another to "Mess. Sweet & Lacosto" both of San Antonio, Texas. Those brief note was published in the American Antiquarian Society journal on page 251 and 252 in its 1928 issue.]

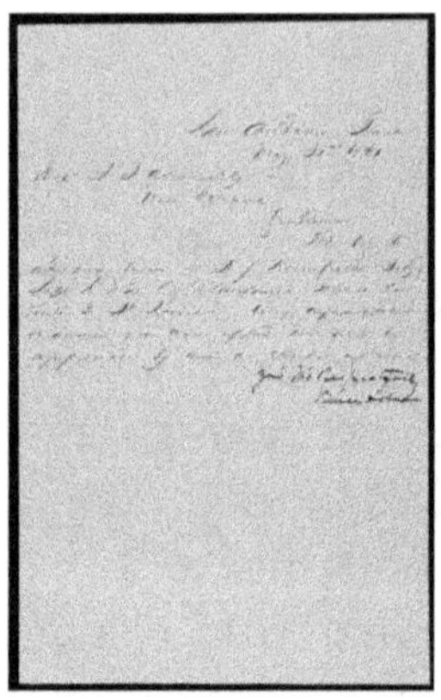

San Antonio, Texas, May 31, 1861

Messr. I. I.. Ad______
New Orleans

We beg to introduce to you Mr. H. S. Rumfield, ____, Supt. O. Mail Co to California, who is en route to St. Louis. Any information or advice you can afford ___ will be appreciated by him and ____ of ____

Yours __ Respectfully
Vance & Bro.

[NOTE: The June 8, 1862 letter below, written to "Dear Doctor" is printed in the 1928 issue of the American Antiquarian Society on page 267-8. The middle part of that letter is included here because it mentions the relocation of the Overland Mail Co. contract to the Central Route and the sub-contract with Russell and eventually with Ben Holladay. This letter also mentions the Overland Mail Co. relationship with the Mormon (Latter Day Saints) church.]

Salt Lake City, June 8, 1862

Dear Doctor,

Amidst the perplexing circumstances by which we have been harassed for the past two months I assure you that I have never ceased to remember the letter so frequently promised you but so long delayed.

As you must be informed of the causes which led to the late suspension of mail service of the "Eastern Division" of the "Overland Route," I need say but little on that subject. It is proper to remark, however, that the Overland Mail Company — incorporated as such — is not directly responsible for the management of that part of the line, lying between this City and Atchison.

The Company's contract with Government embraces the entire line from Missouri to California; but when the transfer was made from the Southern Route, with the full consent of the Department, the Eastern Division was sub-let to Wm. H. Russell and others, who assumed the entire management thereof under a contract which was regarded as advantageous to the Overland Co. These parties failed in December last and the fulfillment of said contract devolved upon their assignees who could not control the means necessary to an efficient operation of the lines. The affairs of the Division continued in bad shape until the 21st day of March, last, when, with the consent of all parties concerned it was transferred to the sole charge and management of Ben Holladay of New York — a gentleman who possesses wealth and energy sufficient for the undertaking. The financial troubles, to which I have alluded, did not cause the stoppage of mail.

Reports have been circulated east, attributing the interruption to that cause; yet the evidence is conclusive that Indians -— and Indians alone, are responsible for the frequent and formidable depredations that compelled a suspension of through service until troops could be brought out, and placed upon the line, to protect it against further violence. The difficulties are now all surmounted, and arrangements made to put the mails in motion tomorrow, and continue daily thereafter.

The Mormons have always been hostile in feeling towards the Eastern Division and its management, though I cannot believe, for a moment that they were in any way implicated in the acts of violence which culminated in the attack on the stage, the destruction of the mails and the wounding of six men, near Ice Springs, on the morning of the 16th of April. Though their ill feeling is undisguised and uncompromising, they have too much sagacity to put themselves in a position that would lead to an open rupture with the Government.

While they are so badly disposed towards the Eastern — because it has been a damage rather than an advantage to them — our Company, (The Overland) on the other hand, commands their undivided confidence, friendship and affection. The principal part of our supplies — amounting in the aggregate, since the 1st day of July last, to several hundred thousand dollars — have been purchased in this valley and paid for in glittering gold! Our dealings with them have been conducted upon principles of firmness and justice. While we permit no person in the service of the company to deal unfairly with them, we will submit to no wrong in turn. We do not hesitate to employ a Mormon — or rather, in this respect, make no distinction between "Saint and Gentile," other things being equal. Whenever a dispute arises between us and any of the people concerning a matter of any consequence, whether involving money or otherwise, we at once refer the case to Brigham who never fails to hear patiently and decide with wisdom and impartiality.

The foregoing is but an imperfect outline of the policy which governs us in our dealings with this "peculiar people." Heber C. Kimball — brother Heber, as he is familiarly called by the "saints," paid me a visit last week, and in conversation gave me the most gratifying assurances of the good feeling cherished by his people towards this company. It was the first and only interview I have had with him — the first time he ever entered this office. Like Brigham, he is seldom seen on the streets, except on Sunday, on his way to or from the Tabernacle. Our interview took place in the back office — was strictly private and continued about an hour. Not a word was said upon the subject of religion — the Mormon religion especially. When the old man was ready to depart he arose from his chair, and placing his right hand on my head, in the most solemn tone and manner pronounced a blessing — almost in the exact words of the good old Apostolic Benediction. The proceeding was so unexpected that it rather startled me. He noticed my momentary confusion and seeming to think that I doubted his sincerity took my hand in his own and looking me squarely in the face, said—*"No one can justly accuse Heber of hypocrisy — I always speak as I am moved by the Holy Spirit; my blessing was from the heart— from the heart."* I assured him that I did not doubt his sincerity in the least, that I fully appreciated his good wishes, and that memory would never cease to revert with pleasure to the visit with which he was pleased to honor me. He then brushed the tears from his eyes — for by this time his feelings had entirely overcome him — and, with a hearty and emphatic *"God bless you,"* took his departure.

Summer is now fairly inaugurated—yet we have had but little hot weather thus far. The nights, especially, are delightfully cool and exhilarating. We can retire to bed with assurances favoring the happiest and most invigorating exercise of our "drowsy powers,"—not an insect to disturb our repose, save an occasional bed-bug, and that, perchance, already gorged to satiety with the "blood of the saints."

NOTE: Reviewing Hiram's additional letters in the files of the Huntington Library, the additional letters in their files seem to be written well before or after the close of the Southern route. Those additional letters were written from Salt Lake City, Fort Fillmore, El Paso, San Antonio, St. Louis, Carson City, or Washington DC.

Additional letters in the 1928 issue of the American Antiquarian Society include: Jan. 7, 1861 letter to his wife, page 250; letters of reference from Sam. Jones, McKnight (2), Sweet & Lacosto; Giddings on pages 251-2; July 17, 1861 letter from Fred Cook, Treasurer on page 253-4; Aug 8, 1861 letter to his wife on page 254-5; Dec. 19, 1861 letter to his wife on page 255-6; Dec. 26, 1861 letter to his wife on page 256-265; Jan. 1, 1862 letter to his daughter, Mary on page 265-6; June 8, 1862 letter to 'Doctor' on page 267-9; and letters to his wife on June 22, 1861, July 6, 1861, Aug. 26, 1862, Sept. 23, 1862, Dec. 29, 1862, Jan. 25, 1863, Feb. 4, 1863, Feb. 12, 1863, and Mar. 5, 1863 on pages 270-288; March 2, 1863 Frank Cook's letter to A. J. Center on page 288-291; letters to his wife Mar. 8, 1863, Mar. 24, 1863, and May 25, 1863, on page 292-7; Apr. 11, 1863 letter from Sam Gilbert; July 21, 1863 letter from S. S. Harding on page 298; Jan. 17, 1864 letter from W. H. Brodhead on page 298; May 8, 1864 letter from L. Wines; July 13, 1864 & June 20, 1865 letters from Brigham Young on page 299 & 301; Feb. 20, 1865, Dec. 4, 1865, and Nov. 2, 1866 letters to his wife on page 300-2.

BURIAL OF H. S. RUMFIELD.

Remains of an Old-Timer Brought Here From Savannah, Ohio.

On Tuesday last the remains of H. S. Rumfield, who died in Savannah, O., on the 22nd of December last, were brought to this city and interred by the side of his wife in the family burying plot at Mount Olivet. There was no funeral service, the remains being conveyed to the cemetery from Evans's undertaking parlors and followed by half a dozen or more intimate friends.

Few there were of the old-timers in this city who did not know Mr. Rumfield. He came to Utah in 1855 and made his home in this State until 1899, when he went to spend the remainder of his life with two of his daughters in Ohio. For ten years after coming to Utah he was manager of the Overland mail, later was connected with the smelter at Stockton, and after that was for seventeen years secretary and treasurer of the George M. Scott Hardware company, and the head of that firm said recently that he was the most accurate bookkeeper ever in the employ of the firm. He was a generous, warm-hearted man and his acts of charity, though unknown to the public, will be cherished by many a man and woman who in the hour of need found a friend in Mr. Rumfield.

Ten years ago Mrs. Rumfield died in this city, and two of the daughters went back to Ohio, where they now live. Mr. Rumfield was born in Tiffin, O., and at the time of his death was 79 years of age. Three daughters survive him, one of whom is married and lives in northern Idaho.

TO BE BURIED HERE.—The remains of H. S. Rumfield, a former Salt Laker who died in Savannah, Ga., last December, will be brought to this city for burial in the family plot beside the remains of his wife. No services of any kind will be held when the remains arrive.

Rumfield death notice,
The Salt Lake Herald,
Tue., March 4, 1902, page 8

Marilyn Heifner located this obituary of Hiram S. Rumfield on page 5 of the March 9, 1902 issue of The Salt Lake Tribune, Salt Lake City, Utah.

Image of Hiram S. Rumfield discovered...

*Overland Mail Co. Employees
on Central Route
Thursday, Oct. 19, 1865*

———————

*Left to right:
James J. Tracy, Treasurer OMCo;
James Street, Constructor;
H. S. Rumfield, General Agent;
Sam Woodward, Agent Ruby Valley;
and Aaron Stein.*
**Hiram Rumfield, seated center,
was Treasurer of the Overland
Mail Co. on the Southern Route.**

———————

*Image courtesy of
Yale University, Beinecke Rare Book
& Manuscript Library*

Envelope addressed by Hiram S. Rumfield discovered...

Enveloped addressed by Hiram S. Rumfield to his wife in Tiffin, Ohio.
From the collection of Bob Crossman

This envelope, from the Postal History collection of Bob Crossman, was addressed by Hiram S. Rumfield *(photo on left)* to his wife in Tipton, Ohio on March 5, 1863.

Hiram has served as Treasurer of the Overland Mail Company. Many of the letters to his wife have been preserved and published for his comments on the company. This particular letter to his wife is more personal in nature.

The stockings you have commenced knitting will certainly be acceptable to me on my return home.
At present, however, I am in no want.
Last Fall I bought half a dozen pairs of factory socks, a very good article, at 45 cents a pair.

Hiram S. Rumfield
Thursday, Oct. 19, 1865
Salt Lake City
Image: Yale University

Office of the Assistant Treasurer
Overland Mail Co.
SALT LAKE CITY, UTAH TERRITORY.
March 5th—1863

MY DEAR FRANK—

Your kind letter of the 11th February, came to hand on Monday evening. I was sorry to hear that Mary was obliged to defer writing her letter on account of the arrival of company, and hope she may have better luck next time.

The stocking you have commenced knitting will certainly be acceptable to me on my return home. At present, however, I am in no want. Last fall I bought half a dozen pairs of factory socks, a very good article, at 45 cents per pair. These, with the old ones brought from home, will suffice until I return to Ohio. As it regards shirts, I am equally well supplied. My old stock would have held out until next fall but for the fact that the muslin became unserviceable from age.

"Overland Mail Stage, Arizona, 1858" signed by William Hayes Hilton

CHAPTER FORTY SEVEN
William Tallack, July 4, 1860
"The California overland express: the longest stage-ride in the world"
by William Tallack, London, 1865
also as reprinted in "The First Overland Mail: Butterfield Trail
St. Louis to San Francisco" by Walter B. Lang, pages 129 to 163

William Tallack writes:

A few months previous to the secession of the Confederate States, the writer found himself in San Francisco on his return from Australia to Europe. He had calculated on taking the usual route, eastward from California to New York, by way of Panama, and, after a sojourn in New England and the central Atlantic seaboard, to return to London by one of the regular steamers from New York.

On reaching San Francisco he was unexpectedly informed that the hitherto double steam line via Panama had just been purchased by a well known millionaire, who had thus been able to establish a monopoly of transit on his own terms. In short, the fares were doubled, and conveniences at least halved; in addition to which the hot season having fully set in rendered the prospect of a return to the oppressive latitudes of the tropics anything but an inviting one, and led the writer to look around for some other route, and finally to take the **Overland Mail Stage** through Arizona, Texas, and

the Indian Territory, to St. Louis...
[His lengthy observations on day one to seventeen focus on his journey through California, New Mexico, Nevada and Texas.]

Eighteenth Day - North Eastern Texas

...We found the muddy water of the Red River much beneath its usual level, and were ferried across by slaves, from one deep red earthy bluff of bank to another similar one on the eastern side, up which we scrambled; and were now in the Indian Territory, the tract of fertile region, five hundred miles long by two hundred broad, permanently guaranteed by the Federal Government to the remnant of the various tribes who once were lords of the whole territory from the Mississippi to the Atlantic.

"Crossing Boggy River, Texas, 1859" signed by William Hayes Hilton
Source: Huntington Library, call number mssHilton Book 3, San Marino, CA.

After supper at a large log-house, we again traveled all night through forest regions, and on awaking in the morning perceived two new companions sitting in our midst, one a government agent for the protection of the Indian tribes hereabouts and the other, a Yankee school-master of a mission-school for the young aborigines. We found both of these to be gentlemen, and, in conversation and politeness, a great improvement compared with the passengers who left us at Sherman.

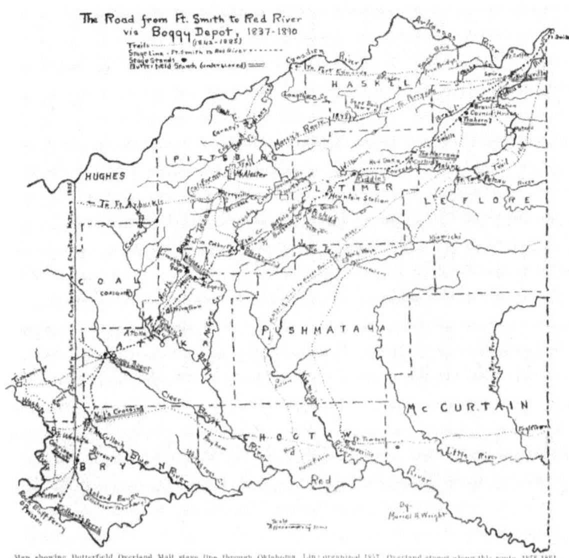

Butterfield Overland National Trail Through Indian Territory
The description for this map reads, "The route of the Butterfield Overland Mail stages in Southeastern Oklahoma along the old road from Fort Smith is shown on the map that accompanies this article (1957). Approximate routes of other trails in this region are shown to aid as illustrations, many of them important in Oklahoma history."
*Chronicles of Oklahoma, Spring 1957, *"The Butterfield Overland Mail One Hundred Years Ago" *by Muriel H. Wright, pages 55-71.*

Nineteenth Day – The Indian Territory

Notwithstanding the general exclusion of whites from the occupation of land in the Indian Territory, we found several in possession of farms in the most fertile districts. Early this morning we breakfasted at one such establishment, taking our meal under the veranda outside an open door, just within which the lady of the house was comfortably smoking a pipe, whilst still in bed, with her daughter at her side. Both watched the operations at the table with the easy nonchalance of backwoods-etiquette. Similarly comfortable, an old negress was smoking at the door of one of the out-buildings, and at the same time keeping a quiet eye upon a number of frolicking curly-headed black children, some of whose seniors might, however, have been less at ease in the establishment than appeared to be the case with themselves; for, in front of the veranda, there was a notice offering *"two hundred and fifty dollars reward for the apprehension of my slave Frank,"* who had run off in search of a happier allotment.

As visitors we could not complain of our fare here, as we had sweet corn and the first potatoes since the commencement of our journey from San Francisco.

The Indian Territory much resembles the better parts of Texas in its fertile openings, abundance of wood, and adaptability for agriculture, more especially for cattle-raising. It is thinly peopled by the surviving representatives of the Choctaw, Cherokees, Chickasaws, Creeks, Shawnees, Kickapoos, Seminoles, Pawnees, Wichitas, and Delawares, an aggregate population of eight thousand, of whom a fourth are Choctaws.

These tribes have always been somewhat superior in character to the Indians of the prairie and desert regions westward, including the Apaches, Comanches, and Arapahoes. All the latter are more treacherous than the eastern races, from whom they differ in various other respects; as, for instance, by the use of bows and arrows instead of rifles, by living more in the saddle than on foot, and by an almost total disuse of agriculture or settle residences. They are also more licentious, but less cruel than the former.

The leading tribes now established in the Territory are the Choctaws and Cherokees. The latter are the most intelligent and civilized, and have amongst them a regular aristocratic organization. They have good houses, and keep slaves. The young Choctaws eagerly seek matrimonial alliances with the Cherokee ladies, many of whom are well dowered both with wealth and education, and have adopted crinolines and pianos. *[NOTE: A crinoline is a stiff or structured petticoat designed to hold out a skirt, popular at various times since the mid-19th century.]*

Open murder and private assassination, together with perjury and miscellaneous outrages, are characteristics of the tribes in the Territory, especially amongst the Chickasaws and Choctaws. Small as the allotted district is which is thus apportioned for the permanent possession of so many, and formerly so extensive nations, there seems every probability that, in spite of the ample opportunities these now enjoy for quiet progress and increase, two or three generations will witness their extinction.

As we traversed the sunny forest glades and fertile undulations of open land, our American passengers expressed, in no gentle terms, their disapprobation of the forbearance of the Federal Government in reserving such an ample and splendid region for a population so scanty and so evidently unable to avail themselves of even a small portion of the West and easily attainable advantages set before them. *[NOTE: **On several days in this travel diary, William Tallack makes stereotypical and racist comments that I find personally repugnant:**]*

The Indian Territory confirms the almost universal experience that, by nations as well as by individuals, permanent establishment and eminent usefulness can only be attained through the means of the many gradations and varieties of a long preliminary discipline. Humanly speaking, it appears absolutely impossible for aboriginal races like the North American Indian to maintain an existence advantageous to their neighbors or to themselves, when brought into contact with superior races; and facts abundantly testify to the wisdom and mercy of that apparently inevitable law of Providence that no such inveterately savage race shall be by any means enabled, in these latter ages of the world's history, to continue as a thorn and stumbling block in the way of the elder and nobler nations, who have been brought, through ages of political and social discipline, to a foremost position of beneficent influence in Christendom and in the world at large. So that, whilst we may mourn, in a poetical and traditionary point of view, over the gradual but certain disappearance of these *"children of the forest,"* after their ages of mere animal enjoyment of an uncivilized and unprogressive existence, and whilst seeking the temporal and spiritual improvement of the survivors, we may thankfully reflect on the incalculable benefits to mankind to be derived from the possession of their vast vacated territories by races who have borne hither, and laboriously established, from beyond the Atlantic, the accumulated treasures both of their own rich civilization and that also of the first-born and pre-eminently favored nations of Palestine, Greece, and Rome.

The southern continuation of the Ozark Mountains extends into the Indian Territory, adding to the picturesqueness of the scenery more than to the facility of travel. We took twelve hours in accomplishing forty-seven miles through this district, which became far more difficult northward. Much of the Territory is carboniferous, and in many parts beautiful fossils are obtained, and, in particular, fine specimens of dendritic rock.

Edwards Store near Red Oak, Oklahoma. The Edwards Store is the only structure remaining in Indian Territory that stood on the Butterfield Overland National Trail. Recognized by Oklahoma's National Historic Places as an unofficial Butterfield stop.

We found the temperature, though extremely warm, hereabouts (98 degrees in the shade) far more endurable than that experienced in the Colorado and Gila deserts.

Twentieth Day – Arkansas

This was the anniversary of the Declaration of Independence, *"the glorious Fourth,"* and accordingly, at midnight, the passengers (all being Americans except the writer) welcomed its advent with loud hurrahs. Yet it had been interesting to the writer to notice repeatedly, during the journey, how his republican companions freely expressed their deep discontent with many of their own political circumstances, especially deploring the hopeless corruption of their executive government.

A radical source of political evil was acknowledged to be the unprecedented place-hunting encouraged by the established practice of compelling all subordinate employees (including post-masters and custom-house officials) to evacuate their situations at every change in the administration, and frequently shorter intervals. Thus personal merit and exemplary performance of duty receive no reward, but actually place their exhibitor in a more unfavorable position as to his own pecuniary interest than that enjoyed by immoral and unprincipled persons. A gentleman remarked to the writer that, during his ten years; residence in San Francisco, he had known almost every desk in the city custom-house officered afresh about six times. Another Californian, speaking of Federal employees generally, added, *"They go in for the stealings,"* more than for their regularly recognized emolument. The recent defalcations and disclosures in the highest circles at Washington abundantly prove the truth of this remark.

Today we breakfasted at Scullyville, a station kept by the governor of the Choctaws, who has here a thriving farm. Near one of the Indian villages we observed a post with a hole at the top, through which balls are driven with sticks by the Indians when playing their national game. This sport requires great skill, and is rough work, often leading to severe injuries or loss of life.

Major Blain (Indian protector under the Federal Government, and one of our passengers) remarks that he has been struck with the poetic beauty of many of the expressions in the aboriginal languages. Thus, the Comanches call the stars *"God's eyes,"* and the moon is the *"night queen."* **[NOTE BY BOB CROSSMAN: On several days *in this travel diary, William Tallack makes stereotypical and racist comments that I find personally repugnant:]***

He adds that this once powerful and dreaded nation are now fearfully wasting away, through their degraded habits imitated from the worst of the whites. It is characteristic generally of savage aborigines that, on contact with superior races, they immediately adopt the worst vices of the latter, whilst obstinately and hopelessly refusing to profit by their virtues.

After a hot and dusty drag of fifteen miles in six hours our horses fairly gave in, and we had to walk the last part of the stage west of Fort Smith. On reaching this town, on the frontier of Arkansas and of civilization, we found every one holiday-keeping, in honor of *"the Fourth."* We were allowed two hours delay — a very welcome opportunity for a bath and a leisurely dinner at a regular hotel. There we emerged on the comforts of ice-water and ice-cream, both such universal requirements of loyal American citizens in summer. Our land-lord had a fat pig in readiness for some western agricultural exhibition, and, in order to restrain any diminution of size by the copious perspiration in the sweltering weather, a large block of ice was placed on the recumbent animal; and the latter seemed very comfortably to appreciate the attention thus given to his personal condition.

At Fort Smith, for once, we met with a really conscientious stage agent, who refused to permit our being crowded with any further addition to our full complement of way passengers, much to the loudly expressed chagrin of an Irishman and a lady, who were desirous of favoring us with their presence, regardless of our convenience, if not so of their own.

In the evening we crossed the Arkansas River, on a ferry propelled by two horses walking round a sort of treadmill, or nearly horizontal wheel, communicating motion to the paddles. This kind of locomotive power we had not previously met with, nor did we see any recurrence of it subsequently.

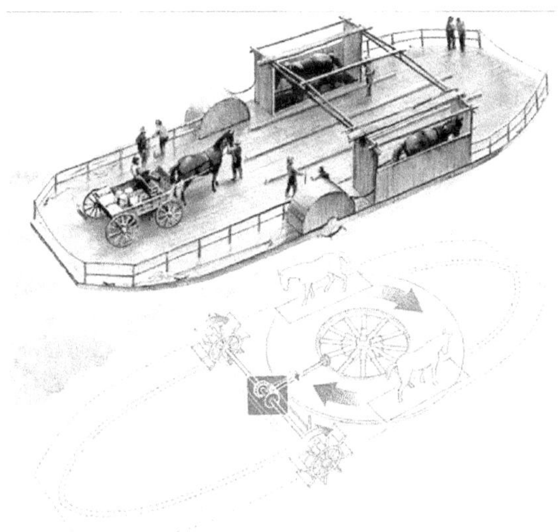

William Tallack seems to be describing a ferry similar to the 63' length x 18' beam 'Superior Horse Boat Eagle' that was operating in 1841 out of Westport, New York seen in this sketch. This New York ferry was featured in the October 1989 issue of The National Geographic. John Russell Young, in August of 1859 described this same Van Buren ferry in his report to Philadephia's The Press.

Our route continues through hilly forests, chiefly of oak, but with many hickories and papaw-trees. The latter somewhat resemble laurels, but their large oval leaves are all pendent.

The population hereabouts is still very scanty, and only a few log-houses have broken the solitude of our journey, with the exception of the two towns of Fort Smith and Van Buren, both of which are close to a navigable river.

Smoking seems to be in frequent favor hereabouts with the gentler sex, if we may judge by our observations of both whites and slaves. At a relay station this morning we saw an announcement offering a reward of a thousand dollars for the apprehension of seven run-away negroes.

This evening our route has become more rugged than at any former stage of the journey, except the San Felipe Pass, west of the Colorado Desert, in California. We have passed several emigrant parties resting at camp-fires and guarded by noisy dogs, all bound to Texas, or still further west.

Twenty-First Day – The Ozarks

Last night we crossed Boston Mountain, a spur of the Ozarks. Hour after hour we clambered literally *"upstairs,"* for our route lay at times in the channel of a mountain stream, over successive ledges of rock. The worst of the ascent we had to walk, which was more comfortable than when inside, as there was bright moonlight. The scenery of the deep gorge was very romantic, and fireflies were swarming around us in every direction. –

night was anything but favorable to sleep continuous succession of unmitigated jolts, knocking our faces, shoulders, knees, and backs against the wagon, or one another

When riding, our night was anything but favorable to sleep, being a continuous succession of unmitigated jolts, knocking our faces, shoulders, knees, and backs against the wagon, or one another. But at last tired nature could hold out no longer, and we sank into the soundest and sweetest unconsciousness of the lively behavior of our vehicle.

Passengers often had to sit and sleep atop mailbags that filled the space between the seats. This image is taken from William Tallack's book, to illustrate the thirteenth day of their journey.

Soon after awaking we entered the town of Fayetteville, a go-ahead place possessing its pillared courthouse, churches, and ladies' college.

Today we have traversed a splendid region of forest and meadow openings, scattered with fertile fields of cotton, maize and especially heavy crops of Hungarian millet-grass.

a good supper of eggs, honey, potatoes, French beans, steaks, and pastry in abundance, and with courtesy

Our commissariat here amply amends for our recent desert fare. This evening we had a good supper of eggs, honey, potatoes, French beans, steaks, and pastry in abundance, and with courtesy: the latter we do not always receive in addition, when in the plains or elsewhere.

During our journey we have had no opportunity for reading, as the hurried relays and motion of the vehicle have effectually confined our employments to conversation and observation. The former had embraced *"things in general,"* with one exception. We have, by common consent, carefully avoided the slightest allusions to slavery, in its moral and political bearings. This topic has always, and especially of late years, been a dangerous one for travelers in the South, whether northerners or foreigners; and, although some of us had our own decided opinions in favor of abolitionism, we felt that for the present silence was wisdom, as very mild expressions of an anti-slavery nature have repeatedly produced most unpleasant and even fatal results to their utters. It would be particularly disagreeable to have one's journey interrupted in the summary manner which has sometimes been the case with the incautious in these parts. We remembered that, in Texas and Arkansas, suspicion is easily roused; and tar, feathers, or a halter, have often been easily improvised by the irresponsible sovereignty of pro-slavery mobs.

So far, however, as our limited opportunities of observation extended to the agricultural and domestic aspects of slavery in the districts through which we passed, and so far, also, as the dress, conversation, and actions of the negroes hereabouts impressed us, there was evidently a large amount of comfort and moderation in their condition and treatment.

The chief objections to slavery are not so much on

the ground of comfort or economy, as on that of the deep and wide-spread moral degradation and spiritual desolation necessarily implied in the existence of the system.

In the vegetation of these districts sumac-trees and the *"jemsen-weed"* are abundantly conspicuous. The bright red foliage of the former is very ornamental; its leaves are used by the Indians as a substitute for tobacco. The *"jemsen-weed"* is so named from its having been mistaken for salad by the early Virginian colonists of Jamestown, an awkward mishap which nearly led to serious results, as it is the stramonium of the pharmacopoeia, or a closely allied species. Other prevalent blossoms hereabouts are those of the mullein, horsemint, iron-weed, red asters, wild carnation, and *"poke-weed."*

This 1858 engraving illustrates the moving of passengers and mail between a stagecoach and a Celerity wagon.
"The Overland Mail – Changing Stage-Coach for Celerity Wagon"
Frank Leslie's Illustrated Newspaper, Oct. 23, 1858, pg. 325-328.
lithograph, hand colored ; 15 3/4 x 10 3/4 in.

Twenty-Second Day – Western Missouri

In Missouri at last. Yesterday we changed at Fayetteville from a light wagon to a regular Western *"coach,"* similar to the one in which we started from San Francisco; but with it we received an accession of five passengers inside – a widow and four small children.

Last night, in accordance with the established habit of our journey, when it became dark we dropped into silence, or tried to, in order to sleep, but in vain: talk, talk, continued the widow, though receiving from us very monosyllabic replies, and then broader and broader hints as to acceptableness of quiet, which at last were complied with till we slept.

Early in the morning we reached Springfield *[Missouri]*, where the mail agent found that it would be impossible to forward all the miscellaneous coach full of passengers, luggage, and letter-bags, so as to reach the Syracuse railroad in time to dispatch the latter by tomorrow's train to St. Louis, which, if missed, would entail a further delay to the mails of forty-eight hours, till Monday morning, as no train would run between that time and tomorrow (Saturday) morning.

Having all along been much incommoded by the bulky mail-sacks, we now gained through them the advantage of an accelerated conclusion to our journey, as the agent here decided to forward the letters and the through passengers by a smaller fast conveyance, leaving the coach, the widow, and her family, with the remaining passengers and baggage, to follow more at leisure. Thus freed from *impedimenta,* we started at a brisk rate.

But we were still one hundred and thirty-five miles from the western terminus of the *"Pacific Railroad,"* at Syracuse, and it was a very doubtful matter whether, with the utmost exertion, we could accomplish this so as to save the Saturday train leaving at eight o'clock tomorrow for St. Louis, as it is now six on Friday morning. However, on we went, driven in the characteristic wild style of Yankee drivers, and, when near a relay, perceived the westward-bound stage coming over a hill.

We knew that, if this reached the station before ourselves, it would secure the right of priority in case of there being only one relay of horses at hand, which would ruin our chance of catching the train, as the last stage in would have to proceed with already jaded horses. Our diver urged on the team, and we drew up at the station just a few minutes before the others came steaming in. The fresh horses were ours, and were also, as we had anticipated, the only animals in waiting. Thus aided, we dashed on again, and kept it up briskly all day.

In the evening we crossed the Osage River at an easily fordable point near the town of Warsaw.

Here one of our through passengers left us. He was a gold-digger, returning after nine years absence in California, to his Missourian home, scarcely richer than when he left it; yet he appeared to be a sober, industrious, and agreeable young man. He reports, as the result of his observation at the diggings, that very few indeed ever succeed in amassing fortunes there.

In Western Missouri we have seen unmistakable traces of the tornadoes which often visit these regions bordering on the open prairies, where the winds sweep along with the gathered force of hundreds of miles of unimpeded momentum.

We continued our race for the train all night, and with success; for, soon after awakening this morning, we saw, rising above the trees before us, the thrice welcome and readily recognized wreaths of the white breath of the *"iron-horse,"* at the Syracuse station and western terminus of the *"Pacific Railroad."* A few minutes more and we had completed our long and uninterrupted ride of twenty-seven hundred miles; and, as we leaped for the last time from the stage, it was not without feeling some emotion of thankfulness to that good Providence who had brought us thus safely to the termination of a journey characterized by extreme interest and variety, and by more than a little peril and physical exertion.

Railroad: Locomotive, 1870 is a photograph by Granger which was uploaded on June 28th, 2012.

1870 Engraving of a Train from a photo by Granger

We had yet an hour before the train started, an interval very essential for changing the condition of our dusty persons and worn-out clothes, etc. Then, after a hearty breakfast, never did a ride seem more luxuriously comfortable than the smooth and rapid motion of the commodious railway-cars, both by their contrast with out three weeks' route over rugged mountain and rolling prairie, as well as by the restful feeling arising from the secure accomplishment of a journey so different from any in our former experiences of travel.

Thus, reclining with a delightful ease and satisfaction on the softly-cushioned seats, we skirted for nearly a hundred miles the whirling waters of the turbid wide Missouri – past Jefferson City, the capital of the State, past white double-tiered steamboats on our left, and neat towns, rich harvests, and tributary rivers on our right, till, in the early afternoon, we rolled into a spacious terminus; from which we emerged once more into the active scenes of city life, amongst the crowded thoroughfares, lofty edifices, hotels, street railways, and bustling wharves of St. Louis the populous and thriving emporium of the Upper Mississippi.

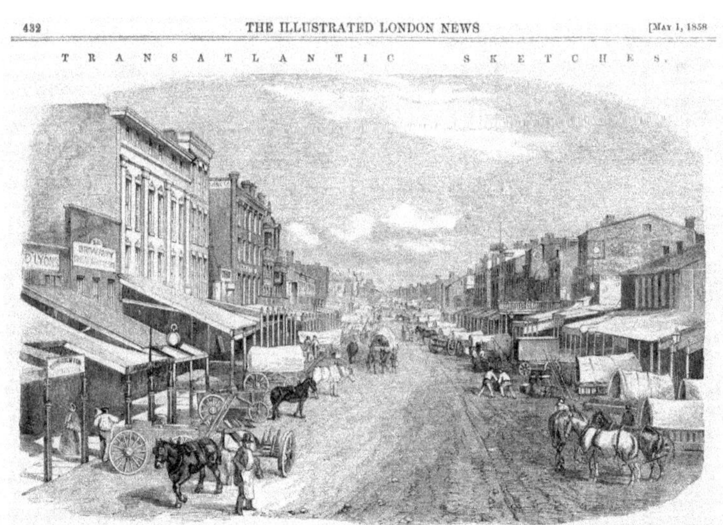

1858 wood engraving from The Illustrated London News, page 432, from May 1, 1858, showing a street scene of the Broadway in St. Louis. Shops line either side of the road and horses and covered wagons are parked in front of the shops, buildings fronted by covered sidewalks.

1867 St. Louis' Eads Bridge Under Construction
This bridge over the Mississippi is still in use today.

William Tallock, continued

Ten years before his death, William Tallock wrote to the London Times, April 10, 1903. That communication was reprinted in The Savannah Morning News, December 25, 1903.

The Savannah Morning News
Savannah, Georgia, December 25, 1903
"The Old Overland Route:
William Tallock Writes to Thunderer About It"
From the *London Times.*

... there was also a southern coach service by way of Arizona and Texas.

This was the line worked by The Butterfield Overland Route Company, established in 1850, and subsidized by the United States government. Its coaches, small light New Hampshire wagons (carrying six inside passengers and sometimes one outside with the driver), left San Francisco or St. Louis twice a week, and usually performed the distance of 2,868 miles in twenty-two days and nights, although the schedule time was twenty-four days... I can testify from personal experience, having traversed its whole length in the summer of 1860.

I can testify from personal experience, having traversed its whole length in the summer of 1860.

... thence over the plains of Texas to the Indian Territory and Arkansas and Missouri, where the passengers were deposited at the Syracuse station which was then the western terminus of the already commenced Pacific Railroad, a few hours distance from St. Louis.

somewhat difficult to sleep in an upright sitting posture and closely wedged together, with mail-bags thrust between our feet

...Travel by the Butterfield route was of an exhilarating nature. The first night or two it was somewhat difficult to sleep in an upright sitting posture and closely wedged together, with mail-bags thrust between our feet; but thenceforward unconsciousness at night was perfect, except when we were rousted out for a walk or a meal.

The stations, mostly rough shanties, were located at distances varying from twelve to thirty miles. At them, either twice or sometimes thrice in the twenty-four hours, meals were provided, consisting chiefly of bread, beans, coffee and bacon, and for which a dollar a meal was charged.

Where the route was particularly rough or mountainous, the passengers were permitted to walk, and the change was mostly a welcome one as the constant crowded sitting up for twenty-two days and nights had rather a cramping effect. At the stations or at some stream we could get a hasty wash, also very welcome, for occasionally the dust and heat were excessive, especially in the valleys of the Colorado and Gila rivers.

...In the three weeks we only had one storm, or rainfall, and there was scarcely a single bridge crossed in the whole distance at that period. The rivers were traversed by broad ferry barges, conveying both vehicle and passengers.

Stage was "smashed up" and the front "wheels became disengaged."
Image: courtesy of Pixabay

CHAPTER FORTY EIGHT

S. P. Nott, Stage Accident, July, 1860

as it appears in the Aug. 3, 1860 issue of The Cincinnati Enquirer, Cincinnati, Ohio, page 3, reprinting an article from a Fort Smith or Van Buren paper.

Appreciation is expressed to Earl Shero for discovering this newspaper clipping.

ACCIDENT TO THE OVERLAND STAGE

We learn from **Mr. S. P. Nott**, of Sherman, Texas who arrived here *[Fort Smith or Van Buren, Ark.]* on Sunday last, and was a passenger *[this stage had left San Francisco, July 2, 1860 according to the Sacramento Bee, Aug. 8, 1860)* in the unfortunate stage which was smashed up fifty miles from this place, in the Choctaw country, on Friday night last, that the stage arrived at the station a little before sundown, and after getting supper, it was about eight o'clock at night when the stage started, with eight passengers, Mr. Stout, road agent, and the driver.

The brake was out of order, ad one of the horses was refractory, and the team started in a run, but was soon checked, and Mr. Stout got upon the seat with the driver, and the latter gave his whip a crack, and away went the team down the hill full tilt, and as the brake was useless, there was no way to stop them. While the stage was at the top of its speed, the curtains being drawn, Dr. Denton took out his knife and cut them, and jumped out, and in cutting the curtains, cut Mr. Nott severely in the back. Dr. Denton was badly bruised in the fall.

The stage soon after struck a tree and smashed to pieces, and the fore wheels became disengaged, and the horses ran some distance, dragging the driver and bruising him severely.

Mr. Nott says he braced himself, and when the stage struck the tree he landed some distance from the place where it struck, and the top of the stage with him.

In recovering he heard the groans of the wounded, and on going to one he found the blood to be gurgling in his throat, and it being dark, he raised him up, and receiving no answer from him, he put his hand to his head and found the forepart of the skull broke in. The man proved to be Mr. Mackey, of Cass County, Missouri. He was killed immediately.

Mr. Nott returned to the station and there he soon fainted from the loss of blood. Mrs. Chapin, the lady of the house, had all the wounded bodies taken to the station, and went to work and dressed their wounds with her own hands. Mr. Nott speaks in the highest terms of the kindness of Mrs. Chapin.

Mr. Stout, the Road Agent, was seriously injured, his face badly bruised, and his upper lip cut through, and the lower lip is not in much better condition, besides his bruises in the chest are very serious.

Most of the passengers were injured more or less, and only two of them, young men from Ohio, were able to walk about.

The names of the passengers are Messrs. Nott, McCarty, Halsey, Denton of New York, and two younger men from Ohio, and Mr. Mackey of Missouri who was killed.

On Saturday, about eleven o'clock, an express arrived here with the news of the accident, and a coach was dispatched immediately, taking Doctors Bomford and Dunlap, to attend to the wounded.

This is the first serious accident to the stage in the region of this place, since the Overland Line when into operation.

The Louisville Daily Courier, Louisville, Kentucky, July 23, 1860 also carried this story and included:

FORT SMITH, ARK., JULY 22

The Overland mail coach with dates to July 2d, arrived at 10:30 this morning, with some of the passengers who received injuries at Mountain Station *[Indian Territory]* by the running away of a team.

The Chicago Tribune issue of July 23, 1860, page 4 also carried this story and included:

VANBUREN, ARK., JULY 21. — Intelligence has reach here this evening that the Overland Mail Coach coming east from California, met with a serious accident at Mountain Pass, Choctaw Nation.... It will be delayed some thirty hours beyond the usual time.

The Daily Exchange, Baltimore, Maryland, July 24, 1860 also carried this story and included:

FORT SMITH, ARK., JULY 23 — The Overland California Mail of the 2nd inst, has arrived by the mail coach, which also brings some passengers who were injured at the Mountain Station... They state that ...the horses became frightened and galloped to the brow of the mountain, when the driver turned them off from the main road, bringing the coach in collision with a tree, shattering it to pieces, and killing a drover who was from Cassville mountain named Macky, and injuring all other passengers...

Crossing the River by Ferry
"Beyond the Mississippi: From the Great River to the Great Ocean,"
by Albert D. Richardson, American Publishing, 1867, page 35

CHAPTER FORTY NINE
W. A. Wallace, July 7, 1860
The St. Joseph Weekly Free Democrat
St. Joseph, Missouri
Saturday, July 7, 1860, page 2

Mr. A. W. Wallace one of the editors of the *Alta Californian*, arrived in our city [St. Joseph, Missouri] last evening from San Francisco having come by the Butterfield Overland mail route. In consequence of sickness he was obliged to quit the stages at Fort Smith, and is consequently four days behind the mail. To him we are indebted for the following highly important and interesting way news, which has not before been communicated to the Press:

The agents of the O. M. Co., have succeeded in breaking up a formidable band of robbers and thieves on the Colorado and Gila rivers. This section has been a place for fugitive villains for a long time, and their numbers have heretofore given them impunity from arrest... On a recent occasion 100 sacks of barley, worth at that point 12¢ per pound, were carried off; animals also were stolen...

Recent discoveries of the gold in the mountains, between Gila and Mimbus rivers, is creating immense excitement thro' all the country. Hundreds of men and women were passed on the road in all sorts of conveyances. Some of the towns on the Rio Grande were nearly depopulated. It was said that when the stage came through not more than forty men were remaining in El Paso. The employees of the Overland Mail company at many of the stations have given notice of their intention to quit the service and follow the crowd.

...The location of the mines is between the foot of Gila and Mimbus rivers, about six miles from either stream, and about thirty miles north of the stage road...

On the 18th ult., a band of Comanches attacked the station at the "Head of Concho," 100 miles east of the "Pecos Crossing," killed the keeper, Mr. J. W. Sheppard, scalped him, and run off all the stock, eleven mules. The stage was delayed seven hours for other animals to be brought up..

On Tuesday morning, 3d inst., at daylight, the Overland Mail Station, twenty-two miles east of Syracuse *[Missouri]*, was burned. — Four horses, one of the finest teams on the road, perished in the flames. The cause of the fire was unknown, but supposed to have arisen from a match having been dropped upon the ground, and ignited by being trodden upon by the horses.

Hannibal Daily Messenger
Wednesday, July 25, 1860, page 2

The Missouri and Western telegraph line was extended to Fort Smith, on the extreme southwest of St. Louis, on the Butterfield Overland Mail route today, and is now open for business.

Map of Indian Territory, 1884

CHAPTER FIFTY
Mountain Station Accident, July 22, 1860
*as reported in the Hannibal Daily Messenger issue of
Wednesday, July 25, 1860, on page 2, apparently based on interviews with the
stage passengers and Overland employees.*

Fort Smith, Ark.

July 22, 1860

The Overland Mail coach, with San Francisco dates to the 2d of July, arrived at half-past ten o'clock this morning, with some of the passengers who received injuries at **Mountain Station** *[Indian Territory, on top of Blue Mountain]*, by the running away of a team, the particulars of which are as follows:

The stage left **Mountain Station** with seven passengers, besides the driver and Mr. Stout, a roadmaster in the employ of the Overland Company, who was acting as conductor. On leaving the station the driver cracked his whip and the horses immediately started on a run. When they arrived at the brow of the mountain the brakes were applied, but were found to be useless. In his efforts to stop the horses, the driver drove out of the road and they came in collision with a tree, literally smashing the coach in pieces, killing one man by the name of Mackey, a drover from Cassville, Missouri, who was on his return from California, and injuring every other person on the stage to a greater or less extent. Mr. Stout was severely cut in the face and had his nose completely flattened. He also complained of internal injuries.

Several of the injured remain here for rest until the next stage.

This stagecoach in the Otero Museum, La Juinta, Colorado was made by the same manufacturer as the ones purchased by Butterfield's Overland Mail Co.

Van Buren Press, Van Buren, Arkansas
July 27, 1860

Passenger Killed in Accident – Runaway Horses

Accident – The California Overland stage met with an accident last week on Thursday night about seventy miles from Fort Smith in the Choctaw nation. On leaving what is called **Mountain Station**, the horses commenced running, and from some defect in the brake became unmanageable and after running nearly a half mile, dashed the stage against a tree, breaking it entirely up.

One passenger whose name we understand was McKay, and who lived in Missouri, was killed, and some four or five others were seriously injured, as were also the conductor and driver. This is the first and only serious accident that within our knowledge has ever before happened to the Overland stage in this part of the country.

Mountain Spring Station in Indian Territory
The spring is still flowing.
Photo by Susan Dragoo, Historian for Butterfield Overland National Historic Trail Through Oklahoma/Indian Territory.

A portion of the Butterfield Overland National Historic Trail near Mountain Spring Station, Indian Territory.

The Overland Mail Company used leather mail bags with brass locks and brass keys.

1859 US Mail padlock is on display at the Smithsonian Postal History Museum. The lock on this russet leather stagecoach bag has patent dates of 1858, 1860 & 1866.

CHAPTER FIFTY ONE
S. H. Shock, August 13, 1860
as reported in the Daily Missouri Republican issue of Monday, August 13, 1860, on page 2, based on interview with Mr. S. H. Shock, agent at Memphis for the Overland Mail Co.

MAIL ROBBERS ARRESTED

Mr. S. H. Shock, agent in this city [Memphis], received news, on Tuesday, that the mail bags, which reached Madison, Arkansas, last Sunday night, had been cut open and robbed of their contents. He immediately started for the above mentioned town, on hearing the intelligence, to investigate the matter and bring the robbers to arrest.

The circumstance of the robbing led to the suspicion that the driver of the stage coach was concerned in the act, and he took him in charge, together with two others, who turned out to be accomplices. There names are Marcelus Noles, Louis Burton and Martin Dox.

The rifled bags were en route for Memphis, but we have not ascertained what amount of money had been abstracted from their contents. Mr. Shock brought his prisoners to this city *[Memphis]* and had them confined in prison to await definite orders from the head of the department, to whom Col. Gallaway telegraphed yesterday. This makes the third instance, within the last ten days, of the imprisonment of mail robbers in the Memphis jail, and two instances when the guilty parties were the carriers of the mail. — *[Memphis Avalanche]*

Note: The Fort Smith Postmaster, in a letter to the editor states that the Overland Mail bags were locked with a brass key. Source: Daily Missouri Republican, Tuesday, July 12, 1859, page 2

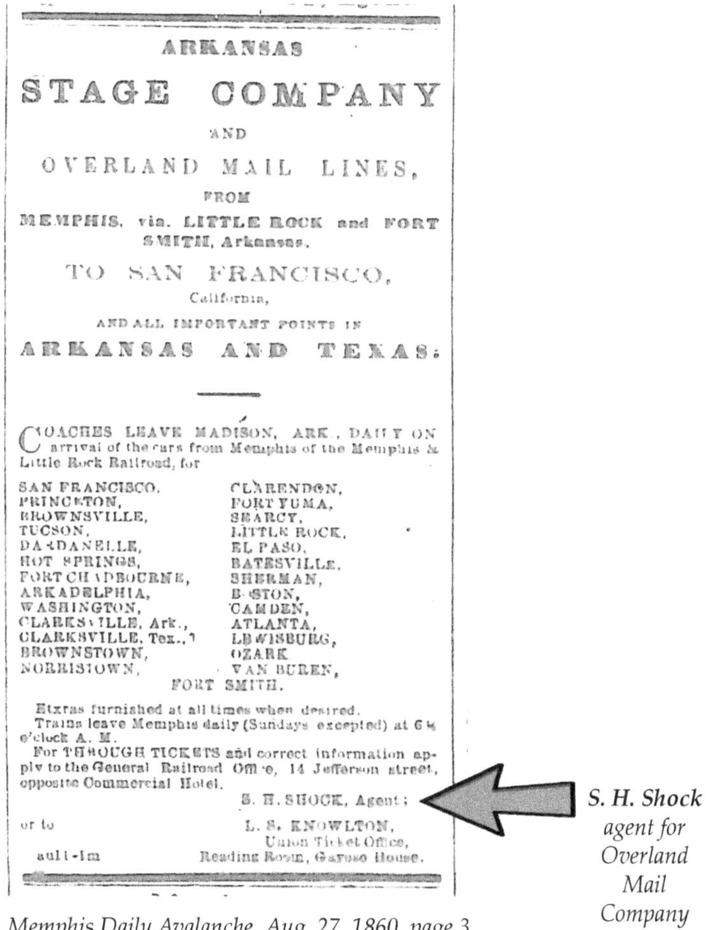

ARKANSAS

STAGE COMPANY

AND

OVERLAND MAIL LINES,

FROM

MEMPHIS, via. LITTLE ROCK and FORT SMITH, Arkansas.

TO SAN FRANCISCO, California,

AND ALL IMPORTANT POINTS IN

ARKANSAS AND TEXAS.

COACHES LEAVE MADISON, ARK., DAILY ON arrival of the cars from Memphis of the Memphis & Little Rock Railroad, for

SAN FRANCISCO,	CLARENDON,
PRINCETON,	FORT YUMA,
BROWNSVILLE,	SEARCY,
TUCSON,	LITTLE ROCK,
DARDANELLE,	EL PASO,
HOT SPRINGS,	BATESVILLE,
FORT CHADBOURNE,	SHERMAN,
ARKADELPHIA,	BOSTON,
WASHINGTON,	CAMDEN,
CLARKSVILLE, Ark.,	ATLANTA,
CLARKSVILLE, Tex.,	LEWISBURG,
BROWNSTOWN,	OZARK
NORRISTOWN,	VAN BUREN,
	FORT SMITH.

Etxras furnished at all times when desired.
Trains leave Memphis daily (Sundays excepted) at 6½ o'clock A. M.
For THROUGH TICKETS and correct information apply to the General Railroad Office, 14 Jefferson street, opposite Commercial Hotel.

S. H. SHOCK, Agent;

or to L. S. KNOWLTON,
Union Ticket Office,
au11-1m Reading Room, Gayoso House.

S. H. Shock agent for Overland Mail Company

Memphis Daily Avalanche, Aug. 27, 1860, page 3

"The Overland Mail — Passing a Bivouac of Emigrants in Western Arkansas"
Frank Leslie's Illustrated Newspaper, Oct. 23, 1858, pg. 325-328.
lithograph, hand colored; 15 3/4 x 10 3/4 in.

CHAPTER FIFTY TWO
Letter to the Editor, September 7, 1860
as reprinted in The Press Argus, Centennial Edition
September 19, 1958, Section B, page 4

The Press Argus
Van Buren, Arkansas
September 7, 1860

Nine persons in the stage, with the sun a 120 degrees hot, pouring its overflowing tide of warmth upon us; no doubt Dante who has so graphically portrayed to man the abodes of the wicked, had he known something of modern traveling, would have placed in his "purgatorio'"and underland mail especially at night, dashing and clashing amidst the rocks. ravines and dry rivers, of the Ozark mountains, where every body's head, searching for a pillow, or, at least, for. some immovable position, and finding none, clashed against another cranium or awoke in alarm the unsuspecting neighbor.

The Butterfield way passenger below was on his way to attend a political rally for the 1860 Presidential campaign of Stephen Douglas, along with his vice-presidential candidate, Herschel Johnson.

This passenger traveled over the Butterfield route from St. Louis to Syracuse, MO by train. While waiting for the Overland stagecoach departure time to Warsaw, he dined at the BRAYTON HOUSE.

CHAPTER FIFTY THREE
1860 Presidential Campaign, Oct. 5, 1860
as reported in the Oct. 6, 1860 issue of the
Weekly Jefferson Inquirer, Jefferson, Missouri, page 2

On Wednesday last at 3 o'clock we left Jefferson City *[Missouri]* for the metropolitan city of South-west Missouri — Warsaw — for the purpose of attending the great DOUGLAS rally to be held at this place.

After a pleasant ride on the P. R. R. *[Pacific Rail Road, whose tracks only reached from St. Louis to Syracuse, Missouri in Oct. of 1860]*, we arrived at Syracuse, and after partaking of an excellent supper at the BRAYTON HOUSE, we mounted the "Overland Mail" coach for this place *[Warsaw, Missouri]*, and arrived here yesterday morning just at daylight.

Long before we reached WARSAW our ears were greeted with the loud roar of the cannon, and on the way for miles we passed, wagons filled with the honest yeomany of the land winding their way to WARSAW to attend the great mass meeting. When the stage would pass them a shout from their honest hearts for DOUGLAS, JOHNSON and the Union would greet us. —

Near the city, the Henry County delegation numbering 300 were encamped. When we passed them they were holding prayer meeting over a BRECKITE who had repented in "sack cloth and ashes," and were singing the familiar hymn of WATTS. *[A 'Breckite" was a supporter of John Breckinridge, Vice President of the US, who ran against Stephen Douglas for the Democratic ticket. He lost to Douglas at the 1860 convention. In the 1860 presidential campaign, Stephen Douglas lost to Abraham Lincoln.]*

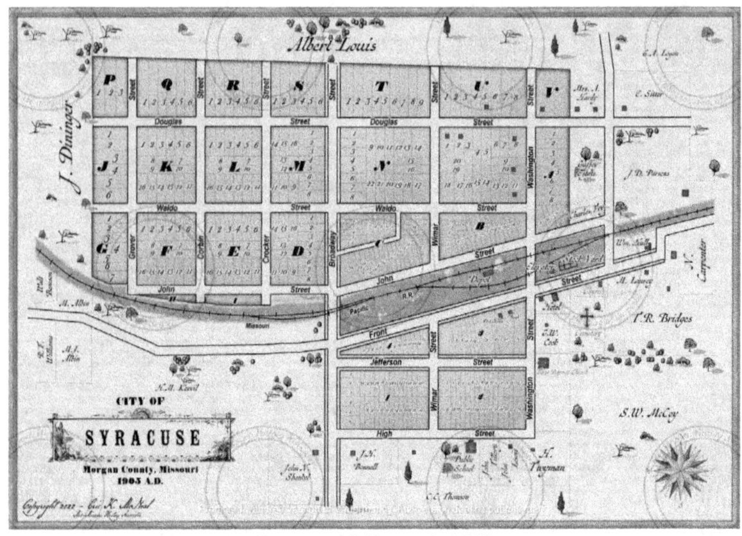

Syracuse, Missouri, 1905
Image courtesy of the Mid-Missouri Historical Association
Reprints of this map (18"x12") are available foe $25 from the association.

THE BRAYTON HOUSE
as reported in the Oct. 6, 1860 issue of the Weekly Jefferson Inquirer, page 3

This house, kept by Col. Thos. R. Brayton, and located at Syracuse, still maintains its well-earned reputation. —

The rooms and bedding are little palaces within themselves. The table is furnished with the greatest variety of vegetables, and cooked to suit the taste of all., We have never stopped at an hotel outside of St. Louis, where we were better treated and where every attention is afforded the guest of the hotel.

Mr. Baldwin, who presides in the office, is affable and courteous to visitors, and seems to delight in laboring to please those who patronize the House. We can, and do most cordially recommend the House to the traveling public, as one of the best outside St. Louis, and equal to the best in that city.

———————

Ralph and Eliza (Shepard) Pumpelly
Wikipedia, "Raphael Pumpelly"

CHAPTER FIFTY FOUR
Ralph Pumpelly, October 8, 1860
"Travels and Adventures of RALPHAEL PLUMPELLY
Mining Engineer, Geologist, Archeologist and Explorer"
by Raphael Plumpelly
New York, Henry Holt and Company, 1920
Chapter XVI, "I Go to Arizona"

In St. Louis on the 8th of October, 1860, I bought my ticket from Syracuse to Tucson, per Overland Mail Stage, Waybill No. 7 of this date. I went by rail to Jefferson City, then the westernmost end of the railroad in Missouri. This finished the first, and in point of time the shortest stage in a journey, the end of which I had not even tried to foresee.

I secured the right to a back seat in the overland coach as far as Tucson, and looked forward, with comparatively little dread, to sixteen days and nights of continuous travel. But the arrival of a woman and her brother dashed my hopes of an easy journey at the very outset, and obliged me to take the front seat, where, with my back to the horses, I began to foresee coming discomfort.

The coach was fitted with three seats, and these were occupied by nine passengers. As the occupants of the front and middle seats faced each other, it was necessary for these six people to interlock their knees ; and there being room inside for only ten of the twelve legs, each side of the coach was graced by a foot, now dangling near the wheel, now trying in vain to find a place of support. An unusually heavy mail in the boot, by weighing down the rear, kept those of us who were on the front seat constantly bent forward, thus, by taking away all support from our backs, rendering rest at all times out of the question.

**The woman, a very hag, ever following the disgusting
habit of dipping - filling the air, and
covering her clothes with snuff;
the girls – overcome by seasickness –
having no regard for the clothes of their neighbors**

My immediate neighbors were a tall Missourian, with his wife and two young daughters; and from this family arose a large part of the discomfort of the journey. The man was a border bully, armed with revolver, knife, and rifle; the woman, a very hag, ever following the disgusting habit of dipping - filling the air, and covering her clothes with snuff; the girls, for several days overcome by seasickness, and in this having no regard for the clothes of their neighbors; - these were circumstances which offered slight promise of pleasure on a journey which, at the best, could only be tedious and difficult.

For several days our road lay through the more barren and uninteresting parts of Missouri and Arkansas ; but when we entered the Indian Territory, and the fertile valley of the Red River, the scenery changed, and we seemed to have come into one of the Edens of the earth. Before reaching Fort Smith every male passenger in the stage had lost his hat, and most of the time allowed for breakfast at that town was used in getting new headgear. It turned out to be a useless expense, however, for in less than two days we were all again bareheaded. As this happened to the passengers of every stage, we estimated that not less than fifteen hundred hats were lost yearly by travelers for the benefit of the population along the road.

After passing the Arkansas River, and traveling two or three days through the cultivated region of northeastern Texas, we came gradually to the outposts of population. The rivers became fewer, and deeper below the surface; the rolling prairie-land covered with grass gave way to dry gravelly plains, on which the increasing preponderance of cacti, and the yucca, warned us of our approach to The Great American Desert. Soon after our entrance into this region we were one morning all startled from a deep sleep by the noise of a party coming up at full gallop, and ordering the driver to halt. They were a rough-looking set of men, and we took them for robbers until their leader told us that they were "regulators," and were in search of a man who had committed a murder the previous day at a town we had passed through.

"He's a tall fellow, with blue eyes and red beard," said the leader. *"So if you've got him in there, driver, you needn't tote him any further."* As I was tall, and had blue eyes and a red beard, I didn't feel perfectly safe until the party left us, convinced that the object of their search was not in the stage...

The fatigue of uninterrupted traveling by day and night ...was producing in me a condition bordering on insanity.

The fatigue of uninterrupted traveling by day and night in a crowded coach, and in the most uncomfortable positions, was beginning to tell seriously upon all the passengers, and was producing in me a condition bordering on insanity. This was increased by the constant anxiety caused by the danger from Comanches. Every jolt of the stage, indeed any occurrence which started a passenger out of the state of drowsiness was instantly magnified into an attack, and the nearest fellow passenger was as likely to be taken for an Indian as for a friend. In some persons, this temporary mania developed itself to such a degree that their own safety and that of their fellow travelers made it necessary to leave them at the nearest station, where sleep usually restored them before the arrival of the next stage, in the following week. Instances have occurred of travelers in this condition jumping from the coach, and wandering off to a death from starvation in the desert...

[NOTE: At this point Raphael Plumpelly *has left the Indian Territory (Oklahoma) and entered into Texas. The remaining portions of Mr. Plumbley's journey are found in "The First Overland Mail: Butterfield Trail - San Francisco to Memphis, 1858-1861, on pages 58-62.]*

"The Overland Mail - The Start from Fort Smith, Arkansas for the Pacific Coast – First Coach Driven by John Butterfield, Jr." Frank Leslie's Illustrated Newspaper, Vol. VI, Oct. 23, 1858 pg. 325-328.
Lithograph, hand colored; 15 ³/₄ x 10 ³/₄

Henry Dwight Barrows (1825 - 1914)
Wikipedia, "Henry Dwight Barrows

CHAPTER FIFTY FIVE

Henry Dwight Barrows, December 1860
*as reprinted in "The First Overland Mail: Butterfield Trail
San Francisco to Memphis" by Walter B. Lang, pages 64 to 70*
From 1856, for nearly ten years, H. D. Barrows was the
Los Angeles correspondent of the San Francisco Bulletin

*"Henry Dwight Barrows was born in Mansfield, Conn., on February 23, 1825. After receiving an education he went to work in Boston. Stimulated by stories of the new West, he departed for New York to take the steamer "Illinois" on April 26, 1852. for Panama and San Francisco... In his 'Reminiscences of Los Angeles in the Fifties and Early Sixties,' he relates that 'I road over it (**Butterfield trail**) from here (Los Angeles) to St. Louis on my wedding trip in 1860-61, a distance of 1,900 miles, traveling night and day for eighteen days and twenty-four hours passing through the then hostile Apache Indian country of Arizona and New Mexico, and of the Comanches of northern Texas...'"*
(Historical Society of Southern California, 1896)

A Two Thousand Mile Stage Ride
by H. D. Barrows
Read at a Pasadena Meeting, Feb. 4, 1896

Thirty-five years ago it was the good fortune of myself and wife to ride over the Butterfield route, which was, I believe, the longest and best conducted stage route in the world. The distance from San Francisco, by way of Los Angeles, El Paso, Fort Chadbourne, Fort Smith, to St. Louis, as indicated by the schedule of the stage stations, was 2881 miles.

I bought our two tickets for $400, gold, at the Overland Stage Office, which was located where the Roeder Block, on Spring Street now stands; and we boarded the delayed stage (delayed by heavy rains and a snow storm in the Tehachape mountains,) from San Francisco, which arrived at the **Bella Union**, now the St. Charles Hotel in this city, at about 10 o'clock Monday night, December 17, 1860.

The Bella Union Hotel in Los Angeles, California, constructed in 1835

We traveled day and night by stage for about eighteen days and five hours, arriving at Smithton, Missouri, the terminus of the railway, to St. Louis, on the morning of January 5, 1861; and at St. Louis on the evening of the same day. Of course the journey was somewhat tedious, but this was more than compensated for by the incidents and variety of scenery of the vast stretch of country passed through, and really, the weariness of stage travel was less disagreeable, than sea-sickness, etc., by water, as we had occasion to realize on our return trip, by way of the Isthmus.

Prior to the establishment of the overland stage route, a trip from Los Angeles to the Atlantic States usually occupied about four weeks; it could not be made in much less time, even with close connections by steamer. But by the stage and rail route, including a stop of two days at St. Louis, we were enabled to see the great tragedians, Booth and Charlotte Cushman, in Shakespeare's *"Merchant of Venice,"* at the Academy of Music in Philadelphia, twenty-three days after we left Los Angeles. About twenty days traveling time across the continent, and mostly by stage, we thought then, was not bad time.

Encouraged and subsidized by the United States Government for carrying of the mails, John Butterfield of Missouri, *[NOTE: actually 'of New York']* a veteran stage man, with others, established the overland stage line between St. Louis and Memphis, and San Francisco, via Los Angeles, in 1858, making trips at first twice a week, each way; and subsequently six times a week *[NOTE: the six times a week did not go into effect until moving to the Central Route.]* receiving, I believe, from the government, under the later contract, $1,000,000 annually. *[NOTE: 1858-1861 it was $600,000, 1861-1864 it was $1,000,000 annually.]*

The first stage from the East, (Memphis) arrived in Los Angeles, October 7, 1858. A driver and conductor accompanied each stage, and they always went armed through the hostile Indian country. The stations were usually ten to fifteen miles, and occasionally twenty to twenty-five miles apart.

Image Soure:"Pokin Around: Historic stagecoach, once at Silver Dollar City, about to embark on 100-mile journey" by Steve Pokin, May 18, 2022. Photo by Dennis Crider

A condensed summary of the itinerary of our journey may not be without interest.

Leaving Los Angeles, Monday...

At Fort Yuma...

At Gila Bend, Sutton's Ranch...

On Saturday... arrived at Tucson.

Apache Pass...

Mesilla on Monday night...

El Paso before daylight...

Fort Chadbourne...

At Phantom Hill...

Sunday we passed Fort Belknap, where we heard the Comanches had been committing depredations. Monday, as we drew near the bright thriving town of Sherman, Texas, we began to see cattle running at large on the hills, which was an indication that we were out of Indian country.

We crossed Red River into the Choctaw or peaceable Indian Territory on the last day of the year. The next morning was biting cold. We ate breakfast at a large farm house, occupied by two well-to-do Choctaw farmers, who dressed and looked like Americans, and who were nearly as white. They had large families. Just as we were leaving, a number of full-blooded Indians came out on to the broad veranda, with their Chief. We were told that they were to leave on the next stage after us, en route for Washington, to see their new Great Father, Lincoln, inaugurated.

In the early spring of 1863 a delegation of Southern Plains Indians, members of the Apache, Arapaho, Caddo, Cheyenne, Comanche, and Kiowa tribes, were invited to Washington to meet with President Abraham Lincoln at the height of the Civil War. The purpose of the visit was to secure peaceful relations with the Indians and to dissuade them from joining forces with the Confederacy.
The subjects seated in the front row, left to right, have been identified as Standing in Water, War Bonnet, and Lean Bear, Cheyenne; and Yellow Wolf, Kiowa. In the middle row at left is the Kiowa woman, Coy, beside her husband, White Bull. Courtesy of www.whitehousehistory.org

George Hudson, Choctaw Chief 1860-1862.
Courtesy of The Oklahoma Historical Society

1867 Fort Smith
Men gather in front of Devany's shoe store on Garrison Avenue on a day in September 1867. The buildings behind them were on the northwest corner of the intersection of Garrison and North Sixth Street. Notice the fiddler seated in the covered wagon and the animal on top of the cover.
Courtesy of Bill and Ann England, and cowboykisses blog spot

The Choctaw Indians had made great progress in civilization; they had schools and churches, and we were told, were industrious and intelligent. They made their own laws, their chief officer being called a Judge. We could see signs of thrift and prosperity as we passed through their Territory.

We reached Fort Smith on the 2nd of January, fifteen and a half days from Los Angeles. I was surprised to find Fort Smith a wide-awake, progressive city, having been under the impression that it was little more than a Fort and log-built frontier settlement.

On our journey thus far we had ridden in what were called thorough-brace mud-wagons. But next morning before light, on a Concord stage coach we arrived at Springfield, a larger and handsomer city. Fayetteville was another fine city, that is, it had less of a frontier aspect than one would expect from its location.

Bird's-eye view of north side of the square in Fayetteville, Arkansas, late 1870s. Includes Central Drug and Gus Albrecht, with Old Main in the background. Credit: Courtesy Shiloh Museum of Ozark History / Peter Harkins Collection (S-90-194-75)

The next day, the 4th, the weather being very cold, it snowed slightly, this being the first snow we had seen on our whole continental trip, albeit, it was made in midwinter. We now had some difficulty in keeping warm, although the stages were adapted to cold weather by being padded, and they could also be closed tight. However, we wrapped our blankets and shawls and fixings about us, and didn't come any where near freezing.

Late that night, or rather about 3 o'clock the next (Saturday) morning, January 5, 1861, we were glad to reach the end of our long stage journey of over 2,000 miles, at Smithton, the terminus of the railway to St. Louis.

The the regular daily train did not leave till 9 o'clock, a.m., we got about two hours sleep on a bed – the first in eighteen days. While this was very welcome, nevertheless it must not be supposed that we were used up, for we were not, by any means.

Missouri Pacific Railroad #152 built by Hinkley Locomotive Works in 1872. The Overland Mail left St. Louis by train. At the end of the tracks in Tipton, and later Syracuse, the mail was handed off to the stagecoach for the balance of the trip to San Francisco.
W. A. Anderson Photo / T. Greuter Collection, ca 1877 Hermann, MO

We took the [train] cars and reached St. Louis between 6 and 7 o'clock that night, eighteen days and twenty hours from Los Angeles. As the train passed along some distance on the bank of the Missouri River, we had an opportunity to see that stream. Next morning we got sight of the vast Mississippi, whose veins and arteries, in a great system of net-work, extend more than thirty thousand miles. Several of us at least, then saw those two mighty rivers for the first time.

At the Planters' House we found an inn, and rest. Next day, Sunday, we took a warm bath and changed our apparel, somewhat the worse for wear and tear and dust, and we felt as good as new.

Planters's House Hotel
Court House on left, and Planters's House Hotel on Right
There were three incarnations of the Planter's House hotel in St. Louis.
This one shown above was built in 1841 and stood until 1891.

After a two days' stay in St. Louis, we went by rail, via Chicago and Pittsburg to Philadelphia, where, for a time our journey was at an end; although we later visited various other Eastern cities. We returned to California, via the Isthmus, the following May.

To many people, doubtless, who think more of their ease than they do of robust physical health, a stage ride of a thousand or two thousand miles, may seem a very formidable undertaking. But for those who had a liking for adventure, and a desire to see something of the world, a long ride of two or three weeks, practically in the open air, not in hot, stuffy *[train]* cars, possesses a wonderful charm, especially in remembrance, when by the necromancy of idealization we segregate the pleasurable from that which was merely disagreeable, and therefore irrelevant. Such a ride is one of the most effective cures for dyspepsia that can be imagined.

The **"Overland Stage"** was the precursor of the Continental Railroad, and the interest taken in the former by the statesmen and especially by Southern and Western statesmen of forty years ago, did them infinite credit. As we look back and see that they grasped the situation accurately; they foresaw the importance of opening up direct communication between the distant sections of our common country; and they labored wisely and patriotically, despite much opposition and innumerable obstacles, for the establishment of such direct and systematic intercommunication, first by means of a continental stage line, which they knew would soon be followed by a continental railroad.

First Charge of Fremont's Bodyguard, Led by Major Zagonyi, on the Confederate Garrison at Springfield, Mo., October 25th, 1861
Image source: Frank Leslie's Illustrated History of the Civil War, 1895

CHAPTER FIFTY SIX

Charles Babcock, Agent of the Overland, June 26, 1861
as reprinted in "The Santa Fe Gazette, July 13, 1861, page 2

This incident occurred during the months that the Overland Mail Company was closing down operations on the Southern Ox-bow Route and relocating personnel and equipment north to begin operation on the Central Route July 1, 1861 to complete their six year contract with the Postmaster General.

Syracuse, Mo.,
July 26, 1861

A gentleman arrived here to-day from the South says he met Gov. Jackson with M. M. Parsons and some 1,200 troops at Pomme De Terre Bridge, eleven miles south of Warsaw, on Sunday morning, at 10 o'clock, moving southward. They had four cannon and about twenty-five baggage wagons, some of which were stage coaches.

He reports that **Charles Babcock**, late Agent of the Overland Mail Company at Warsaw, joined Jackson's forces there, and furnished him with ten full teams belonging to the Mail Company. A good many horses were drowned in crossing the Osage.

Unknown driver and stage line

CHAPTER FIFTY SEVEN
Butterfield Employee Recollections

Drivers Bill Hawes & Dave Milligan
as reported in "Butterfield Overland Mail Company" by F. P. Rose.
Source: The Arkansas Historical Quarterly , Spring, 1956, Vol. 15, No. 1
(Spring, 1956), page 69-70. Published by: Arkansas Historical Association.
Also in The Ozarks Mountaineer, June, 1955, p.13.

"With the death at his home in Lincoln, Arkansas, of Alfred Hossman, on July 9, 1932, the last of the old-time stage drivers passed into history. Mr. Hossman had come to Fayetteville with his parents from Tennessee when he was six years of age. In 1858, when he was about twenty years old, he secured a position as a driver on a Cane Hill route. His greatest ambition was to become a Butterfield driver, but the war ruined his hopes. He was nearly 95 years old at the time of his death.

Mr. Hossman often related his reminiscences, and that on numerous occasions he had seen John Butterfield and his sons, Charles and John, both in Fayetteville and Fort Smith. Charles, who was in charge of the station and hotel in Fayetteville, he once saw break up a Negro camp meeting, just to see them run, by driving a mail wagon and four horses right through the middle of it. He says this was the first intimation that there was a Charles Butterfield, as his existence and connection with the company had not been known up to that time.

There were two old Eastern Butterfield drivers Mr. Hossman said he would never forget, **"Bill" Hawes** and **"Dave" Milligan** by name, who were greatly admired for their dexterity by the aspiring drivers of Fayetteville. *"You could hear the conductor's horn way down the mountain,"* he recalled, *"and it was a grand sight to see that 'Yankee' Hawes handle them six horses and swing his stage–wagon into the square, taking the corners on a dead run!"* He remembered that on one occasion, **Hawes** stopped off on one trip at Hog Eye (now Moffit) just long enough to get married.

Al Hossman, Stage Driver
Interview by W. T. Campbell, Arkansas Gazette, Little Rock, Sunday, Oct. 7, 1945, page 9B Special Features Editorials

Dɪᴅ ʏᴏᴜ ᴇᴠᴇʀ ᴅʀɪᴠᴇ ᴀ sᴛᴀɢᴇ?

"Why man! — I've whipped up and down the land night and day. I drove the 25 mile trip from Evansville t' Dripping Springs stand in Crawford county at night — drove it s'much at night I didn't know it by day. Yes, I drove Butterfield

Al Hosman.
Sketch by W. T. Campbell

stages. Y' see, pa started t' Califony in '49. We got two ox wagons fixed up 'n got t' St. Joe, 'n crossed over into Nebrascy. Stopped there t' let the oxen graze. Pa got t' noticin' that ther's more folks comin' back than they was goin', 'n he jes turned round n' headed fer Arkansaw.

Y' see Doc Wade Pollard's wife's my own cousin, 'n we come t' Fayetteville in 1857. I didn't have a nickle — an' Wade, he says if I go out to Newtown — that's Clyde now, other side of Cane Hill — 't he'd pay me, 'n I could learn the business there. Y' see, I'd worked in a stable in St. Joe — yes, I's born in 1836 — jes you figure that up, will y'?"

But, did he drive out of Fayetteville?

"Why man, I drove from Fayetteville t' Evansville 'n back a long — Yes, four horses, 'n we kep' five teams at Newton. No, I was drivin' on the branch line. No, I didn't drive the Overland — Bill Hawes 'n Dave Milligan did that drivin.' They didn't stop fer anything 'cept fresh horses. Well, Bill did stop long enough 't Hogeye — they call it Moffitt now — t' git married. He was — well, y' should 've seen that yankee!"

Did he know Charley Butterfield?

"Charley Butterfield? He was a case. Yes sir — they used t' have camp meetin's 't Cane Hill. One night Charley hitched up one of his coaches 'n loaded up 'th some of his friends — an' other things — 'n drove over in grand style, drove right up into the cook tent, 'n had t' be backed out by hand."

Did he drive the Old Wire Road?

"No. I said I drove the branch line through Prairie Grove, Cane Hill, Newtown, Dutch Mills t' Evansville. Told y' th' Overland drove the old military road. Y' see, old man Bowens from th' Evansville stand.

Did you make any money? I told y' I didn't have a

nickel. Well, sir, I kep' things right at Newtown, 'n after awhile they put me t' drivin'. Yes, the paymaster come over the line once a month, 'n paid off. They wasn't any shin plasters then — jes paid in silver an' gold — paid me $20 a month. No, they boarded me. I stayed in the boardin' house, where us drivers stayed jes across th' street in front of the stables, 'n the stables 's down there about where th' courthouse is now. No, we didn't stay in any brick house. No, Charley Butterfield didn't live in any brick house — frame house there where the old Van Winkle was."

[In the balance of the interview he shared his experiences as a soldier during the Civil War.[

Employees Are Courteous, Civil & Attentive, Sept. 1858
as reported in The New York Herald, Friday, November 19, 1858; and
as reprinted in The Press Argus, September 19, 1958, Section A, page 16

The employees of the company I found, without exception to be courteous, civil and attentive. They are most of them from the East, and many, especially of the drivers, from New York State.

I found the drivers on the whole line, with but few exceptions, experienced men. Several are a little reckless and too anxious to make fast time; but as a general thing they are very cautious.

All the superintendents are experienced stage men;

Mr. Crocker, who has charge of the division from St. Louis and Memphis to Red River, has line in excellent condition;

Mr. Bates, from Red River to Chadbourne, has worked very hard, especially with his new road and wild mules, and is an old stage man;

Mr. Glover, from Chadbourne to the Rio Grande, has a very wild and unsettled country under his charge, and his arrangements were not very complete and, as I have said, this portion of the road will grow better every month,.

MESSRS. HAWLEY & BUCKLEY, from El Paso to Los Angeles, are both experienced stage men, and attend to their business.

MR. KENYON, who, like **MR. BUCKLEY**, is one of the owners, is, as the perfectness of the arrangements on his end of the stage line indicate, an excellent stage man.

The road agents or sub-superintendents are also all of them men of much experience, and apparently appear to have taken every care to have the employees reliable.

Considering that the contract was signed but just a year before the route went into operation; that an exploring party had to be sent over the road to lay out the details of the line, consuming nearly eight months time; that during this time over 100 wagons had to be built, nearly 1,500 horses and mules bought and stationed, corrals and station houses built, men employed, and all these appurtenances disposed along the route, the work appears to me to be superhuman.

Then it must be taken into consideration that the food and clothing for all these men and horses have to be transported over the line, which is no mean item in itself...

I have no doubt that the work is feasible; that the route will be successful; that the passengers to the Western States and from thence to California will patronize it; that the towns along the route will improve and others spring up; that military protection will be extended; that new mining districts will be discovered and worked; that the great work of the Pacific Railroad will be forwarded; that the people of California will have regular information from the East twice per week, and the contractors will realize handsomely on the investments which they make in this great enterprise of the day.

Mr. Walton, Dec. 11, 1858
as printed in the Memphis Enquirer;
as reprinted in the Dec. 11, 1858 issue of Little Rock's
Weekly Arkansas Gazette on page 3;
and as reprinted in the Dec. 4, 1858 issue of the Des Arc Citizen,
Des Arc, Arkansas on page 2

OVERLAND MAIL – **Mr. Walton**, agent of the California Overland Mail Company, informs the editors of the *Memphis Enquirer* that he has just returned from a visit to ascertain the cause why the route from Fort Smith to Memphis was not as well filled as that to St. Louis.

He finds that owning to other contracts of the sub-contractors, the mail is laid over about 48 hours at Fort Smith, and about 24 at Des Arc. At present this cannot be remedied; but arrangements are in progress for putting stock on the line under the direct supervision of the contractors, Messrs. Butterfield & Co.

As soon as these arrangements are completed, the same grade of work will be done between Memphis and Fort Smith, as between the latter place and St. Louis.

Blast of the Conductor's Horn, March 12, 1859
as reported in The Arkansan, March 12, 1859, page 2

...when the clash and rattle of the Overland Coaches is heard in our streets, and the toot of the driver's 'tin horn' is borne to our ears from the distant environs...

Dr. E. Ridge, passenger, April 2, 1859
as reported in the April 2, 1859 issue of The Arkansan, page 2

PIKES PEAK. — **Dr. E. Ridge** arrived home in the, overland stage Sunday morning. He reports the liveliest enthusiasm in and about St. Louis on the subject of the goldmines.

Numerous companies had organized, and others were organizing and equipping for the new El Dorado. These companies were not confined to St. Louis or the immediate surrounding country, but were from various states — every thing appears to be made expressly for the gold mines. Pike's Peak hats, coats, cigars and whiskey abound at every corner. The, same excitement prevails at Fort Smith, only on a somewhat smaller scale...

Flooding in West Arkansas, April 14, 1859
as reported in The Memphis Daily Avalanche
Thursday, April 14, 1859, page 3

The overland mail arrived here yesterday morning at 7 o'clock A.M., bringing San Francisco dates of the 21st of March. This we believe is the quickest trip on record, being three days and five hours ahead of schedule time.

The mail was delayed eight hours in Helena, awaiting the arrival of a boat to transport it to this place.

James Glover, May 4, 1859
as printed in the Wednesday, May 4, 1859 issue of the
Arkansas True Democrat, Little Rock, Arkansas on page 2.

PERSONAL – We had the pleasure of a short interview with **James Glover**, Esq., Superintendent of the Overland Mail Company. He tells us that they intend stocking the road from Dardanelle to Memphis and carrying their own mails, and to make this, the superior arm of the service. The last three mails from San Francisco arrived at Memphis in 22 days.

Mr. Glover is an energetic man and there is a prospect of his settling in our city. We have great faith in his ability and go-aheaditiveness.

The Memphis Daily Appeal, May 24, 1859

[Report apparently based on an interview of Mr. Crocker, OM Superintendent concerning the end of the sub-contract with the CHIDESTER, REESIDE & CO., and the stocking of the Memphis route with Butterfield owned stock and equipment.]

OVERLAND MAIL — MEMPHIS BRANCH

The Overland Mail Company, we are glad to announce, have determined to stock the road from Memphis to this place, by the way of Little Rock. Already have they started a number of coaches down the road, and **Mr. Crocker**, the Superintendent, proceeds immediately to locate stands and make every other preparation to carry the overland mail on this branch by the company. As soon as their stock is put on the road, the people in the lower part of the State will see staging that is staging.

Memphis Daily Appeal, May 31, 1859, page 3
[This report is apparently based on an interview with passengers as they arrived on May 30, 1859 at St. Louis.]

...A fight occurred between Major VanDorm and a party of Northern Comanches at the fork of the Arkansas river, on the 16th inst. Thirty-six Indians were killed and thirty-six were taken prisoners. Two soldiers were killed and several wounded, among the latter were Lieut. Lee and Capt. Smith.

There was much excitement among the Brazos Reserve Indians on account of there being five hundred Texans encamped twenty miles below, and were threatening an attack.

Overland Employee's Spouse
Dies of Consumption, July 23, 1859
as reported in The Arkansan, July 23, 1859, page 4

On Thursday, the 21st unst., at the Hotel of Mr. Onstott, of consumption, Mrs. Ella Smith, wife of Mr. E. G. Smith of the Overland Mail Co.*[She died at the Byrnside House in Fayetteville, Arkansas, owned by Mr. Onstott, and where the Overland Mail Co. offices were located.]*

Proposed Alternate Route, Sept, 28, 1859
as reported in the September 28, 1859 issue of the Arkansas True Democrat,
Little Rock, Arkansas, page 3

We clip the following from the Times: We learn from **Capt. Fox**, Superintendent of the Overland Mail, that the citizens of Dardanelle are cutting out a new road on the south side of the Arkansas River to intersect the Little Rock road at Perryville. It is thought that as soon as the road is opened, the stages of the Overland Mail Company will run to Little Rock all the way on this side of the river. We understand that the work on the road is well done. The people of Dardanelle are enterprising and liberal, and what they undertake they will go through with. Success to the enterprise.

[This is the only mention in the newspapers of the day concerning this proposed alternate route. Apparently Butterfield's Overland Mail Co. never used this alternate route.]

Road Conditions, Dec. 31, 1859
as reported in the Jan. 6, 1859 issue of Marshall County Democrat,
Plymouth, Indiana, page 2

St. Louis, Dec. 31, 1859

Five passengers left San Francisco, three of whom stopped at Fort Smith.

The roads from San Francisco to Red River, are very good, thence to Tipton very bad.

Appreciation of Butterfield Employees
by a Wagon Train Passenger, July 20, 1860
as printed in the August 25, 1860 issue of the
Arkansas True Democrat, Little Rock, Arkansas

In Camp Lion Holes, July 20, 1860

Friend M – In compliance with my promise on leaving Little Rock, I now write, being the first letter written by me since our departure.

We are now in camp, resting our stock at this place, which you will find by consulting your map, is about

900 miles west of Fort Smith, and about 200 east of the Rio Grande. We have been out fifty-five days, and traveled about 1,100 miles, in the heat of summer, and yet we are yet between 600 and 700 miles short of our destination...

We have now passed, entirely, the Comanche country, and although **during our passage we were continually reminded by the Overland Mail station keepers of the hazard and extreme danger of so small a party as ours attempting to cross the plains,** yet we have made the trip without seeing an isolated Indian...

We have almost universally received at the hands of the employees of the Overland Mail Company, kind treatment, and gentlemanly consideration; in fact, we have met with but one exception, which was at the hands of the station keeper at the crossing of the Colorado, who refused some of our party a drink of water, which so enraged some of our number, that had it not been for the interference of cooler heads, he would undoubtedly have received rough treatment.

This, I am pleased to say, was the only exception, which speaks well for the mail company and those employed by it. No one who has not traveled over the Overland Mail Line can form any just idea of the magnitude of this successful enterprise, and the complete system necessary to its permanent establishment as a means of communication between the Eastern States and the Pacific.

Indeed, I am convinced that it is one of the greatest achievements, as a coach mail line, that the world has ever seen, considering the extreme length of the line (2,700 miles), the character of the country through which it passes, and the immense distance necessary to transport provender *[feed and hay]* for stock, and the additional fact that during the whole time of its existence, but three mail failures have occurred on this line, and they were produced by high water.

There are several "dry stations" on the line, to which water has to be hauled, in some instances, the distance of 25 miles.

Butterfield Stage Accident, Aug. 3, 1860
as reported in the Aug. 3, 1860 issue of the Van Buren Press,
Van Buren, Arkansas

ACCIDENT – The California Overland Stage *[actually it was Butterfield's Overland stage]* upset on Boston Mountain about twenty miles north of this place on Sunday morning last. Nobody was hurt and the only damage done, that of breaking off the top of the stage. For a stage running day and night, and compelled to make by schedule the closest time, there have been the fewest accidents on this line than on any other in this country.

Butterfield Stage Accident, Sept. 28, 1860
as reported in the Sept. 28, 1860 issue of the Van Buren Press,
Van Buren, Arkansas

The California Overland Stage *[actually it was Butterfield's Overland Mail Co. stage]* from St. Louis upset last Sunday about 15 miles north of this city. There were nine passengers on the stage at the time who escaped with slight bruises. The horses, after the upset, ran off with the four wheels attached and two of them were so seriously injured they had to be killed.

Passenger Interview, Nov. 28, 1860
as reported in the Glasgow Weekly Times issue of
Thursday, December 6, 1860, on page 2.

Fort Smith, Nov. 28th, 1860

The Overland Mail from San Francisco, Nov. 9th, passed here *[Fort Smith, Arkansas]* this morning at eight o'clock. **The passengers state** that two men, formerly of St. Louis, named ALFRED PARINGOT and SAMUEL MC-

NEAL, employees of the Overland Mail Company, were scalped by the Comanche Indians five miles east of Riley Station, on the 22nd inst. No interruption, however, happened to the Overland Stage or its passengers.

Butterfield Conductor Interview, Feb. 6, 1861
as reported in The St. Joseph Weekly Free Democrat issue of Saturday, February 9, 1861, on page 2.

Fort Smith, Ark., Feb. 6, 1861

The conductor of the Overland Mail from Little Rock reports the arsenal taken possession of by State troops *[Confederate]* at that place *[Little Rock]* on Saturday evening last.

Conductor Reports, Feb. 8, 1861
as reported in the Feb. 8, 1861 issue of The Arkansian, page 2

FORT SMITH 7TH —The Overland Mail Conductor says, The U. S. Arsenal at Little Rock was taken possession of by the State troops on Saturday evening last.

Butterfield Employees Arrested, Feb. 18, 1861
as reported in the Daily Missouri Republican issue of Monday, February 18, 1861, page 2

Fort Smith, Feb. 15, 1861

A terrible tragedy occurred in this city last night. A party of five Overland Mail and Little Rock coach drivers entered the grocery of a German named HAGGE, and commenced quarreling. Pistols were drawn on both sides. The barkeeper, named BUTCHER, was shot through the head and died instantly. HAGGE received a shot in the forehead, and died at 8 o'clock this morning. Three of the drivers, GEORGE BENNETT, MATT ELLIS, and PONY FARMER, are under arrest and guarded by a company of military. The other two escaped. There is intense excitement among citizens. The prisoners are not undergoing trial before the Mayor. They will undoubtedly be hanged today.

Fort Smith, Feb. 16, 1861

As the trial of the prisoners for the murder of HAGGE and BUTCHER was drawing to a close yesterday, a mob entered the Justices' offices and demanded the prisoners for the purpose of hanging them. One prisoner, named PONY FARMER, broke from custody and attempted to escape. He was fired on and instantly killed. The crown secured the remaining prisoners and made for the place of execution, but, before carrying out their designs, the authorities interfered, secured the prisoners and lodged them in Greenwood jail. The excitement is intense.

Stages Confiscated in Texas, Feb. 20, 1861
as reported in the February 23, 1861 issue of the Weekly Arkansas Gazette, Little Rock, Arkansas, , page 2

Fort Smith, Ark., Feb. 20, 1861

Extra Overland Mail coach from Sherman, Texas reports the Texans had seized the Overland coach with the mail. They also seized the company's property and imprisoned its agents and other employees.

It was reported Forts Chadbourne and Belknap had been captured.

Stages Confiscated In Missouri, June 29, 1861
as reported in the June 29, 1861, issue of the Des Arc Semi-Weekly Citizen Des Arc, Arkansas, , page 3

FROM MISSOURI —

SYRACUSE, JUNE 27 — Jackson is reported at Ponnen Deterre *[Pomme de Terre, Missouri]* with 1,200 men. Overland mail coaches are in Jackson's possession.

THE CALIFORNIA MAIL, JULY 2, 1869
as reported in the Memphis Daily Appeal, July 2, 1859, page 3

The overland mail from this city for California will be transported for the present by way of Helena, and thence overland to Little Rock, avoiding the line of the Memphis and Little Rock Railroad. Passengers for this route will be sent by steamer to Helena, and will there meet Messrs. Chidester, Rapley & Co., splendid stages for Fort Smith. **Mr. Nichols**, the popular agent of the line at this city, will embark for Little Rock today on business connected with the mail service.

1st Steamboat to Reach Little Rock, 1822, by DeSpain 1975
Sketch from collection of Bob Crossman

Frank Clugage, Butterfield Employee, Aug.11, 1892
as reported in the Iron County Register,
Ironton, Missouri, Aug. 11, 1892, p.2

FRANK CLUGAGE, aged 76 years, died at Atchison, Kas., on the 2d, and the body was taken to his old home at Marrysville, O. The deceased in early life was interested with the Ohio Stage Co., operating in Ohio, Indiana and Illinois, and previous to the late war, with the **Southern Overland Mail Co.,** on the line across the continent from St. Louis via El Paso to San Francisco.

"Old Dave" Butterfield Driver, Dec. 3, 1896
as reported in the Platte Valley Lye, Saratoga, Wyoming
December 3, 1896, page 1

"Old Dave," the pioneer driver who has charge of the Sixteen Mile station, is still hale and hearty, despite his advanced age. Dave began to drive stage in 1858, on the old California Overland...

Drivers of Stage Go Overlooked, Sept. 19, 1956
as printed in The Press Argus, Centennial Edition
Van Buren, Arkansas, September 19, 1956, Section B, page 6

There has been very little of a personal nature written about the drivers of the Butterfield Overland Mail Company, but in Crawford county. Arkansas, at least the names of three are known and a few facts concerning them.

Michael Maney and **M. Dudley** were two stage drivers who lived at the home stage-station of George Woosley up in Jasper township two miles south of Cedarville.

Michael was 25 years old in 1860 and was born in New York. **Dudley** also was 25 years old and was born in Virginia.

It is significant to a researcher of history to note that the George and James Woosley families had a neighbor, who had a son by the name of Dudley. This was the case over at the home of Whitfield Bourne.

Whether there was any relationship that might have been the reason for this coincidence is not known.

It is known that the Whitfield Bourne home was a local stage line station stop. At Hiram Brodie's home stage-station at Lee Creek post office in Lee Creek township, there was a stage driver driver by the name of **George Evans**. He was born in Pennsylvania. He was 25 years old in 1860.

Had it not been for the 1860 census, the names of these drivers, or knowledge of them, would never have been recorded in this special edition.

For although books written about the Butterfield story mentions the drivers, yet the facts are in general terms, with little personal detail. The majority of them were picked by John Butterfield Sr. from his drivers in

– 414 –
© 2024 Robert O. Crossman

the east. They were the best from the Mohawk valley and other sections where he had run stages. They were young men, and men versed in the care and driving of horses, under the best or worse conditions.

If either of the three young men who lived in Crawford county and drove the stages remained in Arkansas, their descendants have failed to rise up and call them blessed, for absolutely nothing ever 'turned up" about them after the stage quit running here.

Ahab Bowen, Agent. Sept. 19, 1956
as reported in The Press Argus, Centennial Edition, Van Buren, Arkansas
September 19, 1956, Section B, page 6

Ahab Bowen, pictured here, was the Butterfield Agent at Bolivar, Missouri, 1858-1861. He was also the Proprietor of the Franklin Hotel; Stage Station; general store keeper; owner and operator of livery stable; and the Butterfield corral.

He was a leading citizen and civic leader of Bolivar, Missouri.

He died in Dallas, Texas in 1900.

Photo from Historical Collection
Union Title Co., San Diego, CA.

True Democrat, Saturday, June 23, 1860, Little Rock, Arkansas
This advertisement ran multiple times during 1860.

Witness to the Butterfield Overland National Historic Trail
Just two blocks from Little Rock's Arkansas River Ferry & the Anthony House home station of the Overland Mail Co. stands the oldest structure in Little Rock.
The Henderliter Grog House *stands at the corner of Cumberland and Third street. Built by Jesse Hinderliter in mid 1820's when he moved to Little Rock from St. Louis. The building served as his home, grog house (bar), tavern & boarding house.*   *Photo ca 1935*

Aunt Adeline
Credit: The Slave Narrative "Aunt Adeline,"
Jack Dappa Blues Heritage Radio

CHAPTER FIFTY EIGHT
Aunt Adeline, age 89, Parks Station, Arkansas
Federal Writer's Project: Slave Narrative Project
Arkansas, Volume 1, page 11

I was born a slave about 1848, in Hickmon County, Tennessee. *[Aunt Adeline's mother, with a group of five negroes, was sold into slavery to John P. A. Parks, in Tennessee, about 1840. After moving to Arkansas, John P. A. Parks' home in western Arkansas was a Butterfield Swing Station, 1858-1861.]*

When my mother's master came to Arkansas about 1849, looking for a country residence, he bought what was known as the Old Kidd Place on the Old Wire Road, which was **one of the Stage Coach stops**. I was about one year old when we came. We had a big house and **many times passengers would stay several days and wait for the next stage to come by.**

It was then that I earned my first money. I must have been about six or seven years old. One of Mr. Parks' daughters was about one and a half years older than I was. We had a play house back of the fire place chimney. We didn't have many toys — maybe a doll made of a corn cob, with a dress made from scraps and a head made from a roll of scraps. We were playing church. Miss Fannie was the preacher and I was the audience. We were singing, "Jesus my all to Heaven is gone." When we were half way through with our song we discovered that the **passengers from the stage coach** had stopped to listen. We were so frightened at our audience that we both ran. But we were coaxed to come back for a dime and sing our song over...

I was about 15 years old when the Civil War ended and was still living with Mrs. Blakely and helped care for her little children.

By this time Aunt Adeline was the slave of Mr. Parks' daughter, Elizabeth Parks Blakeley. Aunt Adeline continued to care for children in the family for five generations of Parks' descendants.

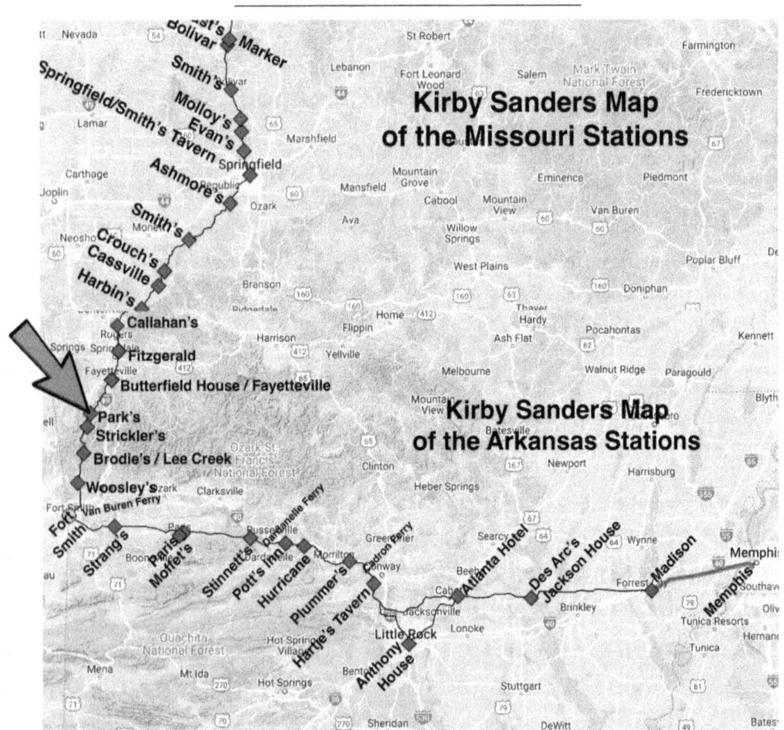

Image from "In History is Herstory: Kiziah Love," by Deborah Love, 2015

CHAPTER FIFTY NINE

Kiziah Love, Enslaved at Colbert's Ferry, Aug. 16, 1937

interview at age 93

Lawd help us, I sho' remembers all about slavery times for I was a grown woman, married and had one baby, when de War done broke out. That was a sorry time for some poor black folks but I guess Master Frank Colbert's Negroes was about as well off as the best of em. I can recollect things that happened way back better than I can things that happen now. Funny aint' it?

Frank Colbert, a full-blood Choctaw Indian, was my owner. He owned my mother but I don't remember much about my father. He died when I was a little youngun. My Mistress' name was Julie Colbert. She and master Frank was de best folks that ever lived. All the negroes loved master Frank and knowned jest what he wanted done and they tried their best to do it, too.

... We lived on Master Frank's farm and Isom went back and forth to work fer his master and I worked ever day fer mine. I don't 'spect we could of done that way iffen we hadn't of had Indian masters. They let us do a lot like we pleased jest so we got our work done and didn't run off.

Old Master Frank never worked us hard and we had plenty of good food to eat. He never did like to put us under white overseers and never tried it but once.

...Master Colbert run a stage stand and a ferry on Red River and he didn't have much time to look after his farm and his Negroes. He had lots of land and lots of slaves. His house was a big log house, three rooms on one side and three on the other, and there was a big open hall *[dog trot]* between them. There was a big gallery clear across the front of the house. Behind the house was the kitchen and the smoke house. The smoke house was always filled with plenty of good meat and lard. They would kill the polecat and dress it and take a sharp stick and turn it up their back jest under the flesh. The would also run one up each leg and then turn him over on his back and put him on top of the house and let him freeze all night. The next morning they'd pull the sticks out and all the scent would be on them sticks and the cat wouldn't smell at all. They'd cook it like they did possum, bake it with taters or make dumplings...

Kiziah (Kissiah) Love's Dawes Census Card, which lists her slave holder Frank Colbert. She was enrolled as a Chickasaw Freedmen because she lived on the Chickasaw reservation, despite being enslaved.

Card list her children: Jack age 22, Mike age 21, Tenanna age 18, Brit age 16, Emma age 14, Janie age 12, Jean age 8. And grandson Jesse, age 7 months.

Concord, New Hampshire made Mail Stagecoach, Otero Museum, La Junta, CO

CHAPTER SIXTY

Fred K. Cook, Treasurer OMCo., July 19, 1861
Wm. Buckley, Supt. OMCo., Aug. 13, 1861

Both of the following letters were written during the chaos of closing of the Southern Ox Bow Route in March of 1861 and relocating the Overland Mail Co. new operations to the north on the Central Route, July 1, 1861.

Office of the Overland Mail Company
84 B. Way, New York, July 17, 1861
H. S. Rumfield, Esq,
Agent Overland Mail Co.
St. Louis, Mo.

Dear Sir:

I rec'd your telegram of the 16th asking how you should raise money to pay off with, late last evening.

I also have your letter of 6th at Syracuse.

It is very difficult for me to decide how to do. I do not know that we can abandon the mail service without consent of the Govt. There seems to be a difference of opinion between you and the others.

Allen thinks it safe to resume. You do not and I do not. If it were only a question as to whether our stock would be taken by federal forces or not, I would say go on and if they take it let them do so. But are not the rebels just as likely to get it?

I do not, on consideration, see that we can move either way for a few days yet. When it is safe, if it should be soon, you will begin again under my former instructions. But perhaps before that I may see you, as I expect to leave for Salt Lake on the 24th (morning).

That I may meet you & say all that may be advisable, I wish you to hover around St. Louis until then, (provided you cannot resume service) that I may communicate with you as occasion requires.

I may not be able to stay in St. Louis, but if you are there you can go with me on R. R. to Hudson and we can determine matters on the way. Or if I should go by Chicago, I can have you meet me on the Hannibal R. Rd. On account of other matters I desire to be at St. Joseph on Saturday p.m. 27th.

I send you herewith or another day, my account against Tuller to the present time, so far as I know it. Nothing is complete since Dec. 31st. But up to that, you and I do not agree, as you will discover. The differences, you must regulate your accounts to, as mine are right. I do not know how things are to be brought up rightly, as Tuller may not be competent to settle when I meet him at Salt Lake. But if no other way the papers must all be sent to me at Salt Lake after you and he have made up your accounts. Recollect, all accounts and papers are to be sent to me at Salt Lake. More of this when we meet.

Perhaps I repeat in the following. When you go over the ground to settle, or collect P. O. orders, you must get affidavits and positive proof of every loss, of stock in order to make claim on the Govt. Get them up in good shape — in style terse and in words brief as may be as yet sufficiently full as to essential facts and figures...

After the 22d, I become Agent and Assist. Treas., and Alexander J. Carter, Treasurer. That change became necessary in sending me to Salt Lake. After that date

any drafts you make must be on him; and when you come to settle, you can draw on him, on such terms as you can make for amt. you need — and if you need for expenses meanwhile you can draw on me. I will write you again soon.   Yours truly, Fred K. Cook,
                                        Treasr. O.M.Co.

The P.O. order returns which you are to collect you are not to send me, but to my successor here.

Placerville
August 13, 1861
JAMES BEGGS, ESQ.
Dear Sir,

On your arrival at Folsom you will call on H. Montfort Agt. Pioneer Stage Co. He will direct what to be done with the Stock & c as I have wrote him to have a place for them. When Smith arrives with his stock, you will have all horses able to work from his band and yours, sent to Carson City. You will send only good stage horses. I shall want about fifty or sixty head if you have them. Send six or eight of the best wagons — and harness for all the horses if you have them. Smith will go over to Carson with the horses.

I want you to remain with the balance of the horses. The horses that are very poor and not able to send over to Smith. I want the best of care taken of them. They had better be fed hay and grain as the grass if very poor.

Mr. Montfort will buy hay and grain for you. I suppose there are some horses that will never be of any use to the Co. for staging. If you can sell them or trade for good horses do so. I do not want much hay and grain bought for them. Those that will make good stage horses have the best of care taken of them, the wagons have all washed, and put under shade. Also the harness that may be left — have good care taken of it. You will discharge all men excepting enough to help take care of the stock — say to Smith to take with him some of the men you have with you — and discharge the men he hired in Visalia, as I want to give the old employees as much work as we have to do.

I want you to remain with the stock until I return. Will find something for you to do. Don't keep any more men with you than necessary to take care of the stock.

You will not feed the horses over six or eight lbs. barley each pr day – have it soaked.

Mr. McLane may want some of the horses. If he should, let him have them & take receipt for same.

Your Truly,
Wm. Buckley, Supt. O.M. Co.

Telegraph me when you arrive in Folsom, also when Smith arrives — and how many horses will be fit to send over by Smith.

Overland Mail Stage in the Snow, artist unknown

Lieutenant William W. Averell
Source: Wikipedia, "William W. Averell"

CHAPTER SIXTY ONE
Lieutenant Averell, Spring 1861
Article by Muriel H. Wright as it appears in The Chronicles of Oklahoma, Spring 1961, "Lieutenant Averell's Ride, 1861" by Muriel H. Wright

Appreciation is expressed to Susan Dragoo and Dr. C. J. Messer for rediscovering Lieutenant Averell's ride in Muriel Wright's article.

Lieutenant Averell's observations by stagecoach between April 23 and April 27, 1861 occurred on the same route used by Butterfield between Springfield, Missouri and Fort Smith, Arkansas. It appears that his journey over this route occurred during the last hours of Butterfield's operations on the Southern Route.

The last westbound Butterfield stage left St. Louis sometime between March 18 and 21, 1861, 30 days ahead of Averell's stage ride.

The last eastbound Butterfield stage left San Francisco on April 13, 1861 and would have passed Averell's stage as it headed northeast arriving in St. Louis on May 1, 1861.

So, it appears that Averell's westbound ride on the route used by Butterfield between Springfield and Fort Smith occurred 30 days after Butterfield's last westbound trip over that same route.

In these beginning weeks of the Civil War, stage travel conditions had deteriorated greatly, as Averill reports, "I was obliged to drive the stage a greater part of the distance between Cassville and Bentonville, on account of the drunkenness of the driver."

Lieutenant Averell writes: Providing myself with a rough traveling suit of citizen 's clothing, I left Washington at 2.45 p. m. on the 17th of April, by the Baltimore and Ohio Railway...

I arrived at Saint Louis on the evening of the 19th, and left on the morning of the 20th by the first train to Rolla, Mo., where I arrived, 115 miles distant, at 5 in the afternoon.

Leaving Rolla by the first stage coach at 5 a.m. the 22d, with several prominent Southern gentlemen as fellow passengers.

[It appears that 100 miles southwest of Rolla, at Springfield, Missouri, Lieut. Averell began to travel on the route used by Butterfield between Springfield, Missouri and Fort Smith, Arkansas.]

I proceeded, with changing horses, mails, and passengers, toward Fort Smith, through towns wild with secession excitement and rumors of war. The unruly temper of the people and their manifest readiness to embrace any pretext for violence made it necessary for the safety of my dispatches and their successful delivery that my name and character should remain unknown.

Having assumed a name and purpose suitable to the emergency, I experienced no great difficulty in passing safely through several inquisitions. I was obliged to drive the stage a greater part of the distance between Cassville and Bentonville, on account of the drunkenness of the driver, there being no other male passenger.

At Evansville I met the intelligence, which momentarily astounded me, that Fort Smith had been captured by a force of secessionists 800 strong, which had come under the command of Colonel Borland from Little Rock. Near the foot of Boston mountain, on the southern side, the rumor was confirmed by the passengers of a coach from Fort Smith which we met, happily in a pitchy dark night, which prevented my recognition by some of the lady passengers, wives of army officers who might have known me.

Crossing the Arkansas River on a ferry-boat, we reached Fort Smith at 9 o'clock on the morning of the

27th. The town was in a political frenzy. The fort had been evacuated by Captain Sturgis, with four companies of the First Cavalry, four or five days before, and the post quartermaster, on whom I had an order for transportation, was a prisoner in the guardhouse. Secession troops were having a "general training" and target practice. It was perilous to make inquiries regarding our troops, and the only information obtainable of them was that they had gone westward, that pursuit up the Arkansas and from the direction of Texas as on foot, and that bridges had been burned and the streams were swollen from recent rains.

[It appears that Lieut. Averell stagecoach ride ended here at Fort Smith, Arkansas. He continues westward by horseback, still following the same route used by Butterfield's Overland Mail Company.]

Exchanging my gold watch and a little money for a horse, saddle, and bridle with a man whose primary incentive to the trade was his apprehension of losing his horse by public seizure, I mounted for the remainder of the journey. It was 260 miles to Fort Arbuckle. Having been out of the saddle two years on account of my wound, and having just completed a toilsome, jilting journey of 300 miles in a coach, I was in poor condition for the struggle before me.

The horse was unbroken to the saddle, and after a fierce but unsuccessful effort to throw me, ran wildly away through the successive lines of drilling troops, but I managed to guide him in a westerly direction and mastered him before reaching the Poteau River. This stream, 100 yards wide, was bank full and the bridge destroyed. Removing my heavy black overcoat, I swam the horse across, after a fearful struggle, in which I lost my overcoat and also suffered some injury from being struck by the horse.

Twenty miles west of Fort Smith the road forks, the right hand going to Fort Arbuckle and the left to Fort

Washita, these points being separated by sixty-five miles. Between the two routes the volcanic protrusion called the San Bois Mountains rise in several ranges about 1,500 feet high and gradually sink to the level of the undulating prairie seventy-five miles west of the fork. The deep trail showed that Sturgis has taken the left-hand road to Washita; therefore I went forward on the other the distance of about a mile to establish my trail in case of pursuit and then crossed over to the other road.

The next morning I was overtaken at Holloway's Overland Station, fifty-four miles west of Fort Smith, by four mounted desperadoes, but my would-be captors, finding me wearing the light-blue uniform overcoat of a private soldier, which I had obtained at a station to replace the black one lost in the river, were easily persuaded that they had missed their man and I was not the one they wanted, but a rancorous secessionist like themselves who was going to fetch a sister from the army on account of the prospective troubles. Permitted to pursue my way, and quitting the road a few hours later to graze my horse, the same party, undeceived by a study of trails, passed me in hot pursuit. Resuming the road after them, a friendly wayfarer, who had met them and heard their inquiries, informed me of their wrathful purpose to shoot me on sight.

With the intention to reach the trail crossing to the Arbuckle road at the western end of the mountains, if possible, and to avail myself of the sheltering woods which covered their southern slopes if necessary, I rode cautiously forward. But ere the desired trail was reached the party was descried *[caught sight of]* returning, whereupon I took to the woods and was fired upon and ordered to halt. Realizing that I could make a trail faster than they could find it, my course was taken directly across the mountains and my escape made good.

The Arbuckle road was found about two hours after midnight, after experiencing considerable trouble in keeping my horse, which I was obliged to lead during the night in the woods through howling packs of wolves. The next day I was headed off by the same party on that road and pursued. After another troublesome night in the woods among wolves and impassable ravines I found a Cherokee cabin, some food for myself and horse, and a guide to the Arbuckle road, ten miles west of Perryville...

[NOTE: At this point, Lieutenant Averell has left the Butterfield Route at Holloway's Station, and turned north a short distance to continue on the Arbuckle Road. Averell spent the next few months in Indian Territory making contact with many of the Indian Nations and including great detail in his writings. The report of the balance of his trip is recorded in The Chronicles of Oklahoma, Spring 1961, "Lieutenant Averell's Ride, 1861" by Muriel H. Wright]

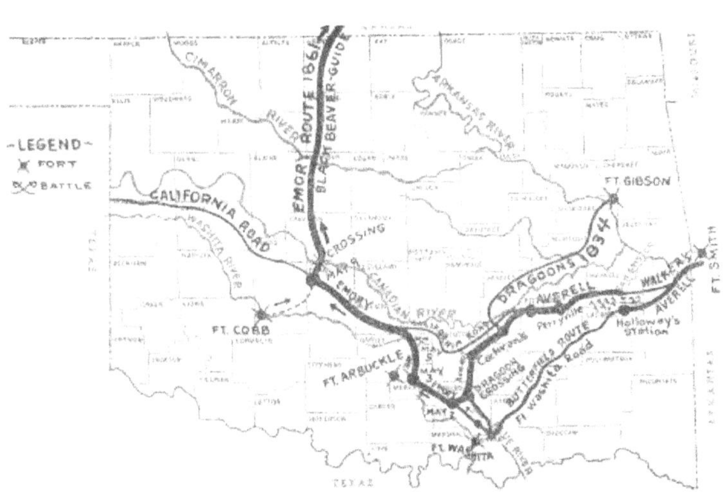

*Map of Lieut. Averell s ride from Fort Smith into Indian Territory
Source: "Lieutenant Averell's Ride, 1861" by Muriel H. Wright,
The Chronicles of Oklahoma, Spring 1961, page 9*

Col. William W. Averell (sitting) of 3rd Pennsylvania Cavalry with staff in August 1862. Source: Wikipedia, "William W. Averell"

General William W. Averell
Rare Cabinet Card Image, compliments of Yankee Rebel Antiques

Image courtesy of The Post-Standard, Syracuse, New York

CHAPTER SIXTY TWO

John Butterfield Jr. & Amos B. Stafford, April 24, 1903
as reported in the April 24, 1904 issue of The Post-Standard, Syracuse, N.Y.

Credit must be expressed to Gerald T. Ahnert who discovered this article in 2014. In Dec. 2023, the article's accompanying photograph was confirmed as the ONLY existing photograph of a Mail Stagecoach used by Butterfield. Image was taken Sept. 1858 on the first day of operations in front of Charles Butterfield's home in Fayetteville, Arkansas.

NOTE: A reporter of Syracuse, New York's "The Post-Standard," sat down on April 23, 1904 in Utica, New York to interview local residents John Butterfield Jr. and stagecoach driver, Amos B. Stafford.

Amos B. Stafford and John Butterfield
— Connected With the First Great Route —
— Reminiscences Like a Novel of Adventure —
Special to the Post-Standard.

Utica, April 23. — The picturesque days of the "overland mail" service on the Western frontier, enlivened by Indian skirmishes, robber raids and exciting rides over mountain passes; have a strange fascination in this era of Pullman cars and more rigorously enforced law.

The schoolboy smuggles into his desk the thrilling tale of some imaginative hero of that period and even more mature readers find an exhilarating pleasure in the authentic accounts of the courage and hardihood of the famous drivers who handled six or eight horses or mules, from the top of the old red coaches, through wild and lawless sections.

Here and there one of these old drivers is to be found, passing the closing years of his life quietly, and when one of them can be induced to "talk" his reminiscences are often as interesting as a good novel of adventure. Among such are two whose figures are familiar in the streets of this city. Amos B. Stafford and John Butterfield, who were connected with the first great route, that running from near St. Louis to San Francisco.

Mr. Stafford is a native of Syracuse. He was born in 1835, and came to Utica eleven years later. His tall form and deep-set eyes are well known throughout the city *[Utica, N.Y.]* One of his chief enjoyments today is driving, not four-in-hand nor six-in-hand, but a single horse attached to a light rig. He is a lover of horse flesh and it is not improbable that his life in the West, in his younger days, had much to do in cultivating this interest. He is out for a drive practically every day when the weather and roads are in reasonably good condition.

Mr. Butterfield is a Utica boy, having been born here in 1827. He has a spacious and comfortable home on Park Avenue *[Utica, N.Y.]* and is taking life quietly. Every day he may be seen in the hotel which bears his name and which belongs to the family.

With Mr. Stafford and others he frequently goes over some of the scenes and incidents of his experience as a stage driver. He has been interested also in other means of transportation,

Amos B Stafford, 1904
Driver for Butterfield
Image courtesy of Gerald T. Ahnert

including street car service in this city.

The St. Louis — San Francisco stage and mail line was 2,770 miles in length and about 3,000 horses and 200 coaches were used in its operation. It was established in the fall of 1858, the first stage over it leaving St. Louis on September 16. Twenty-three days and six hours later the mail reached the Pacific coast terminus.

When the government conceived the idea of inaugurating such a service, to supersede the old pony routes and intrepid mail boys, it advertised for bids.

The reputation of the country through which the line runs, was not the best and no proposals were received. No one seemed to be anxious to sacrifice himself to Indian savagery or bandit recklessness as to human life. The stories of attacks and hold-ups in which there was a free use of firearms and knives were numerous and, in the minds of the majority of people, the "Rocky Road to Dublin" was a fine gravel road as compared with the highways in the "wild and wooly." [*"Rocky Road to Dublin" was an 1863 Irish song about the troubles and travails of a man's travel from Ireland to England.*]

It was the government, therefore, that had to open the negotiations and do the proposing and John Butterfield, Sr., father of the John Butterfield heretofore mentioned, was the man to whom it turned.

The elder Butterfield had for years been interested in transportation problems and he was looked upon as one of the best fitted men in the country for the difficult task that Uncle San had to give out. He had begun life as a driver and had established a thriving livery business and been connected with a system of packet boats and had later been a powerful factor in the development of the street railway business. He had also appreciated the need and feasibility of an express service and had been one of the directors of the Utica City National Bank, which, by the way, has just completed a ten story banking and office building in Genesee Street in this city *[Utica, New York]* and will soon move into it.

The contract eventually entered into between the government and Mr. Butterfield was for six years and called for the equipment and operation of a line from St. Louis in the Pacific. When the papers had been signed, John Butterfield Jr., with whom this article is concerned, set out for California by water. He was then in the prime of his early manhood, 31 years of age, and prepared to meet any experience that the terrible country to the west of his native city might have in store for him. The duty imposed upon him was to journey eastward from San Francisco, laying out the proposed route and arranging to stock it. On January 7, 1858, at high noon, he set out from San Francisco. He reached Utica on May 7, having safely and successfully made the long journey.

The line, as laid out, ran southeasterly from San Francisco to El Paso, Texas along the coast, then over the mountains and off across the level plains. From El Paso the course lay across Texas to Sherman, near the northern boundary, and on to Fort Smith, Arizona *[actually Fort Smith, Arkansas]*, by way of the haunts of the Choctaw, Creek and Cherokee Indians.

From Fort Smith it crossed the mountains to Springfield, ~~MO.~~, and extended on to Bolivar and Warsaw. After fording the Osage river, Mr. Butterfield laid his course off in a long swing to the northwest to Fayetteville, then a town of considerable importance, the home of Charles Butterfield, son of John Butterfield, Sr. Thence the course was due east to Tipton, the terminal of the Missouri Pacific Railroad.

[The reporter mistakenly mixed up Fayetteville, Missouri with Fayetteville, Arkansas, **so the entire paragraph above has a confused geography.** *The paragraph should have read: "From Fort Smith it crossed the mountains to Fayetteville, then a town of considerable importance, the home of Charles Butterfield, son of John Butterfield, Sr. From Fayetteville, Mr. Butterfield laid his course off in a long swing to the northeast to Springfield, MO., and extended on to Bolivar and Warsaw. After fording the Osage river, the course was due north to Tipton, the terminal of the Missouri Pacific Railroad."]*

The line was opened with John Butterfield, Jr., as superintendent of a division and Mr. Stafford as station agent at Fayetteville. Among the coaches were several which, prior to their shipment West, had been displayed in the East. In the celebration in this city *[Utica, N.Y.]* in 1858, of the Atlantic cable enterprise, several of the stages were driven. Freshly painted and drawn by six horses each they were objects of much interest, especially as it was known to what a country they were soon to be sent. Charles E. Butterfield, A. B. Stafford, William Dunn and George Carver each drove one of the coaches.

There were several others from this section who held positions on the new overland route. R. Samuel Reynolds of Utica was a conductor in charge of both mail and passengers between Springfield and Fort Smith. Ex-Sheriff Hugh Croker had charge of the Fort Smith division and Giles Hawley of Rome of the El Paso division. Nelson Davis of Utica was also stationed at El Paso. Mr. Butterfield was superintendent of the division extending from Tipton to Fort Smith, a distance of 500 miles.

In the more thickly settled sections contiguous to St. Louis and San Francisco, Concord overland coaches were used, while in the long stretches over the plains and mountains, vehicles of the hack style were operated. The entire distance was cut up into relays of twelve miles each. A change of horses and drivers was made at each relay. *[Actually horses were changed at each station, drivers were changed about every 60 to 80 miles, and conductors changed every 120 to 160 miles.]* There were two mails each way every week and their progress was never stopped day or night. The approach of a coach to the end of a relay was heralded by the blowing of horns, in the fashion of Merry England. The government did its part toward guarding the mails and passengers, from loss in the one case and injury in the other.

Forts were located at intervals along the line and troops patrolled many sections. Occasionally the troops were on hand to drive away marauding parties of Indians or whites, but as often the drivers and passengers were obliged to be their own defenders and many a true tale of courage and quick action has been told of them.

The portion of the route running between San Francisco and El Paso was particularly wild and dangerous and the drivers and the passengers as well needed nerve of the first order to make the trip. It is said that attacks averaged once a week, but in the majority of cases the soldiers or the drivers and passengers or both, were able to beat the assailants off.

There was often as much danger from the road itself as from the redskins and desperadoes. The typical driver was a bold and daring fellow and breaking records in the matter of time was as popular among the men of those days as with the engineers of the fast trains and steamers of today. Mr. Stafford occasionally took the reins when, for any reason, the regular driver was unable to go out on a relay from Fayetteville.

On one dark night he gave the load of passengers that had come through from San Francisco an experience that greatly pleased them if it did give them something of a shaking up. Along about 1 a.m. it was found that the regular driver was too ill to make the run that night and Mr. Stafford was aroused from bed and asked to mount the box. He did and he covered the twelve miles in just 50 minutes. Journeys at break-neck speed over mountain roads, paved with rocks, and along winding pathways bordering yawning chasms, were fraught with a thrilling excitement and stirring pleasure for the driver and with a sickening fear for the timid passengers.

But the wild driving, the Indian attacks and hold-ups by the desperadoes went on until the Civil War broke out, when they soon came to an end, the "overland mail" being discontinued. The government then found it necessary to withdraw the troops from the Indian country and it was then that the redskins and bandits plundered and stole to an extent that made it impracticable to carry on the business. Some of the old coaches finally found their way into the hands of Buffalo Bill and were the target of blank cartridges in exhibition attacks in the "Wild West Show" for years.

1862 Downtown Utica, New York. Image courtesy of the Observer-Dispatch.

The **Uticans** engaged in the business returned to the East, the family of Charles Butterfield having some difficulty in getting out of Fayetteville, owing to the strong Southern sentiment existing there. The Butterfields had a relative, **General Daniel Butterfield** *[image on following page]*, who was an officer of the Northern army. It was through Mr. Stafford's planning and quick work that they were gotten safely to Springfield *[Missouri]*.

Major General Daniel Butterfield (October 31, 1831 – July 17, 1901)
Son of John Butterfield Sr. and Malinda Baker Butterfield
Image from the collection of Bob Crossman, *8 in x 10 in*
Photograph by James E. McCloes; Engraving by J. C. Buttre of New York

Daniel Butterfield is given credit for helping the Butterfields escape to St. Louis from Fayetteville, Arkansas when the Civil War started.

Daniel is also given credit for making the original time schedule for the Overland Mail stagecoaches in 1858. Daniel spread out a large sheet of paper, fifty or sixty feet long and about two feet wide, where he laid out the stations along the trail, noting the days and hours for arrivals and departures from each.

After working for his father at the American Express, he served in the Civil War. Daniel was soon promoted brigadier general. Daniel either wrote or re-wrote a popular bugle-call for burials, called Taps. Wounded at Gettysburg, Daniel later received the Medal of Honor.

The Butterfield Hotel, Fayetteville, Arkansas

Butterfield Hotel's Location, Fayetteville, AR
The Butterfield Hotel was apparently burned near the time of the Civil War.
The Van Winkle Hotel was built on that site about 1880.
Looking West along Center Street toward the County Court House.
Image source: "When Fayetteville Moved on Four Hooves," by Denele Campbell

Butterfield's stages came down College Street from the north, turned right onto Center Street, and the hotel was on the right. After one block on Center Street, the stage entered the town square. Denele Campbell writes, *"...determining that his Overland Mail route would cross through Fayetteville, John Butterfield purchased a five-acre plot of land along the east side of the main road (now College Avenue) where he built a station, a large barn and stables. This was Butterfield's master plan. "*

The Butterfield Hotel, located in Fayetteville, Arkansas was burned at the time of the Civil War. This image is the 1880 Van Winkle Hotel, built on the same site.

Apparently the Butterfield was similar in appearance, according to local legend.

Image source: Arkansas Historical Quarterly, Spring 1973, page 64.

Van Winkle Hotel. Fayetteville, AR

Alexander Toponce

CHAPTER SIXTY THREE
Alexander Toponce
as reported in his book,
"Reminiscences of Alexander Toponce, Pioneer, 1839-1923"
This 248 page book was written by Mr. Toponce, typewritten under his direction, and was finished on his 80th birthday. It was published after his death by his widow, Katie Toponce.

(page 28) I helped to install the first overland stage line that went through from Missouri to California about 1855. *[actually 1857-8]* This stage line was started by a man named Butterfield, from Buffalo *[actually Utica, NY]*, New York, and run from Tipton, Mo., by way of Texas and New Mexico , but when Johnston's army was sent to Utah in 1858 the route was changed to run by way of Salt Lake. *[actually route changed in 1861]*

(page 22-24) After a few days we went to a place called Coal Camp, now known as Tipton, Missouri. The Missouri Pacific railroad was being built through that part of the state. There was a rich old Missouri planter who owned one hundred negroes and a big tract of rich land. He fought hard against letting the railroad cross his land because it would scare the cattle. But the

railroad came through in spite of him and doubled the value of his land and they located the town of Tipton on his farm...

(page 29, author skips around a great deal. The following may have occurred on the Butterfield Overland or on the West Port to Santa Fe stage line.)

The stage was the old Concord, or "Pitching Betsy" type, with two seats inside, facing each other...

2008 Celebration of the 150th Anniversary of the Stagecoach Route taken at the Fitzgerald Station, Springdale, Arkansas. Replica of a Concord stagecoach.

So we piled the front seat full of mail bags, clear to the roof, and fastened them with a rope. The first class mail was in sacks with a copper padlock, the second class had an iron padlock and the third-class mail was in big sacks fastened with a puckering string. Our orders always were, in case of emergency, to save the copper locks first, the iron locks next and the mail bags with puckering strings last. *[This is the only known description of the types of Overland Mail Co. mail bags and the variety of locks.]*

About that time the Methodist, or someone like that, were sending an awful lot of Bibles and tracts through to the heathen in California, and the government was also shipping great quantities of patent office reports, and these Bibles and reports were in the sacks with puckering strings...

Kirkbride Potts Home Station, on Memphis / Ft. Smith Route
by Joe Gray, 1976

CHAPTER SIXTY FOUR

Thomas Ranahan, stage driver

as reported in the Imperial Valley Press, El Centro, California, March 26, 1923

"Stage Coach Driver of Early 60's Visiting Here
Recounts Thrilling Prairie Wagon Days"

Visiting in El Centro at present is **Thomas Ranahan**, of Boise, Idaho, one of the two survivors of the early stage coach days when that means of transportation was the only way passengers and mail could be carried overland from the east to the Pacific coast.

...ran away from home in Kansas City to become a stage driver, and there after covering all parts of the west as a driver, railroad man, Indian scout and frontiersman.

Mr. Ranahan tells of the mail contract question that was puzzling congress in 1858 as thought it were only yesterday. The Vanderbilt and Gould interests at that time had a contract to transport mail from the Atlantic to the Pacific via the Panama Railroad [*that crossed the Isthmus of Panama*], and as it was desirable to reduce running time as much as possible, plans were formulated... to transport the mail overland instead of having to make the long trip via Panama.

After much wrangling, he finally succeeded in getting a contract from the government, calling for 24 days running time between Ft. Smith, Arkansas and San Francisco *[actually it was St. Louis & Memphis, via Fort Smith to San Francisco.]* Ft. Smith was the junction point for mail for the west from New York and New Orleans, the two important cities of that period. The first trip was made on September 23, 1858 and the mail arrived in San Francisco in a little over 23 days, thus demonstrating that the plan proposed by... Butterfield was feasible.

This aroused the ire of the capitalists *[Vanderbilt and Gould families]* and they determined to put Butterfield out of business. One means adopted was to buy up tons of European magazines, which they had transported across the ocean and then to Ft. Smith, and destined for San Francisco. The magazines were dumped at Ft. Smith and the New Yorkers chuckled with glee as they saw the apparent end of Butterfield's scheme.

However, the latter was a crafty as the Goulds and Vanderbilts and appeared before congress where he explained that his contract called for the delivery of first class mail and certain designated newspapers printed in this country and that he did not have to transport foreign magazines. Congress upheld him and the magazines so carefully brought by the New Yorkers were later burned at Ft. Smith.

The original route of the Overland stage was from Ft. Smith, through Oklahoma, Texas, New Mexico, Arizona and California, but later, when the Civil War broke out, as most of this country lay in rebel territory, the route was moved further north...

Mr. Ranahan relates that the early stage coach routes to San Francisco lay through Yuma. The drive from there across the desert to San Bernardino, was toughest of the whole route, making nearly 200 miles without water. To make it possible to cover this stretch, Butterfield hauled out water tanks which were placed at 40 mile intervals and kept locked…

Despite his strenuous life, Mr. Ranahan is extremely active, though suffering at present from neuritis, which prompted him to leave the rigors of an Idaho winter for the milder climate of Southern California. His experiences in the last 60 years would make a most interesting book and he remains as a fitting reminder of the rugged type of men who lived in one of the most exciting periods of American history, and to whose courage and determination to overcome obstacles, the west of today was made possible.

"Stagecoach Ride Down Steep Grade" 1898, Artist unknown

Muriel Hazel Wright (1889-1975)
Teacher, historian, and editor

CHAPTER SIXTY FIVE
"The Butterfield Overland Mail One Hundred Years Ago"
by Muriel H. Wright
Chronicles of Oklahoma, Spring 1957, pages 55-71

NOTE: This is NOT a personal diary entry. I'm including here because this article by Muriel H. Wright interjects interesting bits of history concerning the first day of operation for Butterfield's Overland Mail, and sets the context for the first person accounts that are printed in this book.

Arrival at Springfield, Missouri, was at 3:15 p.m., Friday, September 17. The blowing of the horn as the stagecoach approached had caused excitement in the town. A crowd gathered to see the first overland mail, and to congratulate Mr. Butterfield and John Jr. A salute of guns was fired. The 143 mile trip from Tipton to Springfield had never before been made in such quick time. There was a forty-five minute stop at Springfield while the mail and baggage and passengers were changed from the stagecoach to a Concord "Celerity" wagon.

Travel night and day again past four stations before reaching the Arkansas line, the rugged Ozark hills, Fayetteville, and then Fort Smith after crossing the Arkansas River on a raft at Van Buren. The mail and passengers from Tipton reached Fort Smith at five minutes past two o'clock in the morning. There was much excitement as the coach drove up to the City Hotel where the mail from Memphis had arrived only fifteen minutes earlier. Ormsby reports, *"Horns were blown, houses were lit up, and many flocked to the hotel to have a look at the wagons and talk over the exciting topics, and have a peep at the first mail bags. The general interest was contagious..."* even this early in the morning.

One hour and twenty-five minutes were used in joining the two mails from Memphis and St. Louis, examining and arranging the way mails and the way bill and changing stages. Then exactly at half past three o'clock in the morning on Sunday, September 19, 1858, the first westbound stage left Fort Smith, exactly twenty-four hours ahead of the time table schedule, gained in the first 468 miles of the journey.

There were only three persons on the stage leaving Fort Smith, MR. ORMSBY of the New York Herald, MR. FOX the mail agent, and the driver (MR. MCDOWELL). The Choctaw line was crossed, the Poteau was forded and they were in the Indian Territory on the way to Colbert's Ferry.

Ormsby wrapped up in blankets and stretched out on the seats, took his first opportunity in three days to get some sleep though he says that it took him *"some time to get accustomed to the jolting over the rough road, the rocks and the log bridges."* The stage arrived at Skullyville about daylight, and stopped at Governor Tandy Walker's house, the station for changing horses...

Source: Chronicles of Oklahoma, Spring 1957, "The Butterfield Overland Mail One Hundred Years Ago," by Muriel H. Wright, pages 55-71

Tom Dillard
Historian and retired archivist

CHAPTER SIXTY SIX
"Butterfield Overland Mail's
Memphis to Fort Smith Route - A Harsh Task"
by Tom Dillard
Arkansas Democrat Gazette, December 23, 2007

NOTE: This is NOT a personal diary entry. I'm including here because this article by Tom Dillard interjects interesting bits of history concerning the route from Fort Smith to Memphis.

John Butterfield of Utica, N.Y., received a large government contract to carry the U.S. mail from St. Louis and Memphis to San Francisco.

Butterfield performed a miracle in establishing 140 stations along the route, procuring handsome coaches from a New England manufacturer, buying more than a thousand horses and mules, and hiring a staff of hundreds — and all within a year.

By Sept. 16, 1858, the system was in place and Butterfield himself oversaw the departure from St. Louis. At the same time as the St. Louis departure another Butterfield Overland Mail Co. mail haul left from Memphis. After meeting in Fort Smith, the Memphis coach returned home.

The experiences and challenges endured by both

teams were remarkably difficult and unpredictable, but the Memphis to Fort Smith leg was especially challenging in some ways. While the route from Memphis did not involve overcoming steep mountains that required even the passengers to get out and help heave the coaches forward, it was in its own way equally grueling — and far more unpredictable.

Butterfield apparently underestimated the challenges in traversing Arkansas in a stagecoach in the years before the Civil War. His plan was to subcontract with riverboat companies to carry the mail the entire distance from Memphis to Fort Smith via steamboats. But in September 1858 low rainfall made river traffic difficult.

Butterfield then decided to transmit the mail overland from Memphis, the first leg to be on a recently completed portion of the Memphis and Little Rock Railroad. The first leg of the trip from St. Louis had also been by railroad — 180 miles due west to Tipton, Mo.

The Memphis and Little Rock Railroad had hired more than 400 Irish laborers to build the roadbed and lay tracks from Hopefield, across the Mississippi River from Memphis, to near modern Forrest City on the St. Francis River. Meantime, construction crews from the western terminus began at modern North Little Rock, then called Huntersville, and proceed eastward to DeValls Bluff on the White River. Keep in mind that almost all Arkansas rivers were unbridged in the 1850s. The 45 mile gap of swampy lands between the White and St. Francis rivers would not be completed until after the Civil War.

The little steam engine puffed clouds of black smoke as it made its way from the terminal in Hopefield, probably never reaching 20 miles per hour. The only passenger on that initial trip from Memphis was R. M. Brummer, an employee of Chidester, Reeside & Co.

Butterfield had already contracted with the company to handle part of the Memphis route. Camden resident John T. Chidester was owner of an extensive network of stagecoach lines, including a daily run from Hot Springs to Little Rock. Government mail contracts were his bread and butter.

The rail line ended at the village of Madison on the St. Francis, whereupon the mail and passenger were transferred to a "light vehicle" for a journey over unimproved roads to Des Arc.

THE GREAT OVERLAND MAIL.—The Overland California United States Mail left Memphis on Thursday morning last. It is brought by the Memphis and Little Rock Rail Road to within twelve miles of Madison, on St. Francis river, thence by light vehicles to Des Arc—thence by Messrs. Chidester, Reeside & Co.'s line of four horse U. S. Mail coaches to Fort Smith, where it meets the St. Louis mail. Messrs. Chidester, Reeside & Co., are sub-contractors under Butterfield & Co., from Memphis to Fort Smith ; the whole then proceeds over the plains to El Paso and California.

R. M. Brummer, Esq., of the firm of Chidester, Reeside & Co., who came with the California Overland Mail, early yesterday morning, has our thanks for Memphis papers of Thursday. This arrangement places Des Arc within fourteen hours of Memphis. We are now "close neighbors" to the Bluff City.

[*Des Arc Citizen.*

On first westward trip, a light vehicle was used between Madison and Des Arc
Weekly Arkansas Gazette, Saturday, Sept. 25, 1858, page 2

Total travel from Hopefield on the Mississippi to Des Arc on the White was 14 hours, probably a record for that era. Citizens of Prairie County were able to read a Memphis newspaper on the same day it was printed.

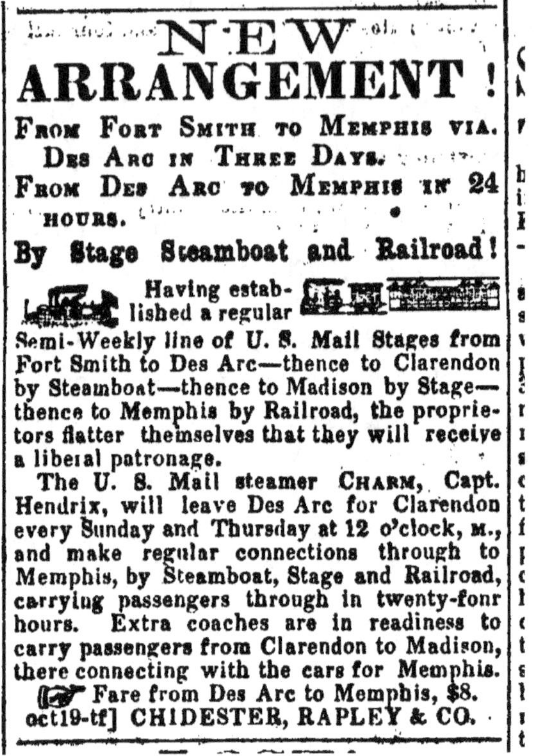

It appears from this newspaper advertisement, that by October 1859 Chidester was using a steamboat for part of the route between Des Arc and the end of tracks at Madison. However, other sources indicate that by this time Butterfield had stopped sub-contracting to Chidester, and was using his own companies equipment and employees between Fort Smith and Memphis.
Source: Des Arc Citizen, Oct. 19, 1859, page 3

A Chidester, Reeside & Co. stagecoach picked up the mail at Des Arc and headed west to Norristown, near modern Russellville. From there Butterfield had his own coaches complete the trip to Fort Smith. Total time on the initial trip from Memphis to Fort Smith took about 66 hours — amazingly enough, the mail coach from St. Louis arrived only 15 minutes later.

To the chagrin of city leaders, Little Rock was not on the original Butterfield line from Memphis. The village of Atlanta, now known as Austin, about 25 miles to the northeast, was the closest stop and Little Rock mail was delivered to that point by horse and buggy — an arrangement that infuriated residents of the capital city, who successfully lobbied to become an official station.

Anthony House hotel home station in Little Rock, Arkansas
The three story Anthony House was a famous landmark in Little Rock.
Following a fire in 1840 the three story hotel was rebuilt with red brick.
Photo courtesy of The Arkansas State Archives (Image #ASA 5300.36)

The **Anthony House** hotel became the Butterfield station in Little Rock. As early as 1843 the Anthony House offered 28 bedrooms, a 60-foot-long dining room, a meat house, ice house and a bar.

Compared to those on the St. Louis route, passengers on the Memphis trip never knew exactly how their trip would proceed. The late Ted R. Worley, who was state historian when the Butterfield centennial was held in 1958, has noted that *"Butterfield route was, as far as the Memphis branch was concerned, really many different routes. Mail, passengers, and freight starting out together from Memphis were not likely to stay together on even to take the same route all the way to Fort Smith."*

Passengers from Memphis, as elsewhere on the Butterfield line, were very much a second priority. Passengers often complained that when stages were halted by mud or high waters, the mail was sent ahead in lighter wagons or on horseback. Passengers were also expected to leave the coaches and help get them through mud holes. Ted Worley noted that *"when Sandford Faulkner [a prominent citizen] related that he paid stagecoach fare from Little Rock to Fort Smith and then walked all the way and carried a fence rail to help pry [the stuck coach] out of the mud, he was not being entirely fanciful."*

Tom W. Dillard is the founding editor of the Encyclopedia of Arkansas History & Culture (www.encyclopediaofarkansas.net), and head of the special collections department at the University of Arkansas in Fayetteville, Arkansas.

MEMPHIS AND LITTLE ROCK RAILROAD.

Passenger Train leaves Ferry Landing daily (Sundays excepted) at 6:30 A. M. Arrives at 5 P. M. Connects at Madison with Arkansas Stage Company and Overland M il Coaches to Little Rock, Fort Smith, San Francisco, California; Hot Springs, Washington, Arkansas; Clarksville, Texas, and all principal points in Arkansas and Texas. Tickets for sale by L. S. Knowlton, sole agent for this line. Union Ticket Office, Gayoso House Reading Room.

Memphis Daily Appeal, Oct. 2, 1860, page 3
Advertisement for the train caring Overland Mail to the end of the tracks.

Approximate locations of known Butterfield stations, and suspected stations, across Arkansas, laid on top of the J. H. Colton & Co. 1855 map of Arkansas.

ABOUT THE AUTHOR

Dr. Robert O. "Bob" Crossman has lived within a few hundred feet of Butterfield's Overland Mail Co. stage route across Arkansas most of his adult life in Russellville 1968-1971, Morrilton 1972, Brightwater 1977, North Little Rock 1977-78, Pottsville 1979-1981, Prairie Grove 1981-1988, and since 1988 in Conway.

He is a member of the Butterfield Overland National Historic Trail Association, Southern Trails Chapter of the Oregon-California Trails Association, Faulkner County Historical Society, Arkansas Historical Association, Shiloh Museum of Ozark History, and Old Colony History Museum. He also serves on the board of the Arkansas Chapter of Butterfield Overland National Historic Trail Association.

He is also a member of several philatelic groups including the American Philatelic Society, State Revenue Society, American Revenue Association, Pinnacle Stamp Club of Little Rock, Carriers and Locals Society, U.S. Philatelic Classics Society, U.S. Stamp Society, Civil War Philatelic Society, U.S. Cancellation Club, Western Cover Society, The Postal History Foundation of Tucson, and the American Association of Philatelic Exhibitors.

After graduating from Russellville High School, Dr. Crossman received a B.A. from Hendrix College in Conway, Arkansas, and received graduate and post-graduate degrees from SMU in Dallas, Texas.

He is the author of four additional books on the Butterfield:
- *"Butterfield's Overland Mail Co. STAGECOACH TRAIL Across Arkansas"* 2021
- *"Butterfield's Overland Mail Co. Use of STEAMBOATS Across Arkansas"* 2022
- *"Butterfield's Overland Mail Co. as REPORTED in the Newspapers of Arkansas"* 2023
- *"POSTAL HISTORY of John Butterfield's Overland Mail Co. on the Southern and Central Routes including Butterfield's Pony Express 1858-1864"*

He has several published articles including: *"I Lived on The Butterfield Mail Route for Decades and Didn't Know It,"* The American Philatelist, Jan. 2023; *"Fort Smith's Connection to the Butterfield's Overland Mail Co.: Stations Between Memphis and Fort Smith"* in the Fort Smith Historical Society Journal, Fall 2021, p. 25-43; *"The Butterfield Overland Mail Company: Faulkner County Connection"* in Faulkner County Facts & Fiddlings, Fall 2021, p. 24-32; and *"Faulkner County and Butterfield's Overland Mail Company Stagecoach Route"* in Faulkner County Facts & Fiddlings, Spring 2024.

Before retiring as a local church pastor, national and state staff member of The United Methodist Church, he wrote several additional books including:
Living Generously / Giving Generously, Ingram Spark Press, 2020
Preach Grace: 480 Sermons from a New Church in Conway, Arkansas, 2020
New Church Handbook: Planting New Churches in the Wesleyan Tradition, 2018
Committed to Christ: Six Steps to a Generous Life, Abingdon Press, 2012

Dr. Bob Crossman • bcrossman@arumc.org
8 Sternwheel Drive, Conway, AR 72034-9391

I just couldn't resist including photos of my family.

Bob & Marcia Crossman

Paul Crossman & Louis Lefebvre

Jessica, Blake Charles, Grayson
with Bob & Marcia Crossman

Owen, David, Cooper & Marlie
Crossman

Fred Borck, Raquel Borck, Brooks Bachamp,
Bailey Bachamp, Dylan Bachamp & Sherry Borck

Gracie & Maggie Mae
Crossman

My Golden Anniversary Edition
of the 1929 Model A

 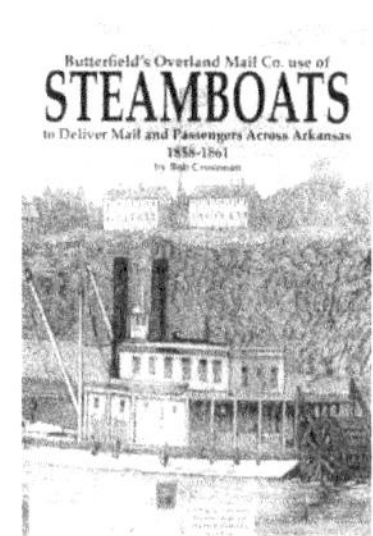  

AVAILABLE IN HARDBACK AND PAPERBACK

*"POSTAL HISTORY of John Butterfield's Overland Mail Co.
on the Southern & Central Routes including
Butterfield's Pony Express 1858-1864"*

To learn about the STAGECOACH LAND ROUTE across Arkansas,
order Bob Crossman's 2021 book:
*"Butterfield's Overland Mail STAGECOACH Route
Across Arkansas: 1858-1861"*

To learn about Butterfield's use of STEAMBOATS across Arkansas,
order Bob Crossman's 2022 book:
*"Butterfield's Overland Mail Co. use of STEAMBOATS
to Deliver Mail and Passengers Across Arkansas 1858-1861"*

To read the history of Butterfield from the newspapers of the time,
order Bob Crossman's 2023 book:
*"Butterfield's Overland Mail Co. as REPORTED in the
Newspapers of Arkansas 1858-1861"*

- DISCOUNTS FOR ORDERING AS A SET OF FOUR FROM THE AUTHOR -

Order copies from your favorite bookseller,
or to obtain signed copies, order from the author at

bcrossman@arumc.org

Explore the Butterfield Overland National Historic Trail by also reading these books by Bob Crossman:

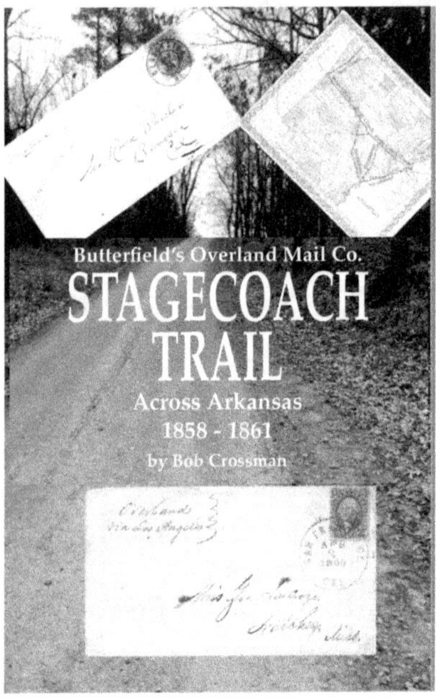

"Butterfield's Overland Mail Co. Stagecoach Trail Across Arkansas: 1858-1861" by Bob Crossman tells the story of the Overland Mail Company stagecoaches which carried passengers and mail west from Memphis and St. Louis to San Francisco through Arkansas. The Overland stagecoaches and stage wagons traveled day and night, completing the 3,293 mile journey is less than twenty five days.

This book pays special attention to each of the twenty Overland Mail Company stations spread across Arkansas. The stations were typically located about fifteen miles apart. The stagecoaches or stage wagons would stop for ten minutes at each station for the quick change of horses. Twice a day the stage would stop at a station for about forty minutes, allowing the passengers to have a moment of rest and purchase a quick meal while the driver obtained a fresh team of horses or mules.

"Butterfield's Overland Mail Co. use of STEAMBOATS to Deliver Mail and Passengers Across Arkansas 1858-1861" explores the untold story of John Butterfield's use of STEAMBOATS to carry the Overland Mail over portions of the Fort Smith to Memphis route of Butterfield's Overland Trail.

While the purpose of my research of the Overland Mail was to satisfy my personal curiosity, hopefully this collection of my research will also make a contribution to the efforts of officially recognizing the route of Butterfield's Overland Mail Co. as a National Historic Trail.

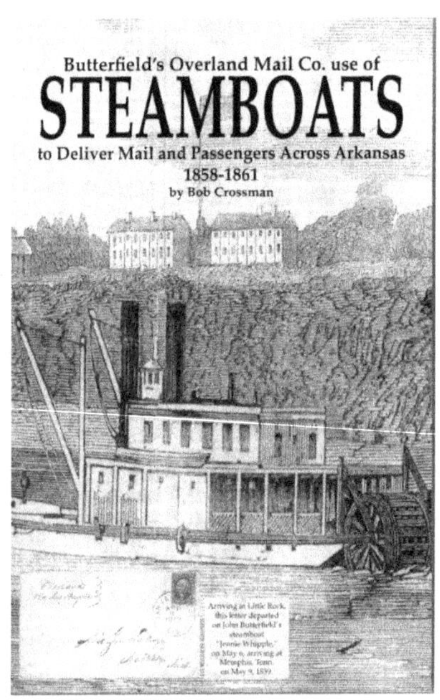

*"Butterfield's Overland Mail Co.
as REPORTED in
Arkansas Newspapers of 1858-1861"*

In this volume, the newspapers of Arkansas do an amazing job of covering the news around Butterfield's Overland Mail Company. Frequently the newspaper editors would draw their information from their exchange of newspapers across the country to bring to their subscribers the most accurate and comprehensive description of facts as possible.

In this book I have let the newspaper reporters tell the story in their own words. It has been difficult, but I have limited my interpretive comments to a brief title I've assigned each article. In this way, today's reader can immerse themselves into the world of the citizens of Arkansas.

This new full color book reports on the mail carried by Butterfield's Overland Mail between September 1858 and March 1861 on the Southern Ox Bow Route, and beginning in July of 1861 on the Central Route. Also, to include additional information and artifacts from US transcontinental mail carried immediately before and immediately after the existence of Butterfield's Overland Mail Co.

In most instances within his previous three books on Butterfield's Overland Mail Co., he focused primarily on the Arkansas route. This volume, by contrast, expands to focus on the entire route of the Butterfield. Also, by contrast, this volume focuses on Butterfield's presence on the Southern Ox-bow Route and later on the northern Central Route. In addition, this volume covers the entire time period of the Overland Mail Company's contract with the postal system: 1858-1864.

While the purpose of this research of the Overland Mail was to satisfy his personal curiosity, he is hopeful that summary of Butterfield Postal History will also make a contribution to Butterfield's Overland Mail Co. new status as a National Historic Trail.

REVIEWS OF STAGECOACH ROUTE VOLUME

"Bob Crossman has filled in a much needed gap for Butterfield's Overland Mail Company by documenting the history of this famous Old West enterprise from Memphis, Tennessee, to Fort Smith, Arkansas." **Gerald T. Ahnert**
Historian and member of the Oregon-California Trails Association who for the last fifty years has been researching Butterfield's Overland Mail Company.

"John Butterfield's Overland Mail Company story is a truly amazing piece of American History. This well researched book gathers information regarding the trail through Arkansas and will be recognized as The Authority on the subject. It makes all of us that are friends of the Butterfield Trail very grateful for this book." **Margaret Motley**
President, Pope County Historical Foundation (Potts Inn)

"Bob Crossman has successfully memorialized the Butterfield's Overland Mail Company's development, operation, and route in Arkansas through meticulous, comprehensive research! This work is a significant contribution to the history of the state which will be referenced for decades to come." **David Plummer**
Descendant of Butterfield Station Agent, Samuel Plummer

"The Fort Smith to San Francisco route of the Butterfield Overland Mail has been covered extensively. This book provides a much-needed history of the Memphis to Fort Smith route, and it contains photos, maps, schedules and news articles making it a great resource." **Glendle Griggs**
McCollum-Chidester House Museum
Ouachita County Historical Society, Camden, AR

"Dr. Crossman has written a book that is a must-have for the history enthusiast, Old West fan, or for reference in libraries and museums. A light has been shown on some historical places that were not widely known in the past." **Jack W. James**
Old Military Road Museum, Lavaca, Arkansas

"With a keen interest and living near the old Butterfield stagecoach road, I'm glad to add this historical Butterfield Trail book to my library." **R. D. Keever**

REVIEWS OF POSTAL HISTORY VOLUME

"The book offers a complete story of the Overland Mail, both Ox Bow and Central Routes, complexities not always understood. Relationships to the Pony Express and Wells Fargo are clarified. Lots of full color illustrations. Lots of contemporary articles and ads. The book gives life to a difficult subject." **Dr. Gordon Nelson, Florida Tech, Melbourne, Florida**

"Bob Crossman's latest book, Postal History of John Butterfield's Overland Mail Co. on the Southern & Central Routes including Butterfield's Pony Express 1858-1864, is an indispensable resource to any collector or historian seeking to understand the challenges and triumphs of mail delivery in the western United States during the middle of the 19th Century.

Profusely illustrated with numerous, detailed route maps, contemporary photographs, drawings, original source documents, colored and black and white engravings and - to delight of postal history collectors - a wide variety of domestic and international covers carried "Via Overland Mail", Crossman's book is both a gold mine of American and philatelic history and a pleasure to read."

Don Chenevert, Jr., APS Life Member

"Bob Crossman has compiled a large number of original documents into a fascinating collection, providing an in-depth understanding of the history and operation of the Butterfield Overland Mail Company's stage line and other components of the postal service prior to the completion of the transcontinental railroad. It's a resource I'm pleased to have on my bookshelf."

Susan Dragoo, Oklahoma Historian

"This book is well written and the use of color adds much to the pleasure of readers. Bob has researched and published yet another book packed with great graphics, thoroughly documented sources, and an in-depth look into his topic.

The best part of these books? They are INTERESTING to read. Between the color, maps, sketches, photos etc, reading them is almost like having a great lunch buffet" **Teresa Harris, Ouachita County, Arkansas historian**
Co-Editor of the Ouachita County Historical Society Quarterly
Administrator, Ouachita County Historical Society Facebook Page

"Bob Crossman explores the audacious history of John Butterfield's Overland Mail Co. with lively prose and vivid narrative. The comprehensive history is delightfully detailed with copious illustrations and newly published research. This fascinating, accurate and exciting book should be of interest to all US western postal history researchers and enthusiasts."
Joe Cody, President, Arizona & New Mexico Postal History Society

"Bob Crossman's chapter on The Overland Mail Company's Pony Express is informative. Unlike most histories of the Pony Express, it does not rely on sentimental or romantic notions of the service. Rather, it sticks to the facts, quoting extensively from primary and secondary sources. It is a good source of information for anyone who wants to learn more about this aspect of the famous enterprise." **Scott Alumbaugh, Author,**
"On the Pony Express Trail: One Man's Journey to
Discover History From a Different Kind of Saddle"

"Thoroughly researched and filled with attractive illustrations and informative and entertaining quotes and excerpts, Bob Crossman has given us an important contribution to the literature on early communication and transportation in the American West. This book is appropriately timed with the recent Congressional designation of the Butterfield Overland National Historic Trail. I look forward to owning my own copy."
Patrick Hearty, Historian/National Trails Liaison
National Pony Express Association

1859 D. McGowan's Map of the United States west of the Mississippi showing the routes to Pike's Peak, Overland Mail Route to California and Pacific rail road surveys. To which are added the new state & territorial boundaries, the principal mail & rail road routes, with all the arrangements & corrections made by Congress up to the date of its issue.
Published by Leopold Gast & Bro.58 cm x 72cm by Leopold Gast & Bro., St. Louis
Image courtesy of: Yale University, Beinecke Rare Book & Manuscript Library

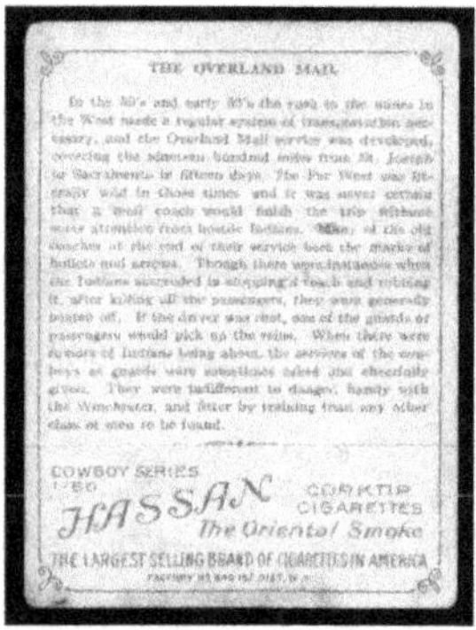

"The Overland Mail," 1910
One of 49 in the 'Cowboy Series' of cards from Hassan,
The Oriental Smoke Cork-tip Cigarettes
Image source: from the personal collection of Bob Crossman